To K
& Co.
Xmas
2002

K. Clerk.

Football
Hearts
& Wolves

Sudsons
+

CARD.

DREAMS *of* ELSEWHERE

THE SELECTED TRAVEL WRITINGS OF
ROBERT LOUIS STEVENSON

DREAMS *of* ELSEWHERE

COMPILED AND EDITED BY JUNE SKINNER SAWYERS

The In Pinn

Published by The In Pinn

The In Pinn is an imprint of
Neil Wilson Publishing
303a The Pentagon Centre
36 Washington Street
GLASGOW
G3 8AZ
Tel: 0141-221-1117
Fax: 0141-221-5363
E-mail: info@nwp.co.uk
www.theinpinn.co.uk
www.nwp.co.uk

A catalogue record for this book is available from the British Library.

ISBN 1-903238-62-5 (hardback)
ISBN 1-903238-69-2 (paperback)

Typeset in New Caledonia
Designed by Belstane
Printed in Finland by WS Bookwell

For my aunt,
Catherine Harvey Mason Keiller Porter Campbell
of Glasgow

The Vagabond

TO AN AIR BY SHUBERT

Give to me the life I love,
Let the lave go by me,
Give the jolly heaven above
And in the byway night me.
Bed in the bush with stars to see,
Bread I dip in the river—
There's the life for a man like me,
There's the life for ever.

Let the blow fall soon or late,
Let what will be o'er me;
Give the face of earth around
And the road before me.
Wealth I seek not, hope nor love,
Nor a friend to know me;
All I seek, the heaven above
And the road below me.

Or let autumn fall on me
Where afield I linger,
Silencing the bird on tree,
Biting the blue finger;
White as meal the frosty field—
Warm the fireside haven—
Not to autumn will I yield,
Not to winter even!

Let the blow fall soon or late,
Let what will be o'er me;
Give the face of earth around,
And the road before me.
Wealth I ask not, hope, nor love,
Nor a friend to know me.
All I ask, the heaven above
And the road below me.

—RLS
from *Songs of Travel* (1895)

Contents

Acknowledgements

ASSEMBLING this collection has been a labour of love. I wish here to thank all Stevenson scholars – past and present. In addition I am indebted to George Cohen for bringing to my attention several years ago a copy of *Stevenson's Travels in Hawaii* (Honolulu: University of Hawaii Press, 1973), edited by A Grove Day at a time when I had still to fathom the extent of RLS's vast travel itinerary.

My neighbours Rick and Ann Selin offered plenty of jokes, smiles, cups of coffee, and lots of support – especially of the computer kind – along the way. I thank Neil Wilson for his encouragement and for giving me the opportunity to be published, once again, in my native Scotland. While doing additional research in northern California, I and a friend had the pleasure of staying at the lovely Santa Rosa home of Bill Thompson and Bob Sigman, who good naturedly put up with my ongoing Stevenson obsessions. As always, I thank Theresa Albini simply for being there.

Foreword

On a high plateau overlooking a broad sweep of the Pacific in Samoa, there is a place that a traveller once described as beautiful beyond dreams. To a friend, he wrote: 'The morning is such a morning as you have never seen; heaven upon earth for sweetness, freshness, depth upon depth of unimaginable colour and a huge silence broken at this moment only by the far-away murmur of the Pacific and the rich piping of a single bird.' After a life of travelling hopefully, Robert Louis Stevenson had arrived at his final destination.

Along the way he had become a celebrated novelist, but also a keen observer of people and places he encountered in a kaleidoscope of travels off the beaten track. He belonged to a generation of writers who did not jet around the world, recording fleeting impressions and drawing superficial conclusions. He took the time to stand and stare, and muse eloquently on his experiences. The result is a set of travel essays as vivid and compelling in their own way as his romantic fiction.

Stevenson was always dreaming of elsewhere. As a young man, he wrote a children's poem:

> I should like to rise and go
> Where the golden apples grow;-
> Where below another sky
> Parrot islands anchored lie.

So he did. Blithely ignoring Victorian conventions and the perils of uncharted seas, off he went. And happily for us, he left detailed accounts of his adventures in Europe, America and the South Seas.

The travel genre is attractive to writers for the freedom it affords to be whatever they wish to be – explorer, historian, geographer, philosopher, story-teller – and RLS was all of them. In the tranquillity of a French pine forest by moonlight he considers the importance of friendship; in a leper colony on Hawaii he reflects on physical horror and moral beauty; in all of his writing there is humanity and compassion.

A measure of his talent is the esteem in which he was held wherever he travelled. In an age when Pacific islanders were considered little better than savages, Stevenson found complex societies with strict codes of honour that had much in common with 17th century Scottish clans. He respected and admired his hosts, and at night they would sit in thatched huts by lagoons swapping tales of their respective homelands. In Samoa, where he spent the last years of his life, he was known affectionately as Tusitala – teller of tales. The essence of good travel writing is simple. It is the facility to take readers in their imagination to wherever the author is – to feel the salt spray of an ocean, to hear the voices of characters met on a country lane – and Stevenson was a master of the art.

Admirers of his work will welcome this judicious selection of sketches from an itinerant life. Those less familiar with his blithe spirit are in for a rare treat, a voyage of discovery with the teller of tales to where the surf murmurs on Parrot islands.

Gavin Bell

Chronology

1850 Born on November 13 at 8 Howard Place in Edinburgh.

1857 The Stevensons move to 17 Heriot Row in the New Town.

1862 Family holiday in London and Hamburg.

1863 Continental trip with family to France, Italy, and Switzerland.

1867 Enrolls at Edinburgh University to study civil engineering.

1868 Summer vacation in the northeast of Scotland, including stopover in Wick, Caithness to learn family lighthouse building trade.

1869 RLS and father to Orkney and the Outer Hebrides.

1870 Visits Mull on another lighthouse building tour.

1871 Switches from studying civil engineering to law.

1872 Three weeks in Germany during summer with friend Walter Simpson.

1873 Meets Frances Sitwell, an important influence in his life. 'Roads' published in. *Portfolio Magazine* in December. To the south of France at the end of the year.

1874 Menton, France. Returns to Edinburgh in May. 'Ordered South' published in *Macmillan's Magazine*. Cruises the Inner Hebrides with Walter Simpson from July–August.

1875 Qualifies as an advocate. Visits his cousin, Bob Stevenson, at the artists' colony at Barbizon, Fontainebleau, France, in March and April.

1876 Winter walking tour in Galloway and Carrick. Begins canoe trip through the canals of northern France in September. Meets Fanny Osbourne, an American from Indiana. 'Forest Notes' published in May, 'Walking Tours' in June, both in *Cornhill Magazine*.

1877 In Edinburgh, London, and Fontainebleau.

1878 In August, Fanny returns to her husband in California; divorce proceedings begin. Stevenson travels through the south of France on a donkey. Both *An Inland Voyage* and *Edinburgh: Picturesque Notes* are published.

1879 In London, Scotland, and France. Sails to join Fanny in California. *Travels with a Donkey* published.

1880 In May marries Fanny Osbourne in San Francisco. Returns to Britain in August. From August-September in Strathpeffer and Edinburgh. Leaves for Davos, Switzerland, in November.

1881 In Pitlochry from June to July. Writes fifteen chapters of *Treasure Island* in Braemar, Scotland. Visits Davos in Switzerland. Publication of *Virginibus Puerisque and other Papers* and 'Swiss Notes' is published in the *Pall Mall Gazette*. Back in Davos in October.

1882 In Kingussie in July and August. Publication of *Familiar Studies of Men and Books* and *New Arabian Nights*.

1883 Stevenson and Fanny move to Hyeres, France. Publication of *The Silverado Squatters* and *Treasure Island*.

1884 Seriously ill in Nice. Louis and Fanny settle in Bournemouth, England. 'Fontainebleau' appears in the May issue of the *Magazine of Art*. Publication of *The Silverado Squatters* and *Treasure Island*.

1885 As a wedding present to Fanny, Stevenson's father, Thomas, buys them a house in Bournemouth, which they name 'Skerryvore.' Publication of *More New Arabian Nights: The Dynamiter* and *Prince Otto*.

1886 Publication of *The Strange Case of Dr. Jekyll and Mr. Hyde* and *Kidnapped*.

1887 Thomas Stevenson dies in May. In August, Stevenson, his mother, Fanny, and stepson Lloyd sail for America. They stay briefly in Newport, Rhode Island, then settle down at Saranac Lake, New York, for several months. Publication of *Memoir of Fleeming Jenkin*, *The Merry Men and Other Tales and Fables*, *Underwoods* and *Memories and Portraits*.

1888 In New York City in April, Manasquan, New Jersey, in May. Voyage on the yacht 'Casco' from San Francisco to the Marquesas, the Paumotus, Tahiti, Sandwich Islands, and Hawaii. Publication of *The Black Arrow: A Tale of Two Roses*.

1889 Maggie Stevenson returns to Scotland. Stevenson, Fanny, and Lloyd remain behind in Hawaii. Voyage on the trading schooner 'Equator' to the Gilbert Islands and then on to Samoa. *The Master of Ballantrae* is published, as is *The Wrong Box*. Stevenson purchases Vailima on Samoa.

1890 Voyage on the steamer Janet Nicholl in the Pacific from Sydney, Australia. Suffers serious haemorrhaging. Publication of *In the South Seas*.

1892 Publication of *Across the Plains, The Wrecker, A Footnote to History: Eight Years of Trouble in Samoa* and *Three Plays* by WE Henley and RL Stevenson.

1893 War erupts in Samoa. Stevenson visits Honolulu for the last time. Publication of *Island Nights' Entertainments* and *Catriona* (in USA: *David Balfour*).

1894 Stevenson dies of a brain haemorrhage at his home in Samoa on 3 December. Publication of *The Ebb-Tide*.

1895 Publication of *Songs of Travel and other Verses*.

1896 *Weir of Hermiston* and *The Amateur Emigrant* and *In the South Seas* published.

1897 Publication of *St. Ives: Being The Adventures of a French Prisoner in England*.

Introduction

I have been after an adventure all my life, a pure, dispassionate adventure, such as befell early and heroic voyagers
Robert Louis Stevenson

I travel not to go anywhere, but to go.
I travel for travel's sake. The great affair is to move.
RLS

'I kept always two books in my pocket, one to read, one to write in,' once remarked Robert Louis Stevenson.

As a child, Stevenson travelled a great deal with his parents. During the summer months, Bridge of Allan and North Berwick and, later, Peebles in Scotland were family favourites. But his mother's 'weak chest' prompted visits to warmer climates: Nice and Mentone in France and Genoa, Naples, Rome, Florence, and Venice in Italy. Stevenson had caught the travelling bug; this restlessness, this urge to go, was something that stayed with him all his life.

Stevenson went in search of adventure and a respite from the inhospitable climate of his native windswept Scotland. He yearned for a place that would gently caress his battered body and nurture his wandering soul. The very thought of getting away energised him, gave him hope that things could be better. But, most of all, he travelled for the sheer joy of travel.

One of the most beloved of nineteenth-century writers – certainly among the most resilient as well as the most humane – Stevenson was known for his kindness and compassion. He was generous of spirit in both his personal life and his professional life. He was, for example, an early admirer of Walt Whitman and Herman Melville – those other idiosyncratic seekers – at a time when American literature was not taken seriously in Europe, certainly not within the literary elite of London. His restlessness and craving for new adventures and appreciation of new vistas predated the likes of Jack London, Jack Kerouac, Bruce Chatwin, and later generations of literary rebels who did things their own way and who found on the road a sense of freedom that eluded them elsewhere.

Stevenson was not only one of the great travellers of literary history but also a graceful writer of stylish prose. Aside from the unpredictability of his questionable health, he was in many ways the perfect traveller – inquisitive, optimistic, and always curious. Every time he travelled, he was like a child with a new toy – in this case, the world was his plaything. He despised routine and yearned for the thrill of the unexpected. No matter how excruciatingly long the journey, or how uncomfortable the circumstances, Stevenson invariably turned his adventures on the road into excellent copy. 'Everything that happened to Louis Stevenson seemed to him worthy of public record ...' wrote James Pope Hennessy, one of his many biographers.[1] He was constantly in search of a good story. The story-teller tells stories; the story-teller finds stories to tell. Stevenson was a consummate story-teller.

His diversity was impressive. Stevenson wrote virtually every type of literary form imaginable: novels, essays, plays, poems, literary criticism, biography, children's literature, fantasies, fables, and short stories. He penned a timeless classic of young adult fiction (*Treasure Island*) as well as several novels that have withstood the test of time (*Kidnapped, The Strange Case of Dr. Jekyll and Mr. Hyde*), and a popular children's book of poems (*A Child's Garden of Verse*). His works have been adapted into films, television dramas, and Broadway musicals and his lyrics and poetry have been set to music by everyone from classical composers Ralph Vaughan Williams to, more recently, Ronald Stevenson and his daughter, harpist Savourna Stevenson.

Like his fiction, his travel writings are full of vivid portraits of flesh-and-blood human beings, human beings that he met on his travels, for the always garrulous Stevenson loved to hear a good tale as well as tell one. To him the human species was endlessly fascinating. He never grew tired of meeting new people, of seeking new adventures. Thus, he left posterity with a quite significant collection of travel books, travel essays, and travel poetry. The description of his fellow passengers in steerage on the long journey across the Atlantic in *The Amateur Emigrant* is one of the finest and most brutally honest depictions of nineteenth-century travel – so graphic in fact that it wasn't published until after his death since his editors as well as his own father found it distasteful and indeed shocking that someone of his social standing should deign to associate with the lower classes. But, Stevenson had no patience with any form of pretence. And in another travel classic, *The Silverado Squatters*, we meet as colourful a cast of characters as to be found in any work of fiction.

Journalist Ian Bell has claimed that Stevenson 'was a product of his circumstances... Three things mattered most to him: illness, Scotland, and travel.'[2] They were all interconnected, of course, each one affecting the other. He both longed to escape from his native land – to unchain his fettered Caledonian soul – and yet he loved Scotland dearly. Adds Bell: 'He had deep roots there he could not sever.'[3] Like James Joyce and other similar literary exiles through the ages, Stevenson wrote best about Scotland when he was away from it.[4]

Sometimes taken for a madman – or at least an eccentric of the first order – by many of his peers – Stevenson certainly was ahead of his time. Bohemian dandy and literary gypsy, he was cosmopolitan before it became fashionable, a verifiable nonconformist to the end of his days. What's more, virtually every place he visited or experienced became fodder for a story. On one level, he would fit quite nicely in the celebrity-obsessed culture of the twenty-first century where nothing truly exists unless a life has been transformed into a book or, better yet, turned into a movie. Stevenson's life was nothing if not cinematic.

At the same time, though, he detested the grovelling mentality of the press and the cult of celebrity that followed him wherever he went after the phenomenal success of *Dr. Jekyll and Mr. Hyde*. One suspects that, if alive today, Stevenson would play along – for a time – before growing weary of the whole charade. On his arrival in New York in September 1887, he was greeted by a barrage of reporters on the quayside. In a letter to his friend and mentor Sidney Colvin, he complained, 'My reception here was idiotic to the last degree; if Jesus Christ came, they would make less fuss.'[5] Even though, he craved attention and needed the company of his fellow human beings – his less charitable detractors have called him a narcissistic nomad – he also appreciated solitude.

Stevenson was popular with critics until World War I when the Modernists turned their back on him. He was effectively shorn from the established literary canon and dismissed as a populist and romance writer, or worse, as a mere writer of children's books, and thus not deemed worthy of academic consideration or serious study. That stubbornly blind and parochial attitude continued until fairly recently.

Fortunately, in the last decade or so, the tide has turned. Since the years leading up to the centenary of his death, several new biographies have been published, including *Louis: A Life of Robert Louis Stevenson* by Philip Callow (Ivan R Dee, 2001), the definitive *Robert Louis Stevenson: A Biography* by Frank McLynn (Random House, 1993), and *Dreams of Exile: Robert Louis Stevenson, A Biography* by Ian Bell (Henry Holt, 1992). These, in addition to the valuable contributions of earlier biographers, especially Jenni Calder, David Daiches, JC Furnas, and James Pope Hennessy.

On the centenary anniversary of his death,[6] BBC Radio broadcast on Radio 4 dramatisations and readings of *The Master of Ballantrae*, *The Strange Case of Dr Jekyll and Mr Hyde*, *Kidnapped*, 'The Bottle Imp,' and *Travels with a Donkey* while BBC Television aired a travel documentary on Stevenson's many journeys. And on a decidedly more populist note, as we go to press, Walt Disney Pictures is scheduled to release an animated version of *Treasure Island* called *Treasure Planet* in late 2002. Clearly, the Stevenson aura has not diminished over time.

° ° °

Robert Lewis (later 'Louis') Balfour Stevenson was born in Edinburgh, Scotland, on 13 November 1850, at 8 Howard Place, on the outskirts of Edinburgh's New Town. Nicknamed 'Smout', a Scots word for a young fish, Louis, as he was also called, was an unusually precocious child. From his earliest memories, he loved the sound of the spoken word. Unlike the unpredictable weather that raged outside his door or the uncertainty of his frail body, language – the use of it – was something he could control, something he could mould to his own liking. He paid especially close attention to the ghost stories that his nurse Alison 'Cummy' Cunningham would recite on cold, windy, storm-racked Edinburgh nights, both terrified and mesmerised at the same time. Young Stevenson was extremely fond of Cummy. She sang the old Scots ballads, read to him from the Bible and *Pilgrim's Progress*, and fired up his already active imagination with tales of the Covenanters and other stories from Scotland's gory and violent past. 'My parents and Cummy brought me up on the Shorter Catechism, porridge, and the Covenanters,' he once said.[7]

Like his mother and maternal grandfather, Louis suffered from various respiratory ailments – something that would stalk him throughout his short life. Truth be told, the flat on Howard Place was a rather damp and gloomy building. Before long, in 1853, the Stevensons were on the move, this time to a larger house across the street at 1 Inverleith Terrace. Unfortunately, it wasn't much of an improvement, still damp and located on a corner that was subject to the fierce northern winds. On advice of doctors who were concerned about both Stevenson and his mother's health, they moved three years later to 17 Heriot Row in the New Town proper, across the street from the newly developed Queen Street Gardens. It was drier, larger, and less exposed to the elements. And it was here, on this pleasant street, that Louis grew up.[8]

At the age of seventeen, Stevenson enrolled at Edinburgh University to study engineering – it was a short-lived and mostly feeble attempt to follow in his engineer father's prestigious footsteps. The Stevensons were highly respected lighthouse builders[9] and during the summer months Louis would occasionally join members of the engineering firm on company trips – Wick in 1868, the Isle of Earraid in 1870. Both places would feature prominently in his writings, especially Earraid. He soon abandoned engineering altogether though, but, still trying to please his father, agreed to study law. In July 1875 he passed his exams, was admitted to the Scottish bar, and joined the firm of Skene, Edwards, & Bilton.

Not surprisingly, his legal career was exceedingly brief. Louis was more interested in learning how to write, of mastering his craft, than courting respectability. He felt a natural affinity toward the essay. He read voraciously and deliberately modelled his writing style on the work of such masters of the craft as William Hazlitt, Daniel Defoe, Charles Lamb, Nathaniel Hawthorne, and Michel de Montaigne. As a student, he sampled the bohemian lifestyle that Edinburgh so richly offered rather than attend to his studies. His gaunt frame was a regular fixture on the city streets. He often could be seen strolling the seedy underbelly of the Old Town or imbibing in the pubs along Lothian Road or on Rose and Jamaica Streets, a short walk from respectable Heriot Row. With his wide-brimmed hat, cravat, and ubiquitous velvet coat, he cut quite a curious and distinctive figure, especially in a town as conservative as Edinburgh.

In 1873, Stevenson published his first essay, 'Roads', in the *Portfolio Magazine*, followed by 'Ordered South' the following year in *Macmillan's Magazine*, and 'Forest Notes' and 'Walking Tours' in 1876 in *Cornhill Magazine*. The fact that he could combine his two loves – writing and travel – came as something of a revelation. During the summer of that year, he spent a considerable amount of time in Fontainebleau, an artist's colony in France, with his arty cousin Bob (Robert Alan Mowbray Stevenson was also the person who introduced him to the many pleasures of bohemian Paris). It was in the adjacent riverside village of Grez where he met his future wife, an American woman from Indiana some ten years his senior named Fanny Osbourne. Louis was smitten with her from the moment he made a dramatic entrance through an open hotel window and sat down next to her at the dinner table. She must have thought this young, rail-thin Scotsman to be a bit odd, but she warmed to him soon enough.

While many of Stevenson's early essays revolved around travel, it is significant that his earliest books were also travel narratives. *An Inland Voyage* (1878), his first full-length book, was an account of a journey he took with his boyhood friend Walter Simpson by canoe down the River Oise in northern France. It is an entertaining, rambling read – too rambling for some critics – but it is also quite funny, as when the shabbily dressed writer is arrested at Chatillon-sur-Loire on suspicion of being a Prussian spy.

The following year (1879), both *Edinburgh: Picturesque Notes* – his scathing but entertaining portrait of his native city – and *Travels with a Donkey in the Cévennes* were published. *Travels with a Donkey* was written during a particularly difficult time in Stevenson's life. Fanny had just returned to America to sort out her messy domestic situation – she was still married to her philandering husband Sam Osbourne – leaving Stevenson dejected and depressed, 'a miserable widower', as he put it. Whenever he found himself in such an ugly mood, he did what came naturally. He went elsewhere. Thus, within a month of Fanny's leaving, the lovelorn Scot was riding the back of a donkey named Modestine in a wild and remote corner of southern France. He knew little about the area nor did he seem to care. He simply needed to get away, to escape from the emotional turmoil and chaos that was running through his head. From this dire experience came *Travels with a Donkey in the Cévennes*, an utterly charming piece of writing that has retained its freshness and strong sense of place over the years.

In July 1879 Stevenson received an urgent cable from Fanny. By this time she had rejoined her estranged husband in California. No one is quite sure of its contents, but whatever it said it was enough to make Louis drop everything and set sail for America. He had always been fascinated by America – by its newness, by its vastness. Now he had a chance to see the country firsthand.

Stevenson left Greenock on 7 August and arrived in New York on 18 August, sick and poor. He then caught the emigrant train, travelling cross country as his already precarious health increasingly worsened. By the time he arrived in California, he was at death's door. Of course, Stevenson kept copious notes throughout the whole ordeal. The result was the marvellous *The Amateur Emigrant*, yet another classic piece of travel writing.

Stevenson lived in Monterey for a short time, recuperating and writing, until Fanny finally obtained her divorce. Louis and Fanny were married in San Francisco in May 1880. Short on cash and desperate to get away from the damp, chilly climate of the Bay area, they spent their honeymoon at an abandoned silver mine in the Napa Valley. From this unusual experience emerged *The Silverado Squatters*, which ranks with some of his finest work and is arguably his best travel book.

From 1880 to 1887 the peripetic Stevensons had several temporary homes: Bournemouth in England, southern France, Switzerland, and Saranac Lake in upstate New York. Stevenson, the erstwhile traveller, adapted quite easily to most places, with the notable exception of England. He wrote about his dislike for Scotland's southern neighbor quite often. England was one of the few countries where he felt like a stranger. 'I cannot get over my astonishment – indeed it increases every day, at the hopeless gulph that there is between England and Scotland, English and Scotch,' he wrote to his mother from Suffolk in 1873. 'Nothing is the same; and I feel as strange and outlandish here, as I do in France and Germany.'[10]

In the spring of 1888, his American publisher offered Stevenson a considerable advance to visit and write about the South Pacific. Since he had been a child, Stevenson had imagined what it would be like to live on an island paradise, far from the sickness that stalked him, the sickness that refused to allow him to live a normal existence. So when the chance came, he took it – with no hesitation.

In 1888, the Stevenson party chartered the yacht 'Casco' and sailed from San Francisco. Their South Sea journey had begun. They travelled to the Marquesas, the Paumotus, the Society Islands, Tahiti, and Hawaii before arriving at their final destination, Samoa, the following year.

He didn't know it, but Stevenson had arrived at his final home: Apia on the island of Upolu. In 1890, he purchased a 314.5-acre tract and began building a house that he called Vailima.[11] Here he enjoyed playing the role of the Highland chieftain – of the Lowland variety, that is – to the hilt. As his strength increased, he did some manual labour – working with his hands was not a task that he was overly familiar with – and rode around his estate on a pony named Jack. 'This is a hard and interesting and beautiful life that we lead now,' he wrote.[12]

And yet Scotland was never far from his mind. 'You ask me,' he replied in a letter to Sidney Colvin, 'if I am ever homesick for the Highlands and the Isles.

Conceive that for the last month I have been living there between 1786 and 1850, in my grandfather's diaries and letters.' He never did complete this family history, though.[13] He did, however, become embroiled in island politics and various domestic and business affairs, while continuing to write. He wrote until his breath was taken from him.

Stevenson lived his life bravely and courageously. He did not allow fear to dictate what he could or could not do. Lesser men with stonger constitutions would have given up years earlier. For someone who came close to death so many times in so many places as he did – often far away from home, wherever home happened to be at the moment – the end came suddenly, irrevocably, without warning, not from the lung ailments that had plagued him all his life but from a devastating brain haemorrhage. Robert Louis Stevenson died on 3 December 1894 in Vailima, lying on a cot in the hallway of his mansion, surrounded by his family. He was 44. A quiet, uneventful conclusion to a life lived well.

At his request, Stevenson was laid to rest at the top of Mount Vaea, a thousand feet or so above sea level overlooking the harbour (he frequently had expressed a desire to be buried in Scotland but he knew that the logistics of his remote island location made it all but impossible). Always aware of the precarious nature of his health, Stevenson had even written his own 'Requiem',[14] which was engraved on his tomb.

On 5 December 1994, Vailima opened to the public as the Robert Louis Stevenson Museum. In an ironic twist, the Church of Jesus Christ of Latter-Day Saints – the Mormons – had purchased the property. One wonders how Stevenson might have reacted to the news. Perhaps a chuckle, perhaps a disbelieving nod of the head? It seems that this atheistic son of devout Presbyterian parents, this voluntary exile who longed for home, could never truly escape the clutches of religion – even in death.

* * *

Dreams of Elsewhere makes no claims to being a comprehensive collection of Stevenson's travel writings. To do so would require several hefty volumes. It is, however, as far as I can tell, the most comprehensive and representative sampling of his prolific travel output, including excerpts from his most famous travel books (*Inland Voyage, Travels with a Donkey in the Cévennes, The Amateur Emigrant, The Silverado Squatters, Travels in Hawaii,* and *In the South Seas*), most of his travel essays, and several travel poems.

The selections have been arranged geographically and in roughly chronological order, except when, in the case of his American writings, it seemed to make more logistical sense to begin with *The Amateur Emigrant*, followed by 'Across the Plains', and concluding with *The Silverado Squatters*.

Because this collection is intended for the general reader, endnotes have been kept to a minimum, and are only included where necessary or helpful. The book is also intended to be used as a guide. It is hoped that after reading these selections, the reader will be inspired to visit the places where Stevenson actually treaded. Hence, Stevenson sites, museums, and libraries as well as clubs and organisations are listed.

Notes

1. James Pope Hennessy, *Robert Louis Stevenson* (New York: Simon and Schuster, 1974), p. 16.
2. Ian Bell, *Dreams of Exile: Robert Louis Stevenson, A Biography* (New York: Henry Holt, 1992), p. xv.
3. Bell, *Dreams of Exile,* p. xvi.
4. 'Singular that I should fulfill the Scots destiny throughout, and live a voluntary exile and have my head filled with the blessed, beastly place all the time!' Letter from RLS to Sidney Colvin, August 1893. Quoted in Bell, *Dreams of Exile,* p. xiii.
5. Ernest Mehew, ed. *Selected Letters of Robert Louis Stevenson* (Hartford, Conn.: Yale University Press, 2001), p. 343.
6. On the 100th anniversary of the death of Robert Louis Stevenson, the Royal Bank of Scotland issued a £1 banknote. In the same year Samoa issued several stamps, including a portrait of RLS and another depicting his tomb on Mount Vaea and his Vailima House estate. On 13 November 2000, Hawaii Post issued a set of two stamps to celebrate the 150th anniversary of the birth of RLS: one shows RLS reading a book to the young Princess Ka'iulani in Waikiki; the other shows RLS sitting with King Kalakaua on the verandah of Iolani Palace in Honolulu.
7. Bell, *Dreams of Exile,* p. 24.
8. The Stevenson House at 17 Heriot Row is now a bed-and-breakfast establishment.
9. According to Bella Bathurst, 'Between 1790 and 1940, eight members of the Stevenson family planned, designed and constructed the ninety-seven manned lighthouses that still speckle the Scottish coast, working in conditions and places that would be daunting even for modern engineers. ... The archetypal lighthouse on its lonely rock in a lonely sea is largely the product of Scottish imagination and a Scottish sense of endeavor.' See Bella Bathurst, *The Lighthouse Stevensons* (New York: HarperCollins Publishers, 1999), pp. xvii and xxii.
10. Mehew, ed., Selected Letters, p. 37. See also 'The Foreigner at Home' and 'The Scot Abroad' from *The Silverado Squatters* in this volume.
11. According to Philip Callow the Stevensons believed Vailima meant Five Waters, 'or so they understood.' See Philip Callow, *Louis: A Life of Robert Louis Stevenson* (Chicago: Ivan R Dee, 2001), p. 275.
12. Letter from RLS to Sidney Colvin, 2 November 1890. In Mehew, ed., *Selected Letters*, p. 433.
13. Letter from RLS to Sidney Colvin, 5[?] September 1891. Ibid., pp. 461–62.
14. An earlier and much longer version of 'Requiem' was originally written in August 1879 when a sickly Stevenson was crossing the country in a crowded emigrant train enroute to meet Fanny in California. See Angus Calder, ed. *Robert Louis Stevenson: Selected Poems* (London: Penguin Books, 1998), p. 258. The famous lines are as follows: Under the wide and starry sky, Dig the grave and let me lie. Glad did I live and gladly die, And I laid me down with a will. This be the verse you grave for me: Here he lies where he longed to be; Home is the sailor, home from sea, And the hunter home from the hill.

Scotland

On the Enjoyment
of Unpleasant Places

On the Enjoyment of Unpleasant Places *was originally published in* Portfolio
Magazine *in November 1874. The 'unpleasant place' of the title is Wick in
Caithness, Scotland, where Stevenson visited in September and October 1868.*

IT is a difficult matter to make the most of any given place, and we have much in
our own power. Things looked at patiently from one side after another generally
end by showing a side that is beautiful. A few months ago some words were said
in the portfolio as to an 'austere regimen in scenery'; and such a discipline was
then recommended as 'healthful and strengthening to the taste'. That is the text,
so to speak, of the present essay. This discipline in scenery, it must be understood,
is something more than a mere walk before breakfast to whet the appetite. For
when we are put down in some unsightly neighbourhood, and especially if we
have come to be more or less dependent on what we see, we must set ourselves
to hunt out beautiful things with all the ardour and patience of a botanist after a
rye plant. Day by day we perfect ourselves in the art of seeing nature more
favourably. We learn to live with her, as people learn to live with fretful or violent
spouses: to dwell lovingly on what is good, and shut our eyes against all that is
bleak or inharmonious. We learn, also, to come to each place in the right spirit.
The traveller, as Brantome quaintly tells us, *'Fait des discourse en soi pour
soutenir en chemin'*; and into these discourses he weaves something out of all that
he sees and suffers by the way; they take their tone greatly from the varying character of the scene; a sharp ascent brings different thoughts from a level road; and
the man's fancies grow lighter as he comes out of the wood into a clearing. Nor
does the scenery any more affect the thoughts than the thoughts affect the
scenery. We see places through our humours as through differently coloured
glasses. We are ourselves a term in the equation, a note of the chord, and make
discord or harmony almost at will. There is no fear for the result, if we can but
surrender ourselves sufficiently to the country that surrounds and follows us, so
that we are ever thinking suitable thoughts or telling ourselves some suitable sort
of story as we go. We become thus, in some sense, a centre of beauty; we are
provocative of beauty, much as a gentle and sincere character is provocative of
sincerity and gentleness in others. And even where there is no harmony to be
elicited by the quickest and most obedient of spirits, we may still embellish a
place with some attraction of romance. We may learn to go far afield for associations, and handle them lightly when we have found them. Sometimes an old print
comes to our aid; I have seen many a spot lit up at once with picturesque imagi-

3

nations, by a reminiscence of Callot, or Sadeler, or Paul Brill. Dick Turpin has been my lay figure for many an English lane. And I suppose the Trossachs would hardly be the Trossachs for most tourists if a man of admirable romantic instinct had not peopled it for them with harmonious figures, and brought them thither with minds rightly prepared for the impression[1]. There is half the battle in this preparation. For instance: I have rarely been able to visit, in the proper spirit, the wild and inhospitable places of our own Highlands. I am happier where it is tame and fertile, and not readily pleased without trees. I understand that there are some phases of mental trouble that harmonise well with such surroundings, and that some persons, by the dispensing power of the imagination, can go back several centuries in spirit, and put themselves into sympathy with the hunted, houseless, unsociable way of life that was in its place upon these savage hills. Now, when I am sad, I like nature to charm me out of my sadness, like David before Saul; and the thought of these past ages strikes nothing in me but an unpleasant pity; so that I can never hit on the right humour for this sort of landscape, and lose much pleasure in consequence. Still, even here, if I were only let alone, and time enough were given, I should have all manner of pleasures, and take many clear and beautiful images away with me when I left. When we cannot think ourselves into sympathy with the great features of a country, we learn to ignore them, and put our head among the grass for flowers, or pore, for long times together, over the changeful current of a stream. We come down to the sermon in stones, when we are shut out from any poem in the spread landscape. We begin to peep and botanise, we take an interest in birds and insects, we find many things beautiful in miniature. The reader will recollect the little summer scene in *Wuthering Heights* – the one warm scene, perhaps, in all that powerful, miserable novel – and the great feature that is made therein by grasses and flowers and a little sunshine: this is in the spirit of which I now speak. And, lastly, we can go indoors; interiors are sometimes as beautiful, often more picturesque, than the shows of the open air, and they have that quality of shelter of which I shall presently have more to say.

With all this in mind, I have often been tempted to put forth the paradox that any place is good enough to live a life in, while it is only in a few, and those highly favoured, that we can pass a few hours agreeably. For, if we only stay long enough we become at home in the neighbourhood. Reminiscences spring up, like flowers, about uninteresting corners. We forget to some degree the superior loveliness of other places, and fall into a tolerant and sympathetic spirit which is its own reward and justification. Looking back the other day on some recollections of my own, I was astonished to find how much I owed to such a residence; six weeks in one unpleasant country-side had done more, it seemed, to quicken and educate my sensibilities than many years in places that jumped more nearly with my inclination.

The country to which I refer was a level and tree-less plateau, over which the winds cut like a whip[2]. For miles and miles it was the same. A river, indeed, fell into the sea near the town[3] where I resided; but the valley of the river was shallow and bald, for as far up as ever I had the heart to follow it. There were roads, certainly, but roads that had no beauty or interest; for, as there was no timber, and but little irregularity of surface, you saw your whole walk exposed to you from the beginning: there was nothing left to fancy, nothing to expect, nothing to see by the wayside, save here and there an unhomely-looking homestead, and here and there a solitary, spectacled stone-breaker; and you were only accompanied, as you went doggedly forward, by the gaunt telegraph-posts and the hum of the resonant wires in the keen sea-wind. To one who had learned to know their song in warm pleasant places by the Mediterranean, it seemed to taunt the country, and make it still bleaker by suggested contrast. Even the waste places by the side of the road were not, as Hawthorne[4] liked to put it, 'taken back to Nature' by any decent covering of vegetation. Wherever the land had the chance, it seemed to lie fallow. There is a certain tawny nudity of the South, bare sunburnt plains, coloured like a lion, and hills clothed only in the blue transparent air; but this was of another description – this was the nakedness of the North; the earth seemed to know that it was naked, and was ashamed and cold.

It seemed to be always blowing on that coast. Indeed, this had passed into the speech of the inhabitants, and they saluted each other when they met with 'Breezy, breezy,' instead of the customary 'Fine day' of farther south. These continual winds were not like the harvest breeze, that just keeps an equable pressure against your face as you walk, and serves to set all the trees talking over your head, or bring round you the smell of the wet surface of the country after a shower. They were of the bitter, hard, persistent sort, that interferes with sight and respiration, and makes the eyes sore. Even such winds as these have their own merit in proper time and place. It is pleasant to see them brandish great masses of shadow. And what a power they have over the colour of the world! How they ruffle the solid woodlands in their passage, and make them shudder and whiten like a single willow! There is nothing more vertiginous than a wind like this among the woods, with all its sights and noises; and the effect gets between some painters and their sober eyesight, so that, even when the rest of their picture is calm, the foliage is coloured like foliage in a gale. There was nothing, however, of this sort to be noticed in a country where there were no trees and hardly any shadows, save the passive shadows of clouds or those of rigid houses and walls. But the wind was nevertheless an occasion of pleasure; for nowhere could you taste more fully the pleasure of a sudden lull, or a place of opportune shelter. The reader knows what I mean; he must remember how, when he has sat himself down behind a dyke on a hillside, he delighted to hear the wind hiss vainly through the crannies at his back; how his body tingled all over with warmth, and it began to dawn upon him, with a sort of slow surprise, that the country was beautiful, the heather purple, and the far-away hills all marbled with sun and shadow. Wordsworth, in a beautiful passage of the 'Prelude'[5], has used this as a figure for the feeling struck in us by the quiet by-streets of London after the uproar of the great thoroughfares; and the comparison may be turned the other way with as good effect:

> Meanwhile the roar continues, till at length
> Escaped as from an enemy, we turn
> Abruptly into some sequester'd nook,
> Still as a shelter'd place when winds blow loud!

I remember meeting a man once, in a train, who told me of what must have been quite the most perfect instance of this pleasure of escape. He had gone up, one sunny, windy morning, to the top of a great cathedral somewhere abroad; I think it was Cologne Cathedral, the great unfinished marvel by the Rhine; and after a long while in dark stairways, he issued at last into the sunshine, on a platform high above the town. At that elevation it was quite still and warm; the gale was only in the lower strata of the air, and he had forgotten it in the quiet interior of the church and during his long ascent; and so you may judge of his surprise when, resting his arms on the sunlit balustrade and looking over into the *place* far below him, he saw the good people holding on their hats and leaning hard against the wind as they walked. There is something, to my fancy, quite perfect in this little experience of my fellow-traveller's. The ways of men seem always very trivial to us when we find ourselves alone on a church-top, with the blue sky and a few tall pinnacles, and see far below us the steep roofs and foreshortened buttresses, and the silent activity of the city streets; but how much more must they not have seemed so to him as he stood, not only above other men's business, but above other men's climate, in a golden zone like Apollo's!

This was the sort of pleasure I found in the country of which I write. The pleasure was to be out of the wind, and to keep it in memory all the time, and hug oneself upon the shelter. And it was only by the sea that any such sheltered places were to be found. Between the black worm-eaten head-lands there are little bights and havens, well screened from the wind and the commotion of the external sea, where the sand and weeds look up into the gazer's face from a depth of tranquil water, and the sea-birds, screaming and flickering from the ruined crags, alone disturb the silence and the sunshine. One such place has impressed itself on my memory beyond all others. On a rock by the water's edge, old fighting men of the Norse breed had planted a double castle; the two stood wall to wall like semi-detached villas; and yet feud had run so high between their owners, that one, from out of a window, shot the other as he stood in his own doorway. There is something in the juxtaposition of these two enemies full of tragic irony. It is grim to think of bearded men and bitter women taking hateful counsel together about the two hall-fires at night, when the sea boomed against the foundations and the wild winter wind was loose over the battlements. And in the study we may reconstruct for ourselves some pale figure of what life then was. Not so when we are there; when we are there such thoughts come to us only to intensify a contrary impression, and association is turned against itself. I remember walking thither three afternoons in succession, my eyes weary with being set against the wind, and how, dropping suddenly over the edge of the down, I found myself in a new world of warmth and shelter. The wind, from which I had escaped, 'as from an enemy', was seemingly quite local. It carried no clouds with it, and came from such a quarter that it did not trouble the sea within view. The two castles, black and ruinous as the rocks about them, were still distinguishable from these by something more insecure and fantastic in the outline, something that the last storm had left imminent and the next would demolish entirely. It would be diffi-cult to render in words the sense of peace that took possession of me on these three afternoons. It was helped out, as I have said, by the contrast. The shore was battered and bemauled by previous tempests; I had the memory at heart of the insane strife of the pigmies who had erected these two castles and lived in them in mutual distrust and enmity, and knew I had only to put my head out of this lit-tle cup of shelter to find the hard wind blowing in my eyes; and yet there were the two great tracts of motionless blue air and peaceful sea looking on, uncon-cerned and apart, at the turmoil of the present moment and the memorials of the precarious past. There is ever something transitory and fretful in the impression of a high wind under a cloudless sky; it seems to have no root in the constitution of things; it must speedily begin to faint and wither away like a cut flower. And on those days the thought of the wind and the thought of human life came very near together in my mind. Our noisy years did indeed seem moments in the being of the eternal silence; and the wind, in the face of that great field of stationary blue, was as the wind of a butterfly's wing. The placidity of the sea was a thing likewise to be remembered. Shelley[6] speaks of the sea as 'hungering for calm', and in this place one learned to understand the phrase. Looking down into these green waters from the broken edge of the rock, or swimming leisurely in the sunshine, it seemed to me that they were enjoying their own tranquility; and when now and again it was disturbed by a wind ripple on the surface, or the quick black passage of a fish far below, they settled back again (one could fancy) with relief.

On shore too, in the little nook of shelter, everything was so subdued and still that the least particular struck in me a pleasurable surprise. The desultory crack-ling of the whin-pods in the afternoon sun usurped the ear. The hot, sweet breath of the bank, that had been saturated all day long with sunshine, and now exhaled it into my face, was like the breath of a fellow-creature. I remember that I was haunted by two lines of French verse; in some dumb way they seemed to fit my surroundings and give expression to the contentment that was in me, and I kept repeating to myself –

Mon coeur est un luth suspendu,
Sitot qu'on le touche, il resonne.

I can give no reason why these lines came to me at this time; and for that very cause I repeat them here. For all I know, they may serve to complete the impression in the mind of the reader, as they were certainly a part of it for me.

And this happened to me in the place of all others where I liked least to stay. When I think of it I grow ashamed of my own ingratitude. 'Out of the strong came forth sweetness.' There, in the bleak and gusty North, I received, perhaps, my strongest impression of peace. I saw the sea to be great and calm; and the earth, in that little corner, was all alive and friendly to me. So, wherever a man is, he will find something to please and pacify him: in the town he will meet pleasant faces of men and women, and see beautiful flowers at a window, or hear a cage-bird singing at the corner of the gloomiest street; and for the country, there is no country without some amenity – let him only look for it in the right spirit, and he will surely find.

Notes

1. Dick Turpin was a famous English highwayman; Sir Walter Scott (1771–1832), the Scots novelist and poet and most popular author of his day, set many of his novels in the Trossachs, the wooded glen between Loch Katrine and Loch Achray in central Scotland north of Loch Lomond.
2. Caithness in the far north of Scotland.
3. The town of Wick.
4. Nathaniel Hawthorne (1804–1864), American novelist.
5. William Wordsworth (1770–1850), English poet.
6. Percy Bysshe Shelley (1792–1822), English poet.

FROM *Edinburgh: Picturesque Notes*

Edinburgh: Picturesque Notes first ran in Portfolio Magazine from June to December 1878 before appearing in book form in 1879. It was condemned by the Scotsman for its 'sarcastic, if poetic, descriptions'.

INTRODUCTION

THE ancient and famous metropolis of the North sits overlooking a windy estuary from the slope and summit of three hills. No situation could be more commanding for the head city of a kingdom; none better chosen for noble prospects. From her tall precipice and terraced gardens she looks far and wide on the sea and broad champaigns. To the east you may catch at sunset the spark of the May lighthouse, where the Firth expands into the German Ocean; and away to the west, over all the carse of Stirling, you can see the first snows upon Ben Ledi.

But Edinburgh pays cruelly for her high seat in one of the vilest climates under heaven. She is liable to be beaten upon by all the winds that blow, to be drenched with rain, to be buried in cold sea fogs out of the east, and powdered with the snow as it comes flying southward from the Highland hills. The weather is raw and boisterous in winter, shiftly and ungenial in summer, and a downright meteorological purgatory in the spring. The delicate die early, and I, as a survivor, among bleak winds and plumping rain, have been sometimes tempted to envy them their fate. For all who love shelter and the blessings of the sun, who hate dark weather and perpetual tilting against squalls, there could scarcely be found a more unhomely and harassing place of residence. Many such aspire angrily after that Somewhere-else of the imagination, where all troubles are supposed to end. They lean over the great bridge which joins the New Town with the Old[1] – that windiest spot, or high altar, in this northern temple of the winds – and watch the trains[2] smoking out from under them and vanishing into the tunnel on a voyage to brighter skies. Happy the passengers who shake off the dust of Edinburgh, and have heard for the last time the cry of the east wind among her chimney-tops! And yet the place establishes an interest in people's hearts; go where they will, they find no city of the same distinction; go where they will, they take a pride in their old home.

Venice, it has been said, differs from other cities in the sentiment which she inspires. The rest may have admirers; she only, a famous fair one, counts lovers in her train. And, indeed, even by her kindest friends, Edinburgh is not considered in a similar sense. These like her for many reasons, not any one of which is satisfactory in itself. They like her whimsically, if you will, and somewhat as a virtuoso dotes upon his cabinet. Her attraction is romantic in the narrowest meaning of the term. Beautiful as she is, she is not so much beautiful as interesting. She is pre-eminently Gothic, and all the more so since she has set herself off with some Greek airs, and erected classic temples on her crags.[3] In a word, and above all, she is a curiosity. The Palace of Holyrood[4] has been left aside in the growth of Edinburgh, and stands grey and silent in a workman's quarter and among brew-eries and gas works. It is a house of many memories. Great people of yore, kings and queens, buffoons and grave ambassadors, played their stately farce for cen-turies in Holyrood. Wars have been plotted, dancing has lasted deep into the night, – murder has been done in its chambers.[5] There Prince Charlie[6] held his phantom levées, and in a very gallant manner represented a fallen dynasty for some hours. Now, all these things of clay are mingled with the dust, the king's crown itself is shown for sixpence to the vulgar; but the stone palace has outlived these charges. For fifty weeks together, it is no more than a show for tourists and a museum of old furniture; but on the fifty-first, behold the palace reawakened and mimicking its past. The Lord Commissioner, a kind of stage sovereign, sits among stage courtiers; a coach and six and clattering escort come and go before the gate; at night, the windows are lighted up, and its near neighbours, the work-men, may dance in their own houses to the palace music. And in this the palace is typical. There is a spark among the embers; from time to time the old volcano smokes. Edinburgh has been partly abdicated, and still wears, in parody, her met-ropolitan trappings. Half a capital and half a country town, the whole city leads a double existence; it has long trances of the one and flashes of the other; like the king of the Black Isles, it is half alive and half a monumental marble. There are armed men and cannon in the old citadel overhead; you may see the troops mar-shalled in the high parade; and at night after the early winter even-fall, and in the morning before the laggard winter dawn, the wind carries abroad over Edinburgh the sound of drums and bugles. Grave judges sit bewigged in what was once the scene of imperial deliberations. Close by in the High Street perhaps the trumpets may sound about the stroke of noon; and you see a troop of citizens in tawdry masquerade; tabard above, heather-mixture trowser below, and the men them-selves trudging in the mud among unsympathetic bystanders. The grooms of a well-appointed circus tread the streets with a better presence. And yet these are the Heralds and Pursuivants of Scotland, who are about to proclaim a new law of the United Kingdom before two-score boys, and thieves, and hackney-coachmen. Meanwhile every hour the bell of the University rings out over the hum of the streets, and every hour a double tide of students, coming and going, fills the deep archways. And lastly, one night in the springtime – or say one morning rather, at the peep of day – late folk may hear voices of many men singing a psalm in uni-son from a church on one side of the old High Street; and a little later after, or perhaps a little before, the sound of many men singing a psalm in unison from another church on the opposite side of the way. There will be something in the words above the dew of Hermon, and how goodly it is to see brethren dwelling together in unity. And the late folk will tell themselves that all this singing denotes the conclusion of two yearly ecclesiastical parliaments – the parliaments of Churches which are brothers in many admirable virtues, but not especially like brothers in this particular of a tolerant and peaceful life.

Again, meditative people will find a charm in a certain consonancy between the aspect of the city and its odd and stirring history. Few places, if any, offer a more barbaric display of contrasts to the eye. In the very midst stands one of the most satisfactory crags in nature – a Bass Rock upon dry land, rooted in a garden shaken by passing trains, carrying a crown of battlements and turrets, and describing its war-like shadow over the liveliest and brightest thoroughfare of the new town. From their smoky beehives, ten stories high, the unwashed look down upon the open squares and gardens of the wealthy; and gay people sunning themselves along Princes Street, with its mile of commercial palaces all beflagged upon some great occasion, see, across a gardened valley set with statues, where the washings of the Old Town flutter in the breeze at its high windows. And then, upon all sides, what a clashing of architecture! In this one valley, where the life of the town goes most busily forward, there may be seen, shown one above and behind another by the accidents of the ground, buildings in almost every style upon the globe. Egyptian and Greek temples, Venetian palaces and Gothic spires, are huddled one over another in a most admired disorder; while, above all, the brute mass of the Castle and the summit of Arthur's Seat look down upon these imitations with a becoming dignity, as the works of Nature may look down the monuments of Art. But Nature is a more indiscriminate patroness than we imagine, and in no way frightened of a strong effect. The birds roost as willingly among the Corinthian capitals as in the crannies of the crag; the same atmosphere and daylight clothe the eternal rock and yesterday's imitation portico; and as the soft northern sunshine throws out everything into a glorified distinctness – or easterly mists, coming up with the blue evening, fuse all these incongruous features into one, and the lamps begin to glitter along the street, and faint lights to burn in the high windows across the valley – the feeling grows upon you that this also is a piece of nature in the most intimate sense; that this profusion of eccentricities, this dream in masonry and living rock, is not a drop-scene in a theatre, but a city in the world of everyday reality, connected by railway and telegraph-wire with all the capitals of Europe, and inhabited by citizens of the familiar type, who keep ledgers, and attend church, and have sold their immortal portion to a daily paper. By all the canons of romance, the place demands to be half deserted and leaning towards decay; birds we might admit in profusion, the play of the sun and winds, and a few gipsies encamped in the chief thoroughfare; but these citizens with their cabs and tramways, their trains and posters, are altogether out of key. Chartered tourists, they make free with historic localities, and rear their young among the most picturesque sites with a grand human indifference. To see them thronging by, in their neat clothes and conscious moral rectitude, and with a little air of possession that verges on the absurd, is not the least striking feature of the place.'[1]

And the story of the town is as eccentric as its appearance. For centuries it was a capital thatched with heather, it has gone up in flame to heaven, a beacon to ships at sea. It was the jousting-ground of jealous nobles, not only on Greenside, or by the King's Stables, where the tournaments were fought to the sound of trumpets and under the authority of the royal presence, but in every alley where there was room to cross swords, and in the main street, where popular tumult under the Blue Blanket alternated with the brawls of outlandish clansmen and retainers. Down in the palace John Knox reproved his queen in the accents of modern democracy.[7] In the town, in one of those little shops plastered like so many swallows' nests among the buttresses of the old Cathedral, that familiar autocrat, James VI,[8] would gladly share a bottle of wine with George Heriot[9] the goldsmith. Upon the Pentland Hills, that so quietly look down on the Castle with the city lying in waves around it, those mad and dismal fanatics, the Sweet Singers, haggard from long exposure on the moors, sat day and night with the 'tearful psalmns' to see Edinburgh consumed with fire from heaven, like another Sodom or Gomorrah. There, in the Grass-market, stiff-necked, convenanting heroes, offered up the often unnecessary, but not less honourable, sacrifice of their lives, and bade eloquent farewell to sun, moon, and stars, and earthly friendships, or died silent to the roll of drums. Down by yon outlet rode Grahame of Claverhouse[10] and his thirty dragoons, with the town beating to arms behind their horses' tails – a sorry handful thus riding for their lives, but with a man at the head who was to return in a different temper, make a dash that staggered Scotland to the heart, and die happily in the thick of fight. There Aikenhead was hanged for a piece of boyish incredulity;[11] there, a few years afterwards, David Hume[12] ruined Philosophy and Faith, an undisturbed and well-reputed citizen; and thither, in yet a few years more, Burns came from the plough-tail, as to an academy of gilt unbelief and artificial letters.[13] There, when the great exodus was made across the valley, and the New Town began to spread abroad its draughty parallelograms, and rear its long frontage on the opposing hill, there was such a flitting, such a change of domicile and dweller, as was never excelled in the history of cities: the cobbler succeeded the earl; the beggar ensconced himself by the judge's chimney; what had been a palace was used as a pauper refuge; and great mansions were so parcelled out among the least and lowest in society, that the hearthstone of the old proprietor was thought large enough to be partitioned off into a bedroom by the new.

Notes

1. The Old Town, a former slum, stretches from Edinburgh Castle to the Palace of Holyrood. Overcrowding and general squalor led to the creation of the New Town in 1725, although actual construction did not begin until some fifty years later. James Craig (1744–1795) was the architect of the New Town.

2. Waverley Station.

3. The plethora of classically-inspired buildings and monuments earned Edinburgh the sobriquet of the 'Athens of the North'.

4. The official residence of the royal family when in Edinburgh.

5. In March 1566, Mary Queen of Scot's Italian secretary David Rizzio was murdered on the orders of her husband Lord Darnley.

6. Prince Charles Edward Stuart (1720–1788), claimant to the throne of Great Britain and the 'Bonnie Prince Charlie' of legend. On 17 September 1745, the prince marched triumphantly into Edinburgh and converted Holyrood Palace into his headquarters. In 1840 Thomas Duncan (1807–1845) of Kinclaven in Perthshire, painted his best-known work, *Prince Charles's Entry into Edinburgh after Prestonpans*.

7. John Knox (c. 1513–1572), the fiery Protestant reformer and author of *First Blast of the Trumpet against the Monstrous Regiment of Women* (1558), as well as uncompromising foe of the very Catholic Mary, Queen of Scots.

8. James VI (1566–1701), King of Scotland from 1567, King of England from 1603; son of Mary, Queen of Scots and Lord Darnley (1566–1625).

9. George Heriot (1563–1624), Scottish goldsmith and philanthropist.

10. 1st Viscount Dundee, John Graham of Claverhouse (c. 1649–1689), soldier, also known as 'Bonny Dundee'.

11. Thomas Aikenhead, or Aitkenhead, an Edinburgh student, who in 1696 at the age of eighteen, was tried for heresy for professing to be an atheist and hanged.

12. David Hume (1711–1776), Scots philosopher and historian.

13. After the wild success of his *Poems Chiefly in the Scottish Dialect* in 1786, Robert Burns (1759–1796) became the toast of Edinburgh's literary and cultural elite.

°1. These sentences have, I hear, given offence in my native town, and a proportionable pleasure to our rivals of Glasgow. I confess the news caused me both pain and merriment. May I remark, as a balm for wounded fellow-townsmen, that there is nothing deadly in my accusations. Small blame to them if they keep ledgers: 'tis an excellent business habit. Churchgoing is not, that ever I heard, a subject of reproach; decency of linen is a mark of prosperous affairs, and conscious moral rectitude one of the tokens of good living. It is not their fault if the city calls for something more specious by way of inhabitants. A man in a frock-coat looks out of place upon an Alp or Pyramid, although he has the virtues of a Peabody and the talents of a Bentham. And let them console themselves – they do as well as anybody else; the population of (let us say) Chicago would cut quite as rueful a figure on the same romantic stage. To the Glasgow people I would say only one word, but that is of gold; *I have not yet written a book about Glasgow.*

The Foreigner at Home

The Foreigner at Home *was published in* Cornhill Magazine *in May 1882.*
Stevenson often commented on the profound differences between Scotland and
England. See The Scot Abroad *in this volume.*

This is no my ain house; I ken by the biggin' o't. [1]

Two recent books one by Mr. Grant White on England, one on France by the dia-
bolically clever Mr. Hillebrand, may well have set people thinking on the divisions
of races and nations. Such thoughts should arise with particular congruity and
force to inhabitants of that United Kingdom, peopled from so many different
stocks, babbling so many different dialects, and offering in its extent such singular contrasts, from the busiest over-population to the unkindliest desert, from the
Black Country to the Moor of Rannoch. It is not only when we cross the seas that
we go abroad; there are foreign parts of England; and the race that has conquered
so wide an empire has not yet managed to assimilate the islands whence she
sprang. Ireland, Wales, and the Scottish mountains still cling, in part, to their old
Gaelic speech. It was but the other day that English triumphed in Cornwall, and
they still show in Mousehole, on St. Michael's Bay, the house of the last Cornish-
speaking woman.[2] English itself, which will now frank the traveller through the
most of North America, through the greater South Sea Islands, in India, along
much of the coast of Africa, and in the ports of China and Japan, is still to be
heard, in its home country, in half a hundred varying stages of transition. You may
go all over the States, and – setting aside the actual intrusion and influence of foreigners, negro, French, or Chinese – you shall scarce meet with so marked a difference of accent as in the forty miles between Edinburgh and Glasgow, or of
dialect as in the hundred miles between Edinburgh and Aberdeen. Book English
has gone round the world, but at home we still preserve the racy idioms of our
fathers, and every county, in some parts every dale, has its own quality of speech,
vocal or verbal. In like manner, local custom and prejudice, even local religion and
local law, linger on into the latter end of the nineteenth century – *imperia in
imperio*, foreign things at home.

In spite of these promptings to reflection, ignorance of his neighbours is the
character of the typical John Bull. His is a domineering nature, steady in fight,
imperious to command, but neither curious nor quick about the life of others. In
French colonies, and still more in the Dutch, I have read that there is an immediate and lively contact between the dominant and the dominated race, that a certain sympathy is begotten, or at the least a transfusion of prejudices, making life
easier for both. But the Englishman sits apart, bursting with pride and ignorance.

He figures among his vassal in the hour of peace with the same disdainful air that led him on to victory. A passing enthusiasm for some foreign art or fashion may deceive the world, it cannot impose upon his intimates. He may be amused by a foreigner as by a monkey, but he will never condescend to study him with any patience. Miss Bird,[3] an authoress with whom I profess myself in love, declares all the viands of Japan to be uneatable – a staggering pretension. So, when the Prince of Wales's marriage was celebrated at Mentone by a dinner to the Mentonese, it was proposed to give them solid English fare – roast beef and plum pudding, and no tomfoolery. Here we have either pole of the Britannic folly. We will not eat the food of any foreigner; nor, when we have the chance, will we eager him to eat of it himself. The same spirit inspired Miss Bird's American missionaries, who had come thousands of miles to change the faith of Japan, and openly professed their ignorance of the religions they were trying to supplant.

I quote an American in this connection without scruple. Uncle Sam is better than John Bull, but he is tarred with the English stick. For Mr. Grant White the States are the New England States and nothing more. He wonders at the amount of drinking in London; let him try San Francisco. He wittily reproves English ignorance as to the status of women in America; but has he not himself forgotten Wyoming? The name Yankee, of which he is so tenacious, is used over the most of the great Union as a term of reproach. The Yankee States, of which he is so staunch a subject, are but a drop in the bucket. And we find in his book a vast virgin ignorance of the life and prospects of America; every view partial, parochial, not raised to the horizon; the moral feeling proper, at the largest, to a clique of states; and the whole scope and atmosphere not American, but merely Yankee. I will go far beyond him in reprobating the assumption and the incivility of my countryfolk to their cousins from beyond the sea; I grill in my blood over the silly rudeness of our newspaper articles; and I do not know where to look when I find myself in company with an American and see my countrymen unbending to him as to a performing dog. But in the case of Mr. Grant White example were better than precept. Wyoming is, after all, more readily accessible to Mr. White than Boston to the English, and the New England self-sufficiency no better justified than the Britannic.

It is so, perhaps, in all countries; perhaps in all, men are most ignorant of the foreigners at home. John Bull is ignorant of the States; he is probably ignorant of India; but considering his opportunities, he is far more ignorant of countries nearer his own door. There is one country, for instance – its frontier not so far from London, its people closely akin, its language the same in all essentials with the English – of which I will go bail he knows nothing. His ignorance of the sister kingdom cannot be described; it can only be illustrated by anecdote. I once travelled with a man of plausible manners and good intelligence – a University man, as the phrase goes – a man, besides, who had taken his degree in life and knew a thing or two about the age we live in. We were deep in talk, whirling between Peterborough and London; among other things, he began to describe some piece of legal injustice he had recently encountered, and I observed in my innocence that things were not so in Scotland. 'I beg your pardon,' said he, 'this is a matter of law.' He had never heard of the Scots law; nor did he choose to be informed. The law was the same for the whole country, he told me roundly; every child knew that. At last, to settle matters, I explained to him that I was a member of a Scottish legal body, and had stood the brunt of an examination in the very law in question. Thereupon he looked me for a moment full in the face and dropped the conversation. This is a monstrous instance, if you like, but it does not stand alone in the experience of Scots.

England and Scotland differ, indeed, in law, in history, in religion, in education, and in the very look of nature and men's faces, not always widely, but always trenchantly. Many particulars that struck Mr. Grant White, a Yankee, struck me, a Scot, no less forcibly; he and I felt ourselves foreigners on many common provocations. A Scotchman may tramp the better part of Europe and the United States, and never again receive so vivid an impression of foreign travel and strange lands and manners as on his first excursion into England. The change from a hilly to a level country strikes him with delighted wonder. Along the flat horizon there arise the frequent venerable towers of churches. He sees at the end of airy vistas the revolution of the windmill sails. He may go where he pleases in the future; he may see Alps, and Pyramids, and lions; but it will be hard to beat the pleasure of that moment. There are, indeed, few merrier spectacles than that of many windmills bickering together in a fresh breeze over a woody country; their halting alacrity of movement, their pleasant business, making bread all day with uncouth gesticulations, their air, gigantically human, as of a creature half alive, put a spirit of romance into the tamest landscape. When the Scotch child sees them first he falls immediately in love; and from that time forward windmills keep turning in his dreams. And so, in their degree, with every feature of the life and landscape. The warm, habitable age of towns and hamlets, the green, settled, ancient look of the country; the lush hedgerows, stiles, and privy path-ways in the fields; the sluggish, brimming rivers; chalk and smock-frocks; chimes of bells and the rapid, pertly-sounding English speech – they are all new to the curiosity; they are all set to English airs in the child's story that he tells himself at night. The sharp edge of novelty wears off; the feeling is scotched, but I doubt whether it is ever killed. Rather it keeps returning, ever the more rarely and strangely, and even in scenes to which you have been long accustomed suddenly awakes and gives a relish to enjoyment or heightens the sense of isolation.

One thing especially continues unfamiliar to the Scotchman's eye – the domestic architecture, the look of streets and buildings; the quaint, venerable age of many, and the thin walls and warm colouring of all. We have, in Scotland, far fewer ancient buildings, above all in country places; and those that we have are all of hewn or harled masonry. Wood has been sparingly used in their construction; the window-frames are sunken in the wall, not flat to the front, as in England; the roofs are steeper-pitched; even a hill farm will have a massy, square, cold and permanent appearance. English houses, in comparison, have the look of cardboard toys, such as a puff might shatter. And to this the Scotchman never becomes used. His eye can never rest consciously on one of these brick houses – rickles of brick, as he might call them – or on one of these flat-chested streets, but he is instantly reminded where he is, and instantly travels back in fancy to his home. 'This is no my ain house; I ken by the biggin' o't.' And yet perhaps it is his own, bought with his own money, the key of it long polished in his pocket; but it has not yet, and never will be, thoroughly adopted by his imagination; nor does he cease to remember that, in the whole length and breadth of his native country, there was no building even distantly resembling it.

But it is not alone in scenery and architecture that we count England foreign. The constitution of society, the very pillars of the empire, surprise and even pain us. The dull, neglected peasant, sunk in matter, insolent, gross and servile, makes a startling contrast with our own long-legged, long-headed, thoughtful, Bible-quoting ploughman. A week or two in such a place as Suffolk leaves the Scotchman gasping. It seems incredible that within the boundaries of his own island a class should have been thus forgotten. Even the educated and intelligent, who hold our own opinions and speak in our own words, yet seem to hold them with a difference or, from another reason, and to speak on all things with less interest and conviction. The first shock of English society is like a cold plunge. It is possible that the Scot comes looking for too much, and to be sure his first experiment will be in the wrong direction. Yet surely his complaint is grounded; surely the speech of Englishmen is too often lacking in generous ardour, the better part of the man too often withheld from the social commerce, and the contact of mind with mind evaded as with terror. A Scotch peasant will talk more liberally out of his own experience. He will not put you by with conversational counters and small jests; he will give you the best of himself, like one interested in life and man's chief end. A Scotchman is vain, interested in himself and others, eager for sympathy, setting forth his thoughts and experience in the best light. The egoism of the Englishman is self-contained. He does not seek to proselytise. He takes no interest in Scotland or the Scotch, and, what is the unkindest cut of all, he does not care to justify his indifference. Give him the wages of going on and being an Englishman, that is all he asks; and in the meantime, while you continue to associate, he would rather not be reminded of your baser origin. Compared with the grand, tree-like self-sufficiency of his demeanour, the vanity and curiosity of the Scot seem uneasy, vulgar, and immodest. That you should continually try to establish human and serious relations, that you should actually feel an interest in John

Bull, and desire and invite a return of interest from him, may argue something more awake and lively in your mind, but it still puts you in the attitude of a suitor and a poor relation. Thus even the lowest class of the educated English towers over a Scotchman by the head and shoulders.

Different indeed is the atmosphere in which Scotch and English youth begin to look about them, come to themselves in life, and gather up those first apprehensions which are the material of future thought and, to a great extent, the rule of future conduct. I have been to school in both countries, and I found, in the boys of the North, something at once rougher and more tender, at once more reserve and more expansion, a greater habitual distance chequered by glimpses of a nearer intimacy, and on the whole wider extremes of temperament and sensibility. The boy of the South seems more wholesome, but less thoughtful; he gives himself to games as to a business, striving to excel, but is not readily transported by imagination; the type remains with me as cleaner in mind and body, more active, fonder of eating, endowed with a lesser and a less romantic sense of life and of the future, and more immersed in present circumstances. And certainly, for one thing, English boys are younger for their age. Sabbath observance makes a series of grim, and perhaps serviceable, pauses in the tenor of Scotch boyhood – days of great stillness and solitude for the rebellious mind, when in the dearth of books and play, and in the intervals of studying the Shorter Catechism, the intellect and senses prey upon and test each other. The typical English Sunday, with the huge midday dinner and the plethoric afternoon, leads perhaps to different results. About the very cradle of the Scot there goes a hum of metaphysical divinity; and the whole of two divergent systems is summed up, not merely speciously, in the two first questions of the rival catechisms, the English tritely inquiring, 'What is your name?' the Scottish striking at the very roots of life with, 'What is the chief end of man?' and answering nobly, if obscurely, 'To glorify God and to enjoy Him for ever.' I do not wish to make an idol of the Shorter Catechism; but the fact of such a question being asked opens to us Scotch a great field of speculation; and the fact that it is asked of all of us, from the peer to the ploughboy, binds us more nearly together. No Englishman of Byron's age, character, and history would have had patience for long theological discussions on the way to fight for Greece; but the daft Gordon blood and the Aberdonian school-days kept their influence to the end. We have spoken of the material conditions; nor need much more be said of these: of the land lying everywhere more exposed, of the wind always louder and bleaker, of the black, roaring winters, of the gloom of high-lying, old stone cities, imminent on the windy seaboard; compared with the level streets, the warm colouring of the brick, the domestic quaintness of the architecture, among which English children begin to grow up and come to themselves in life. As the stage of the University approaches, the contrast becomes more express. The English lad goes to Oxford or Cambridge; there, in an ideal world of gardens, to lead a semi-scenic life, costumed, disciplined and drilled by proctors. Nor is this to be regarded merely as a stage of education; it is a piece of privilege besides, and a step that separates him further from the bulk of his compatriots. At an earlier age the Scottish lad begins his greatly different experience of crowded class-rooms, of a gaunt quadrangle, of a bell hourly booming over the traffic of the city to recall him from the public-house where he has been lunching, or the streets where he has been wandering fancy-free. His college life has little of restraint, and nothing of necessary gentility. He will find no quiet clique of the exclusive, studious and cultured; no rotten borough of the arts. All classes rub shoulders on the greasy benches. The raffish young gentleman in gloves must measure his scholarship with the plain, clownish laddie from the parish school. They separate, at the session's end, one to smoke cigars about a watering-place, the other to resume the labours of the field beside his peasant family. The first muster of a college class in Scotland is a scene of curious and painful interest; so many lads, fresh from the heather, hang round the stove in cloddish embarrassment, ruffled by the presence of their smarter comrades, and afraid of the sound of their own rustic voices. It was in these early days, I think, that Professor Blackie[4] won the affection of his pupils, putting these uncouth, umbrageous students at their ease with ready human geniality. Thus, at least, we have a healthy democratic atmosphere to breathe in while at work; even when there is no cordiality there is always a juxtaposition of the different classes, and in the competition of study the intellectual power of each is plainly demonstrated to the other. Our tasks ended, we of the North go forth as freemen into the humming, lamplit city. At five o'clock you may see the last of us hiving from the college gates, in the glare of the shop windows, under the green glimmer of the winter sunset. The frost tingles in our blood; no proctor lies in wait to intercept us; till the bell sounds again, we are the masters of the world; and some portion of our lives is always Saturday, *la treve de dieu*.

Nor must we omit the sense of the nature of his country and his country's history gradually growing in the child's mind from story and from observation. A Scottish child hears much of shipwreck, outlying iron skerries, pitiless breakers, and great sea-lights; much of heathery mountains, wild clans, and hunted Covenanters. Breaths come to him in song of the distant Cheviots and the ring of foraying hoofs. He glories in his hard-fisted forefathers, of the iron girdle and the handful of oat-meal, who rode so swiftly and lived so sparely on their raids. Poverty, ill-luck, enterprise, and constant resolution are the fibres of the legend of his country's history. The heroes and kings of Scotland have been tragically fated; the most marking incidents in Scottish history – Flodden, Darien, or the Forty-five[5] were still either failures or defeats; and the fall of Wallace and the repeated reverses of the Bruce[6] combine with the very smallness of the country to teach rather a moral than a material criterion for life. Britain is altogether small, the mere taproot of her extended empire: Scotland, again, which alone the

Scottish boy adopts in his imagination, is but a little part of that, and avowedly cold, sterile and unpopulous. It is not so for nothing. I once seemed to have perceived in an American boy a greater readiness of sympathy for lands that are great, and rich, and growing, like his own. It proved to be quite otherwise: a mere dumb piece of boyish romance, that I had lacked penetration to divine. But the error serves the purpose of my argument; for I am sure, at least, that the heart of young Scotland will be always touched more nearly by paucity of number and Spartan poverty of life.

So we may argue, and yet the difference is not explained. That Shorter Catechism which I took as being so typical of Scotland, was yet composed in the city of Westminster. The division of races is more sharply marked within the borders of Scotland itself than between the countries. Galloway and Buchan, Lothian and Lochaber, are like foreign parts; yet you may choose a man from any of them, and, ten to one, he shall prove to have the headmark of a Scot. A century and a half ago the Highlander wore a different costume, spoke a different language, worshipped in another church, held different morals, and obeyed a different social constitution from his fellow-countrymen either of the south or north. Even the English, it is recorded, did not loathe the Highlander and the Highland costume as they were loathed by the remainder of the Scotch. Yet the Highlander felt himself a Scot. He would willingly raid into the Scotch lowlands; but his courage failed him at the border, and he regarded England as a perilous, unhomely land. When the Black Watch, after years of foreign service, returned to Scotland, veterans leaped out and kissed the earth at Port Patrick. They had been in Ireland, stationed among men of their own race and language, where they were well liked and treated with affection; but it was the soil of Galloway that they kissed at the extreme end of the hostile lowlands, among a people who did not understand their speech, and who had hated, harried, and hanged them since the dawn of history. Last, and perhaps most curious, the sons of chieftains were often educated on the continent of Europe. They went abroad speaking Gaelic; they returned speaking, not English, but the broad dialect of Scotland. Now, what idea had they in their minds when they thus, in thought, identified themselves with their ancestral enemies? What was the sense in which they were Scotch and not English, or Scotch and not Irish? Can a bare name be thus influential on the minds and affections of men, and a political aggregation blind them to the nature of facts? The story of the Austrian Empire would seem to answer, NO; the far more galling business of Ireland clenches the negative from nearer home. Is it common education, common morals, a common language or a common faith, that join men into nations? There were practically none of these in the case we are considering.

The fact remains: in spite of the difference of blood and language, the Lowlander feels himself the sentimental countryman of the Highlander. When they meet abroad, they fall upon each other's necks in spirit; even at home there is a kind of clannish intimacy in their talk. But from his compatriot in the south the Lowlander stands consciously apart. He has had a different training; he obeys different laws; he makes his will in other terms, is otherwise divorced and married; his eyes are not at home in an English landscape or with English houses; his ear continues to remark the English speech; and even though his tongue acquire the Southern knack, he will still have a strong Scotch accent of the mind.

Notes

1. *This Is No My Ain House*. Jacobite song written to lament Bonnie Prince Charlie's loss at Culloden in his failed attempt to recapture the British crown from the Hanover dynasty for the Stuarts.

2. Thought to be a fishwife from Mousehole named Dolly Pentreath, who died in 1777. Others say the last exclusively Cornish speaker was actually John Davey of Zennor, who died in 1891.

3. Isabella Bird, nineteenth-century English traveller and an early visitor to Japan.

4. John Stuart Blackie (1809–1895), Professor of Greek at Edinburgh University. Stevenson was one of his students.

5. The Scots suffered heavy casualties at the Battle of Flodden in 1513, including the Scots king James IV (1473–1513) and his son Alexander (1493–1513). The Darien Scheme was the brainchild of William Paterson (1658–1719), the Scots-born founder of the Bank of England, who planned a Scottish colony on the isthmus of Darien in Central America, which proved to be a disaster for everyone involved. For a fictional account of the disaster – spirited and well told – see *The Rising Sun* by Douglas Galbraith (New York: Grove Press, 2001). The Forty-five refers to the failed attempt by Charles Edward Stuart to reclaim the throne of his ancestors.

6. William Wallace (c.1274–1305), Scots patriot; Robert the Bruce (1274–1329), King of Scotland from 1306 and hero of the Scottish War of Independence.

Memoirs of an Islet

Earraid is an islet off the western coast of the Isle of Mull. In August 1870,
Stevenson travelled on the steamer Iona *from Glasgow to Oban[1] to the tiny*
island, where he joined his father's engineering firm during the construction of
the Dhu Heartach lighthouse. He writes about his visit to Earraid in Memoirs of
an Islet, *which first appeared in* Memories and Portraits *(1887). The islet also*
became the setting for his short story The Merry Men *(1881) and, once again, in*
chapter 14 of Kidnapped *(1886).*

THOSE who try to be artists use, time after time, the matter of their recollections, setting and resetting little coloured memories of men and scenes, rigging
up (it may be) some especial friend in the attire of a buccaneer, and decreeing
armies to manoeuvre, or murder to be done, on the playground of their
youth. But the memories are a fairy gift which cannot be worn out in using. After
a dozen services in various tales, the little sunbright pictures of the past still shine
in the mind's eye with not a lineament defaced, not a tint impaired. *Gluck und
ungluck wird gesang*, if Goethe[2] pleases; yet only by endless avatars, the original
re-embodying after each. So that a writer, in time, begins to wonder at the perdurable life of these impressions; begins, perhaps, to fancy that he wrongs them
when he weaves them in with fiction; and looking back on them with ever-grow-
ing kindness, puts them at last, substantive jewels, in a setting of their own.

One or two of these pleasant spectres I think I have laid. I used one but the
other day: a little eyot of dense, freshwater sand, where I once waded deep in butterburrs, delighting to hear the song of the river on both sides, and to tell myself
that I was indeed and at last upon an island. Two of my puppets lay there a summer's day, hearkening to the shearers at work in riverside fields and to the drums
of the gray old garrison upon the neighbouring hill. And this was, I think, done
rightly: the place was rightly peopled – and now belongs not to me but to my puppets – for a time at least. In time, perhaps, the puppets will grow faint; the original memory swim up instant as ever; and I shall once more lie in bed, and see the
little sandy isle in Allan Water as it is in nature, and the child (that once was me)
wading there in butterburrs; and wonder at the instancy and virgin freshness of
that memory; and be pricked again, in season and out of season, by the desire to
weave it into art.

There is another isle in my collection, the memory of which besieges me. I put
a whole family there, in one of my tales;[3] and later on, threw upon its shores, and
condemned to several days of rain and shellfish on its tumbled boulders, the hero
of another.[4] The ink is not yet faded; the sound of the sentences is still in my
mind's ear; and I am under a spell to write of that island again.

I

The little isle of Earraid lies close to the south-west corner of the Ross of Mull: the sound of Iona on one side, across which you may see the isle and church of Columba;[5] the open sea to the other, where you shall be able to mark, on a clear, surfy day, the breakers running white on many sunken rocks. I first saw it, or first remembered seeing it, framed in the round bull's-eye of a cabin port, the sea lying smooth along its shores like the waters of a lake, the colourless clear light of the early morning making plain its heathery and rocky hummocks. There stood upon it, in these days, a single rude house of uncemented stones, approached by a pier of wreckwood. It must have been very early, for it was then summer, and in summer, in that latitude, day scarcely withdraws; but even at that hour the house was making a sweet smoke of peats which came to me over the bay, and the bare-legged daughters of the cotter were wading by the pier. The same day we visited the shores of the isle in the ship's boats; rowed deep into Fiddler's Hole, sounding as we went, and having taken stock of all possible accommodation, pitched on the northern inlet as the scene of operations. For it was no accident that had brought the lighthouse steamer to anchor in the Bay of Earraid. Fifteen miles away to seaward, a certain black rock stood environed by the Atlantic rollers, the outpost of the Torran reefs. Here was a tower to be built, and a star lighted, for the conduct of seamen.[6] But as the rock was small, and hard of access, and far from land, the work would be one of years; and my father was now looking for a shore station, where the stones might be quarried and dressed, the men live, and the tender, with some degree of safety, lie at anchor.

I saw Earraid next from the stern thwart of an Iona lugger, Sam Bough[7] and I sitting there cheek by jowl, with our feet upon our baggage, in a beautiful, clear, northern summer eve. And behold! there was now a pier of stone, there were rows of sheds, railways, travelling-cranes, a street of cottages, an iron house for the resident engineer, wooden bothies for the men, a stage where the courses of the tower were put together experimentally, and behind the settlement a great gash in the hillside where granite was quarried. In the bay, the steamer lay at her moorings. All day long there hung about the place the music of chinking tools; and even in the dead of night, the watchman carried his lantern to and fro in the dark settlement and could light the pipe of any midnight muser. It was, above all, strange to see Earraid on the Sunday, when the sound of the tools ceased and there fell a crystal quiet. All about the green compound men would be sauntering in their Sunday's best, walking with those lax joints of the reposing toiler, thoughtfully smoking, talking small, as if in honour of the stillness, or hearkening to the wailing of the gulls. And it was strange to see our Sabbath services, held, as they were, in one of the bothies, with Mr. Brebner reading at a table, and the congregation perched about in the double tier of sleeping bunks; and to hear the singing of the psalms, 'the chapters', the inevitable Spurgeon's sermon, and the old, eloquent lighthouse prayer.

In fine weather, when by the spy-glass on the hill the sea was observed to run low upon the reef, there would be a sound of preparation in the very early morning; and before the sun had risen from behind Ben More, the tender would steam out of the bay. Over fifteen sea-miles of the great blue Atlantic rollers she ploughed her way, trailing at her tail a brace of wallowing stone-lighters. The open ocean widened upon either board, and the hills of the mainland began to go down on the horizon, before she came to her unhomely destination, and lay-to at last where the rock clapped its black head above the swell, with the tall iron barrack on its spider legs, and the truncated tower, and the cranes waving their arms, and the smoke of the engine-fire rising in the mid-sea. An ugly reef is this of the Dhu Heartach; no pleasant assemblage of shelves, and pools, and creeks, about which a child might play for a whole summer without weariness, like the Bell Rock or the Skerryvore,[8] but one oval nodule of black-trap, sparsely bedabbled with an inconspicuous fucus, and alive in every crevice with a dingy insect between a slater and a bug. No other life was there but that of sea-birds, and of the sea itself, that here ran like a mill-race, and growled about the outer reef for ever, and ever and again, in the calmest weather, roared and spouted on the rock itself. Times were different upon Dhu-Heartach when it blew, and the night fell dark, and the neighbour lights of Skerryvore and Rhu-val were quenched in fog, and the men sat prisoned high up in their iron drum, that then resounded with the lashing of the sprays. Fear sat with them in their sea-beleaguered dwelling; and the colour changed in anxious faces when some greater billow struck the barrack, and its pillars quivered and sprang under the blow. It was then that the foreman builder, Mr. Goodwillie, whom I see before me still in his rock-habit of undecipherable rags, would get his fiddle down and strike up human minstrelsy amid the music of the storm. But it was in sunshine only that I saw Dhu-Heartach; and it was in sunshine, or the yet lovelier summer afterglow, that the steamer would return to Earraid, ploughing an enchanted sea; the obedient lighters, relieved of their deck cargo, riding in her wake more quietly; and the steersman upon each, as she rose on the long swell, standing tall and dark against the shining west.

But it was in Earraid itself that I delighted chiefly. The lighthouse settlement scarce encroached beyond its fences; over the top of the first brae the ground was all virgin, the world all shut out, the face of things unchanged by any of man's doings. Here was no living presence, save for the limpets on the rocks, for some old, gray, rain-beaten ram that I might rouse out of a ferny den betwixt two boulders, or for the haunting and the piping of the gulls. It was older than man; it was found so by incoming Celts, and seafaring Norsemen, and Columba's priests. The earthy savour of the bog-plants, the rude disorder of the boulders, the inimitable seaside brightness of the air, the brine and the iodine, the lap of the billows among the weedy reefs, the sudden springing up of a great run of dashing surf along the sea-front of the isle, all that I saw and felt my predecessors must have seen and felt with scarce a difference. I steeped myself in open air and in past ages.

Delightful would it be to me to be in Uchd Ailiun
On the pinnacle of a rock.
That I might often see
The face of the ocean;
That I might hear the song of the wonderful birds.
Source of happiness;
That I might hear the thunder of the crowding waves
Upon the rocks;
At times at work without compulsion –
This would be delightful;
At times plucking dulse from the rocks
At times at fishing.[9]

So, about the next island of Iona, sang Columba himself twelve hundred years before. And so might I have sung of Earraid.

And all the while I was aware that this life of sea-bathing and sun-burning was for me but a holiday. In that year cannon were roaring for days together on French battlefields;[10] and I would sit in my isle (I call it mine, after the use of lovers) and think upon the war, and the loudness of these far-away battles, and the pain of the men's wounds, and the weariness of their marching. And I would think too of that other war which is as old as mankind, and is indeed the life of man: the unsparing war, the grinding slavery of competition; the toil of seventy years, dear-bought bread, precarious honour, the perils and pitfalls, and the poor rewards. It was a long look forward; the future summoned me as with trumpet calls, it warned me back as with a voice of weeping and beseeching; and I thrilled and trembled on the brink of life, like a childish bather on the beach.

There was another young man on Earraid in these days, and we were much together, bathing, clambering on the boulders, trying to sail a boat and spinning round instead in the oily whirlpools of the roost. But the most part of the time we spoke of the great uncharted desert of our futures; wondering together what should there befall us; hearing with surprise the sound of our own voices in the empty vestibule of youth. As far, and as hard, as it seemed then to look forward to the grave, so far it seems now to look backward upon these emotions; so hard to recall justly that loath submission, as of the sacrificial bull, with which we stooped our necks under the yoke of destiny. I met my old companion but the other day; I cannot tell of course what he was thinking; but, upon my part, I was wondering to see us both so much at home, and so composed and sedentary in the world; and how much we had gained, and how much we had lost, to attain to that composure; and which had been upon the whole our best estate: when we sat there prating sensibly like men of some experience, or when we shared our timorous and hopeful counsels in a western islet.

Notes

1. In a letter to his parents, Stevenson describes the night spent at Oban as 'delicious ... The waters of the bay were as smooth as a millpond; and in the dusk, the black shadows of the hills stretched across to our very feet and the lights were reflected in long lines.' See Ernest Mehew, ed. *Selected Letters of Robert Louis Stevenson* (New Haven, Conn: Yale University Press, 1997), p. 13.

2. Johann Wolfgang von Goethe (1749–1832), German poet and dramatist.

3. 'The Merry Men'.

4. David Balfour in *Kidnapped*.

5. Columba (521–597), abbot of Iona.

6. Dhu Heartach lighthouse.

7. Sam Bough (1822–1878), born in Carlisle, an erstwhile bohemian friend of Stevenson who later became a respected landscape painter and member of the Royal Scottish Academy.

8. Stevenson's grandfather Robert Stevenson (1772–1850) constructed the Bell Rock lighthouse near Arbroath in 1807; his uncle Alan Stevenson (1807–1865) built 'Skerryvore' on the west coast in 1844.

9. For additional examples of Saint Columba's work, see *Iona: The Earliest Poetry of a Celtic Monastery* by Thomas Owen Clancy and Gilbert Markus (Edinburgh: Edinburgh University Press, 1995).

10. The Franco-Prussian War began in July 1870.

The Manse:

A FRAGMENT

The Manse was published in Scribner's Magazine *in May 1887 and later appeared that same year as an essay in* Memories and Portraits.

I HAVE named, among many rivers that make music in my memory, that dirty Water of Leith.[1] Often and often I desire to look upon it again; and the choice of a point of view is easy to me. It should be at a certain water-door, embowered in shrubbery. The river is there dammed back for the service of the flour-mill just below, so that it lies deep and darkling, and the sand slopes into brown obscurity with a glint of gold; and it has but newly been recruited by the borrowings of the snuff-mill just above, and these, tumbling merrily in, shake the pool to its black heart, fill it with drowsy eddies, and set the curded froth of many other mills solemnly steering to and fro upon the surface. Or so it was when I was young; for change, and the masons, and the pruning-knife, have been busy; and if I could hope to repeat a cherished experience, it must be on many and impossible conditions. I must choose, as well as the point of view, a certain moment in my growth, so that the scale may be exaggerated, and the trees on the steep opposite side may seem to climb to heaven, and the sand by the water-door, where I am standing, seem as low as Styx. And I must choose the season also, so that the valley may be brimmed like a cup with sunshine and the songs of birds; – and the year of grace, so that when I turn to leave the riverside I may find the old manse and its inhabitants unchanged.

It was a place in that time like no other: the garden cut into provinces by a great hedge of beech, and over-looked by the church and the terrace of the churchyard, where the tombstones were thick, and after nightfall 'spunkies' might be seen to dance at least by children; flower-plots lying warm in sunshine; laurels and the great yew making elsewhere a pleasing horror of shade; the smell of water rising from all round, with an added tang of paper-mills; the sound of water everywhere, and the sound of mills – the wheel and the dam singing their alternate strain; the birds on every bush and from every corner of the overhanging woods pealing out their notes until the air throbbed with them; and in the midst of this, the manse.[2] I see it, by the standard of my childish stature, as a great and roomy house. In truth, it was not so large as I supposed, nor yet so convenient, and, standing where it did, it is difficult to suppose that it was healthful. Yet a large family of stalwart sons and tall daughters were housed and reared, and came to man and womanhood in that nest of little chambers; so that the face of the earth was peppered with the children of the manse, and letters with outlandish stamps became familiar to the local postman, and the walls of the little chambers brightened with the wonders of the East. The dullest could see this was a house that had a pair of hands in divers foreign places: a well-beloved house – its image fondly dwelt on by many travellers.

Here lived an ancestor of mine, who was a herd of men.[3] I read him, judging with older criticism the report of childish observation, as a man of singular simplicity of nature; unemotional, and hating the display of what he felt; standing contented on the old ways; a lover of his life and innocent habits to the end. We children admired him: partly for his beautiful face and silver hair, for none more than children are concerned for beauty and, above all, for beauty in the old; partly for the solemn light in which we beheld him once a week, the observed of all observers, in the pulpit. But his strictness and distance, the effect, I now fancy, of old age, slow blood, and settled habit, oppressed us with a kind of terror. When not abroad, he sat much alone, writing sermons or letters to his scattered family in a dark and cold room with a library of bloodless books – or so they seemed in those days, although I have some of them now on my own shelves and like well enough to read them; and these lonely hours wrapped him in the greater gloom for our imaginations. But the study had a redeeming grace in many Indian pictures, gaudily coloured and dear to young eyes. I cannot depict (for I have no such passions now) the greed with which I beheld them; and when I was once sent in to say a psalm to my grandfather, I went, quaking indeed with fear, but at the same time glowing with hope that, if I said it well, he might reward me with an Indian picture.

Thy foot He'll not let slide, nor will He slumber that thee keeps,

it ran: a strange conglomerate of the unpronounceable, a sad model to set in childhood before one who was himself to be a versifier, and a task in recitation that really merited reward. And I must suppose the old man thought so too, and was either touched or amused by the performance; for he took me in his arms with most unwonted tenderness, and kissed me, and gave me a little kindly sermon for my psalm; so that, for that day, we were clerk and parson. I was struck by this reception into so tender a surprise that I forgot my disappointment. And indeed the hope was one of those that childhood forges for a pastime, and with no design upon reality. Nothing was more unlikely than that my grandfather should strip himself of one of those pictures, love-gifts and reminders of his absent sons; nothing more unlikely than that he should bestow it upon me. He had no idea of spoiling children, leaving all that to my aunt; he had fared hard himself, and blubbered under the rod in the last century; and his ways were still Spartan for the young. The last word I heard upon his lips was in this Spartan key. He had over-walked in the teeth of an east wind, and was now near the end of his many days. He sat by the dining-room fire, with his white hair, pale face and bloodshot eyes, a somewhat awful figure; and my aunt had given him a dose of our good old Scotch medicine, Dr. Gregory's powder. Now that remedy, as the work of a near kinsman of Rob Roy himself, may have a savour of romance for the imagination; but it comes uncouthly to the palate. The old gentleman had taken it with a wry face; and that being accomplished, sat with perfect simplicity, like a child's, munching a 'barley-sugar kiss'. But when my aunt, having the canister open in her hands, proposed to let me share in the sweets, he interfered at once. I had had no Gregory; then I should have no barley-sugar kiss: so he decided with a touch of irritation. And just then the phaeton coming opportunely to the kitchen door – for such was our unlordly fashion – I was taken for the last time from the presence of my grandfather.

Now I often wonder what I have inherited from this old minister. I must suppose, indeed, that he was fond of preaching sermons, and so am I, though I never heard it maintained that either of us loved to hear them. He sought health in his youth in the Isle of Wight, and I have sought it in both hemispheres; but whereas he found and kept it, I am still on the quest. He was a great lover of Shakespeare, whom he read aloud, I have been told, with taste; well, I love my Shakespeare also, and am persuaded I can read him well, though I own I never have been told so. He made embroidery, designing his own patterns; and in that kind of work I never made anything but a kettle-holder in Berlin wool, and an odd garter of knitting, which was as black as the chimney before I had done with it. He loved port, and nuts, and porter; and so do I, but they agreed better with my grandfather, which seems to me a breach of contract. He had chalk-stones in his fingers; and these, in good time, I may possibly inherit, but I would much rather have inherited his noble presence. Try as I please, I cannot join myself on with the reverend doctor; and all the while, no doubt, and even as I write the phrase, he moves in my blood, and whispers words to me, and sits efficient in the very knot and centre of my being. In his garden, as I played there, I learned the love of mills – or had I an ancestor a miller? – and a kindness for the neighbourhood of graves, as homely things not without their poetry – or had I an ancestor a sexton? But what of the garden where he played himself? – for that, too, was a scene of my education. Some part of me played there in the eighteenth century, and ran races under the green avenue at Pilrig; some part of me trudged up Leith Walk, which was still a country place, and sat on the High School benches, and was thrashed, perhaps, by Dr. Adam. The house where I spent my youth was not yet thought upon; but we made holiday parties among the cornfields on its site, and ate strawberries and cream near by at a gardener's. All this I had forgotten; only my grandfather remembered and once reminded me. I have forgotten, too, how we grew up, and took orders, and went to our first Ayrshire parish, and fell in love with and married a daughter of Burns's Dr. Smith – 'Smith opens out his cauld harangues.' I have forgotten, but I was there all the same, and heard stories of Burns[4] at first hand.

And there is a thing stranger than all that; for this HOMUNCULUS or part-man of mine that walked about the eighteenth century with Dr. Balfour in his youth, was in the way of meeting other HOMUNCULOS or part-men, in the persons of my other ancestors. These were of a lower order, and doubtless we looked down upon them duly. But as I went to college with Dr. Balfour, I may have seen the lamp and oil man taking down the shutters from his shop beside the Tron; – we may have had a rabbit-hutch or a bookshelf made for us by a certain carpenter in I know not what wynd of the old, smoky city; or, upon some holiday excursion, we may have looked into the windows of a cottage in a flower-garden and seen a certain weaver plying his shuttle. And these were all kinsmen of mine upon the other side; and from the eyes of the lamp and oil man one-half of my unborn father, and one-quarter of myself, looked out upon us as we went by to college. Nothing of all this would cross the mind of the young student, as he posted up the Bridges with trim, stockinged legs, in that city of cocked hats and good Scotch still unadulterated. It would not cross his mind that he should have a daughter; and the lamp and oil man, just then beginning, by a not unnatural metastasis, to bloom into a lighthouse-engineer, should have a grandson; and that these two, in the fulness of time, should wed; and some portion of that student himself should survive yet a year or two longer in the person of their child.

But our ancestral adventures are beyond even the arithmetic of fancy; and it is the chief recommendation of long pedigrees, that we can follow backward the careers of our HOMUNCULOS and be reminded of our antenatal lives. Our conscious years are but a moment in the history of the elements that build us. Are you a bank-clerk, and do you live at Peckham? It was not always so. And though to-day I am only a man of letters, either tradition errs or I was present when there landed at St. Andrews a French barber- surgeon, to tend the health and the beard of the great Cardinal Beaton;[5] I have shaken a spear in the Debateable Land and shouted the slogan of the Elliots;[6] I was present when a skipper, plying from Dundee, smuggled Jacobites to France after the '15; I was in a West India merchant's office, perhaps next door to Bailie Nicol Jarvie's, and managed the business of a plantation in St. Kitt's; I was with my engineer-grandfather (the son-in-law of the lamp and oil man) when he sailed north about Scotland on the famous cruise that gave us the *Pirate* and the *Lord of the Isles;*[7] I was with him, too, on the Bell Rock, in the fog, when the *Smeaton* had drifted from her moorings, and the Aberdeen men, pick in hand, had seized upon the only boats, and he must stoop and lap sea-water before his tongue could utter audible words; and once more with him when the Bell Rock beacon took a 'thrawe', and his workmen fled into the tower, then nearly finished, and he sat unmoved reading in his Bible – or affecting to read – till one after another slunk back with confusion of countenance to their engineer. Yes, parts of me have seen life, and met adventures, and sometimes met them well. And away in the still cloudier past, the threads that make me up can be traced by fancy into the bosoms of thousands and millions of ascendants: Picts who rallied round Macbeth and the old (and highly preferable) system of descent by females, fleers from before the legions of Agricola, marchers in Pannonian morasses, star-gazers on Chaldaean plateaus; and, furthest of all, what face is this that fancy can see peering through the disparted branches? What sleeper in green tree-tops, what muncher of nuts, concludes my pedigree? Probably arboreal in his habits ...

And I know not which is the more strange, that I should carry about with me some fibres of my minister-grandfather; or that in him, as he sat in his cool study, grave, reverend, contented gentleman, there was an aboriginal frisking of the blood that was not his; tree-top memories, like undeveloped negatives, lay dormant in his mind; tree-top instincts awoke and were trod down; and Probably Arboreal (scarce to be distinguished from a monkey) gambolled and chattered in the brain of the old divine.

Notes
1. Leith is Edinburgh's seaport and until 1920 was a separate town.
2. The house of Stevenson's maternal grandfather, the Reverend Lewis Balfour, in Colinton, several miles southwest of Edinburgh. A young Stevenson played in the garden.
3. Reverend Lewis Balfour (1777–1860).
4. Robert Burns (1759–1796), Scotland's national bard.
5. Cardinal David Beaton (1494–1546).
6. Stevenson is referring to the Border country between Scotland and England, which was the scene of much feuding for centuries. Elliot is a common Border name.
7. Robert Stevenson (1772–1850), Stevenson's grandfather, began work on the famous Bell Rock lighthouse, near Arbroath, in 1807. Sir Walter Scott was on tour with the Lighthouse Commission in 1814, collecting material that would later be used in his novel *The Pirate*.

The Lantern-Bearers

*The Lantern-Bearers was first published in February 1888 in Scribner's
Magazine and it also appeared in Across the Plains (1892). In 1988, Farrar,
Straus & Giroux published* The Lantern-Bearers and Other Essays *edited by
Jeremy Treglown (Cooper Square Press released the paperback edition in 1999).
The title refers to a childhood game that Stevenson played as a boy during
family holidays in North Berwick. He and his mates would fasten tin lanterns to
their waists, button their jackets over them, and meet in a secluded cove or cave.
Once safely inside, they would utter a secret password and then remove the lit
lanterns from underneath their heavy coats. 'The lantern,' writes Treglown in his
introduction, serves 'as a metaphor for the secret imaginative life'.*

I

THESE boys congregated every autumn about a certain easterly fisher-village,
where they tasted in a high degree the glory of existence.[1] The place was created
seemingly on purpose for the diversion of young gentlemen. A street or two of
houses, mostly red and many of them tiled; a number of fine trees clustered about
the manse and the kirkyard, and turning the chief street into a shady alley; many
little gardens more than usually bright with flowers; nets a-drying, and fisher-
wives scolding in the backward parts; a smell of fish, a genial smell of seaweed;
whiffs of blowing sand at the street-corners; shops with golf-balls and bottled lollipops; another shop with penny pickwicks (that remarkable cigar) and the
London Journal, dear to me for its startling pictures, and a few novels, dear for
their suggestive names: such, as well as memory serves me, were the ingredients
of the town. These, you are to conceive posted on a spit between two sandy bays,
and sparsely flanked with villas enough for the boys to lodge in with their sub-
sidiary parents, not enough (not yet enough) to cocknify the scene: a haven in the
rocks in front: in front of that, a file of gray islets: to the left, endless links and sand
wreaths, a wilderness of hiding-holes, alive with popping rabbits and soaring gulls:
to the right, a range of seaward crags, one rugged brow beyond another; the ruins
of a mighty and ancient fortress on the brink of one; coves between – now
charmed into sunshine quiet, now whistling with wind and clamorous with bursting surges; the dens and sheltered hollows redolent of thyme and southernwood,
the air at the cliff's edge brisk and clean and pungent of the sea – in front of all,
the Bass Rock,[2] tilted seaward like a doubtful bather, the surf ringing it with
white, the solan-geese hanging round its summit like a great and glittering smoke.
This choice piece of seaboard was sacred, besides, to the wrecker; and the Bass,
in the eye of fancy, still flew the colours of King James; and in the ear of fancy the

arches of Tantallon still rang with horse-shoe iron, and echoed to the commands of Bell-the-Cat.[3]

There was nothing to mar your days, if you were a boy summering in that part, but the embarrassment of pleasure. You might golf if you wanted; but I seem to have been better employed. You might secrete yourself in the Lady's Walk, a certain sunless dingle of elders, all mossed over by the damp as green as grass, and dotted here and there by the stream-side with roofless walls, the cold homes of anchorites. To fit themselves for life, and with a special eye to acquire the art of smoking, it was even common for the boys to harbour there; and you might have seen a single penny pickwick, honestly shared in lengths with a blunt knife, bestrew the glen with these apprentices. Again, you might join our fishing parties, where we sat perched as thick as solan-geese,[4] a covey of little anglers, boy and girl, angling over each other's heads, to the much entanglement of lines and loss of podleys and consequent shrill recrimination – shrill as the geese themselves. Indeed, had that been all, you might have done this often; but though fishing be a fine pastime, the podley is scarce to be regarded as a dainty for the table; and it was a point of honour that a boy should eat all that he had taken. Or again, you might climb the Law,[5] where the whale's jawbone stood landmark in the buzzing wind, and behold the face of many counties, and the smoke and spires of many towns, and the sails of distant ships. You might bathe, now in the flaws of fine weather, that we pathetically call our summer, now in a gale of wind, with the sand scourging your bare hide, your clothes thrashing abroad from underneath their guardian stone, the froth of the great breakers casting you headlong ere it had drowned your knees. Or you might explore the tidal rocks, above all in the ebb of springs, when the very roots of the hills were for the nonce discovered; following my leader from one group to another, groping in slippery tangle for the wreck of ships, wading in pools after the abominable creatures of the sea, and ever with an eye cast backward on the march off the tide and the menaced line of your retreat. And then you might go Crusoeing, a word that covers all extempore eating in the open air: digging perhaps a house under the margin of the links, kindling a fire of the sea-ware, and cooking apples there – if they were truly apples, for I sometimes suppose the merchant must have played us off with some inferior and quite local fruit capable of resolving, in the neighbourhood of fire, into mere sand and smoke and iodine; or perhaps pushing to Tantallon, you might lunch on sandwiches and visions in the grassy court, while the wind hummed in the crumbling turrets; or clambering along the coast, eat geans (the worst, I must suppose, in Christendom) from an adventurous gean tree that had taken root under a cliff, where it was shaken with an ague of east wind, and silvered after gales with salt, and grew so foreign among its bleak surroundings that to eat of its produce was an adventure in itself.

There are mingled some dismal memories with so many that were joyous. Of the fisher-wife, for instance, who had cut her throat at Canty Bay; and of how I ran with the other children to the top of the Quadrant, and beheld a posse of silent people escorting a cart, and on the cart, bound in a chair, her throat bandaged, and the bandage all bloody – horror! – the fisher-wife herself, who continued thenceforth to hag-ride my thoughts, and even to-day (as I recall the scene) darkens daylight. She was lodged in the little old jail in the chief street; but whether or no she died there, with a wise terror of the worst, I never inquired. She had been tippling; it was but a dingy tragedy; and it seems strange and hard that, after all these years, the poor crazy sinner should be still pilloried on her cart in the scrap-book of my memory. Nor shall I readily forget a certain house in the Quadrant where a visitor died, and a dark old woman continued to dwell alone with the dead body; nor how this old woman conceived a hatred to myself and one of my cousins, and in the dread hour of the dusk, as we were clambering on the garden-walls, opened a window in that house of mortality and cursed us in a shrill voice and with a marrowy choice of language. It was a pair of very colourless urchins that fled down the lane from this remarkable experience! But I recall with a more doubtful sentiment, compounded out of fear and exultation, the coil of equinoctial tempests; trumpeting squalls, scouring flaws of rain; the boats with their reefed lugsails scudding for the harbour mouth, where danger lay, for it was hard to make when the wind had any east in it; the wives clustered with blowing shawls at the pier-head, where (if fate was against them) they might see boat and husband and sons – their whole wealth and their whole family – engulfed under their eyes; and (what I saw but once) a troop of neighbours forcing such an unfortunate homeward, and she squalling and battling in their midst, a figure scarcely human, a tragic Maenad.

These are things that I recall with interest; but what my memory dwells upon the most, I have been all this while withholding. It was a sport peculiar to the place, and indeed to a week or so of our two months' holiday there. Maybe it still flourishes in its native spot; for boys and their pastimes are swayed by periodic forces inscrutable to man; so that tops and marbles reappear in their due season, regular like the sun and moon; and the harmless art of knucklebones has seen the fall of the Roman empire and the rise of the United States. It may still flourish in its native spot, but nowhere else, I am persuaded; for I tried myself to introduce it on Tweedside, and was defeated lamentably; its charm being quite local, like a country wine that cannot be exported.

The idle manner of it was this: –

Toward the end of September, when school-time was drawing near and the nights were already black, we would begin to sally from our-respective villas, each equipped with a tin bull's-eye lantern. The thing was so well known that it had worn a rut in the commerce of Great Britain; and the grocers, about the due time, began to garnish their windows with our particular brand of luminary. We wore them buckled to the waist upon a cricket belt, and over them, such was the rigour of the game, a buttoned top-coat. They smelled noisomely of blistered tin; they never burned aright, though they would always burn our fingers; their use was naught; the pleasure of them merely fanciful; and yet a boy with a bull's-eye under his top-coat asked for nothing more. The fishermen used lanterns about their boats, and it was from them, I suppose, that we had got the hint; but theirs were not bull's-eyes, nor did we ever play at being fishermen. The police carried them at their belts, and we had plainly copied them in that; yet we did not pretend to be policemen. Burglars, indeed, we may have had some haunting thoughts of; and we had certainly an eye to past ages when lanterns were more common, and to certain story-books in which we had found them to figure very largely. But take it for all in all, the pleasure of the thing was substantive; and to be a boy with a bull's-eye under his top-coat was good enough for us.

When two of these asses met, there would be an anxious 'Have you got your lantern?' and a gratified 'Yes!' That was the shibboleth, and very needful too; for, as it was the rule to keep our glory contained, none could recognise a lantern-bearer, unless (like the polecat) by the smell. Four or five would sometimes climb into the belly of a ten-man lugger, with nothing but the thwarts above them – for the cabin was usually locked, or choose out some hollow of the links where the wind might whistle overhead. There the coats would be unbuttoned and the bull's-eyes discovered; and in the chequering glimmer, under the huge windy hall of the night, and cheered by a rich steam of toasting tinware, these fortunate young gentlemen would crouch together in the cold sand of the links or on the scaly bilges of the fishing-boat, and delight themselves with inappropriate talk. Woe is me that I may not give some specimens – some of their foresights of life, or deep inquiries into the rudiments of man and nature, these were so fiery and so innocent, they were so richly silly, so romantically young. But the talk, at any rate, was but a condiment; and these gatherings themselves only accidents in the career of the lantern-bearer. The essence of this bliss was to walk by yourself in the black night; the slide shut, the top-coat buttoned; not a ray escaping, whether to conduct your footsteps or to make your glory public: a mere pillar of darkness in the dark; and all the while, deep down in the privacy of your fool's heart, to know you had a bull's-eye at your belt, and to exult and sing over the knowledge.

Notes
1. North Berwick was a popular resort in East Lothian, where Stevenson raced ponies across the beaches as a boy with his cousins during family holidays in the early 1860s.
2. The 350-foot Bass Rock lies a mile out in the Firth of Forth.
3. Tantallon Castle, a fourteenth-century castle, is perched on the cliffs above the Firth of Forth.
4. Gannets.
5. North Berwick Law, a 613-foot volcanic plug that lies south of North Berwick.

Contributions to the History of Fife:

RANDOM MEMORIES

This evocative essay first appeared in Scribner's Magazine *in October 1888.*

I. – THE COAST OF FIFE

MANY writers have vigorously described the pains of the first day or the first night at school; to a boy of any enterprise, I believe, they are more often agreeably exciting. Misery – or at least misery unrelieved – is confined to another period, to the days of suspense and the 'dreadful looking-for' of departure; when the old life is running to an end, and the new life, with its new interests, not yet begun: and to the pain of an imminent parting, there is added the unrest of a state of conscious pre-existence. The area railings, the beloved shop-window, the smell of semi- suburban tanpits, the song of the church bells upon a Sunday, the thin, high voices of compatriot children in a playing-field – what a sudden, what an overpowering pathos breathes to him from each familiar circumstance! The assaults of sorrow come not from within, as it seems to him, but from without. I was proud and glad to go to school; had I been let alone, I could have borne up like any hero; but there was around me, in all my native town, a conspiracy of lamentation: 'Poor little boy, he is going away – unkind little boy, he is going to leave us'; so the unspoken burthen followed me as I went, with yearning and reproach. And at length, one melancholy afternoon in the early autumn, and at a place where it seems to me, looking back, it must be always autumn and generally Sunday, there came suddenly upon the face of all I saw – the long empty road, the lines of the tall houses, the church upon the hill, the woody hillside garden – a look of such a piercing sadness that my heart died; and seating myself on a doorstep, I shed tears of miserable sympathy. A benevolent cat cumbered me the while with consolations – we two were alone in all that was visible of the London Road: two poor waifs who had each tasted sorrow – and she fawned upon the weeper, and gambolled for his entertainment, watching the effect it seemed, with motherly eyes.

For the sake of the cat, God bless her! I confessed at home the story of my weakness; and so it comes about that I owed a certain journey, and the reader owes the present paper, to a cat in the London Road. It was judged, if I had thus brimmed over on the public highway, some change of scene was (in the medical sense) indicated; my father at the time was visiting the harbour lights of Scotland;

and it was decided he should take me along with him around a portion of the shores of Fife; my first professional tour, my first journey in the complete character of man, without the help of petticoats.

The Kingdom of Fife (that royal province) may be observed by the curious on the map, occupying a tongue of land between the firths of Forth and Tay. It may be continually seen from many parts of Edinburgh (among the rest, from the windows of my father's house) dying away into the distance and the easterly *haar* with one smoky seaside town beyond another, or in winter printing on the gray heaven some glittering hill-tops. It has no beauty to recommend it, being a low, sea-salted, wind-vexed promontory; trees very rare, except (as common on the east coast) along the dens of rivers; the fields well cultivated, I understand, but not lovely to the eye. It is of the coast I speak: the interior may be the garden of Eden. History broods over that part of the world like the easterly *haar*. Even on the map, its long row of Gaelic place-names bear testimony to an old and settled race. Of these little towns, posted along the shore as close as sedges, each with its bit of harbour, its old weather-beaten church or public building, its flavour of decayed prosperity and decaying fish, not one but has its legend, quaint or tragic: Dunfermline, in whose royal towers the king may be still observed (in the ballad) drinking the blood-red wine [1] somnolent Inverkeithing, once the quarantine of Leith; Aberdour, hard by the monastic islet of Inchcolm, hard by Donibristle where the 'bonny face was spoiled'; Burntisland where, when Paul Jones[2] was off the coast, the Reverend Mr. Shirra had a table carried between tidemarks, and publicly prayed against the rover at the pitch of his voice and his broad lowland dialect; Kinghorn, where Alexander 'brak's neckbane' and left Scotland to the English wars;[3] Kirkcaldy, where the witches once prevailed extremely and sank tall ships and honest mariners in the North Sea; Dysart, famous – well famous at least to me for the Dutch ships that lay in its harbour, painted like toys and with pots of flowers and cages of song-birds in the cabin windows, and for one particular Dutch skipper who would sit all day in slippers on the break of the poop, smoking a long German pipe; Wemyss (pronounce Weems) with its bat-haunted caves, where the Chevalier Johnstone, on his flight from Culloden, passed a night of superstitious terrors; Leven, a bald, quite modern place, sacred to summer visitors, whence there has gone but yesterday the tall figure and the white locks of the last Englishman in Delhi, my uncle Dr. Balfour, who was still walking his hospital rounds, while the troopers from Meerut clattered and cried 'Deen Deen' along the streets of the imperial city, and Willoughby mustered his handful of heroes at the magazine, and the nameless brave one in the telegraph office was perhaps already fingering his last despatch; and just a little beyond Leven, Largo Law and the smoke of Largo town mounting about its feet, the town of Alexander Selkirk, better known under the name of Robinson Crusoe.[4] So on, the list might be pursued (only for private reasons, which the reader will shortly have an opportunity to guess) by St. Monance, and Pittenweem, and the two Anstruthers, and Cellardyke, and Crail, where Primate Sharpe was once a humble and innocent country minister: on to the heel of the land, to Fife Ness, overlooked by a sea-wood of matted elders and the quaint old mansion of Balcomie, itself overlooking but the breach or the quiescence of the deep – the Carr Rock beacon rising close in front, and as night draws in, the star of the Inchcape reef springing up on the one hand, and the star of the May Island on the other, and farther off yet a third and a greater on the craggy foreland of St. Abb's. And but a little way round the corner of the land, imminent itself above the sea, stands the gem of the province and the light of mediaeval Scotland, St. Andrews, where the great Cardinal Beaton held garrison against the world, and the second of the name and title perished (as you may read in Knox's jeering narrative) under the knives of true-blue Protestants, and to this day (after so many centuries) the current voice of the professor is not hushed.

Here it was that my first tour of inspection began, early on a bleak easterly morning. There was a crashing run of sea upon the shore, I recollect, and my father and the man of the harbour light must sometimes raise their voices to be audible. Perhaps it is from this circumstance, that I always imagine St. Andrews to be an ineffectual seat of learning, and the sound of the east wind and the bursting surf to linger in its drowsy classrooms and confound the utterance of the professor, until teacher and taught are alike drowned in oblivion, and only the sea-gull beats on the windows and the draught of the sea-air rustles in the pages of the open lecture. But upon all this, and the romance of St. Andrews in general, the reader must consult the works of Mr. Andrew Lang [5] who has written of it but the other day in his dainty prose and with his incommunicable humour, and long ago in one of his best poems, with grace, and local truth, and a note of unaffected pathos. Mr. Lang knows all about the romance, I say, and the educational advantages, but I doubt if he had turned his attention to the harbour lights; and it may be news even to him, that in the year 1863 their case was pitiable. Hanging about with the east wind humming in my teeth, and my hands (I make no doubt) in my pockets, I looked for the first time upon that tragi-comedy of the visiting engineer which I have seen so often re-enacted on a more important stage. Eighty years ago, I find my grandfather[6] writing: 'It is the most painful thing that can occur to me to have a correspondence of this kind with any of the keepers, and when I come to the Light House, instead of having the satisfaction to meet them with approbation and welcome their Family, it is distressing when one is obliged to put on a most angry countenance and demeanour.' This painful obligation has been hereditary in my race. I have myself, on a perfectly amateur and unauthorised inspection of Turnberry Point, bent my brows upon the keeper on the question of storm-panes; and felt a keen pang of self-reproach, when we went down stairs again and I found he was making a coffin for his infant child; and then regained my equanimity with the thought that I had done the man a service, and when the proper inspector came, he would be readier with his panes. The human race is perhaps credited with more duplicity than it deserves. The visitation of a lighthouse at least is a business of the most transparent nature. As soon as the boat grates on the shore, and the keepers step forward in their uniformed coats, the very slouch of the fellows' shoulders tells their story, and the engineer may begin at once to assume his 'angry countenance'. Certainly the brass of the handrail will be clouded; and if the brass be not immaculate, certainly all will be to match – the reflectors scratched, the spare lamp unready, the storm-panes in the storehouse. If a light is not rather more than middling good, it will be radically bad. Mediocrity (except in literature) appears to be unattainable by man. But of course the unfortunate of St. Andrews was only an amateur, he was not in the Service, he had no uniform coat, he was (I believe) a plumber by his trade and stood (in the mediaeval phrase) quite out of the danger of my father; but he had a painful interview for all that, and perspired extremely.

From St. Andrews, we drove over Magus Muir. My father had announced we were 'to post', and the phrase called up in my hopeful mind visions of top-boots and the pictures in Rowlandson's *Dance of Death*; [7] but it was only a jingling cab that came to the inn door, such as I had driven in a thousand times at the low price of one shilling on the streets of Edinburgh. Beyond this disappointment, I remember nothing of that drive. It is a road I have often travelled, and of not one of these journeys do I remember any single trait. The fact has not been suffered to encroach on the truth of the imagination. I still see Magus Muir two hundred years ago; a desert place, quite uninclosed; in the midst, the primate's carriage fleeing at the gallop; the assassins loose-reined in pursuit, Burley Balfour, pistol in hand, among the first. No scene of history has ever written itself so deeply on my mind; not because Balfour, that questionable zealot, was an ancestral cousin of my own; not because of the pleadings of the victim and his daughter; not even because of the live bum-bee that flew out of Sharpe's 'bacco-box, thus clearly indicating his complicity with Satan; nor merely because, as it was after all a crime of a fine religious flavour, it figured in Sunday books and afforded a grateful relief from *Ministering Children* or the *Memoirs of Mrs. Kathatine Winslowe*. The figure that always fixed my attention is that of Hackston of Rathillet, sitting in the saddle with his cloak about his mouth, and through all that long, bungling, vociferous hurly-burly, revolving privately a case of conscience. He would take no hand in the deed, because he had a private spite against the victim, and 'that action' must be sullied with no suggestion of a worldly motive; on the other hand, 'that action', in itself, was highly justified, he had cast in his lot with 'the actors', and he must stay there, inactive but publicly sharing the responsibility. 'You are a gentleman – you will protect me!' cried the wounded old man, crawling towards him. 'I will never lay a hand on you,' said Hackston, and put his cloak about his mouth.

It is an old temptation with me, to pluck away that cloak and see the face – to open that bosom and to read the heart. With incomplete romances about Hackston, the drawers of my youth were lumbered. I read him up in every printed book that I could lay my hands on. I even dug among the Wodrow manuscripts, sitting shame-faced in the very room where my hero had been tortured two centuries before, and keenly conscious of my youth in the midst of other and (as I fondly thought) more gifted students. All was vain: that he had passed a riotous nonage, that he was a zealot, that he twice displayed (compared with his grotesque companions) some tincture of soldierly resolution and even of military common sense, and that he figured memorably in the scene on Magus Muir, so much and no more could I make out. But whenever I cast my eyes backward, it is to see him like a landmark on the plains of history, sitting with his cloak about his mouth, inscrutable. How small a thing creates an immortality! I do not think he can have been a man entirely commonplace; but had he not thrown his cloak about his mouth, or had the witnesses forgot to chronicle the action, he would not thus have haunted the imagination of my boyhood, and to-day he would scarce delay me for a paragraph. An incident, at once romantic and dramatic, which at once awakes the judgment and makes a picture for the eye, how little do we realise its perdurable power! Perhaps no one does so but the author, just as none but he appreciates the influence of jingling words; so that he looks on upon life, with something of a covert smile, seeing people led by what they fancy to be thoughts and what are really the accustomed artifices of his own trade, or roused by what they take to be principles and are really picturesque effects. In a pleasant book about a school-class club, Colonel Fergusson has recently told a little anecdote. A 'Philosophical Society' was formed by some Academy boys – among them, Colonel Fergusson himself, Fleeming Jenkin,[8] and Andrew Wilson, the Christian Buddhist and author of *The Abode of Snow*. Before these learned pundits, one member laid the following ingenious problem: 'What would be the result of putting a pound of potassium in a pot of porter?' 'I should think there would be a number of interesting bi-products,' said a smatterer at my elbow; but for me the tale itself has a bi-product, and stands as a type of much that is most human. For this inquirer who conceived himself to burn with a zeal entirely chemical, was really immersed in a design of a quite different nature; unconsciously to his own recently breeched intelligence, he was engaged in literature. Putting, pound, potassium, pot, porter; initial p, mediant t – that was his idea, poor little boy! So with politics and that which excites men in the present, so with history and that which rouses them in the past: there lie at the root of what appears, most serious unsuspected elements.

The triple town of Anstruther Wester, Anstruther Easter, and Cellardyke, all three Royal Burghs – or two Royal Burghs and a less distinguished suburb, I forget which – lies continuously along the seaside, and boasts of either two or three

40

separate parish churches, and either two or three separate harbours. These ambiguities are painful; but the fact is (although it argue me uncultured), I am but poorly posted upon Cellardyke. My business lay in the two Anstruthers. A tricklet of a stream divides them, spanned by a bridge; and over the bridge at the time of my knowledge, the celebrated Shell House stood outpost on the west. This had been the residence of an agreeable eccentric; during his fond tenancy, he had illustrated the outer walls, as high (if I remember rightly) as the roof, with elaborate patterns and pictures, and snatches of verse in the vein of *exegi monumentum*; shells and pebbles, artfully contrasted and conjoined, had been his medium; and I like to think of him standing back upon the bridge, when all was finished, drinking in the general effect and (like Gibbon) already lamenting his employment.

The same bridge saw another sight in the seventeenth century. Mr. Thomson, the 'curat' of Anstruther Easter, was a man highly obnoxious to the devout: in the first place, because he was a 'curat'; in the second place, because he was a person of irregular and scandalous life; and in the third place, because he was generally suspected of dealings with the Enemy of Man. These three disqualifications, in the popular literature of the time, go hand in hand; but the end of Mr. Thomson was a thing quite by itself, and in the proper phrase, a manifest judgment. He had been at a friend's house in Anstruther Wester, where (and elsewhere, I suspect) he had partaken of the bottle; indeed, to put the thing in our cold modern way, the reverend gentleman was on the brink of *delirium tremens*. It was a dark night, it seems; a little lassie came carrying a lantern to fetch the curate home; and away they went down the street of Anstruther Wester, the lantern swinging a bit in the child's hand, the barred lustre tossing up and down along the front of slumbering houses, and Mr. Thomson not altogether steady on his legs nor (to all appearance) easy in his mind. The pair had reached the middle of the bridge when (as I conceive the scene) the poor tippler started in some baseless fear and looked behind him; the child, already shaken by the minister's strange behaviour, started also; in so doing, she would jerk the lantern; and for the space of a moment the lights and the shadows would be all confounded. Then it was that to the unhinged toper and the twittering child, a huge bulk of blackness seemed to sweep down, to pass them close by as they stood upon the bridge, and to vanish on the farther side in the general darkness of the night. 'Plainly the devil come for Mr. Thomson!' thought the child. What Mr. Thomson thought himself, we have no ground of knowledge; but he fell upon his knees in the midst of the bridge like a man praying. On the rest of the journey to the manse, history is silent; but when they came to the door, the poor caitiff, taking the lantern from the child, looked upon her with so lost a countenance that her little courage died within her, and she fled home screaming to her parents. Not a soul would venture out; all that night, the minister dwelt alone with his terrors in the manse; and when the day dawned, and men made bold to go about the streets, they found the devil had come indeed for Mr. Thomson.

This manse of Anstruther Easter has another and a more cheerful association. It was early in the morning, about a century before the days of Mr. Thomson, that his predecessor was called out of bed to welcome a Grandee of Spain, the Duke of Medina Sidonia, just landed in the harbour underneath. But sure there was never seen a more decayed grandee; sure there was never a duke welcomed from a stranger place of exile. Half-way between Orkney and Shetland, there lies a certain isle; on the one hand the Atlantic, on the other the North Sea, bombard its pillared cliffs; sore-eyed, short-living, inbred fishers and their families herd in its few huts; in the graveyard pieces of wreck-wood stand for monuments; there is nowhere a more inhospitable spot. *Belle-Isle-En-Mer* – Fair-Isle-at-Sea – that is a name that has always rung in my mind's ear like music; but the only 'Fair Isle' on which I ever set my foot, was this unhomely, rugged turret-top of submarine sierras.[9] Here, when his ship was broken, my lord Duke joyfully got ashore; here for long months he and certain of his men were harboured; and it was from this durance that he landed at last to be welcomed (as well as such a papist deserved, no doubt) by the godly incumbent of Anstruther Easter; and after the Fair Isle, what a fine city must that have appeared! and after the island diet, what a hospitable spot the minister's table! And yet he must have lived on friendly terms with his outlandish hosts. For to this day there still survives a relic of the long winter evenings when the sailors of the great Armada[10] crouched about the hearths of the Fair-Islanders, the planks of their own lost galleon perhaps lighting up the scene, and the gale and the surf that beat about the coast contributing their melancholy voices. All the folk of the north isles are great artificers of knitting: the Fair-Islanders alone dye their fabrics in the Spanish manner. To this day, gloves and nightcaps, innocently decorated, may be seen for sale in the Shetland warehouse at Edinburgh, or on the Fair Isle itself in the catechist's house; and to this day, they tell the story of the Duke of Medina Sidonia's adventure.

It would seem as if the Fair Isle had some attraction for 'persons of quality'. When I landed there myself, an elderly gentleman, unshaved, poorly attired, his shoulders wrapped in a plaid, was seen walking to and fro, with a book in his hand, upon the beach. He paid no heed to our arrival, which we thought a strange thing in itself; but when one of the officers of the *Pharos*,[11] passing narrowly by him, observed his book to be a Greek Testament, our wonder and interest took a higher flight. The catechist was cross-examined; he said the gentleman had been put across some time before in Mr. Bruce of Sumburgh's schooner, the only link between the Fair Isle and the rest of the world; and that he held services and was doing 'good'. So much came glibly enough; but when pressed a little farther, the catechist displayed embarrassment. A singular diffidence appeared upon his face: 'They tell me,' said he, in low tones, 'that he's a lord.' And a lord he was; a peer of the realm pacing that inhospitable beach with his Greek Testament, and his plaid about his shoulders, set upon doing good, as he understood it, worthy man! And his grandson, a good-looking little boy, much better dressed than the lordly evangelist, and speaking with a silken English accent very foreign to the scene, accompanied me for a while in my exploration of the island. I suppose this little fellow is now my lord, and wonder how much he remembers of the Fair Isle. Perhaps not much; for he seemed to accept very quietly his savage situation; and under such guidance, it is like that this was not his first nor yet his last adventure.

Notes

1. Stevenson is referring to the old Scots ballad, 'Sir Patrick Spens', where the king 'sits in Dumferling toune,/Drinking the blude-reid wine.'
2. John Paul Jones (1747–1792), Scottish-born American naval officer during the War of Independence.
3. Alexander III (1241–1286) fell to his death as he rode in the dark along the cliffs between Burntisland and Kinghorn in Fife. His untimely demise led to a disputed succession.
4. Alexander Selkirk (1676–1721) was a sailor who was born in Largo, the son of a shoemaker, and said to be the model for Daniel Defoe's *Robinson Crusoe*.
5. Andrew Lang (1844–1912), born in Selkirk and a fellow of Merton College, Oxford, specialised in mythology and folklore.
6. Robert Stevenson (1772–1850), Stevenson's grandfather, was an engineer who was born in Glasgow.
7. Thomas Rowlandson (1756–1827), English illustrator known for his biting humour and social commentary.
8. Henry Charles Fleeming Jenkin (1833–1885), professor of engineering at Edinburgh University. Stevenson was one of his students.
9. Fair Isle is the most remote inhabited island in Britain, located midway between Orkney and Shetland.
10. In 1588, 300 soldiers and sailors from the Spanish Armada were stranded on Fair Isle when their ship, *El Gran Grifon*, grounded off shore.
11. 'In June 1869 Stevenson accompanied his father on the yacht *Pharos* on a trip to Orkney and Shetland to inspect the North Uist Lighthouse, the most northerly dwelling house in the realm.' See Frank McLynn, *Robert Louis Stevenson: A Biography* (New York: Random House, 1993), p. 36

The Education of an Engineer:

MORE RANDOM MEMORIES

*The Education of an Engineer originally appeared in
Scribner's Magazine in November 1888.*

ANSTRUTHER is a place sacred to the Muse; she inspired (really to a considerable extent) Tennant's vernacular poem *Anst'er Fair;*[1] and I have there waited
upon her myself with much devotion. This was when I came as a young man to
glean engineering experience from the building of the breakwater. What I
gleaned, I am sure I do not know; but indeed I had already my own private deter-
mination to be an author; I loved the art of words and the appearances of life; and
Travellers, and Headers, and Rubble, and Polished Ashlar, and Pierres Perdues,
and even the thrilling question of the String-Course, interested me only (if they
interested me at all) as properties for some possible romance or as words to add
to my vocabulary. To grow a little catholic is the compensation of years; youth is
one-eyed; and in those days, though I haunted the breakwater by day, and even
loved the place for the sake of the sunshine, the thrilling seaside air, the wash of
waves on the sea-face, the green glimmer of the divers' helmets far below, and the
musical chinking of the masons, my one genuine preoccupation lay elsewhere,
and my only industry was in the hours when I was not on duty. I lodged with a
certain Bailie Brown, a carpenter by trade; and there, as soon as dinner was
despatched, in a chamber scented with dry rose-leaves, drew in my chair to the
table and proceeded to pour forth literature, at such a speed, and with such inti-
mations of early death and immortality, as I now look back upon with wonder.
Then it was that I wrote *Voces Fidelium*, a series of dramatic monologues in verse;
then that I indited the bulk of a covenanting novel – like so many others, never
finished.[2] Late I sat into the night, toiling (as I thought) under the very dart of
death, toiling to leave a memory behind me. I feel moved to thrust aside the curtain of the years, to hail that poor feverish idiot, to bid him go to bed and clap
Voces Fidelium on the fire before he goes; so clear does he appear before me, sitting there between his candles in the rose-scented room and the late night; so
ridiculous a picture (to my elderly wisdom) does the fool present! But he was driv-
en to his bed at last without miraculous intervention; and the manner of his driving sets the last touch upon this eminently youthful business. The weather was
then so warm that I must keep the windows open; the night without was populous
with moths. As the late darkness deepened, my literary tapers beaconed forth

more brightly; thicker and thicker came the dusty night-fliers, to gyrate for one brilliant instant round the flame and fall in agonies upon my paper. Flesh and blood could not endure the spectacle; to capture immortality was doubtless a noble enterprise, but not to capture it at such a cost of suffering; and out would go the candles, and off would I go to bed in the darkness raging to think that the blow might fall on the morrow, and there was *Voces Fidelium* still incomplete. Well, the moths are – all gone, and *Voces Fidelium* along with them; only the fool is still on hand and practises new follies.

Only one thing in connection with the harbour tempted me, and that was the diving, an experience I burned to taste of. But this was not to be, at least in Anstruther; and the subject involves a change of scene to the sub-arctic town of Wick.[3] You can never have dwelt in a country more unsightly than that part of Caithness, the land faintly swelling, faintly falling, not a tree, not a hedgerow, the fields divided by single slate stones set upon their edge, the wind always singing in your ears and (down the long road that led nowhere) thrumming in the telegraph wires. Only as you approached the coast was there anything to stir the heart. The plateau broke down to the North Sea in formidable cliffs, the tall out-stacks rose like pillars ringed about with surf, the coves were over-brimmed with clamorous froth, the sea-birds screamed, the wind sang in the thyme on the cliff's edge; here and there, small ancient castles toppled on the brim; here and there, it was possible to dip into a dell of shelter, where you might lie and tell yourself you were a little warm, and hear (near at hand) the whin-pods bursting in the afternoon sun, and (farther off) the rumour of the turbulent sea. As for Wick itself, it is one of the meanest of man's towns, and situate certainly on the baldest of God's bays. It lives for herring, and a strange sight it is to see (of an afternoon) the heights of Pulteney[4] blackened by seaward-looking fishers, as when a city crowds to a review – or, as when bees have swarmed, the ground is horrible with lumps and clusters; and a strange sight, and a beautiful, to see the fleet put silently out against a rising moon, the sea-line rough as a wood with sails, and ever and again and one after another, a boat flitting swiftly by the silver disk. This mass of fishers, this great fleet of boats, is out of all proportion to the town itself; and the oars are manned and the nets hauled by immigrants from the Long Island (as we call the outer Hebrides), who come for that season only, and depart again, if 'the take' be poor, leaving debts behind them. In a bad year, the end of the herring fishery is therefore an exciting time; fights are common, riots often possible; an apple knocked from a child's hand was once the signal for something like a war; and even when I was there, a gunboat lay in the bay to assist the authorities. To contrary interests, it should be observed, the curse of Babel is here added; the Lews men are Gaelic speakers. Caithness has adopted English; an odd circumstance, if you reflect that both must be largely Norsemen by descent. I remember seeing one of the strongest instances of this division: a thing like a

Punch-and-Judy box erected on the flat grave-stones of the churchyard; from the hutch or proscenium – I know not what to call it – an eldritch- looking preacher laying down the law in Gaelic about some one of the name of Powl, whom I at last divined to be the apostle to the Gentiles; a large congregation of the Lews men very devoutly listening; and on the outskirts of the crowd, some of the town's children (to whom the whole affair was Greek and Hebrew) profanely playing tigg. The same descent, the same country, the same narrow sect of the same religion, and all these bonds made very largely nugatory by an accidental difference of dialect!

Into the bay of Wick stretched the dark length of the unfinished breakwater, in its cage of open staging; the travellers (like frames of churches) over-plumbing all; and away at the extreme end, the divers toiling unseen on the foundation. On a platform of loose planks, the assistants turned their air-mills; a stone might be swinging between wind and water; underneath the swell ran gaily; and from time to time, a mailed dragon with a window-glass snout came dripping up the ladder. Youth is a blessed season after all; my stay at Wick was in the year of *Voces Fidelium* and the rose-leaf room at Bailie Brown's; and already I did not care two straws for literary glory. Posthumous ambition perhaps requires an atmosphere of roses; and the more rugged excitant of Wick east winds had made another boy of me. To go down in the diving-dress, that was my absorbing fancy; and with the countenance of a certain handsome scamp of a diver, Bob Bain by name, I gratified the whim.

It was gray, harsh, easterly weather, the swell ran pretty high, and out in the open there were 'skipper's daughters', when I found myself at last on the diver's platform, twenty pounds of lead upon each foot and my whole person swollen with ply and ply of woollen underclothing.[5] One moment, the salt wind was whistling round my night-capped head; the next, I was crushed almost double under the weight of the helmet. As that intolerable burthern was laid upon me, I could have found it in my heart (only for shame's sake) to cry off from the whole enterprise. But it was too late. The attendants began to turn the hurdy-gurdy, and the air to whistle through the tube; some one screwed in the barred window of the visor; and I was cut off in a moment from my fellow-men; standing there in their midst, but quite divorced from intercourse: a creature deaf and dumb, pathetically looking forth upon them from a climate of his own. Except that I could move and feel, I was like a man fallen in a catalepsy. But time was scarce given me to realise my isolation; the weights were hung upon my back and breast, the signal rope was thrust into my unresisting hand; and setting a twenty-pound foot upon the ladder, I began ponderously to descend.

Some twenty rounds below the platform, twilight fell. Looking up, I saw a low green heaven mottled with vanishing bells of white; looking around, except for the weedy spokes and shafts of the ladder, nothing but a green gloaming, somewhat opaque but very restful and delicious. Thirty rounds lower, I stepped off on the Pierres Perdues of the foundation; a dumb helmeted figure took me by the hand, and made a gesture (as I read it) of encouragement; and looking in at the creature's window, I beheld the face of Bain. There we were, hand to hand and (when it pleased us) eye to eye; and either might have burst himself with shouting, and not a whisper come to his companion's hearing. Each, in his own little world of air, stood incommunicably separate.

Bob had told me ere this a little tale, a five minutes' drama at the bottom of the sea, which at that moment possibly shot across my mind. He was down with another, settling a stone of the sea-wall. They had it well adjusted, Bob gave the signal, the scissors were slipped, the stone set home; and it was time to turn to something else. But still his companion remained bowed over the block like a mourner on a tomb, or only raised himself to make absurd contortions and mysterious signs unknown to the vocabulary of the diver. There, then, these two stood for awhile, like the dead and the living; till there flashed a fortunate thought into Bob's mind, and he stooped, peered through the window of that other world, and beheld the face of its inhabitant wet with streaming tears. Ah! the man was in pain! And Bob, glancing downward, saw what was the trouble: the block had been lowered on the foot of that unfortunate – he was caught alive at the bottom of the sea under fifteen tons of rock.

That two men should handle a stone so heavy, even swinging in the scissors, may appear strange to the inexpert. These must bear in mind the great density of the water of the sea, and the surprising results of transplantation to that medium. To understand a little what these are, and how a man's weight, so far from being an encumbrance, is the very ground of his agility, was the chief lesson of my submarine experience. The knowledge came upon me by degrees. As I began to go forward with the hand of my estranged companion, a world of tumbled stones was visible, pillared with the weedy uprights of the staging: overhead, a flat roof of green: a little in front, the sea-wall, like an unfinished rampart. And presently in our upward progress, Bob motioned me to leap upon a stone; I looked to see if he were possibly in earnest, and he only signed to me the more imperiously. Now the block stood six feet high; it would have been quite a leap to me unencumbered; with the breast and back weights, and the twenty pounds upon each foot, and the staggering load of the helmet, the thing was out of reason. I laughed aloud in my tomb; and to prove to Bob how far he was astray, I gave a little impulse from my toes. Up I soared like a bird, my companion soaring at my side. As high as to the stone, and then higher, I pursued my impotent and empty flight. Even when the strong arm of Bob had checked my shoulders, my heels continued their ascent; so that I blew out sideways like an autumn leaf, and must be hauled in, hand over hand, as sailors haul in the slack of a sail, and propped upon my feet again like an intoxicated sparrow. Yet a little higher on the foundation, and we began to be affected by the bottom of the swell, running there like a strong breeze of wind. Or so I must suppose; for, safe in my cushion of air, I was conscious of no impact; only swayed idly like a weed, and was now borne helplessly abroad, and now swiftly – and yet with dream-like gentleness – impelled against my guide. So does a child's balloon divagate upon the currents of the air, and touch, and slide off again from every obstacle. So must have ineffectually swung, so resented their inefficiency, those light crowds that followed the Star of Hades, and uttered exiguous voices in the land beyond Cocytus.

There was something strangely exasperating, as well as strangely wearying, in these uncommanded evolutions. It is bitter to return to infancy, to be supported, and directed, and perpetually set upon your feet, by the hand of some one else. The air besides, as it is supplied to you by the busy millers on the platform, closes the eustachian tubes and keeps the neophyte perpetually swallowing, till his throat is grown so dry that he can swallow no longer. And for all these reasons – although I had a fine, dizzy, muddle-headed joy in my surroundings, and longed, and tried, and always failed, to lay hands on the fish that darted here and there about me, swift as humming-birds – yet I fancy I was rather relieved than otherwise when Bain brought me back to the ladder and signed to me to mount. And there was one more experience before me even then. Of a sudden, my ascending head passed into the trough of a swell. Out of the green, I shot at once into a glory of rosy, almost of sanguine light – the multitudinous seas incarnadined, the heaven above a vault of crimson. And then the glory faded into the hard, ugly daylight of a Caithness autumn, with a low sky, a gray sea, and a whistling wind.

Bob Bain had five shillings for his trouble, and I had done what I desired. It was one of the best things I got from my education as an engineer: of which, however, as a way of life, I wish to speak with sympathy. It takes a man into the open air; it keeps him hanging about harbour-sides, which is the richest form of idling; it carries him to wild islands; it gives him a taste of the genial dangers of the sea; it supplies him with dexterities to exercise; it makes demands upon his ingenuity; it will go far to cure him of any taste (if ever he had one) for the miserable life of cities. And when it has done so, it carries him back and shuts him in an office! From the roaring skerry and the wet thwart of the tossing boat, he passes to the stool and desk; and with a memory full of ships, and seas, and perilous headlands, and the shining pharos, he must apply his long-sighted eyes to the petty niceties of drawing, or measure his inaccurate mind with several pages of consecutive figures. He is a wise youth, to be sure, who can balance one part of genuine life against two parts of drudgery between four walls, and for the sake of the one, manfully accept the other.

Wick was scarce an eligible place of stay. But how much better it was to hang in the cold wind upon the pier, to go down with Bob Bain among the roots of the staging, to be all day in a boat coiling a wet rope and shouting orders – not always very wise – than to be warm and dry, and dull, and dead-alive, in the most comfortable office. And Wick itself had in those days a note of originality. It may have still, but I misdoubt it much. The old minister of Keiss would not preach, in these degenerate times, for an hour and a half upon the clock. The gipsies must be gone from their cavern; where you might see, from the mouth, the women tending their fire, like Meg Merrilies, and the men sleeping off their coarse potations; and where, in winter gales, the surf would beleaguer them closely, bursting in their very door. A traveller to-day upon the Thurso coach would scarce observe a little cloud of smoke among the moorlands, and be told, quite openly, it marked a private still. He would not indeed make that journey, for there is now no Thurso coach. And even if he could, one little thing that happened to me could never happen to him, or not with the same trenchancy of contrast.

We had been upon the road all evening; the coach-top was crowded with Lews fishers going home, scarce anything but Gaelic had sounded in my ears; and our way had lain throughout over a moorish country very northern to behold. Latish at night, though it was still broad day in our subarctic latitude, we came down upon the shores of the roaring Pentland Firth,[6] that grave of mariners; on one hand, the cliffs of Dunnet Head ran seaward; in front was the little bare, white town of Castleton, its streets full of blowing sand; nothing beyond, but the North Islands, the great deep, and the perennial ice-fields of the Pole. And here, in the last imaginable place, there sprang up young outlandish voices and a chatter of some foreign speech; and I saw, pursuing the coach with its load of Hebridean fishers – as they had pursued Vetturini up the passes of the Apennines or perhaps along the grotto under Virgil's tomb – two little dark-eyed, white-toothed Italian vagabonds, of twelve to fourteen years of age, one with a hurdy-gurdy, the other with a cage of white mice. The coach passed on, and their small Italian chatter died in the distance; and I was left to marvel how they had wandered into that country, and how they fared in it, and what they thought of it, and when (if ever) they should see again the silver wind-breaks run among the olives, and the stone-pine stand guard upon Etruscan sepulchres.

Upon any American, the strangeness of this incident is somewhat lost. For as far back as he goes in his own land, he will find some alien camping there; the Cornish miner, the French or Mexican half-blood, the negro in the South, these are deep in the woods and far among the mountains. But in an old, cold, and rugged country such as mine, the days of immigration are long at an end; and away up there, which was at that time far beyond the northernmost extreme of railways, hard upon the shore of that ill-omened strait of whirlpools, in a land of moors where no stranger came, unless it should be a sportsman to shoot grouse or an antiquary to decipher runes, the presence of these small pedestrians struck the mind as though a bird-of-paradise had risen from the heather or an albatross come fishing in the bay of Wick. They were as strange to their surroundings as my lordly evangelist or the old Spanish grandee on the Fair Isle.

Notes

1. William Tennant (1784–1848), Scots poet, born in Anstruther, who published 'Anster Fair', a mock heroic poem in 1812.

2. He never completed *Heathercat*.

3. Stevenson, accompanied by his father, Thomas Stevenson (1818–1887), was in Wick from 27 August to 6 October 1868. He wrote about his experiences in 'On the Enjoyment of Unpleasant Places,' which is included in this volume. Stevenson's grandfather, Robert Stevenson, completed Bell Rock Lighthouse in 1811, which was acclaimed as one of the engineering marvels of its day. See also, *Selected Letters of Robert Louis Stevenson*. Edited by Ernest Mehew (New Haven, Conn.: Yale University Press, 2001), p. 8.

4. Built by the British Fisheries Society, Pultneytown is the commercial and fisheries area of Wick.

5. ' ... the nineteenth-century diver in 'inner space' looked like a modern astronaut in the outer dimension.' See Frank McLynn, *Robert Louis Stevenson: A Biography* (New York: Random House, 1993), p. 35.

6. The Pentland Firth, the body of water between the Scottish mainland and the Orkney Islands, is known for its rough crossing.

Sing Me a Song of a Lad that is Gone

FROM SONGS OF TRAVEL

This is Stevenson's adaptation of the famous Skye Boat Song. *The original tune was composed by Annie MacLeod. The lyrics by Englishman Sir Harold Boulton were written in 1884 with decidedly pro-Jacobite sympathies.[1]*
Sing Me a Song of a Lad that is Gone *appears in* Songs of Travel *(1895).*

Sing me a song of a lad that is gone,
Say, could that lad be I?
Merry of soul he sailed on a day
Over the sea to Skye.

Mull was astern, Rum on the port,
Eigg on the starboard bow;
Glory of youth glowed in his soul:
Where is that glory now?

Sing me a song of a lad that is gone,
Say, could that lad be I?
Merry of soul he sailed on a day
Over the sea to Skye.

Give me again all that was there,
Give me the sun that shone!
Give me the eyes, give me the soul,
Give me the lad that's gone!

Sing me a song of a lad that is gone,
Say, could that lad be I?
Merry of soul he sailed on a day
Over the sea to Skye.

Billow and breeze, islands and seas,
Mountains of rain and sun,
All that was good, all that was fair,
All that was me is gone

Notes

1. Stevenson loved music both instrumental and song. 'It is helpful to "listen" to some of RLS's best lyrics ... as essentially "musical" in impetus.' *Robert Louis Stevenson: Selected Poems* edited by Angus Calder (London: Penguin Books, 1998), p. 269. Several composers have set his lyrics to music. See the appendix.

A Winter's Walk in Carrick and Galloway

A FRAGMENT

The uncompleted essay A Winter's Walk in Carrick and Galloway *was originally published posthumously in the* Illustrated London News, *summer 1896, although the actual tour took place in January 1876.*

AT the famous bridge of Doon, Kyle, the central district of the shire of Ayr, marches with Carrick, the most southerly.[1] On the Carrick side of the river rises a hill of somewhat gentle conformation, cleft with shallow dells, and sown here and there with farms and tufts of wood. Inland, it loses itself, joining, I suppose, the great herd of similar hills that occupies the centre of the Lowlands. Towards the sea it swells out the coast-line into a protuberance, like a bay- window in a plan, and is fortified against the surf behind bold crags. This hill is known as the Brown Hill of Carrick, or, more shortly, Brown Carrick.

It had snowed overnight. The fields were all sheeted up; they were tucked in among the snow, and their shape was modelled through the pliant counterpane, like children tucked in by a fond mother. The wind had made ripples and folds upon the surface, like what the sea, in quiet weather, leaves upon the sand. There was a frosty stifle in the air. An effusion of coppery light on the summit of Brown Carrick showed where the sun was trying to look through; but along the horizon clouds of cold fog had settled down, so that there was no distinction of sky and sea. Over the white shoulders of the headlands, or in the opening of bays, there was nothing but a great vacancy and blackness; and the road as it drew near the edge of the cliff seemed to skirt the shores of creation and void space.

The snow crunched under foot, and at farms all the dogs broke out barking as they smelt a passer-by upon the road. I met a fine old fellow, who might have sat as the father in 'The Cottar's Saturday Night',[2] [sic] and who swore most heathenishly at a cow he was driving. And a little after I scraped acquaintance with a poor body tramping out to gather cockles. His face was wrinkled by exposure; it was broken up into flakes and channels, like mud beginning to dry, and weathered in two colours, an incongruous pink and grey. He had a faint air of being surprised – which, God knows he might well be – that life had gone so ill with him. The shape of his trousers was in itself a jest, so strangely were they bagged and ravelled about his knees; and his coat was all bedaubed with clay as though he had lain in a rain- dub during the New Year's festivity. I will own I was not sorry to think he had had a merry New Year, and been young again for an evening; but I was sorry to see the mark still there. One could not expect such an old gentleman to be much of a dandy or a great student of respectability in dress; but there might have been a wife at home, who had brushed out similar stains after fifty New Years, now become old, or a round-armed daughter, who would wish to have him neat, were it only out of self-respect and for the ploughman sweetheart when he looks round at night. Plainly, there was nothing of this in his life, and years and loneliness hung heavily on his old arms. He was seventy-six, he told me; and nobody would give a day's work to a man that age: they would think he couldn't do it. 'And, 'deed,' he went on, with a sad little chuckle, ''deed, I doubt if I could.' He said goodbye to me at a footpath, and crippled wearily off to his work. It will make your heart ache if you think of his old fingers groping in the snow.

He told me I was to turn down beside the school-house for Dunure. And so, when I found a lone house among the snow, and heard a babble of childish voices from within, I struck off into a steep road leading downwards to the sea. Dunure lies close under the steep hill: a haven among the rocks, a breakwater in consummate disrepair, much apparatus for drying nets, and a score or so of fishers' houses. Hard by, a few shards of ruined castle[3] overhang the sea, a few vaults, and one tall gable honeycombed with windows. The snow lay on the beach to the tidemark. It was daubed on to the sills of the ruin: it roosted in the crannies of the rock like white sea-birds; even on outlying reefs there would be a little cock of snow, like a toy lighthouse. Everything was grey and white in a cold and dolorous sort of shepherd's plaid. In the profound silence, broken only by the noise of oars at sea, a horn was sounded twice; and I saw the postman, girt with two bags, pause a moment at the end of the clachan for letters.

It is, perhaps, characteristic of Dunure that none were brought him.

The people at the public-house did not seem well pleased to see me, and though I would fain have stayed by the kitchen fire, sent me 'ben the hoose' into the guest-room. This guest-room at Dunure was painted in quite aesthetic fashion. There are rooms in the same taste not a hundred miles from London, where persons of an extreme sensibility meet together without embarrassment. It was all in a fine dull bottle-green and black; a grave harmonious piece of colouring, with nothing, so far as coarser folk can judge, to hurt the better feelings of the most exquisite purist. A cherry-red half window-blind kept up an imaginary warmth in the cold room, and threw quite a glow on the floor. Twelve cockle-shells and a half-penny china figure were ranged solemnly along the mantel-shelf. Even the spittoon was an original note, and instead of sawdust contained sea-shells. And as for the hearthrug, it would merit an article to itself, and a coloured diagram to help the text. It was patchwork, but the patchwork of the poor; no glowing shreds of old brocade and Chinese silk, shaken together in the kaleidoscope of some tasteful housewife's fancy; but a work of art in its own way, and plainly a labour of love. The patches came exclusively from people's raiment. There was no colour more brilliant than a heather mixture; 'My Johnny's grey breeks,' well polished over the oar on the boat's thwart, entered largely into its composition. And the spoils of an old black cloth coat, that had been many a Sunday to church, added something (save the mark!) of preciousness to the material.

While I was at luncheon four carters came in – long-limbed, muscular Ayrshire Scots, with lean, intelligent faces. Four quarts of stout were ordered; they kept filling the tumbler with the other hand as they drank; and in less time than it takes me to write these words the four quarts were finished – another round was proposed, discussed, and negatived – and they were creaking out of the village with their carts.

The ruins drew you towards them. You never saw any place more desolate from a distance, nor one that less belied its promise near at hand. Some crows and gulls flew away croaking as I scrambled in. The snow had drifted into the vaults. The clachan dabbled with snow, the white hills, the black sky, the sea marked in the coves with faint circular wrinkles, the whole world, as it looked from a loop- hole in Dunure, was cold, wretched, and out-at-elbows. If you had been a wicked baron and compelled to stay there all the afternoon, you would have had a rare fit of remorse. How you would have heaped up the fire and gnawed your fingers! I think it would have come to homicide before the evening – if it were only for the pleasure of seeing something red! And the masters of Dunure, it is to be noticed, were remarkable of old for inhumanity. One of these vaults where the snow had drifted was that 'black route' where 'Mr. Alane Stewart, Commendatour of Crossraguel,' endured his fiery trials.⁴ The 1st and 7th of September 1570 (ill dates for Mr. Alan!), Gilbert, Earl of Cassilis, his chaplain, his baker, his cook, his pantryman, and another servant, bound the Poor Commendator 'betwix an iron chimlay and a fire', and there cruelly roasted him until he signed away his abbacy. It is one of the ugliest stories of an ugly period, but not, somehow, without such a flavour of the ridiculous as makes it hard to sympathise quite seriously with the victim. And it is consoling to remember that he got away at last, and kept his abbacy, and, over and above, had a pension from the Earl until he died.

Some way beyond Dunure a wide bay, of somewhat less unkindly aspect, opened out. Colzean plantations lay all along the steep shore, and there was a wooded hill towards the centre, where the trees made a sort of shadowy etching over the snow. The road went down and up, and past a blacksmith's cottage that made fine music in the valley. Three compatriots of Burns drove up to me in a cart. They were all drunk, and asked me jeeringly if this was the way to Dunure. I told them it was; and my answer was received with unfeigned merriment. One gentleman was so much tickled he nearly fell out of the cart; indeed, he was only saved by a companion, who either had not so fine a sense of humour or had drunken less.

'The toune of Mayboll,' says the inimitable Abercrummie, 'stands upon an

ascending ground from east to west, and lyes open to the south. It hath one principal street, with houses upon both sides, built of freestone; and it is beautifyed
with the situation of two castles, one at each end of this street. That on the east
belongs to the Erle of Cassilis. On the west end is a castle, which belonged sometime to the laird of Blairquan, which is now the tolbooth, and is adorned with a
pyremide [conical roof], and a row of ballesters round it raised from the top of the
staircase, into which they have mounted a fyne clock. There be four lanes which
pass from the principal street; one is called the Black Vennel, which is steep,
declining to the south-west, and leads to a lower street, which is far larger than
the high chief street, and it runs from the Kirkland to the Well Trees, in which
there have been many pretty buildings, belonging to the several gentry of the
country, who were wont to resort thither in winter, and divert themselves in converse together at their own houses. It was once the principal street of the town;
but many of these houses of the gentry having been decayed and ruined, it has
lost much of its ancient beauty. Just opposite to this vennel, there is another that
leads north-west, from the chief street to the green, which is a pleasant plot of
ground, enclosed round with an earthen wall, wherein they were wont to play
football, but now at the Gowff and byasse-bowls. The houses of this town, on both
sides of the street, have their several gardens belonging to them; and in the lower
street there be some pretty orchards, that yield store of good fruit.' 5

As Patterson says, this description is near enough even to- day, and is mighty
nicely written to boot. I am bound to add, of my own experience, that Maybole is
tumbledown and dreary. Prosperous enough in reality, it has an air of decay; and
though the population has increased, a roofless house every here and there seems
to protest the contrary. The women are more than well-favoured, and the men
fine tall fellows; but they look slipshod and dissipated. As they slouched at street
corners, or stood about gossiping in the snow, it seemed they would have been
more at home in the slums of a large city than here in a country place betwixt a
village and a town. I heard a great deal about drinking, and a great deal about religious revivals: two things in which the Scottish character is emphatic and most
unlovely. In particular, I heard of clergymen who were employing their time in
explaining to a delighted audience the physics of the Second Coming. It is not
very likely any of us will be asked to help. If we were, it is likely we should receive
instructions for the occasion, and that on more reliable authority. And so I can
only figure to myself a congregation truly curious in such flights of theological
fancy, as one of veteran and accomplished saints, who have fought the good fight
to an end and outlived all worldly passion, and are to be regarded rather as a part
of the Church Triumphant than the poor, imperfect company on earth. And yet I
saw some young fellows about the smoking-room who seemed, in the eyes of one
who cannot count himself strait-laced, in need of some more practical sort of
teaching. They seemed only eager to get drunk, and to do so speedily. It was not

much more than a week after the New Year; and to hear them return on their past bouts with a gusto unspeakable was not altogether pleasing. Here is one snatch of talk, for the accuracy of which I can vouch –

'Ye had a spree here last Tuesday?'

'We had that!'

'I wasna able to be oot o' my bed. Man, I was awful bad on Wednesday.'

'Ay, ye were gey bad.'

And you should have seen the bright eyes, and heard the sensual accents! They recalled their doings with devout gusto and a sort of rational pride. Schoolboys, after their first drunkenness, are not more boastful; a cock does not plume himself with a more unmingled satisfaction as he paces forth among his harem; and yet these were grown men, and by no means short of wit. It was hard to suppose they were very eager about the Second Coming: it seemed as if some elementary notions of temperance for the men and seemliness for the women would have gone nearer the mark. And yet, as it seemed to me typical of much that is evil in Scotland, Maybole is also typical of much that is best. Some of the factories, which have taken the place of weaving in the town's economy, were originally founded and are still possessed by self-made men of the sterling, stout old breed – fellows who made some little bit of an invention, borrowed some little pocketful of capital, and then, step by step, in courage, thrift and industry, fought their way upwards to an assured position.

Abercrummie has told you enough of the Tolbooth; but, as a bit of spelling, this inscription on the Tolbooth bell seems too delicious to withhold: 'This bell is founded at Maiboll Bi Danel Geli, a Frenchman, the 6th November, 1696, Bi appointment of the heritors of the parish of Maiyboll.' The Castle deserves more notice. It is a large and shapely tower, plain from the ground upwards, but with a zone of ornamentation running about the top. In a general way this adornment is perched on the very summit of the chimney-stacks; but there is one corner more elaborate than the rest. A very heavy string-course runs round the upper story, and just above this, facing up the street, the tower carries a small oriel window, fluted and corbelled and carved about with stone heads. It is so ornate it has somewhat the air of a shrine. And it was, indeed, the casket of a very precious jewel, for in the room to which it gives light lay, for long years, the heroine of the sweet old ballad of 'Johnnie Faa' – she who, at the call of the gipsies' songs, 'came tripping down the stair, and all her maids before her'. Some people say the ballad has no basis in fact, and have written, I believe, unanswerable papers to the proof. But in the face of all that, the very look of that high oriel window convinces the imagination, and we enter into all the sorrows of the imprisoned dame. We conceive the burthen of the long, lack-lustre days, when she leaned her sick head against the mullions, and saw the burghers loafing in Maybole High Street, and the children at play, and ruffling gallants riding by from hunt or foray. We conceive the passion of odd moments, when the wind threw up to her some snatch of song, and her heart grew hot within her, and her eyes overflowed at the memory of the past. And even if the tale be not true of this or that lady, or this or that old tower, it is true in the essence of all men and women: for all of us, some time or other, hear the gipsies singing; over all of us is the glamour cast. Some resist and sit resolutely by the fire. Most go and are brought back again, like Lady Cassilis. A few, of the tribe of Waring, go and are seen no more; only now and again, at springtime, when the gipsies' song is afloat in the amethyst evening, we can catch their voices in the glee.

By night it was clearer, and Maybole more visible than during the day. Clouds coursed over the sky in great masses; the full moon battled the other way, and lit up the snow with gleams of flying silver; the town came down the hill in a cascade of brown gables, bestridden by smooth white roofs, and sprangled here and there with lighted windows. At either end the snow stood high up in the darkness, on the peak of the Tolbooth and among the chimneys of the Castle. As the moon flashed a bull's-eye glitter across the town between the racing clouds, the white roofs leaped into relief over the gables and the chimney-stacks, and their shadows over the white roofs. In the town itself the lit face of the clock peered down the street; an hour was hammered out on Mr. Geli's bell, and from behind the red curtains of a public-house some one trolled out – a compatriot of Burns, again! – 'The saut tear blin's my e'e.'

Next morning there was sun and a flapping wind. From the street corners of Maybole I could catch breezy glimpses of green fields. The road underfoot was wet and heavy – part ice, part snow, part water, and any one I met greeted me, by way of salutation, with 'A fine thowe' (thaw). My way lay among rather bleak bills, and past bleak ponds and dilapidated castles and monasteries, to the Highland-looking village of Kirkoswald. It has little claim to notice, save that Burns came there to study surveying in the summer of 1777, and there also, in the kirkyard, the original of Tam o' Shanter sleeps his last sleep. It is worth noticing, however, that this was the first place I thought 'Highland-looking'. Over the bill from Kirkoswald a farm-road leads to the coast. As I came down above Turnberry, the sea view was indeed strangely different from the day before. The cold fogs were all blown away; and there was Ailsa Craig, like a refraction, magnified and deformed, of the Bass Rock; and there were the chiselled mountain-tops of Arran, veined and tipped with snow; and behind, and fainter, the low, blue land of Cantyre. Cottony clouds stood in a great castle over the top of Arran, and blew out in long streamers to the south. The sea was bitten all over with white; little ships, tacking up and down the Firth, lay over at different angles in the wind. On Shanter they were ploughing lea; a cart foal, all in a field by himself, capered and whinnied as if the spring were in him.

The road from Turnberry to Girvan lies along the shore, among sand- hills and by wildernesses of tumbled bent. Every here and there a few cottages stood together beside a bridge. They had one odd feature, not easy to describe in words: a triangular porch projected from above the door, supported at the apex by a single upright post; a secondary door was hinged to the post, and could be hasped on either cheek of the real entrance; so, whether the wind was north or south, the cotter could make himself a triangular bight of shelter where to set his chair and finish a pipe with comfort. There is one objection to this device; for, as the post stands in the middle of the fairway, any one precipitately issuing from the cottage must run his chance of a broken head. So far as I am aware, it is peculiar to the little corner of country about Girvan. And that corner is noticeable for more reasons: it is certainly one of the most characteristic districts in Scotland, It has this movable porch by way of architecture; it has, as we shall see, a sort of remnant of provincial costume, and it has the handsomest population in the Lowlands ...

Notes
1. Stevenson began his walking tour of the area in January 1876, which took him from Ayr to Wigtown. ' ... this was the occasion,' notes Frank McLynn, ' when he passed through the village of Ballantrae and noted its name.' See Frank McLynn, *Robert Louis Stevenson: A Biography* (New York: Random House, 1993), p. 100.
2. Robert Burns's classic poem, ' The Cotter's Saturday Night', was based upon experiences from the author's boyhood and youth in rural Ayrshire.
3. The ruins of Dunure Castle, seat of the Scottish Kennedys, sits five miles south of Ayr, perched on a cliff.
4. In 1570 Gilbert Kennedy, the 4th Earl of Cassillis, kidnapped Alan Stewart of Crossraguel Abbey and forced him to sign away the abbey lands by setting fire to him. Stewart eventually was rescued by the Laird of Bargany.
5. Maybole, the capital of the ancient kingdom of Carrick, is a small town that lies forty-four miles southwest of Glasgow and 5 miles east of the Firth of Clyde.

The Light-Keeper

*The Light-Keeper was first published in 1898 and refers to the years 1869–70
when Stevenson was in training as a lighthouse engineer.*[1]

I

The brilliant kernel of the night,
The flaming lightroom circles me:
I sit within a blaze of light
Held high above the dusky sea.
Far off the surf doth break and roar
Along bleak miles of moonlit shore,
Where through the tides the tumbling wave
Falls in an avalanche of foam
And drives its churned waters home
Up many an undercliff and cave.

The clear bell chimes: the clockworks strain,
The turning lenses flash and pass,
Frame turning within glittering frame
With frosty gleam of moving glass:
Unseen by me, each dusky hour
The sea-waves welter up the tower
Or in the ebb subside again;
And ever and anon all night,
Drawn from afar by charm of light,
A sea bird beats against the pan.

And lastly when dawn ends the night
And belts the semi-orb of sea,
The tall, pale pharos in the light
Looks white and spectral as may be.
The early ebb is out: the green
Straight belt of seaweed now is seen,
That round the basement of the tower
Marks out the interspace of tide;
And watching men are heavy-eyed,
And sleepless lips are dry and sour.

The night is over like a dream:
The sea-birds cry and dip themselves:
And in the early sunlight, steam
The newly bared and dripping shelves,
Around whose verge the glassy wave
With lisping wash is heard to lave;
While, on the white tower lifted high,
The circling lenses flash and pass
With yellow light in faded glass
And sickly shine against the sky.

II

As the steady lenses circle
With a frosty gleam of glass;
And the clear bell chimes,
And the oil brims over the lip of the burner,
Quiet and still at his desk,
The lonely Light-Keeper
Holds his vigil.

Lured from far,
The bewildered seagull beats
Dully against the lantern;
Yet he stirs not, lifts not his head
From the desk where he reads,
Lifts not his eyes to see
The chill blind circle of night
Watching him through the panes.
This is his country's guardian,
The outmost sentry of peace.
This is the man
Who gives up that is lovely in living
For the means to live.

Poetry cunningly gilds
The life of the Light-Keeper,
Held on high in the blackness
In the burning kernel of night,
The seaman sees and blesses him,
The Poet, deep in a sonnet,
Numbers his inky fingers
Fitly to praise him,
Sitting, patient and stolid,
Martyr to a salary.

Notes

1. 'There were, ultimately, five generations of "Lighthouse Stevensons". Together they built every lighthouse in Scotland and many more overseas.' See Ian Bell, *Dreams of Exile: Robert Louis Stevenson, A Biography* (New York: Henry Holt, 1992), p. 7. See also Bella Bathurst, *The Lighthouse Stevensons: The extraordinary story of the building of the Scottish lighthouses by the ancestors of Robert Louis Stevenson* (New York: HarperCollins Publishers, 1999).

England

Roads

It is somehow significant that Roads, *Stevenson's first published essay for which he was paid, is on travel. In a sense, this rambling, evocative piece on travel sums up – in less than 2,700 words – his entire philosophy of travel and his 'passion for what is ever beyond'. It originally ran in the December 1873 issue of* Portfolio Magazine *and was planned during walks at Cockfield in Suffolk, England.*

No amateur will deny that he can find more pleasure in a single drawing, over which he can sit a whole quiet forenoon, and so gradually study himself into humour with the artist, than he can ever extract from the dazzle and accumulation of incongruous impressions that send him, weary and stupefied, out of some famous picture- gallery. But what is thus admitted with regard to art is not extended to the (so-called) natural beauties no amount of excess in sublime mountain outline or the graces of cultivated lowland can do anything, it is supposed, to weaken or degrade the palate. We are not at all sure, however, that moderation, and a regimen tolerably austere, even in scenery, are not healthful and strengthening to the taste; and that the best school for a lover of nature is not to be found in one of those countries where there is no stage effect – nothing salient or sudden, – but a quiet spirit of orderly and harmonious beauty pervades all the details, so that we can patiently attend to each of the little touches that strike in us, all of them together, the subdued note of the landscape. It is in scenery such as this that we find ourselves in the right temper to seek out small sequestered loveliness. The constant recurrence of similar combinations of colour and outline gradually forces upon us a sense of how the harmony has been built up, and we become familiar with something of nature's mannerism. This is the true pleasure of your 'rural voluptuary', – not to remain awe-stricken before a Mount Chimborazo; not to sit deafened over the big drum in the orchestra, but day by day to teach himself some new beauty – to experience some new vague and tranquil sensation that has before evaded him. It is not the people who 'have pined and hungered after nature many a year, in the great city pent,' as Coleridge[1] said in the poem that made Charles Lamb[2] so much ashamed of himself; it is not those who make the greatest progress in this intimacy with her, or who are most quick to see and have the greatest gusto to enjoy. In this, as in everything else, it is minute knowledge and long-continued loving industry that make the true dilettante. A man must have thought much over scenery before he begins fully to enjoy it. It is no youngling enthusiasm on hilltops that can possess itself of the last essence of beauty. Probably most people's heads are growing bare before they can see all in a landscape that they have the capability of seeing; and, even then, it will be only for one little moment of consummation before the faculties are again on the decline, and they that look out of the windows begin to be darkened and restrained in sight. Thus the study of nature should be carried forward thoroughly and with system. Every gratification should be rolled long under the tongue, and we should be always eager to analyse and compare, in order that we may be able to give some plausible reason for our admirations. True, it is difficult to put even approximately into words the kind of feelings thus called into play. There is a dangerous vice inherent in any such intellectual refining upon vague sensation. The analysis of such satisfactions lends itself very readily to literary affectations; and we can all think of instances where it has shown itself apt to exercise a morbid influence, even upon an author's choice of language and the turn of his sentences. And yet there is much that makes the attempt attractive; for any expression, however imperfect, once given to a cherished feeling, seems a sort of legitimation of the pleasure we take in it. A common sentiment is one of those great goods that make life palatable and ever new. The knowledge that another has felt as we have felt, and seen things, even if they are little things, not much otherwise than we have seen them, will continue to the end to be one of life's choicest pleasures.

Let the reader, then, betake himself in the spirit we have recommended to some of the quieter kinds of English landscape. In those homely and placid agricultural districts, familiarity will bring into relief many things worthy of notice, and urge them pleasantly home to him by a sort of loving repetition; such as the wonderful life-giving speed of windmill sails above the stationary country; the occurrence and recurrence of the same church tower at the end of one long vista after another: and, conspicuous among these sources of quiet pleasure, the character and variety of the road itself, along which he takes his way. Not only near at hand, in the lithe contortions with which it adapts itself to the interchanges of level and slope, but far away also, when he sees a few hundred feet of it upheaved against a hill and shining in the afternoon sun, he will find it an object so changeful and enlivening that he can always pleasurably busy his mind about it. He may leave the river- side, or fall out of the way of villages, but the road he has always with him; and, in the true humour of observation, will find in that sufficient company. From its subtle windings and changes of level there arises a keen and continuous interest, that keeps the attention ever alert and cheerful. Every sensitive adjustment to the contour of the ground, every little dip and swerve, seems instinct with life and an exquisite sense of balance and beauty. The road rolls upon the easy slopes of the country, like a long ship in the hollows of the sea. The very margins of waste ground, as they trench a little farther on the beaten way, or recede again to the shelter of the hedge, have something of the same free delicacy of line – of the same swing and wilfulness. You might think for a whole summer's day (and not have thought it any nearer an end by evening) what concourse and succession of circumstances has produced the least of these deflections; and it is, perhaps, just in this that we should look for the secret of their interest. A foot-path across a meadow – in all its human waywardness and unaccountability, in all the *grata protervitas* of its varying direction – will always be more to us than a rail-road well engineered through a difficult country. No reasoned sequence is thrust upon our attention: we seem to have slipped for one lawless little moment out of the iron rule of cause and effect; and so we revert at once to some of the pleasant old heresies of personification, always poetically orthodox, and attribute a sort of free-will, an active and spontaneous life, to the white riband of road that length-ens out, and bends, and cunningly adapts itself to the inequalities of the land before our eyes. We remember, as we write, some miles of fine wide highway laid out with conscious aesthetic artifice through a broken and richly cultivated tract of country. It is said that the engineer had Hogarth's[3] line of beauty in his mind as he laid them down. And the result is striking. One splendid satisfying sweep pass-es with easy transition into another, and there is nothing to trouble or dislocate the strong continuousness of the main line of the road. And yet there is something wanting. There is here no saving imperfection, none of those secondary curves and little trepidations of direction that carry, in natural roads, our curiosity active-ly along with them. One feels at once that this road has not been laboriously grown like a natural road, but made to pattern; and that, while a model may be academically correct in outline, it will always be inanimate and cold. The traveller is also aware of a sympathy of mood between himself and the road he travels. We have all seen ways that have wandered into heavy sand near the sea-coast, and trail wearily over the dunes like a trodden serpent. Here we too must plod for-ward at a dull, laborious pace; and so a sympathy is preserved between our frame of mind and the expression of the relaxed, heavy curves of the roadway. Such a phenomenon, indeed, our reason might perhaps resolve with a little trouble. We might reflect that the present road had been developed out of a tract sponta-neously followed by generations of primitive wayfarers; and might see in its expression a testimony that those generations had been affected at the same ground, one after another, in the same manner as we are affected to-day. Or we might carry the reflection further, and remind ourselves that where the air is invigorating and the ground firm under the traveller's foot, his eye is quick to take advantage of small undulations, and he will turn carelessly aside from the direct way wherever there is anything beautiful to examine or some promise of a wider view; so that even a bush of wild roses may permanently bias and deform the straight path over the meadow; whereas, where the soil is heavy, one is preoccu-pied with the labour of mere progression, and goes with a bowed head heavily and unobservantly forward. Reason, however, will not carry us the whole way; for the sentiment often recurs in situations where it is very hard to imagine any possible explanation; and indeed, if we drive briskly along a good, well-made road in an open vehicle, we shall experience this sympathy almost at its fullest. We feel the sharp settle of the springs at some curiously twisted corner; after a steep ascent, the fresh air dances in our faces as we rattle precipitately down the other side, and we find it difficult to avoid attributing something headlong, a sort of *abandon*, to the road itself.

The mere winding of the path is enough to enliven a long day's walk in even a commonplace or dreary country-side. Something that we have seen from miles back, upon an eminence, is so long hid from us, as we wander through folded valleys or among woods, that our expectation of seeing it again is sharpened into a violent appetite, and as we draw nearer we impatiently quicken our steps and turn every corner with a beating heart. It is through these prolongations of expectancy, this succession of one hope to another, that we live out long seasons of pleasure in a few hours' walk. It is in following these capricious sinuosities that we learn, only bit by bit and through one coquettish reticence after another, much as we learn the heart of a friend, the whole loveliness of the country. This disposition always preserves something new to be seen, and takes us, like a careful cicerone, to many different points of distant view before it allows us finally to approach the hoped-for destination.

In its connection with the traffic, and whole friendly intercourse with the country, there is something very pleasant in that succession of saunterers and brisk and business-like passers-by, that peoples our ways and helps to build up what Walt Whitman calls 'the cheerful voice of the public road, the gay, fresh sentiment of the road.'[4] But out of the great network of ways that binds all life together from the hill-farm to the city, there is something individual to most, and, on the whole, nearly as much choice on the score of company as on the score of beauty or easy travel. On some we are never long without the sound of wheels, and folk pass us by so thickly that we lose the sense of their number. But on others, about little-frequented districts, a meeting is an affair of moment; we have the sight far off of some one coming towards us, the growing definiteness of the person, and then the brief passage and salutation, and the road left empty in front of us for perhaps a great while to come. Such encounters have a wistful interest that can hardly be understood by the dweller in places more populous. We remember standing beside a countryman once, in the mouth of a quiet by-street in a city that was more than ordinarily crowded and bustling; he seemed stunned and bewildered by the continual passage of different faces; and after a long pause, during which he appeared to search for some suitable expression, he said timidly that there seemed to be a *great deal of meeting thereabouts*. The phrase is significant. It is the expression of town-life in the language of the long, solitary country highways. A meeting of one with one was what this man had been used to in the pastoral uplands from which he came; and the concourse of the streets was in his eyes only an extraordinary multiplication of such 'meetings'.

And now we come to that last and most subtle quality of all, to that sense of prospect, of outlook, that is brought so powerfully to our minds by a road. In real nature, as well as in old landscapes, beneath that impartial daylight in which a whole variegated plain is plunged and saturated, the line of the road leads the eye forth with the vague sense of desire up to the green limit of the horizon. Travel is brought home to us, and we visit in spirit every grove and hamlet that tempts us in the distance. *Sehnsucht* – the passion for what is ever beyond – is livingly expressed in that white riband of possible travel that severs the uneven country; not a ploughman following his plough up the shining furrow, not the blue smoke of any cottage in a hollow, but is brought to us with a sense of nearness and attainability by this wavering line of junction. There is a passionate paragraph in Werther that strikes the very key. 'When I came hither,' he writes, 'how the beautiful valley invited me on every side, as I gazed down into it from the hill-top! There the wood – ah, that I might mingle in its shadows! there the mountain summits – ah, that I might look down from them over the broad country! the interlinked hills! the secret valleys! Oh to lose myself among their mysteries! I hurried into the midst, and came back without finding aught I hoped for. Alas! the distance is like the future. A vast whole lies in the twilight before our spirit; sight and feeling alike plunge and lose themselves in the prospect, and we yearn to surrender our whole being, and let it be filled full with all the rapture of one single glorious sensation; and alas! when we hasten to the fruition, when *there* is changed to *here*, all is afterwards as it was before, and we stand in our indigent and cramped estate, and our soul thirsts after a still ebbing elixir.' It is to this wandering and uneasy spirit of anticipation that roads minister. Every little vista, every little glimpse that we have of what lies before us, gives the impatient imagination rein, so that it can outstrip the body and already plunge into the shadow of the woods, and overlook from the hill-top the plain beyond it, and wander in the windings of the valleys that are still far in front. The road is already there – we shall not be long behind. It is as if we were marching with the rear of a great army, and, from far before, heard the acclamation of the people as the vanguard entered some friendly and jubilant city. Would not every man, through all the long miles of march, feel as if he also were within the gates?

Notes
1. Samuel Taylor Coleridge (1772–1834), English poet.
2. Charles Lamb (1775–1834), English essayist and critic.
3. William Hogarth (1697–1764), socially conscious English painter and engraver.
4. Walt Whitman (1819–1892), the quintessential American poet; Stevenson was a great admirer of Whitman's work.

Cockermouth and Keswick

Although the tour in question took place in 1871,
the essay probably was written in 1873.

VERY much as a painter half closes his eyes so that some salient unity may disengage itself from among the crowd of details, and what he sees may thus form itself into a whole; very much on the same principle, I may say, I allow a considerable lapse of time to intervene between any of my little journeyings and the attempt to chronicle them. I cannot describe a thing that is before me at the moment, or that has been before me only a very little while before; I must allow my recollections to get thoroughly strained free from all chaff till nothing be except the pure gold; allow my memory to choose out what is truly memorable by a process of natural selection; and I piously believe that in this way I ensure the Survival of the Fittest. If I make notes for future use, or if I am obliged to write letters during the course of my little excursion, I so interfere with the process that I can never again find out what is worthy of being preserved, or what should be given in full length, what in torso, or what merely in profile. This process of incubation may be unreasonably prolonged; and I am somewhat afraid that I have made this mistake with the present journey. Like a bad daguerreotype, great part of it has been entirely lost; I can tell you nothing about the beginning and nothing about the end; but the doings of some fifty or sixty hours about the middle remain quite distinct and definite, like a little patch of sunshine on a long, shadowy plain, or the one spot on an old picture that has been restored by the dexterous hand of the cleaner. I remember a tale of an old Scots minister called upon suddenly to preach, who had hastily snatched an old sermon out of his study and found himself in the pulpit before he noticed that the rats had been making free with his manuscript and eaten the first two or three pages away; he gravely explained to the congregation how he found himself situated: 'And now,' said he, 'let us just begin where the rats have left off.' I must follow the divine's example, and take up the thread of my discourse where it first distinctly issues from the limbo of forgetfulness.

COCKERMOUTH

I was lighting my pipe as I stepped out of the inn at Cockermouth,[1] and did not raise my head until I was fairly in the street. When I did so, it flashed upon me that I was in England; the evening sunlight lit up English houses, English faces, an English conformation of street, – as it were, an English atmosphere blew against my face. There is nothing perhaps more puzzling (if one thing in sociology can ever really be more unaccountable than another) than the great gulf that is set between England and Scotland – a gulf so easy in appearance, in reality so difficult to traverse.[2] Here are two people almost identical in blood; pent up together on one small island, so that their intercourse (one would have thought) must be as close as that of prisoners who shared one cell of the Bastille; the same in language and religion; and yet a few years of quarrelsome isolation – a mere forenoon's tiff, as one may call it, in comparison with the great historical cycles – has so separated their thoughts and ways that not unions, not mutual dangers, nor steamers, nor railways, nor all the king's horses and all the king's men, seem able to obliterate the broad distinction. In the trituration of another century or so the corners may disappear; but in the meantime, in the year of grace 1871, I was as much in a new country as if I had been walking out of the Hotel St. Antoine at Antwerp.

I felt a little thrill of pleasure at my heart as I realised the change, and strolled away up the street with my hands behind my back, noting in a dull, sensual way how foreign, and yet how friendly, were the slopes of the gables and the colour of the tiles, and even the demeanour and voices of the gossips round about me.

Wandering in this aimless humour, I turned up a lane and found myself following the course of the bright little river. I passed first one and then another, then a third, several couples out love-making in the spring evening; and a consequent feeling of loneliness was beginning to grow upon me, when I came to a dam across the river, and a mill – a great, gaunt promontory of building, – half on dry ground and half arched over the stream. The road here drew in its shoulders and crept through between the landward extremity of the mill and a little garden enclosure, with a small house and a large signboard within its privet hedge. I was pleased to fancy this an inn, and drew little etchings in fancy of a sanded parlour, and three-cornered spittoons, and a society of parochial gossips seated within over their churchwardens; but as I drew near, the board displayed its superscription, and I could read the name of Smethurst, and the designation of 'Canadian Felt Hat Manufacturers'. There was no more hope of evening fellowship, and I could only stroll on by the river- side, under the trees. The water was dappled with slanting sunshine, and dusted all over with a little mist of flying insects. There were some amorous ducks, also, whose lovemaking reminded me of what I had seen a little farther down. But the road grew sad, and I grew weary; and as I was perpetually haunted with the terror of a return of the tie that had been playing such ruin in my head a week ago, I turned and went back to the inn, and supper, and my bed.

The next morning, at breakfast, I communicated to the smart waitress my intention of continuing down the coast and through Whitehaven to Furness,[3] and, as I might have expected, I was instantly confronted by that last and most worrying form of interference, that chooses to introduce tradition and authority into the choice of a man's own pleasures. I can excuse a person combating my religious or philosophical heresies, because them I have deliberately accepted, and am ready to justify by present argument. But I do not seek to justify my pleasures. If I prefer tame scenery to grand, a little hot sunshine over lowland parks and woodlands to the war of the elements round the summit of Mont Blanc; or if I prefer a pipe of mild tobacco, and the company of one or two chosen companions, to a ball where I feel myself very hot, awkward, and weary, I merely state these preferences as facts, and do not seek to establish them as principles. This is not the general rule, however, and accordingly the waitress was shocked, as one might be at a heresy, to hear the route that I had sketched out for myself. Everybody who came to Cockermouth for pleasure, it appeared, went on to Keswick.[4] It was in vain that I put up a little plea for the liberty of the subject; it was in vain that I said I should prefer to go to Whitehaven. I was told that there was 'nothing to see there' – that weary, hackneyed, old falsehood; and at last, as the handmaiden began to look really concerned, I gave way, as men always do in such circumstances, and agreed that I was to leave for Keswick by a train in the early evening.

AN EVANGELIST

Cockermouth itself, on the same authority, was a Place with 'nothing to see'; nevertheless I saw a good deal, and retain a pleasant, vague picture of the town and all its surroundings. I might have dodged happily enough all day about the main street and up to the castle and in and out of byways, but the curious attraction that leads a person in a strange place to follow, day after day, the same round, and to make set habits for himself in a week or ten days, led me half unconsciously up the same, road that I had gone the evening before. When I came up to the hat manufactory, Smethurst himself was standing in the garden gate. He was brushing one Canadian felt hat, and several others had been put to await their turn one above the other on his own head, so that he looked something like the typical Jew old-clothes man. As I drew near, he came sidling out of the doorway to accost me, with so curious an expression on his face that I instinctively prepared myself to apologise for some unwitting trespass. His first question rather confirmed me in this belief, for it was whether or not he had seen me going up this way last night; and after having answered in the affirmative, I waited in some alarm for the rest of my indictment. But the good man's heart was full of peace; and he stood there brushing his hats and prattling on about fishing, and walking, and the pleasures of convalescence, in a bright shallow stream that kept me pleased and interested, I could scarcely say how. As he went on, he warmed to his subject, and laid his hats aside to go along the water-side and show me where the large trout commonly lay, underneath an overhanging bank; and he was much disappointed, for my sake, that there were none visible just then. Then he wandered off on to another tack, and stood a great while out in the middle of a meadow in the hot sunshine, trying to make out that he had known me before, or, if not me, some friend of mine, merely, I believe, out of a desire that we should feel more friendly and at our ease with one another. At last he made a little speech to me, of which I wish I could recollect the very words, for they were so simple and unaffected that they put all the best writing and speaking to the blush; as it is, I can recall only the sense, and that perhaps imperfectly. He began by saying that he had little things in his past life that it gave him especial pleasure to recall; and that the faculty of receiving such sharp impressions had now died out in himself, but must at my age be still quite lively and active. Then he told me that he had a little raft afloat on the river above the dam which he was going to lend me, in order that I might be able to look back, in after years, upon having done so, and get great pleasure from the recollection. Now, I have a friend of my own who will forgo present enjoyments and suffer much present inconvenience for the sake of manufacturing 'a reminiscence' for himself; but there was something singularly refined in this pleasure that the hatmaker found in making reminiscences for others; surely no more simple or unselfish luxury can be imagined. After he had unmoored his little embarkation, and seen me safely shoved off into midstream, he ran away back to his hats with the air of a man who had only just recollected that he had anything to do.

I did not stay very long on the raft. It ought to have been very nice punting about there in the cool shade of the trees, or sitting moored to an over-hanging root; but perhaps the very notion that I was bound in gratitude specially to enjoy my little cruise, and cherish its recollection, turned the whole thing from a pleasure into a duty. Be that as it may, there is no doubt that I soon wearied and came ashore again, and that it gives me more pleasure to recall the man himself and his simple, happy conversation, so full of gusto and sympathy, than anything possibly connected with his crank, insecure embarkation. In order to avoid seeing him, for I was not a little ashamed of myself for having failed to enjoy his treat sufficiently, I determined to continue up the river, and, at all prices, to find some other way back into the town in time for dinner. As I went, I was thinking of Smethurst with admiration; a look into that man's mind was like a retrospect over the smiling champaign of his past life, and very different from the Sinai-gorges up which one looks for a terrified moment into the dark souls of many good, many wise, and many prudent men. I cannot be very grateful to such men for their excellence, and wisdom, and prudence. I find myself facing as stoutly as I can a hard, combative existence, full of doubt, difficulties, defeats, disappointments, and dangers, quite a hard enough life without their dark countenances at my elbow, so that what I want is a happy-minded Smethurst placed here and there at ugly corners of my life's wayside, preaching his gospel of quiet and contentment.

ANOTHER

I was shortly to meet with an evangelist of another stamp. After I had forced my way through a gentleman's grounds, I came out on the high road, and sat down to rest myself on a heap of stones at the top of a long hill, with Cockermouth lying snugly at the bottom. An Irish beggar-woman, with a beautiful little girl by her side, came up to ask for alms, and gradually fell to telling me the little tragedy of her life. Her own sister, she told me, had seduced her husband from her after many years of married life, and the pair had fled, leaving her destitute, with the little girl upon her hands. She seemed quite hopeful and cheery, and, though she was unaffectedly sorry for the loss of her husband's earnings, she made no pretence of despair at the loss of his affection; some day she would meet the fugitives, and the law would see her duly righted, and in the meantime the smallest contribution was gratefully received. While she was telling all this in the most matter-of-fact way, I had been noticing the approach of a tall man, with a high white hat and darkish clothes. He came up the hill at a rapid pace, and joined our little group with a sort of half-salutation. Turning at once to the woman, he asked her in a business-like way whether she had anything to do, whether she were a Catholic or a Protestant, whether she could read, and so forth; and then, after a few kind words and some sweeties to the child, he despatched the mother with some tracts about Biddy and the Priest, and the Orangeman's Bible. I was a little amused at his abrupt manner, for he was still a young man, and had somewhat the air of a navy officer; but he tackled me with great solemnity. I could make fun of what he said, for I do not think it was very wise; but the subject does not appear to me just now in a jesting light, so I shall only say that he related to me his own conversion, which had been effected (as is very often the case) through the agency of a gig accident, and that, after having examined me and diagnosed my case, he selected some suitable tracts from his repertory, gave them to me, and, bidding me God-speed, went on his way.

LAST OF SMETHURST

That evening I got into a third-class carriage on my way for Keswick, and was followed almost immediately by a burly man in brown clothes. This fellow-passenger was seemingly ill at ease, and kept continually putting his head out of the window, and asking the bystanders if they saw *him* coming. At last, when the train was already in motion, there was a commotion on the platform, and a way was left clear to our carriage door. *He* had arrived. In the hurry I could just see Smethurst, red and panting, thrust a couple of clay pipes into my companion's outstretched band, and hear him crying his farewells after us as we slipped out of the station at an ever accelerating pace. I said something about it being a close run, and the broad man, already engaged in filling one of the pipes, assented, and went on to tell me of his own stupidity in forgetting a necessary, and of how his friend had good-naturedly gone down town at the last moment to supply the omission. I mentioned that I had seen Mr. Smethurst already, and that he had been very polite to me; and we fell into a discussion of the hatter's merits that lasted some time and left us quite good friends at its conclusion. The topic was productive of goodwill. We exchanged tobacco and talked about the season, and agreed at last that we should go to the same hotel at Keswick and sup in company. As he had some business in the town which would occupy him some hour or so, on our arrival I was to improve the time and go down to the lake, that I might see a glimpse of the promised wonders.[5]

The night had fallen already when I reached the water-side, at a place where many pleasure-boats are moored and ready for hire; and as I went along a stony path, between wood and water, a strong wind blew in gusts from the far end of the lake. The sky was covered with flying scud; and, as this was ragged, there was quite a wild chase of shadow and moon-glimpse over the surface of the shuddering water. I had to hold my hat on, and was growing rather tired, and inclined to go back in disgust, when a little incident occurred to break the tedium. A sudden and violent squall of wind sundered the low underwood, and at the same time there came one of those brief discharges of moonlight, which leaped into the opening thus made, and showed me three girls in the prettiest flutter and disorder. It was as though they had sprung out of the ground. I accosted them very politely in my capacity of stranger, and requested to be told the names of all manner of hills and woods and places that I did not wish to know, and we stood together for a while and had an amusing little talk. The wind, too, made himself of the party, brought the colour into their faces, and gave them enough to do to repress their drapery; and one of them, amid much giggling, had to pirouette round and round upon her toes (as girls do) when some specially strong gust had got the advantage over her. They were just high enough up in the social order not to be afraid to speak to a gentleman; and just low enough to feel a little tremor, a nervous consciousness of wrong- doing – of stolen waters, that gave a considerable zest to our most innocent interview. They were as much discomposed and fluttered, indeed, as if I had been a wicked baron proposing to elope with the whole trio; but they showed no inclination to go away, and I had managed to get them off hills and waterfalls and on to more promising subjects, when a young man was descried coming along the path from the direction of Keswick. Now whether he was the young man of one of my friends, or the brother of one of them, or indeed the brother of all, I do not know; but they incontinently said that they must be going, and went away up the path with friendly salutations. I need not say that I found the lake and the moonlight rather dull after their departure, and speedily found my way back to potted herrings and whisky-and-water in the commercial room with my late fellow- traveller. In the smoking-room there was a tall dark man with a moustache, in an ulster coat, who had got the best place and was monopolising most of the talk; and, as I came in, a whisper came round to me from both sides, that this was the manager of a London theatre. The presence of such a man was a great event for Keswick, and I must own that the manager showed himself equal to his position. He had a large fat pocket-book, from which he produced poem after poem, written on the backs of letters or hotel-bills; and nothing could be more humorous than his recitation of these elegant extracts, except perhaps the anecdotes with which he varied the entertainment. Seeing, I suppose, something less countrified in my appearance than in most of the company, he singled me out to corroborate some statements as to the depravity and vice of the aristocracy, and when he went on to describe some gilded saloon experiences, I am proud to say that he honoured my sagacity with one little covert wink before a second time appealing to me for confirmation. The wink was not thrown away; I went in up to the elbows with the manager, until I think that some of the glory of that great man settled by reflection upon me, and that I was as noticeably the second person in the smoking-room as he was the first. For a young man, this was a position of some distinction, I think you will admit …

Notes
1. Cockermouth is a market town at the mouth of the River Cocker in England's Lake District.
2. The profound cultural differences between Scotland and England is a common Stevenson theme.
3. Whitehaven is a town on the Cumbrian coast developed in the seventeenth and eighteenth centuries.
4. Keswick was and remains a popular market town and unofficial 'capital' of the Lake District.
5. Keswick is situated between lakes Derwentwater and Bassenthwaite.

An Autumn Effect

An Autumn Effect, in which Stevenson describes a walking tour of the Chiltern Hills in Buckinghamshire, England, was originally published in Portfolio Magazine *in April and May, 1875.*

A COUNTRY rapidly passed through under favourable auspices may leave upon us a unity of impression that would only be disturbed and dissipated if we stayed longer. Clear vision goes with the quick foot. Things fall for us into a sort of natural perspective when we see them for a moment in going by; we generalise boldly and simply, and are gone before the sun is overcast, before the rain falls, before the season can steal like a dial-hand from his figure, before the lights and shadows, shifting round towards nightfall, can show us the other side of things, and belie what they showed us in the morning. We expose our mind to the landscape (as we would expose the prepared plate in the camera) for the moment only during which the effect endures; and we are away before the effect can change. Hence we shall have in our memories a long scroll of continuous wayside pictures, all imbued already with the prevailing sentiment of the season, the weather and the landscape, and certain to be unified more and more, as time goes on, by the unconscious processes of thought. So that we who have only looked at a country over our shoulder, so to speak, as we went by, will have a conception of it far more memorable and articulate than a man who has lived there all his life from a child upwards, and had his impression of to-day modified by that of to-morrow, and belied by that of the day after, till at length the stable characteristics of the country are all blotted out from him behind the confusion of variable effect.

I begin my little pilgrimage in the most enviable of all humours: that in which a person, with a sufficiency of money and a knapsack, turns his back on a town and walks forward into a country of which he knows only by the vague report of others. Such a one has not surrendered his will and contracted for the next hundred miles, like a man on a railway. He may change his mind at every finger-post, and, where ways meet, follow vague preferences freely and go the low road or the high, choose the shadow or the sun-shine, suffer himself to be tempted by the lane that turns immediately into the woods, or the broad road that lies open before him into the distance, and shows him the far-off spires of some city, or a range of mountain-tops, or a rim of sea, perhaps, along a low horizon. In short, he may gratify his every whim and fancy, without a pang of reproving conscience, or the least jostle to his self-respect. It is true, however, that most men do not possess the faculty of free action, the priceless gift of being able to live for the moment only; and as they begin to go forward on their journey, they will find that they have made for themselves new fetters. Slight projects they may have entertained for a moment, half in jest, become iron laws to them, they know not why. They will be led by the nose by these vague reports of which I spoke above; and the mere fact that their informant mentioned one village and not another will compel their footsteps with inexplicable power. And yet a little while, yet a few days of this fictitious liberty, and they will begin to hear imperious voices calling on them to return; and some passion, some duty, some worthy or unworthy expectation, will set its hand upon their shoulder and lead them back into the old paths. Once and again we have all made the experiment. We know the end of it right well. And yet if we make it for the hundredth time to-morrow: it will have the same charm as ever; our heart will beat and our eyes will be bright, as we leave the town behind us, and we shall feel once again (as we have felt so often before) that we are cutting ourselves loose for ever from our whole past life, with all its sins and follies and circumscriptions, and go forward as a new creature into a new world.

It was well, perhaps, that I had this first enthusiasm to encourage me up the long hill above High Wycombe[1]; for the day was a bad day for walking at best, and now began to draw towards afternoon, dull, heavy, and lifeless. A pall of grey cloud covered the sky, and its colour reacted on the colour of the landscape. Near at hand, indeed, the hedgerow trees were still fairly green, shot through with bright autumnal yellows, bright as sunshine. But a little way off, the solid bricks of woodland that lay squarely on slope and hill-top were not green, but russet and grey, and ever less russet and more grey as they drew off into the distance. As they drew off into the distance, also, the woods seemed to mass themselves together, and lie thin and straight, like clouds, upon the limit of one's view. Not that this massing was complete, or gave the idea of any extent of forest, for every here and there the trees would break up and go down into a valley in open order, or stand in long Indian file along the horizon, tree after tree relieved, foolishly enough, against the sky. I say foolishly enough, although I have seen the effect employed cleverly in art, and such long line of single trees thrown out against the customary sunset of a Japanese picture with a certain fantastic effect that was not to be despised; but this was over water and level land, where it did not jar, as here, with the soft contour of hills and valleys. The whole scene had an indefinable look of being painted, the colour was so abstract and correct, and there was something so sketchy and merely impressional about these distant single trees on the horizon that one was forced to think of it all as of a clever French landscape. For it is rather in nature that we see resemblance to art, than in art to nature; and we say a hundred times, 'How like a picture!' for once that we say, 'How like the truth!' The forms in which we learn to think of landscape are forms that we have got from painted canvas. Any man can see and understand a picture; it is reserved for the few to separate anything out of the confusion of nature, and see that distinctly and with intelligence.

The sun came out before I had been long on my way; and as I had got by that time to the top of the ascent, and was now treading a labyrinth of confined by-roads, my whole view brightened considerably in colour, for it was the distance only that was grey and cold, and the distance I could see no longer. Overhead there was a wonderful carolling of larks which seemed to follow me as I went. Indeed, during all the time I was in that country the larks did not desert me. The air was alive with them from High Wycombe to Tring;[2] and as, day after day, their 'shrill delight' fell upon me out of the vacant sky, they began to take such a prominence over other conditions, and form so integral a part of my conception of the country, that I could have baptised it 'The Country of Larks'. This, of course, might just as well have been in early spring; but everything else was deeply imbued with the sentiment of the later year. There was no stir of insects in the grass. The sunshine was more golden, and gave less heat than summer sunshine; and the shadows under the hedge were somewhat blue and misty. It was only in autumn that you could have seen the mingled green and yellow of the elm foliage, and the fallen leaves that lay about the road, and covered the surface of wayside pools so thickly that the sun was reflected only here and there from little joints and pinholes in that brown coat of proof; or that your ear would have been troubled, as you went forward, by the occasional report of fowling-pieces from all directions and all degrees of distance.

For a long time this dropping fire was the one sign of human activity that came to disturb me as I walked. The lanes were profoundly still. They would have been sad but for the sunshine and the singing of the larks. And as it was, there came over me at times a feeling of isolation that was not disagreeable, and yet was enough to make me quicken my steps eagerly when I saw some one before me on the road. This fellow-voyager proved to be no less a person than the parish constable. It had occurred to me that in a district which was so little populous and so well wooded, a criminal of any intelligence might play hide-and-seek with the authorities for months; and this idea was strengthened by the aspect of the portly constable as he walked by my side with deliberate dignity and turned-out toes. But a few minutes' converse set my heart at rest. These rural criminals are very tame birds, it appeared. If my informant did not immediately lay his hand on an offender, he was content to wait; some evening after nightfall there would come a tap at his door, and the outlaw, weary of outlawry, would give himself quietly up to undergo sentence, and resume his position in the life of the country-side. Married men caused him no disquietude whatever; he had them fast by the foot. Sooner or later they would come back to see their wives, a peeping neighbour would pass the word, and my portly constable would walk quietly over and take the bird sitting. And if there were a few who had no particular ties in the neighbourhood, and preferred to shift into another county when they fell into trouble, their departure moved the placid constable in no degree. He was of Dogberry's opinion; and if a man would not stand in the Prince's name, he took no note of him, but let him go, and thanked God he was rid of a knave. And surely the crime and the law were in admirable keeping; rustic constable was well met with rustic offender. The officer sitting at home over a bit of fire until the criminal came to visit him, and the criminal coming – it was a fair match. One felt as if this must have been the order in that delightful seaboard Bohemia where Florizel and Perdita courted in such sweet accents, and the Puritan sang Psalms to hornpipes, and the four-and-twenty shearers danced with nosegays in their bosoms, and chanted their three songs apiece at the old shepherd's festival; and one could not help picturing to oneself what havoc among good peoples purses, and tribulation for benignant constables, might be worked here by the arrival, over stile and foot-path, of a new Autolycus.

Bidding good-morning to my fellow-traveller, I left the road and struck across country. It was rather a revelation to pass from between the hedgerows and find quite a bustle on the other side, a great coming and going of school-children upon by-paths, and, in every second field, lusty horses and stout country-folk a-plough-ing. The way I followed took me through many fields thus occupied, and through many strips of plantation, and then over a little space of smooth turf, very pleas-ant to the feet, set with tall fir-trees and clamorous with rooks making ready for the winter, and so back again into the quiet road. I was now not far from the end of my day's journey. A few hundred yards farther, and, passing through a gap in the hedge, I began to go down hill through a pretty extensive tract of young beeches. I was soon in shadow myself, but the afternoon sun still coloured the upmost boughs of the wood, and made a fire over my head in the autumnal foliage. A little faint vapour lay among the slim tree-stems in the bottom of the hollow; and from farther up I heard from time to time an outburst of gross laugh-ter, as though clowns were making merry in the bush. There was something about the atmosphere that brought all sights and sounds home to one with a singular purity, so that I felt as if my senses had been washed with water. After I had crossed the little zone of mist, the path began to remount the hill; and just as I, mounting along with it, had got back again, from the head downwards, into the thin golden sunshine, I saw in front of me a donkey tied to a tree. Now, I have a certain liking for donkeys, principally, I believe, because of the delightful things that Sterne has written of them.[3] But this was not after the pattern of the ass at Lyons. He was of a white colour, that seemed to fit him rather for rare festal occa-sions than for constant drudgery. Besides, he was very small, and of the daintiest portions you can imagine in a donkey. And so, sure enough, you had only to look at him to see he had never worked. There was something too roguish and wanton in his face, a look too like that of a schoolboy or a street Arab, to have survived much cudgelling. It was plain that these feet had kicked off sportive children oftener than they had plodded with a freight through miry lanes. He was alto-

gether a fine-weather, holiday sort of donkey; and though he was just then somewhat solemnised and rueful, he still gave proof of the levity of his disposition by
impudently wagging his ears at me as I drew near. I say he was somewhat solemnised just then; for, with the admirable instinct of all men and animals under
restraint, he had so wound and wound the halter about the tree that he could go
neither back nor forwards, nor so much as put down his head to browse. There he
stood, poor rogue, part puzzled, part angry, part, I believe, amused. He had not
given up hope, and dully revolved the problem in his head, giving ever and again
another jerk at the few inches of free rope that still remained unwound. A humorous sort of sympathy for the creature took hold upon me. I went up, and, not without some trouble on my part, and much distrust and resistance on the part of
Neddy, got him forced backwards until the whole length of the halter was set
loose, and he was once more as free a donkey as I dared to make him. I was
pleased (as people are) with this friendly action to a fellow- creature in tribulation, and glanced back over my shoulder to see how he was profiting by his freedom. The brute was looking after me; and no sooner did he catch my eye than he
put up his long white face into the air, pulled an impudent mouth at me, and
began to bray derisively. If ever any one person made a grimace at another, that
donkey made a grimace at me. The hardened ingratitude of his behaviour, and the
impertinence that inspired his whole face as he curled up his lip, and showed his
teeth, and began to bray, so tickled me, and was so much in keeping with what I
had imagined to myself about his character, that I could not find it in my heart to
be angry, and burst into a peal of hearty laughter. This seemed to strike the ass as
a repartee, so he brayed at me again by way of rejoinder; and we went on for a
while, braying and laughing, until I began to grow aweary of it, and, shouting a
derisive farewell, turned to pursue my way. In so doing – it was like going suddenly into cold water – I found myself face to face with a prim little old maid. She
was all in a flutter, the poor old dear! She had concluded beyond question that this
must be a lunatic who stood laughing aloud at a white donkey in the placid beech-
woods. I was sure, by her face, that she had already recommended her spirit most
religiously to Heaven, and prepared herself for the worst. And so, to reassure her,
I uncovered and besought her, after a very staid fashion, to put me on my way to
Great Missenden.⁴ Her voice trembled a little, to be sure, but I think her mind
was set at rest; and she told me, very explicitly, to follow the path until I came to
the end of the wood, and then I should see the village below me in the bottom of
the valley. And, with mutual courtesies, the little old maid and I went on our
respective ways.

Nor had she misled me. Great Missenden was close at hand, as she had said, in
the trough of a gentle valley, with many great elms about it. The smoke from its
chimneys went up pleasantly in the afternoon sunshine. The sleepy hum of a
threshing-machine filled the neighbouring fields and hung about the quaint street

corners. A little above, the church sits well back on its haunches against the hill-side – an attitude for a church, you know, that makes it look as if it could be ever so much higher if it liked; and the trees grew about it thickly, so as to make a density of shade in the churchyard. A very quiet place it looks; and yet I saw many boards and posters about threatening dire punishment against those who broke the church windows or defaced the precinct, and offering rewards for the apprehension of those who had done the like already. It was fair day in Great Missenden. There were three stalls set up, sub jove, for the sale of pastry and cheap toys; and a great number of holiday children thronged about the stalls and noisily invaded every corner of the straggling village. They came round me by coveys, blowing simultaneously upon penny trumpets as though they imagined I should fall to pieces like the battlements of Jericho. I noticed one among them who could make a wheel of himself like a London boy, and seemingly enjoyed a grave pre-eminence upon the strength of the accomplishment. By and by, however, the trumpets began to weary me, and I went indoors, leaving the fair, I fancy, at its height.

Night had fallen before I ventured forth again. It was pitch-dark in the village street, and the darkness seemed only the greater for a light here and there in an uncurtained window or from an open door. Into one such window I was rude enough to peep, and saw within a charming genre picture. In a room, all white wainscot and crimson wall-paper, a perfect gem of colour after the black, empty darkness in which I had been groping, a pretty girl was telling a story, as well as I could make out, to an attentive child upon her knee, while an old woman sat placidly dozing over the fire. You may be sure I was not behindhand with a story for myself – a good old story after the manner of GPR James and the village melodramas, with a wicked squire, and poachers, and an attorney, and a virtuous young man with a genius for mechanics, who should love, and protect, and ultimately marry the girl in the crimson room. Baudelaire[5] has a few dainty sentences on the fancies that we are inspired with when we look through a window into other people's lives; and I think Dickens has somewhere enlarged on the same text. The subject, at least, is one that I am seldom weary of entertaining. I remember, night after night, at Brussels, watching a good family sup together, make merry, and retire to rest; and night after night I waited to see the candles lit, and the salad made, and the last salutations dutifully exchanged, without any abatement of interest. Night after night I found the scene rivet my attention and keep me awake in bed with all manner of quaint imaginations. Much of the pleasure of the *Arabian Nights* hinges upon this Asmodean interest; and we are not weary of lifting other people's roofs, and going about behind the scenes of life with the Caliph and the serviceable Giaffar. It is a salutary exercise, besides; it is salutary to get out of ourselves and see people living together in perfect unconsciousness of our existence, as they will live when we are gone. If to-morrow the blow falls, and the worst of our ill fears is realised, the girl will none the less tell stories to the child on her lap in the cottage at Great Missenden, nor the good Belgians light their candle, and mix their salad, and go orderly to bed.

The next morning was sunny overhead and damp underfoot, with a thrill in the air like a reminiscence of frost. I went up into the sloping garden behind the inn and smoked a pipe pleasantly enough, to the tune of my landlady's lamentations over sundry cabbages and cauliflowers that had been spoiled by caterpillars. She had been so much pleased in the summer-time, she said, to see the garden all hovered over by white butterflies. And now, look at the end of it! She could nowise reconcile this with her moral sense. And, indeed, unless these butterflies are created with a side-look to the composition of improving apologues, it is not altogether easy, even for people who have read Hegel[6] and Dr. M'Cosh, to decide intelligibly upon the issue raised. Then I fell into a long and abstruse calculation with my landlord; having for object to compare the distance driven by him during eight years' service on the box of the Wendover coach with the girth of the round world itself. We tackled the question most conscientiously, made all necessary allowance for Sundays and leap-years, and were just coming to a triumphant conclusion of our labours when we were stayed by a small lacuna in my information. I did not know the circumference of the earth. The landlord knew it, to be sure – plainly he had made the same calculation twice and once before, – but he wanted confidence in his own figures, and from the moment I showed myself so poor a second seemed to lose all interest in the result.

Wendover (which was my next stage) lies in the same valley with Great Missenden, but at the foot of it, where the hills trend off on either hand like a coast-line, and a great hemisphere of plain lies, like a sea, before one, I went up a chalky road, until I had a good outlook over the place. The vale, as it opened out into the plain, was shallow, and a little bare, perhaps, but full of graceful convolutions.[7] From the level to which I have now attained the fields were exposed before me like a map, and I could see all that bustle of autumn field-work which had been hid from me yesterday behind the hedgerows, or shown to me only for a moment as I followed the footpath. Wendover lay well down in the midst, with mountains of foliage about it. The great plain stretched away to the northward, variegated near at hand with the quaint pattern of the fields, but growing ever more and more indistinct, until it became a mere hurly- burly of trees and bright crescents of river, and snatches of slanting road, and finally melted into the ambiguous cloud-land over the horizon. The sky was an opal-grey, touched here and there with blue, and with certain faint russets that looked as if they were reflections of the colour of the autumnal woods below. I could hear the ploughmen shouting to their horses, the uninterrupted carol of larks innumerable overhead, and, from a field where the shepherd was marshalling his flock, a sweet tumultuous tinkle of sheep-bells. All these noises came to me very thin and distinct in the clear air. There was a wonderful sentiment of distance and atmosphere about the day and the place.

I mounted the hill yet farther by a rough staircase of chalky footholds cut in the turf. The hills about Wendover and, as far as I could see, all the hills in Buckinghamshire, wear a sort of hood of beech plantation; but in this particular case the hood had been suffered to extend itself into something more like a cloak, and hung down about the shoulders of the hill in wide folds, instead of lying flatly along the summit. The trees grew so close, and their boughs were so matted together, that the whole wood looked as dense as a bush of heather.[8] The prevailing colour was a dull, smouldering red touched here and there with vivid yellow. But the autumn had scarce advanced beyond the outworks; it was still almost summer in the heart of the wood; and as soon as I had scrambled through the hedge, I found myself in a dim green forest atmosphere under eaves of virgin foliage. In places where the wood had itself for a background and the trees were massed together thickly, the colour became intensified and almost gem-like: a perfect fire green, that seemed none the less green for a few specks of autumn gold. None of the trees were of any considerable age or stature; but they grew well together, I have said; and as the road turned and wound among them, they fell into pleasant groupings and broke the light up pleasantly. Sometimes there would be a colonnade of slim, straight tree-stems with the light running down them as down the shafts of pillars, that looked as if it ought to lead to something, and led only to a corner of sombre and intricate jungle. Sometimes a spray of delicate foliage would be thrown out flat, the light lying flatly along the top of it, so that against a dark background it seemed almost luminous. There was a great bush over the thicket (for, indeed, it was more of a thicket than a wood); and the vague rumours that went among the tree-tops, and the occasional rustling of big birds or hares among the undergrowth, had in them a note of almost treacherous stealthiness, that put the imagination on its guard and made me walk warily on the russet carpeting of last year's leaves. The spirit of the place seemed to be all attention; the wood listened as I went, and held its breath to number my footfalls. One could not help feeling that there ought to be some reason for this stillness; whether, as the bright old legend goes, Pan lay somewhere near in siesta, or whether, perhaps, the heaven was meditating rain, and the first drops would soon come pattering through the leaves. It was not unpleasant, in such an humour, to catch sight, ever and anon, of large spaces of the open plain. This happened only where the path lay much upon the slope, and there was a flaw in the solid leafy thatch of the wood at some distance below the level at which I chanced myself to be walking; then, indeed, little scraps of foreshortened distance, miniature fields, and Lilliputian houses and hedgerow trees would appear for a moment in the aperture, and grow larger and smaller, and change and melt one into another, as I continued to go forward, and so shift my point of view.

For ten minutes, perhaps, I had heard from somewhere before me in the wood a strange, continuous noise, as of clucking, cooing, and gobbling, now and again interrupted by a harsh scream. As I advanced towards this noise, it began to grow lighter about me, and I caught sight, through the trees, of sundry gables and enclosure walls, and something like the tops of a rickyard. And sure enough, a rickyard it proved to be, and a neat little farm-steading, with the beech- woods growing almost to the door of it. Just before me, however, as I came upon the path, the trees drew back and let in a wide flood of daylight on to a circular lawn. It was here that the noises had their origin. More than a score of peacocks (there are altogether thirty at the farm), a proper contingent of peahens, and a great multitude that I could not number of more ordinary barn-door fowls, were all feeding together on this little open lawn among the beeches. They fed in a dense crowd, which swayed to and fro, and came hither and thither as by a sort of tide, and of which the surface was agitated like the surface of a sea as each bird guzzled his head along the ground after the scattered corn. The clucking, cooing noise that had led me thither was formed by the blending together of countless expressions of individual contentment into one collective expression of contentment, or general grace during meat. Every now and again a big peacock would separate himself from the mob and take a stately turn or two about the lawn, or perhaps mount for a moment upon the rail, and there shrilly publish to the world his satisfaction with himself and what he had to eat. It happened, for my sins, that none of these admirable birds had anything beyond the merest rudiment of a tail. Tails, it seemed, were out of season just then. But they had their necks for all that; and by their necks alone they do as much surpass all the other birds of our grey climate as they fall in quality of song below the blackbird or the lark. Surely the peacock, with its incomparable parade of glorious colour and the scannel voice of it issuing forth, as in mockery, from its painted throat, must, like my landlady's butterflies at Great Missenden, have been invented by some skilful fabulist for the consolation and support of homely virtue: or rather, perhaps, by a fabulist not quite so skilful, who made points for the moment without having a studious enough eye to the complete effect; for I thought these melting greens and blues so beautiful that afternoon, that I would have given them my vote just then before the sweetest pipe in all the spring woods. For indeed there is no piece of colour of the same extent in nature, that will so flatter and satisfy the lust of a man's eyes; and to come upon so many of them, after these acres of stone-coloured heavens and russet woods, and grey-brown ploughlands and white roads, was like going three whole days' journey to the southward, or a month back into the summer.

I was sorry to leave Peacock Farm – for so the place is called, after the name of its splendid pensioners – and go forwards again in the quiet woods. It began to grow both damp and dusk under the beeches; and as the day declined the colour faded out of the foliage; and shadow, without form and void, took the place of all the fine tracery of leaves and delicate gradations of living green that had before accompanied my walk. I had been sorry to leave Peacock Farm, but I was not sorry to find myself once more in the open road, under a pale and somewhat troubled-looking evening sky, and put my best foot foremost for the inn at Wendover.

Wendover, in itself, is a straggling, purposeless sort of place. Everybody seems to have had his own opinion as to how the street should go; or rather, every now and then a man seems to have arisen with a new idea on the subject, and led away a little sect of neighbours to join in his heresy. It would have somewhat the look of an abortive watering-place, such as we may now see them here and there along the coast, but for the age of the houses, the comely quiet design of some of them, and the look of long habitation, of a life that is settled and rooted, and makes it worth while to train flowers about the windows, and otherwise shape the dwelling to the humour of the inhabitant. The church, which might perhaps have served as rallying-point for these loose houses, and pulled the township into something like intelligible unity, stands some distance off among great trees; but the inn (to take the public buildings in order of importance) is in what I understand to be the principal street: a pleasant old house, with bay-windows, and three peaked gables, and many swallows' nests plastered about the eaves.

The interior of the inn was answerable to the outside: indeed, I never saw any room much more to be admired than the low wainscoted parlour in which I spent the remainder of the evening. It was a short oblong in shape, save that the fireplace was built across one of the angles so as to cut it partially off, and the opposite angle was similarly truncated by a corner cupboard. The wainscot was white, and there was a Turkey carpet on the floor, so old that it might have been imported by Walter Shandy before he retired, worn almost through in some places, but in others making a good show of blues and oranges, none the less harmonious for being somewhat faded. The corner cupboard was agreeable in design; and there were just the right things upon the shelves – decanters and tumblers, and blue plates, and one red rose in a glass of water. The furniture was old- fashioned and stiff. Everything was in keeping, down to the ponderous leaden inkstand on the round table. And you may fancy how pleasant it looked, all flushed and flickered over by the light of a brisk companionable fire, and seen, in a strange, tilted sort of perspective, in the three compartments of the old mirror above the chimney. As I sat reading in the great armchair, I kept looking round with the tail of my eye at the quaint, bright picture that was about me, and could not help some pleasure and a certain childish pride in forming part of it. The book I read was about Italy in the early Renaissance, the pageantries and the light loves of princes, the passion of men for learning, and poetry, and art; but it was written, by good luck, after a solid, prosaic fashion, that suited the room infinitely more nearly than the matter; and the result was that I thought less, perhaps, of Lippo Lippi, or Lorenzo, or Politian, than of the good Englishman who had written in that volume what he knew of them, and taken so much pleasure in his solemn polysyllables.

I was not left without society. My landlord had a very pretty little daughter, whom we shall call Lizzie. If I had made any notes at the time, I might be able to tell you something definite of her appearance. But faces have a trick of growing more and more spiritualised and abstract in the memory, until nothing remains of them but a look, a haunting expression; just that secret quality in a face that is apt to slip out somehow under the cunningest painter's touch, and leave the portrait dead for the lack of it. And if it is hard to catch with the finest of camel's-hair pencils, you may think how hopeless it must be to pursue after it with clumsy words. If I say, for instance, that this look, which I remember as Lizzie, was something wistful that seemed partly to come of slyness and in part of simplicity, and that I am inclined to imagine it had something to do with the daintiest suspicion of a cast in one of her large eyes, I shall have said all that I can, and the reader will not be much advanced towards comprehension. I had struck up an acquaintance with this little damsel in the morning, and professed much interest in her dolls, and an impatient desire to see the large one which was kept locked away for great occasions. And so I had not been very long in the parlour before the door opened, and in came Miss Lizzie with two dolls tucked clumsily under her arm. She was followed by her brother John, a year or so younger than herself, not simply to play propriety at our interview, but to show his own two whips in emulation of his sister's dolls. I did my best to make myself agreeable to my visitors, showing much admiration for the dolls and dolls' dresses, and, with a very serious demeanour, asking many questions about their age and character. I do not think that Lizzie distrusted my sincerity, but it was evident that she was both bewildered and a little contemptuous. Although she was ready herself to treat her dolls as if they were alive, she seemed to think rather poorly of any grown person who could fall heartily into the spirit of the fiction. Sometimes she would look at me with gravity and a sort of disquietude, as though she really feared I must be out of my wits. Sometimes, as when I inquired too particularly into the question of their names, she laughed at me so long and heartily that I began to feel almost embarrassed. But when, in an evil moment, I asked to be allowed to kiss one of them, she could keep herself no longer to herself. Clambering down from the chair on which she sat perched to show me, Cornelia-like, her jewels, she ran straight out of the room and into the bar – it was just across the passage, – and I could hear her telling her mother in loud tones, but apparently more in sorrow than in merriment, that *the gentleman in the parlour wanted to kiss Dolly*. I fancy she was determined to save me from this humiliating action, even in spite of myself, for she never gave me the desired permission. She reminded me of an old dog I once knew, who would never suffer the master of the house to dance, out of an exaggerated sense of the dignity of that master's place and carriage.

After the young people were gone there was but one more incident ere I went to bed. I heard a party of children go up and down the dark street for a while, singing together sweetly. And the mystery of this little incident was so pleasant to me that I purposely refrained from asking who they were, and wherefore they went singing at so late an hour. One can rarely be in a pleasant place without meeting with some pleasant accident. I have a conviction that these children would not have gone singing before the inn unless the inn-parlour had been the delightful place it was. At least, if I had been in the customary public room of the modern hotel, with all its disproportions and discomforts, my ears would have been dull, and there would have been some ugly temper or other uppermost in my spirit, and so they would have wasted their songs upon an unworthy hearer.

Next morning I went along to visit the church. It is a long-backed red-and-white building, very much restored, and stands in a pleasant graveyard among those great trees of which I have spoken already. The sky was drowned in a mist. Now and again pulses of cold wind went about the enclosure, and set the branches busy overhead, and the dead leaves scurrying into the angles of the church buttresses. Now and again, also, I could hear the dull sudden fall of a chestnut among the grass – the dog would bark before the rectory door – or there would come a clinking of pails from the stable-yard behind. But in spite of these occasional interruptions – in spite, also, of the continuous autumn twittering that filled the trees – the chief impression somehow was one as of utter silence, insomuch that the little greenish bell that peeped out of a window in the tower disquieted me with a sense of some possible and more inharmonious disturbance. The grass was wet, as if with a hoar frost that had just been melted. I do not know that ever I saw a morning more autumnal. As I went to and fro among the graves, I saw some flowers set reverently before a recently erected tomb, and drawing near, was almost startled to find they lay on the grave a man seventy-two years old when he died. We are accustomed to strew flowers only over the young, where love has been cut short untimely, and great possibilities have been restrained by death. We strew them there in token, that these possibilities, in some deeper sense, shall yet be realised, and the touch of our dead loves remain with us and guide us to the end. And yet there was more significance, perhaps, and perhaps a greater consolation, in this little nosegay on the grave of one who had died old. We are apt to make so much of the tragedy of death, and think so little of the enduring tragedy of some men's lives, that we see more to lament for in a life cut off in the midst of usefulness and love, than in one that miserably survives all love and usefulness, and goes about the world the phantom of itself, without hope, or joy, or any consolation. These flowers seemed not so much the token of love that survived death, as of something yet more beautiful – of love that had lived a man's life out to an end with him, and been faithful and companionable, and not weary of loving, throughout all these years.

The morning cleared a little, and the sky was once more the old stone-coloured vault over the sallow meadows and the russet woods, as I set forth on a dog-cart from Wendover to Tring. The road lay for a good distance along the side of the hills, with the great plain below on one hand, and the beech-woods above on the other. The fields were busy with people ploughing and sowing; every here and there a jug of ale stood in the angle of the hedge, and I could see many a team wait smoking in the furrow as ploughman or sower stepped aside for a moment to take a draught. Over all the brown ploughlands, and under all the leafless hedgerows, there was a stout piece of labour abroad, and, as it were, a spirit of picnic. The horses smoked and the men laboured and shouted and drank in the sharp autumn morning; so that one had a strong effect of large, open-air existence. The fellow who drove me was something of a humourist; and his conversation was all in praise of an agricultural labourer's way of life. It was he who called my attention to these jugs of ale by the hedgerow; he could not sufficiently express the liberality of these men's wages; he told me how sharp an appetite was given by breaking up the earth in the morning air, whether with plough or spade, and cordially admired this provision of nature. He sang *O Fortunatos Agricolas!* indeed, in every possible key, and with many cunning inflections, till I began to wonder what was the use of such people as Mr. Arch, and to sing the same air myself in a more diffident manner.

Tring was reached, and then Tring railway-station; for the two are not very near, the good people of Tring having held the railway, of old days, in extreme apprehension, lest some day it should break loose in the town and work mischief. I had a last walk, among russet beeches as usual, and the air filled, as usual, with the carolling of larks; I heard shots fired in the distance, and saw, as a new sign of the fulfilled autumn, two horsemen exercising a pack of fox-hounds. And then the train came and carried me back to London.

Notes
1. High Wycombe is a town in Buckinghamshire under the shadow of the Chiltern Hills.
2. Tring is a small town slightly northwest of St. Albans in west Hertfordshire.
3. Laurence Sterne (1713–1768), English novelist.
4. Great Missenden is considered to form the heart of the Chilterns.
5. Charles-Pierre Baudelaire (1821–1867), French poet.
6. Georg Wilhelm Friedrich Hegel (1770–1831), German philosopher.
7. Wendover is an ancient town northwest of Great Missenden. The 845-foot summit of Coombe Hill offers fine views over the Vale of Aylesbury to the north.
8. The 600-acre forest of Burnham Beeches is part of a vast forest that dates back to prehistoric times.

France and Belgium

Ordered South

Ordered South *was originally published in* Macmillan's Magazine,
30 May 1874.

BY a curious irony of fate, the places to which we are sent when health deserts us are often singularly beautiful.[1] Often, too, they are places we have visited in former years, or seen briefly in passing by, and kept ever afterwards in pious memory; and we please ourselves with the fancy that we shall repeat many vivid and pleasurable sensations, and take up again the thread of our enjoyment in the same spirit as we let it fall. We shall now have an opporAmericayears, the recollection of some valley into which we have just looked down for a moment before we lost sight of it in the disorder of the hills; it may be that we have lain awake at night, and agreeably tantalised ourselves with the thought of corners we had never turned, or summits we had all but climbed: we shall now be able, as we tell ourselves, to complete all these unfinished pleasures, and pass beyond the barriers that confined our recollections.

The promise is so great, and we are all so easily led away when hope and memory are both in one story, that I daresay the sick man is not very inconsolable when he receives sentence of banishment, and is inclined to regard his ill- health as not the least fortunate accident of his life. Nor is he immediately undeceived. The stir and speed of the journey, and the restlessness that goes to bed with him as he tries to sleep between two days of noisy progress, fever him, and stimulate his dull nerves into something of their old quickness and sensibility. And so he can enjoy the faint autumnal splendour of the landscape, as he sees hill and plain, vineyard and forest, clad in one wonderful glory of fairy gold, which the first great winds of winter will transmute, as in the fable, into withered leaves. And so too he can enjoy the admirable brevity and simplicity of such little glimpses of country and country ways as flash upon him through the windows of the train; little glimpses that have a character all their own; sights seen as a travelling swallow might see them from the wing, or Iris as she went abroad over the land on some Olympian errand. Here and there, indeed, a few children huzzah and wave their hands to the express; but for the most part it is an interruption too brief and isolated to attract much notice; the sheep do not cease from browsing; a girl sits balanced on the projecting tiller of a canal boat, so precariously that it seems as if a fly or the splash of a leaping fish would be enough to overthrow the dainty equilibrium, and yet all these hundreds of tons of coal and wood and iron have been precipitated roaring past her very ear, and there is not a start, not a tremor, not a turn of the averted head, to indicate that she has been even conscious of its passage. Herein, I think, lies the chief attraction of railway travel. The speed is so easy, and the train disturbs so little the scenes through which it takes us, that our heart becomes full of the placidity and stillness of the country; and while the body is borne forward in the flying chain of carriages, the thoughts alight, as the humour moves them, at unfrequented stations; they make haste up the poplar alley that leads toward the town; they are left behind with the signalman as, shading his eyes with his hand, he watches the long train sweep away into the golden distance.

Moreover, there is still before the invalid the shock of wonder and delight with which he will learn that he has passed the indefinable line that separates South from North. And this is an uncertain moment; for sometimes the consciousness is forced upon him early, on the occasion of some slight association, a colour, a flower, or a scent; and sometimes not until, one fine morning, he wakes up with the southern sunshine peeping through the *persiennes*, and the southern patois confusedly audible below the windows.[2] Whether it come early or late, however, this pleasure will not end with the anticipation, as do so many others of the same family. It will leave him wider awake than it found him, and give a new significance to all he may see for many days to come. There is something in the mere name of the South that carries enthusiasm along with it. At the sound of the word, he pricks up his ears; he becomes as anxious to seek out beauties and to get by heart the permanent lines and character of the landscape, as if he had been told that it was all his own – an estate out of which he had been kept unjustly, and which he was now to receive in free and full possession. Even those who have never been there before feel as if they had been; and everybody goes comparing, and seeking for the familiar, and finding it with such ecstasies of recognition, that one would think they were coming home after a weary absence, instead of travelling hourly farther abroad.

It is only after he is fairly arrived and settled down in his chosen corner, that the invalid begins to understand the change that has befallen him. Everything about him is as he had remembered, or as he had anticipated. Here, at his feet, under his eyes, are the olive gardens and the blue sea. Nothing can change the eternal magnificence of form of the naked Alps behind Mentone; nothing, not even the crude curves of the railway, can utterly deform the suavity of contour of one bay after another along the whole reach of the Riviera. And of all this, he has only a cold head knowledge that is divorced from enjoyment. He recognises with his intelligence that this thing and that thing is beautiful, while in his heart of hearts he has to confess that it is not beautiful for him. It is in vain that he spurs his discouraged spirit; in vain that he chooses out points of view, and stands there, looking with all his eyes, and waiting for some return of the pleasure that he remembers in other days, as the sick folk may have awaited the coming of the angel at the pool of Bethesda.[3] He is like an enthusiast leading about with him a stolid, indifferent tourist. There is some one by who is out of sympathy with the scene, and is not moved up to the measure of the occasion; and that some one is himself. The world is disenchanted for him. He seems to himself to touch things with muffled hands, and to see them through a veil. His life becomes a palsied fumbling after notes that are silent when he has found and struck them. He cannot recognise that this phlegmatic and unimpressionable body with which he now goes burthened, is the same that he knew heretofore so quick and delicate and alive.

He is tempted to lay the blame on the very softness and amenity of the climate, and to fancy that in the rigours of the winter at home, these dead emotions would revive and flourish. A longing for the brightness and silence of fallen snow seizes him at such times. He is homesick for the hale rough weather; for the tracery of the frost upon his window- panes at morning, the reluctant descent of the first flakes, and the white roofs relieved against the sombre sky. And yet the stuff of which these yearnings are made, is of the flimsiest: if but the thermometer fall a little below its ordinary Mediterranean level, or a wind come down from the snow-clad Alps behind, the spirit of his fancies changes upon the instant, and many a doleful vignette of the grim wintry streets at home returns to him, and begins to haunt his memory. The hopeless, huddled attitude of tramps in doorways; the flinching gait of barefoot children on the icy pavement; the sheen of the rainy streets towards afternoon; the meagreanatomy of the poor defined by the clinging of wet garments; the high canorous note of the North-easter on days when the very houses seem to stiffen with cold: these, and such as these, crowd back upon him, and mockingly substitute themselves for the fanciful winter scenes with which he had pleased himself a while before. He cannot be glad enough that he is where he is. If only the others could be there also; if only those tramps could lie down for a little in the sunshine, and those children warm their feet, this once, upon a kindlier earth; if only there were no cold anywhere, and no nakedness, and no hunger; if only it were as well with all men as it is with him!

For it is not altogether ill with the invalid, after all. If it is only rarely that anything penetrates vividly into his numbed spirit, yet, when anything does, it brings with it a joy that is all the more poignant for its very rarity. There is something pathetic in these occasional returns of a glad activity of heart. In his lowest hours he will be stirred and awakened by many such; and they will spring perhaps from very trivial sources; as a friend once said to me, the 'spirit of delight' comes often on small wings. For the pleasure that we take in beautiful nature is essentially capricious. It comes sometimes when we least look for it; and sometimes, when we expect it most certainly, it leaves us to gape joylessly for days together, in the very home-land of the beautiful. We may have passed a place a thousand times and one; and on the thousand and second it will be transfigured, and stand forth in a certain splendour of reality from the dull circle of surroundings; so that we see it 'with a child's first pleasure,' as Wordsworth[4] saw the daffodils by the lake side. And if this falls out capriciously with the healthy, how much more so with the invalid. Some day he will find his first violet, and be lost in pleasant wonder, by what alchemy the cold earth of the clods, and the vapid air and rain, can be transmuted into colour so rich and odour so touchingly sweet. Or perhaps he may see a group of washerwomen relieved, on a spit of shingle, against the blue sea, or a meeting of flower- gatherers in the tempered daylight of an olive-garden; and something significant or monumental in the grouping, something in the harmony of faint colour that is always characteristic of the dress of these southern women, will come borne to him unexpectedly, and awake in him that satisfaction with which we tell ourselves that we are the richer by one more beautiful experience. Or it may be something even slighter: as when the opulence of the sunshine, which somehow gets lost and fails to produce its effect on the large scale, is suddenly revealed to him by the chance isolation – as he changes the position of his sunshade – of a yard or two of roadway with its stones and weeds. And then, there is no end to the infinite variety of the olive-yards themselves. Even the colour is indeterminate and continually shifting: now you would say it was green, now gray, now blue; now tree stands above tree, like 'cloud on cloud,' massed into filmy indistinctness; and now, at the wind's will, the whole sea of foliage is shaken and broken up with little momentary silverings and shadows. But every one sees the world in his own way. To some the glad moment may have arrived on other provocations; and their recollection may be most vivid of the stately gait of women carrying burthens on their heads; of tropical effects, with canes and naked rock and sunlight; of the relief of cypresses; of the troubled, busy-looking groups of sea-pines, that seem always as if they were being wielded and swept together by a whirlwind; of the air coming, laden with virginal perfumes, over the myrtles and the scented underwood; of the empurpled hills standing up, solemn and sharp, out of the green-gold air of the east at evening.

There go many elements, without doubt, to the making of one such moment of intense perception; and it is on the happy agreement of these many elements, on the harmonious vibration of many nerves, that the whole delight of the moment must depend. Who can forget how, when he has chanced upon some attitude of complete restfulness, after long uneasy rolling to and fro on grass or heather, the whole fashion of the landscape has been changed for him, as though the sun had just broken forth, or a great artist had only then completed, by some cunning touch, the composition of the picture? And not only a change of posture – a snatch of perfume, the sudden singing of a bird, the freshness of some pulse of air from an invisible sea, the light shadow of a travelling cloud, the merest nothing that sends a little shiver along the most infinitesimal nerve of a man's body – not one of the least of these but has a hand somehow in the general effect, and brings some refinement of its own into the character of the pleasure we feel.

And if the external conditions are thus varied and subtle, even more so are those within our own bodies. No man can find out the world, says Solomon, from beginning to end, because the world is in his heart; and so it is impossible for any of us to understand, from beginning to end, that agreement of harmonious circumstances that creates in us the highest pleasure of admiration, precisely because some of these circumstances are hidden from us for ever in the constitution of our own bodies. After we have reckoned up all that we can see or hear or feel, there still remains to be taken into account some sensibility more delicate than usual in the nerves affected, or some exquisite refinement in the architecture of the brain, which is indeed to the sense of the beautiful as the eye or the ear to the sense of hearing or sight. We admire splendid views and great pictures; and yet what is truly admirable is rather the mind within us, that gathers together these scattered details for its delight, and makes out of certain colours, certain distributions of graduated light and darkness, that intelligible whole which alone we call a picture or a view. Hazlitt,[5] relating in one of his essays how he went on foot from one great man's house to another's in search of works of art, begins suddenly to triumph over these noble and wealthy owners, because he was more capable of enjoying their costly possessions than they were; because they had paid the money and he had received the pleasure. And the occasion is a fair one for self- complacency. While the one man was working to be able to buy the picture, the other was working to be able to enjoy the picture. An inherited aptitude will have been diligently improved in either case; only the one man has made for himself a fortune, and the other has made for himself a living spirit. It is a fair occasion for self-complacency, I repeat, when the event shows a man to have chosen the better part, and laid out his life more wisely, in the long run, than those who have credit for most wisdom. And yet even this is not a good unmixed; and like all other possessions, although in a less degree, the possession of a brain that has been thus improved and cultivated, and made into the prime organ of a man's enjoyment, brings with it certain inevitable cares and disappointments. The happiness of such an one comes to depend greatly upon those fine shades of sensation that heighten and harmonise the coarser elements of beauty. And thus a degree of nervous prostration, that to other men would be hardly disagreeable, is enough to overthrow for him the whole fabric of his life, to take, except at rare moments, the edge off his pleasures, and to meet him wherever he goes with failure, and the sense of want, and disenchantment of the world and life.

It is not in such numbness of spirit only that the life of the invalid resembles a premature old age. Those excursions that he had promised himself to finish, prove too long or too arduous for his feeble body; and the barrier-hills are as impassable as ever. Many a white town that sits far out on the promontory, many a comely fold of wood on the mountain side, beckons and allures his imagination day after day, and is yet as inaccessible to his feet as the clefts and gorges of the clouds. The sense of distance grows upon him wonderfully; and after some feverish efforts and the fretful uneasiness of the first few days, he falls contentedly in with the restrictions of his weakness. His narrow round becomes pleasant and familiar to him as the cell to a contented prisoner. Just as he has fallen already out of the mid race of active life, he now falls out of the little eddy that circulates in the shallow waters of the sanatorium. He sees the country people come and go about their everyday affairs, the foreigners stream out in goodly pleasure parties; the stir of man's activity is all about him, as he suns himself inertly in some sheltered corner; and he looks on with a patriarchal impersonality of interest, such as a man may feel when he pictures to himself the fortunes of his remote descendants, or the robust old age of the oak he has planted over-night.

In this falling aside, in this quietude and desertion of other men, there is no inharmonious prelude to the last quietude and desertion of the grave; in this dulness of the senses there is a gentle preparation for the finalinsensibility of death. And to him the idea of mortality comes in a shape less violent and harsh than is its wont, less as an abrupt catastrophe than as a thing of infinitesimal gradation, and the last step on a long decline of way. As we turn to and fro in bed, and every moment the movements grow feebler and smaller and the attitude more restful and easy, until sleep overtakes us at a stride and we move no more, so desire after desire leaves him; day by day his strength decreases, and the circle of his activity grows ever narrower; and he feels, if he is to be thus tenderly weaned from the passion of life, thus gradually inducted into the slumber of death, that when at last the end comes, it will come quietly and fitly. If anything is to reconcile poor spirits to the coming of the last enemy, surely it should be such a mild approach as this; not to hale us forth with violence, but to persuade us from a place we have no further pleasure in. It is not so much, indeed, death that approaches as life that withdraws and withers up from round about him. He has outlived his own usefulness, and almost his own enjoyment; and if there is to be no recovery; if never again will he be young and strong and passionate, if the actual present shall be to him always like a thing read in a book or remembered out of the far-away past; if, in fact, this be veritably nightfall, he will not wish greatly for the continuance of a twilight that only strains and disappoints the eyes, but steadfastly await the perfect darkness. He will pray for Medea: when she comes, let her either rejuvenate or slay.

And yet the ties that still attach him to the world are many and kindly. The sight of children has a significance for him such as it may have for the aged also, but not for others. If he has been used to feel humanely, and to look upon life somewhat more widely than from the narrow loophole of personal pleasure and advancement, it is strange how small a portion of his thoughts will be changed or embittered by this proximity of death. He knows that already, in English counties, the sower follows the ploughman up the face of the field, and the rooks follow the sower; and he knows also that he may not live to go home again and see the corn spring and ripen, and be cut down at last, and brought home with gladness. And yet the future of this harvest, the continuance of drought or the coming of rain unseasonably, touch him as sensibly as ever. For he has long been used to wait with interest the issue of events in which his own concern was nothing; and to be joyful in a plenty, and sorrowful for a famine, that did not increase or diminish, by one half loaf, the equable sufficiency of his own supply. Thus there remain unaltered all the disinterested hopes for mankind and a better future which have been the solace and inspiration of his life. These he has set beyond the reach of any fate that only menaces himself; and it makes small difference whether he die five thousand years, or five thousand and fifty years, before the good epoch for which he faithfully labours. He has not deceived himself; he has known from the beginning that he followed the pillar of fire and cloud, only to perish himself in the wilderness, and that it was reserved for others to enter joyfully into possession of the land. And so, as everything grows grayer and quieter about him, and slopes towards extinction, these unfaded visions accompany his sad decline, and follow him, with friendly voices and hopeful words, into the very vestibule of death. The desire of love or of fame scarcely moved him, in his days of health, more strongly than these generous aspirations move him now; and so life is carried forward beyond life, and a vista kept open for the eyes of hope, even when his hands grope already on the face of the impassable.

Lastly, he is bound tenderly to life by the thought of his friends; or shall we not say rather, that by their thought for him, by their unchangeable solicitude and love, he remains woven into the very stuff of life, beyond the power of bodily dissolution to undo? In a thousand ways will he survive and be perpetuated. Much of Etienne de la Boetie survived during all the years in which Montaigne[6] continued to converse with him on the pages of the ever-delightful essays. Much of what was truly Goethe[7] was dead already when he revisited places that knew him no more, and found no better consolation than the promise of his own verses, that soon he too would be at rest. Indeed, when we think of what it is that we most seek and cherish, and find most pride and pleasure in calling ours, it will sometimes seem to us as if our friends, at our decease, would suffer loss more truly than ourselves. As a monarch who should care more for the outlying colonies he knows on the map or through the report of his vicegerents, than for the trunk of his empire under his eyes at home, are we not more concerned about the shadowy life that we have in the hearts of others, and that portion in their thoughts and fancies which, in a certain far-away sense, belongs to us, than about the real knot of our identity – that central metropolis of self, of which alone we are immediately aware – or the diligent service of arteries and veins and infinitesimal activity of ganglia, which we know (as we know a proposition in Euclid) to be the source and substance of the whole? At the death of every one whom we love, some fair and honourable portion of our existence falls away, and we are dislodged from one of these dear provinces; and they are not, perhaps, the most fortunate who survive a long series of such impoverishments, till their life and influence narrow gradually into the meager limit of their own spirits, and death, when he comes at last, can destroy them at one blow.

NOTE. – To this essay I must in honesty append a word or two of qualification; for this is one of the points on which a slightly greater age teaches us a slightly different wisdom:

A youth delights in generalities, and keeps loose from particular obligations; he jogs on the footpath way, himself pursuing butterflies, but courteously lending his applause to the advance of the human species and the coming of the kingdom of justice and love. As he grows older, he begins to think more narrowly of man's action in the general, and perhaps more arrogantly of his own in the particular. He has not that same unspeakable trust in what he would have done had he been spared, seeing finally that that would have been little; but he has a far higher notion of the blank that he will make by dying. A young man feels himself one too many in the world; his is a painful situation: he has no calling; no obvious utility; no ties, but to his parents. And these he is sure to disregard. I do not think that a proper allowance has been made for this true cause of suffering in youth; but by the mere fact of a prolonged existence, we outgrow either the fact or else the feeling. Either we become so callously accustomed to our own useless figure in the world, or else – and this, thank God, in the majority of cases – we so collect about us the interest or the love of our fellows, so multiply our effective part in the affairs of life, that we need to entertain no longer the question of our right to be.

And so in the majority of cases, a man who fancies himself dying, will get cold comfort from the very youthful view expressed in this essay. He, as a living man, has some to help, some to love, some to correct; it may be, some to punish. These duties cling, not upon humanity, but upon the man himself. It is he, not another, who is one woman's son and a second woman's husband and a third woman's father. That life which began so small, has now grown, with a myriad filaments, into the lives of others. It is not indispensable; another will take the place and shoulder the discharged responsibility; but the better the man and the nobler his purposes, the more will he be tempted to regret the extinction of his powers and the deletion of his personality. To have lived a generation, is not only to have grown at home in that perplexing medium, but to have assumed innumerable duties. To die at such an age, has, for all but the entirely base, something of the air of a betrayal. A man does not only reflect upon what he might have done in a future that is never to be his; but beholding himself so early a deserter from the fight, he eats his heart for the good he might have done already. To have been so useless and now to lose all hope of being useful any more – there it is that death and memory assail him. And even if mankind shall go on, founding heroic cities, practising heroic virtues, rising steadily from strength to strength; even if his work shall be fulfilled, his friends consoled, his wife remarried by a better than he; how shall this alter, in one jot, his estimation of a career which was his only business in this world, which was so fitfully pursued, and which is now so ineffectively to end?

Notes

1. Dr. Andrew Clark, a London-based specialist in diseases of the lung, recommended that Stevenson spend some time in the South of France. He is the 'invalid' of the essay.

2. Stevenson left Paris on 6 November 1873 and travelled south toward Lyons and Avignon, reaching Mentone on the 12th.

3. While in a particularly dark mood, Stevenson complained, 'Being sent to the South is not much good unless you take your soul with you ... and my soul is rarely with me here ... Go south! Why I saw more beauty with my eyes healthfully alert to see in two wet windy February afternoons in Scotland, than I can see in my beautiful olive gardens and grey hills in a whole week in my low and lost estate ... It is a pitiable blindness, this blindness of the soul ... ' Letter from Stevenson to Frances Sitwell, 20 November 1873. In *Selected Letters of Robert Louis Stevenson*. Edited by Ernest Mehew (New Haven, Conn.: Yale University Press, 2001), p. 63.

4. William Wordsworth (1770–1850), English poet.

5. William Hazlitt (1778–1830), English essayist who exerted a major influence on Stevenson.

6. Michel Eyquem de Montaigne (1533–1592), French essayist.

7. Johann Wolfgang von Goethe (1749–1832), German poet and dramatist.

Forest Notes

Forest Notes *was originally published in* Cornhill Magazine *in May 1876.*

ON THE PLAIN

PERHAPS the reader knows already the aspect of the great levels of the Gâtinais, where they border with the wooded hills of Fontainebleau. Here and there a few grey rocks creep out of the forest as if to sun themselves. Here and there a few apple-trees stand together on a knoll. The quaint, undignified tartan of a myriad small fields dies out into the distance; the strips blend and disappear; and the dead flat lies forth open and empty, with no accident save perhaps a thin line of trees or faint church spire against the sky. Solemn and vast at all times, in spite of pettiness in the near details, the impression becomes more solemn and vast towards evening. The sun goes down, a swollen orange, as it were into the sea. A blue-clad peasant rides home, with a harrow smoking behind him among the dry clods. Another still works with his wife in their little strip. An immense shadow fills the plain; these people stand in it up to their shoulders; and their heads, as they stoop over their work and rise again, are relieved from time to time against the golden sky.[1]

These peasant farmers are well off nowadays, and not by any means over-worked; but somehow you always see in them the historical representative of the serf of yore, and think not so much of present times, which may be prosperous enough, as of the old days when the peasant was taxed beyond possibility of payment, and lived, in Michelet's image,[2] like a hare between two furrows. These very people now weeding their patch under the broad sunset, that very man and his wife, it seems to us, have suffered all the wrongs of France. It is they who have been their country's scapegoat for long ages; they who, generation after generation, have sowed and not reaped, reaped and another has garnered; and who have now entered into their reward, and enjoy their good things in their turn. For the days are gone by when the Seigneur ruled and profited. 'Le Seigneur,' says the old formula, 'enferme ses manants comme sous porte et gonds, du ciel a la terre. Tout est a lui, foret chenue, oiseau dans l'air, poisson dans l'eau, bete an buisson, l'onde qui coule, la cloche dont le son au loin roule.'[3] Such was his old state of sovereignty, a local god rather than a mere king. And now you may ask yourself where he is, and look round for vestiges of my late lord, and in all the country- side there is no trace of him but his forlorn and fallen mansion. At the end of a long avenue, now sown with grain, in the midst of a close full of cypresses and lilacs, ducks and crowing chanticleers and droning bees, the old chateau lifts its red chimneys and peaked roofs and turning vanes into the wind and sun. There is a glad spring bustle in the air, perhaps, and the lilacs are all in flower, and the creepers green about the broken balustrade: but no spring shall revive the honour of the place. Old women of the people, little, children of the people, saunter and gambol in the walled court or feed the ducks in the neglected moat. Plough-horses, mighty of limb, browse in the long stables. The dial-hand on the clock waits for some better hour. Out on the plain, where hot sweat trickles into men's eyes, and the spade goes in deep and comes up slowly, perhaps the peasant may feel a movement of joy at his heart when he thinks that these spacious chimneys are now cold, which have so often blazed and flickered upon gay folk at supper, while he and his hollow-eyed children watched through the night with empty bellies and cold feet. And perhaps, as he raises his head and sees the forest lying like a coast-line of low hills along the sea-level of the plain, perhaps forest and chateau hold no unsimilar place in his affections.

If the chateau was my lord's, the forest was my lord the king's; neither of them for this poor Jacques. If he thought to eke out his meagre way of life by some petty theft of wood for the fire, or for a new roof-tree, he found himself face to face with a whole department, from the Grand Master of the Woods and Waters, who was a high-born lord, down to the common sergeant, who was a peasant like himself, and wore stripes or a bandoleer by way of uniform. For the first offence, by the Salic law, there was a fine of fifteen sols; and should a man be taken more than once in fault, or circumstances aggravate the colour of his guilt, he might be whipped, branded, or hanged. There was a hangman over at Melun, and, I doubt not, a fine tall gibbet hard by the town gate, where Jacques might see his fellows dangle against the sky as he went to market.

And then, if he lived near to a cover, there would be the more hares and rabbits to eat out his harvest, and the more hunters to trample it down. My lord has a new horn from England. He has laid out seven francs in decorating it with silver and gold, and fitting it with a silken leash to hang about his shoulder. The hounds have been on a pilgrimage to the shrine of Saint Mesmer, or Saint Hubert in the Ardennes, or some other holy intercessor who has made a speciality of the health of hunting-dogs. In the grey dawn the game was turned and the branch broken by our best piqueur. A rare day's hunting lies before us. Wind a jolly flourish, sound the *bien-aller* with all your lungs. Jacques must stand by, hat in hand, while the quarry and hound and huntsman sweep across his field, and a year's sparing and labouring is as though it had not been. If he can see the ruin with a good enough grace, who knows but he may fall in favour with my lord; who knows but his son may become the last and least among the servants at his lordship's kennel – one of the two poor varlets who get no wages and sleep at night among the hounds?

For all that, the forest has been of use to Jacques, not only warming him with fallen wood, but giving him shelter in days of sore trouble, when my lord of the chateau, with all his troopers and trumpets, had been beaten from field after field into some ultimate fastness, or lay over-seas in an English prison. In these dark days, when the watch on the church steeple saw the smoke of burning villages on the sky-line, or a clump of spears and fluttering pensions drawing nigh across the plain, these good folk gat them up, with all their household gods, into the wood, whence, from some high spur, their timid scouts might overlook the coming and going of the marauders, and see the harvest ridden down, and church and cottage go up to heaven all night in flame. It was but an unhomely refuge that the woods afforded, where they must abide all change of weather and keep house with wolves and vipers. Often there was none left alive, when they returned, to show the old divisions of field from field. And yet, as times went, when the wolves entered at night into depopulated Paris, and perhaps De Retz was passing by with a company of demons like himself, even in these caves and thickets there were glad hearts and grateful prayers.

Once or twice, as I say, in the course of the ages, the forest may have served the peasant well, but at heart it is a royal forest, and noble by old associations. These woods have rung to the horns of all the kings of France, from Philip Augustus downwards. They have seen Saint Louis exercise the dogs he brought with him from Egypt; Francis I go a-hunting with ten thousand horses in his train; and Peter of Russia following his first stag. And so they are still haunted for the imagination by royal hunts and progresses, and peopled with the faces of memorable men of yore. And this distinction is not only in virtue of the pastime of dead monarchs. Great events, great revolutions, great cycles in the affairs of men, have here left their note, here taken shape in some significant and dramatic situation. It was hence that Guise and his leaguers led Charles the Ninth a prisoner to Paris. Here, booted and spurred, and with all his dogs about him, Napoleon[4] met the Pope beside a woodland cross. Here, on his way to Elba not so long after, he kissed the eagle of the Old Guard, and spoke words of passionate farewell to his soldiers. And here, after Waterloo, rather than yield its ensign to the new power, one of his faithful regiments burned that memorial of so much toil and glory on the Grand Master's table, and drank its dust in brandy, as a devout priest consumes the remnants of the Host.

IN THE SEASON

Close into the edge of the forest, so close that the trees of the *bornage* stand pleasantly about the last houses, sits a certain small and very quiet village.[5] There is but one street, and that, not long ago, was a green lane, where the cattle browsed between the doorsteps. As you go up this street, drawing ever nearer the beginning of the wood, you will arrive at last before an inn where artists lodge.[6] To the door (for I imagine it to be six o'clock on some fine summer's even), half a dozen, or maybe half a score, of people have brought out chairs, and now sit sunning themselves, and waiting the omnibus from Melun. If you go on into the court you will find as many more, some in billiard-room over absinthe and a match of corks some without over a last cigar and a vermouth. The doves coo and flutter from the dovecot; Hortense is drawing water from the well; and as all the rooms open into the court, you can see the white-capped cook over the furnace in the kitchen, and some idle painter, who has stored his canvases and washed his brushes, jangling a waltz on the crazy, tongue-tied piano in the salle-a-manger. *'Edmond, encore un vermouth,'* cries a man in velveteen, adding in a tone of apologetic afterthought, *'Un double, s'il vous plait.'* 'Where are you working?' asks one in pure white linen from top to toe. 'At the Carrefour de l'Epine,' returns the other in corduroy (they are all gaitered, by the way). 'I couldn't do a thing to it. I ran out of white. Where were you?' 'I wasn't working. I was looking for motives.' Here is an outbreak of jubilation, and a lot of men clustering together about some new-comer with outstretched hands; perhaps the 'correspondence' has come in and brought So-and-so from Paris, or perhaps it is only So-and-so who has walked over from Chailly to dinner.

'A table, Messieurs!' cries M. Siron, bearing through the court the first tureen of soup. And immediately the company begins to settle down about the long tables in the dining-room, framed all round with sketches of all degrees of merit and demerit. There's the big picture of the huntsman winding a horn with a dead boar between his legs, and his legs – well, his legs in stockings. And here is the little picture of a raw mutton-chop, in which Such-a-one knocked a hole last summer with no worse a missile than a plum from the dessert. And under all these works of art so much eating goes forward, so much drinking, so much jabbering in French and English, that it would do your heart good merely to peep and listen at the door. One man is telling how they all went last year to the fete at Fleury, and another how well so-and-so would sing of an evening: and here are a third and fourth making plans for the whole future of their lives; and there is a fifth imitating a conjurer and making faces on his clenched fist, surely of all arts the most difficult and admirable! A sixth has eaten his fill, lights a cigarette, and resigns himself to digestion. A seventh has just dropped in, and calls for soup. Number eight, meanwhile, has left the table, and is once more trampling the poor piano under powerful and uncertain fingers.

Dinner over, people drop outside to smoke and chat. Perhaps we go along to visit our friends at the other end of the village, where there is always a good welcome and a good talk, and perhaps some pickled oysters and white wine to close the evening. Or a dance is organised in the dining-room, and the piano exhibits all its paces under manful jockeying, to the light of three or four candles and a lamp or two, while the waltzers move to and fro upon the wooden floor, and sober men, who are not given to such light pleasures, get up on the table or the sideboard, and sit there looking on approvingly over a pipe and a tumbler of wine. Or sometimes – suppose my lady moon looks forth, and the court from out the half-lit dining-room seems nearly as bright as by day, and the light picks out the window-panes, and makes a clear shadow under every vine-leaf on the wall – sometimes a picnic is proposed, and a basket made ready, and a good procession formed in front of the hotel. The two trumpeters in honour go before; and as we file down the long alley, and up through devious footpaths among rocks and pine-trees, with every here and there a dark passage of shadow, and every here and there a spacious outlook over moonlit woods, these two precede us and sound many a jolly flourish as they walk. We gather ferns and dry boughs into the cavern, and soon a good blaze flutters the shadows of the old bandits' haunt, and shows shapely beards and comely faces and toilettes ranged about the wall. The bowl is lit, and the punch is burnt and sent round in scalding thimblefuls. So a good hour or two may pass with song and jest. And then we go home in the moonlit morning, straggling a good deal among the birch tufts and the boulders, but ever called together again, as one of our leaders winds his horn. Perhaps some one of the party will not heed the summons, but chooses out some by-way of his own. As he follows the winding sandy road, he hears the flourishes grow fainter and fainter in the distance, and die finally out, and still walks on in the strange coolness and silence and between the crisp lights and shadows of the moonlit woods, until suddenly the bell rings out the hour from far- away Chailly, and he starts to find himself alone. No surf-bell on forlorn and perilous shores, no passing knell over the busy market- place, can speak with a more heavy and disconsolate tongue to human ears. Each stroke calls up a host of ghostly reverberations in his mind. And as he stands rooted, it has grown once more so utterly silent that it seems to him he might hear the church bells ring the hour out all the world over, not at Chailly only, but in Paris, and away in outlandish cities, and in the village on the river, where his childhood passed between the sun and flowers.

IDLE HOURS

The woods by night, in all their uncanny effect, are not rightly to be understood until you can compare them with the woods by day. The stillness of the medium, the floor of glittering sand, these trees that go streaming up like monstrous seaweeds and waver in the moving winds like the weeds in submarine currents, all these set the mind working on the thought of what you may have seen off a foreland or over the side of a boat, and make you feel like a diver, down in the quiet water, fathoms below the tumbling, transitory surface of the sea. And yet in itself, as I say, the strangeness of these nocturnal solitudes is not to be felt fully without the sense of contrast. You must have risen in the morning and seen the woods as they are by day, kindled and coloured in the sun's light; you must have felt the odour of innumerable trees at even, the unsparing heat along the forest roads, and the coolness of the groves.

And on the first morning you will doubtless rise betimes. If you have not been wakened before by the visit of some adventurous pigeon, you will be wakened as soon as the sun can reach your window – for there are no blind or shutters to keep him out – and the room, with its bare wood floor and bare whitewashed walls, shines all round you in a sort of glory of reflected lights. You may doze a while longer by snatches, or lie awake to study the charcoal men and dogs and horses with which former occupants have defiled the partitions: Thiers, with wily profile; local celebrities, pipe in hand; or, maybe, a romantic landscape splashed in oil. Meanwhile artist after artist drops into the salle-a-manger for coffee, and then shoulders easel, sunshade, stool, and paint-box, bound into a fagot, and sets of for what he calls his 'motive.' And artist after artist, as he goes out of the village, carries with him a little following of dogs. For the dogs, who belong only nominally to any special master, hang about the gate of the forest all day long, and whenever any one goes by who hits their fancy, profit by his escort, and go forth with him to play an hour or two at hunting. They would like to be under the trees all day. But they cannot go alone. They require a pretext. And so they take the passing artist as an excuse to go into the woods, as they might take a walking-stick as an excuse to bathe. With quick ears, long spines, and bandy legs, or perhaps as tall as a greyhound and with a bulldog's head, this company of mongrels will trot by your side all day and come home with you at night, still showing white teeth and wagging stunted tail. Their good humour is not to be exhausted. You may pelt them with stones if you please, and all they will do is to give you a wider berth. If once they come out with you, to you they will remain faithful, and with you return; although if you meet them next morning in the street, it is as like as not they will cut you with a countenance of brass.

The forest – a strange thing for an Englishman – is very destitute of birds. This is no country where every patch of wood among the meadows gibes up an increase of song, and every valley wandered through by a streamlet rings and reverberates from side to with a profusion of clear notes. And this rarity of birds is not to be regretted on its own account only. For the insects prosper in their absence, and become as one of the plagues of Egypt. Ants swarm in the hot sand; mosquitos drone their nasal drone; wherever the sun finds a hole in the roof of the forest, you see a myriad transparent creatures coming and going in the shaft of light; and even between- whiles, even where there is no incursion of sun-rays into the dark arcade of the wood, you are conscious of a continual drift of insects, an ebb and flow of infinitesimal living things between the trees. Nor are insects the only evil creatures that haunt the forest. For you may plump into a cave among the rocks, and find yourself face to face with a wild boar, or see a crooked viper slither across the road.

Perhaps you may set yourself down in the bay between two spreading beech-roots with a book on your lap, and be awakened all of a sudden by a friend: 'I say, just keep where you are, will you? You make the jolliest motive.' And you reply: 'Well, I don't mind, if I may smoke.' And thereafter the hours go idly by. Your friend at the easel labours doggedly a little way off, in the wide shadow of the tree; and yet farther, across a strait of glaring sunshine, you see another painter, encamped in the shadow of another tree, and up to his waist in the fern. You cannot watch your own effigy growing out of the white trunk, and the trunk beginning to stand forth from the rest of the wood, and the whole picture getting dappled over with the flecks of sun that slip through the leaves overhead, and, as a wind goes by and sets the trees a-talking, flicker hither and thither like butterflies of light. But you know it is going forward; and, out of emulation with the painter, get ready your own palette, and lay out the colour for a woodland scene in words.

Your tree stands in a hollow paved with fern and heather, set in a basin of low hills, and scattered over with rocks and junipers. All the open is steeped in pitiless sunlight. Everything stands out as though it were cut in cardboard, every colour is strained into its highest key. The boulders are some of them upright and dead like monolithic castles, some of them prone like sleeping cattle. The junipers – looking, in their soiled and ragged mourning, like some funeral procession that has gone seeking the place of sepulchre three hundred years and more in wind and rain – are daubed in forcibly against the glowing ferns and heather. Every tassel of their rusty foliage is defined with pre-Raphaelite minuteness. And a sorry figure they make out there in the sun, like misbegotten yew-trees! The scene is all pitched in a key of colour so peculiar, and lit up with such a discharge of violent sunlight, as a man might live fifty years in England and not see.

Meanwhile at your elbow some one tunes up a song, words of Ronsard[7] to a pathetic tremulous air, of how the poet loved his mistress long ago, and pressed on her the flight of time, and told her how white and quiet the dead lay under the stones, and how the boat dipped and pitched as the shades embarked for the passionless land. Yet a little while, sang the poet, and there shall be no more love; only to sit and remember loves that might have been. There is a falling flourish in the air that remains in the memory and comes back in incongruous places, on the seat of hansoms or in the warm bed at night, with something of a forest savour.

'You can get up now,' says the painter; 'I'm at the background.'

And so up you get, stretching yourself, and go your way into the wood, the daylight becoming richer and more golden, and the shadows stretching farther into the open. A cool air comes along the highways, and the scents awaken. The fir-trees breathe abroad their ozone. Out of unknown thickets comes forth the soft, secret, aromatic odour of the woods, not like a smell of the free heaven, but as though court ladies, who had known these paths in ages long gone by, still walked

in the summer evenings, and shed from their brocades a breath of musk or berg-
amot upon the woodland winds. One side of the long avenues is still kindled with
the sun, the other is plunged in transparent shadow. Over the trees the west
begins to burn like a furnace; and the painters gather up their chattels, and go
down, by avenue or footpath, to the plain.

A PLEASURE PARTY

As this excursion is a matter of some length, and, moreover, we go in force, we
have set aside our usual vehicle, the pony-cart, and ordered a large wagonette
from Lejosne's. It has been waiting for near an hour, while one went to pack a
knapsack, and t'other hurried over his toilette and coffee; but now it is filled from
end to end with merry folk in summer attire, the coachman cracks his whip, and
amid much applause from round the inn door off we rattle at a spanking trot. The
way lies through the forest, up hill and down dale, and by beech and pine wood,
in the cheerful morning sunshine. The English get down at all the ascents and
walk on ahead for exercise; the French are mightily entertained at this, and keep
coyly underneath the tilt. As we go we carry with us a pleasant noise of laughter
and light speech, and some one will be always breaking out into a bar or two of
opera bouffe. Before we get to the Route Ronde here comes Desprez, the
colourman from Fontainebleau, trudging across on his weekly peddle with a case
of merchandise; and it is 'Desprez, leave me some malachite green'; 'Desprez,
leave me so much canvas'; 'Desprez, leave me this, or leave me that'; M. Desprez
standing the while in the sunlight with grave face and many salutations. The next
interruption is more important. For some time back we have had the sound of
cannon in our ears; and now, a little past Franchard, we find a mounted trooper
holding a led horse, who brings the wagonette to a stand. The artillery is practising in the Quadrilateral, it appears; passage along the Route Ronde formally inter-
dicted for the moment. There is nothing for it but to draw up at the glaring cross-
roads and get down to make fun with the notorious Cocardon, the most ungainly
and ill-bred dog of all the ungainly and ill-bred dogs of Barbizon, or clamber
about the sandy banks. And meanwhile the doctor, with sun umbrella, wide
Panama, and patriarchal beard, is busy wheedling and (for aught the rest of us
know) bribing the too facile sentry. His speech is smooth and dulcet, his manner
dignified and insinuating. It is not for nothing that the Doctor has voyaged all the
world over, and speaks all languages from French to Patagonian. He has not come
borne from perilous journeys to be thwarted by a corporal of horse. And so we
soon see the soldier's mouth relax, and his shoulders imitate a relenting heart. '*En
voiture, Messieurs, Mesdames,*' sings the Doctor; and on we go again at a good
round pace, for black care follows hard after us, and discretion prevails not a little over valour in some timorous spirits of the party. At any moment we may meet

the sergeant, who will send us back. At any moment we may encounter a flying shell, which will send us somewhere farther off than Grez.

Grez – for that is our destination – has been highly recommended for its beauty. *'Il y a de l'eau,'*[8] people have said, with an emphasis, as if that settled the question, which, for a French mind, I am rather led to think it does. And Grez, when we get there, is indeed a place worthy of some praise. It lies out of the forest, a cluster of houses, with an old bridge, an old castle in ruin, and a quaint old church. The inn garden descends in terraces to the river; stable-yard, kailyard, orchard, and a space of lawn, fringed with rushes and embellished with a green arbour. On the opposite bank there is a reach of English-looking plain, set thickly with willows and poplars. And between the two lies the river, clear and deep, and full of reeds and floating lilies. Water-plants cluster about the starlings of the long low bridge, and stand half-way up upon the piers in green luxuriance. They catch the dipped oar with long antennae, and chequer the slimy bottom with the shadow of their leaves. And the river wanders and thither hither among the islets, and is smothered and broken up by the reeds, like an old building in the lithe, hardy arms of the climbing ivy. You may watch the box where the good man of the inn keeps fish alive for his kitchen, one oily ripple following another over the top of the yellow deal. And you can hear a splashing and a prattle of voices from the shed under the old kirk, where the village women wash and wash all day among the fish and water-lilies. It seems as if linen washed there should be specially cool and sweet.

We have come here for the river. And no sooner have we all bathed than we board the two shallops and push off gaily, and go gliding under the trees and gathering a great treasure of water-lilies. Some one sings; some trail their hands in the cool water; some lean over the gunwale to see the image of the tall poplars far below, and the shadow of the boat, with the balanced oars and their own head protruded, glide smoothly over the yellow floor of the stream. At last, the day declining – all silent and happy, and up to the knees in the wet lilies – we punt slowly back again to the landing-place beside the bridge. There is a wish for solitude on all. One hides himself in the arbour with a cigarette; another goes a walk in the country with Cocardon; a third inspects the church. And it is not till dinner is on the table, and the inn's best wine goes round from glass to glass, that we begin to throw off the restraint and fuse once more into a jolly fellowship.

Half the party are to return to-night with the wagonette; and some of the others, loath to break up company, will go with them a bit of the way and drink a stirrup-cup at Marlotte. It is dark in the wagonette, and not so merry as it might have been. The coachman loses the road. So-and-so tries to light fireworks with the most indifferent success. Some sing, but the rest are too weary to applaud; and it seems as if the festival were fairly at an end –

'Nous avons fait la noce,
Rentrons â nos foyers!'

And such is the burthen, even after we have come to Marlotte and taken our places in the court at Mother Antonine's. There is punch on the long table out in the open air, where the guests dine in summer weather. The candles flare in the night wind, and the faces round the punch are lit up, with shifting emphasis, against a background of complete and solid darkness. It is all picturesque enough; but the fact is, we are aweary. We yawn; we are out of the vein; we have made the wedding, as the song says, and now, for pleasure's sake, let's make an end on't. When here comes striding into the court, booted to mid-thigh, spurred and splashed, in a jacket of green cord, the great, famous, and redoubtable Blank; and in a moment the fire kindles again, and the night is witness of our laughter as he imitates Spaniards, Germans, Englishmen, picture- dealers, all eccentric ways of speaking and thinking, with a possession, a fury, a strain of mind and voice, that would rather suggest a nervous crisis than a desire to please. We are as merry as ever when the trap sets forth again, and say farewell noisily to all the good folk going farther. Then, as we are far enough from thoughts of sleep, we visit Blank in his quaint house, and sit an hour or so in a great tapestried chamber, laid with furs, littered with sleeping hounds, and lit up, in fantastic shadow and shine, by a wood fire in a mediaeval chimney. And then we plod back through the darkness to the inn beside the river.

How quick bright things come to confusion! When we arise next morning, the grey showers fall steadily, the trees hang limp, and the face of the stream is spoiled with dimpling raindrops. Yesterday's lilies encumber the garden walk, or begin, dismally enough, their voyage towards the Seine and the salt sea. A sickly shimmer lies upon the dripping house-roofs, and all the colour is washed out of the green and golden landscape of last night, as though an envious man had taken a water-colour sketch and blotted it together with a sponge. We go out a-walking in the wet roads. But the roads about Grez have a trick of their own. They go on for a while among clumps of willows and patches of vine, and then, suddenly and without any warning, cease and determine in some miry hollow or upon some bald knowe; and you have a short period of hope, then right-about face, and back the way you came! So we draw about the kitchen fire and play a round game of cards for ha'pence, or go to the billiard-room, for a match at corks and by one consent a messenger is sent over for the wagonette – Grez shall be left to-morrow.

To-morrow dawns so fair that two of the party agree to walk back for exercise, and let their kidnap-sacks follow by the trap. I need hardly say they are neither of them French; for, of all English phrases, the phrase 'for exercise' is the least comprehensible across the Straits of Dover. All goes well for a while with the pedestrians. The wet woods are full of scents in the noontide. At a certain cross, where there is a guardhouse, they make a halt, for the forester's wife is the daughter of their good host at Barbizon. And so there they are hospitably received by the comely woman, with one child in her arms and another prattling and tottering at her gown, and drink some syrup of quince in the back parlour, with a map of the forest on the wall, and some prints of love-affairs and the great Napoleon hunting. As they draw near the Quadrilateral, and hear once more the report of the big guns, they take a by-road to avoid the sentries, and go on a while somewhat vaguely, with the sound of the cannon in their ears and the rain beginning to fall. The ways grow wider and sandier; here and there there are real sand-hills, as though by the sea-shore; the fir-wood is open and grows in clumps upon the hillocks, and the race of sign-posts is no more. One begins to look at the other doubtfully. 'I am sure we should keep more to the right,' says one; and the other is just as certain they should hold to the left. And now, suddenly, the heavens open, and the rain falls 'sheer and strong and loud,' as out of a shower-bath. In a moment they are as wet as shipwrecked sailors. They cannot see out of their eyes for the drift, and the water churns and gurgles in their boots. They leave the track and try across country with a gambler's desperation, for it seems as if it were impossible to make the situation worse; and, for the next hour, go scrambling from boulder to boulder, or plod along paths that are now no more than rivulets, and across waste clearings where the scattered shells and broken fir-trees tell all too plainly of the cannon in the distance. And meantime the cannon grumble out responses to the grumbling thunder. There is such a mixture of melodrama and sheer discomfort about all this, it is at once so grey and so lurid, that it is far more agreeable to read and write about by the chimney-corner than to suffer in the person. At last they chance on the right path, and make Franchard in the early evening, the sorriest pair of wanderers that ever welcomed English ale. Thence, by the Bois d'Hyver, the Ventes-Alexandre, and the Pins Brules, to the clean hostelry, dry clothes, and dinner.

THE WOODS IN SPRING

I think you will like the forest best in the sharp early springtime, when it is just beginning to reawaken, and innumerable violets peep from among the fallen leaves; when two or three people at most sit down to dinner, and, at table, you will do well to keep a rug about your knees, for the nights are chill, and the salle-a-manger opens on the court. There is less to distract the attention, for one thing, and the forest is more itself. It is not bedotted with artists' sunshades as with unknown mushrooms, nor bestrewn with the remains of English picnics. The hunting still goes on, and at any moment your heart may be brought into your mouth as you hear far-away horns; or you may be told by an agitated peasant that the Vicomte has gone up the avenue, not ten minutes since, 'A *fond de train,*

Monsieur, et avec douze pipuers.'

If you go up to some coign of vantage in the system of low hills that permeates the forest, you will see many different tracts of country, each of its own cold and melancholy neutral tint, and all mixed together and mingled the one into the other at the seams. You will see tracts of leafless beeches of a faint yellowish grey, and leafless oaks a little ruddier in the hue. Then zones of pine of a solemn green; and, dotted among the pines, or standing by themselves in rocky clearings, the delicate, snow-white trunks of birches, spreading out into snow-white branches yet more delicate, and crowned and canopied with a purple haze of twigs. And then a long, bare ridge of tumbled boulders, with bright sand-breaks between them, and wavering sandy roads among the bracken and brown heather. It is all rather cold and unhomely. It has not the perfect beauty, nor the gem-like colouring, of the wood in the later year, when it is no more than one vast colonnade of verdant shadow, tremulous with insects, intersected here and there by lanes of sunlight set in purple heather. The loveliness of the woods in March is not, assuredly, of this blowzy rustic type. It is made sharp with a grain of salt, with a touch of ugliness. It has a sting like the sting of bitter ale; you acquire the love of it as men acquire a taste for olives. And the wonderful clear, pure air wells into your lungs the while by voluptuous inhalations, and makes the eyes bright, and sets the heart tinkling to a new tune – or, rather, to an old tune; for you remember in your boyhood something akin to this spirit of adventure, this thirst for exploration, that now takes you masterfully by the hand, plunges you into many a deep grove, and drags you over many a stony crest. it is as if the whole wood were full of friendly voice, calling you farther in, and you turn from one side to another, like Buridan's donkey, in a maze of pleasure.

Comely beeches send up their white, straight, clustered branches, barred with green moss, like so many fingers from a half-clenched hand. Mighty oaks stand to the ankles in a fine tracery of underwood; thence the tall shaft climbs upwards, and the great forest of stalwart boughs spreads out into the golden evening sky, where the rooks are flying and calling. On the sward of the Bois d'Hyver the firs stand well asunder with outspread arms, like fencers saluting; and the air smells of resin all around, and the sound of the axe is rarely still. But strangest of all, and in appearance oldest of all, are the dim and wizard upland districts of young wood. The ground is carpeted with fir-tassel, and strewn with fir-apples and flakes of fallen bark. Rocks lie crouching in the thicket, guttered with rain, tufted with lichen, white with years and the rigours of the changeful seasons. Brown and yellow butterflies are sown and carried away again by the light air – like thistledown. The loneliness of these coverts is so excessive, that there are moments when pleasure draws to the verge of fear. You listen and listen for some noise to break the silence, till you grow half mesmerised by the intensity of the strain; your sense of your own identity is troubled; your brain reels, like that of some gymnosophist poring on his own nose in Asiatic jungles; and should you see your own outspread feet, you see them, not as anything of yours, but as a feature of the scene around you.

Still the forest is always, but the stillness is not always unbroken. You can hear the wind pass in the distance over the tree-tops; sometimes briefly, like the noise of a train; sometimes with a long steady rush, like the breaking of waves. And sometimes, close at band, the branches move, a moan goes through the thicket, and the wood thrills to its heart. Perhaps you may hear a carriage on the road to Fontainebleau, a bird gives a dry continual chirp, the dead leaves rustle under-foot, or you may time your steps to the steady recurrent strokes of the woodman's axe. From time to time, over the low grounds, a flight of rooks goes by; and from time to time the cooing of wild doves falls upon the ear, not sweet and rich and near at hand as in England, but a sort of voice of the woods, thin and far away, as fits these solemn places. Or you hear suddenly the hollow, eager, violent barking of dogs; scared deer flit past you through the fringes of the wood; then a man or two running, in green blouse, with gun and game-bag on a bandoleer; and then, out of the thick of the trees, comes the jar of rifle-shots. Or perhaps the hounds are out, and horns are blown, and scarlet-coated huntsmen flash through the clearings, and the solid noise of horses galloping passes below you, where you sit perched among the rocks and heather. The boar is afoot, and all over the forest, and in all neighbouring villages, there is a vague excitement and a vague hope; for who knows whither the chase may lead? and even to have seen a single piqueur, or spoken to a single sportsman, is to be a man of consequence for the night.

Besides men who shoot and men who ride with the hounds, there are few peo-ple in the forest, in the early spring, save woodcutters plying their axes steadily, and old women and children gathering wood for the fire. You may meet such a party coming home in the twilight: the old woman laden with a fagot of chips, and the little ones hauling a long branch behind them in her wake. That is the worst of what there is to encounter; and if I tell you of what once happened to a friend of mine, it is by no means to tantalise you with false hopes; for the adventure was unique. It was on a very cold, still, sunless morning, with a flat grey sky and a frosty tingle in the air, that this friend (who shall here be nameless) heard the notes of a key-bugle played with much hesitation, and saw the smoke of a fire spread out along the green pine-tops, in a remote uncanny glen, hard by a hill of naked boulders. He drew near warily, and beheld a picnic party seated under a tree in an open. The old father knitted a sock, the mother sat staring at the fire. The eldest son, in the uniform of a private of dragoons, was choosing out notes on a key- bugle. Two or three daughters lay in the neighbourhood picking violets. And the whole party as grave and silent as the woods around them! My friend watched for a long time, he says; but all held their peace; not one spoke or smiled; only the dragoon kept choosing out single notes upon the bugle, and the father knitted away at his work and made strange movements the while with his flexible eyebrows. They took no notice whatever of my friend's presence, which was disquieting in itself, and increased the resemblance of the whole party to mechanical waxworks. Certainly, he affirms, a wax figure might have played the bugle with more spirit than that strange dragoon. And as this hypothesis of his became more certain, the awful insolubility of why they should be left out there in the woods with nobody to wind them up again when they ran down, and a growing disquietude as to what might happen next, became too much for his courage, and he turned tail, and fairly took to his heels. It might have been a singing in his ears, but he fancies he was followed as he ran by a peal of Titanic laughter. Nothing has ever transpired to clear up the mystery; it may be they were automata; or it may be (and this is the theory to which I lean myself) that this is all another chapter of Heine's *Gods in Exile*; that the upright old man with the eyebrows was no other than Father Jove, and the young dragoon with the taste for music either Apollo or Mars.

MORALITY

Strange indeed is the attraction of the forest for the minds of men. Not one or two only, but a great chorus of grateful voices have arisen to spread abroad its fame. Half the famous writers of modern France have had their word to say about Fontainebleau. Chateaubriand, Michelet, Beranger, George Sand, de Senancour, Flaubert, Murger, the brothers Goncourt, Theodore de Banville, each of these has done something to the eternal praise and memory of these woods. Even at the very worst of times, even when the picturesque was anathema in the eyes of all Persons of Taste, the forest still preserved a certain reputation for beauty. It was in 1730 that the Abbe Guilbert published his *Historical Description of the Palace, Town, and Forest of Fontainebleau*. And very droll it is to see him, as he tries to set forth his admiration in terms of what was then permissible. The monstrous rocks, etc., says the Abbe *'sont admirees avec surprise des voyageurs qui s'ecrient aussitot avec Horace: Ut mihi devio rupee et vacuum nemus mirari libet.'* The good man is not exactly lyrical in his praise; and you see how he sets his back against Horace[9] as against a trusty oak. Horace, at any rate, was classical. For the rest, however, the Abbe likes places where many alleys meet; or which, like the Belle-Etoile, are kept up 'by a special gardener,' and admires at the Table du Roi the labours of the Grand Master of Woods and Waters, the Sieur de la Falure, *'qui a fait faire ce magnifique endroit.'*

But indeed, it is not so much for its beauty that the forest makes a claim upon men's hearts, as for that subtle something, that quality of the air, that emanation from the old trees, that so wonderfully changes and renews a weary spirit. Disappointed men, sick Francis Firsts and vanquished Grand Monarchs, time out of mind have come here for consolation. Hither perplexed folk have retired out of the press of life, as into a deep bay-window on some night of masquerade, and here found quiet and silence, and rest, the mother of wisdom. It is the great moral spa; this forest without a fountain is itself the great fountain of Juventius. It is the best place in the world to bring an old sorrow that has been a long while your friend and enemy; and if, like Beranger's[10] your gaiety has run away from home and left open the door for sorrow to come in, of all covers in Europe, it is here you may expect to find the truant hid. With every hour you change. The air penetrates through your clothes, and nestles to your living body. You love exercise and slumber, long fasting and full meals. You forget all your scruples and live a while in peace and freedom, and for the moment only. For here, all is absent that can stimulate to moral feeling. Such people as you see may be old, or toil-worn, or sorry; but you see them framed in the forest, like figures on a painted canvas; and for you, they are not people in any living and kindly sense. You forget the grim contrariety of interests. You forget the narrow lane where all men jostle together in unchivalrous contention, and the kennel, deep and unclean, that gapes on either hand for the defeated. Life is simple enough, it seems, and the very idea of sacrifice becomes like a mad fancy out of a last night's dream.

Your ideal is not perhaps high, but it is plain and possible. You become enamoured of a life of change and movement and the open air, where the muscles shall be more exercised than the affections. When you have had your will of the forest, you may visit the whole round world. You may buckle on your knapsack and take the road on foot. You may bestride a good nag, and ride forth, with a pair of saddle- bags, into the enchanted East. You may cross the Black Forest, and see Germany wide-spread before you, like a map, dotted with old cities, walled and spired, that dream all day on their own reflections in the Rhine or Danube. You may pass the spinal cord of Europe and go down from Alpine glaciers to where Italy extends her marble moles and glasses her marble palaces in the midland sea. You may sleep in flying trains or wayside taverns. You may be awakened at dawn by the scream of the express or the small pipe of the robin in the hedge. For you the rain should allay the dust of the beaten road; the wind dry your clothes upon you as you walked. Autumn should hang out russet pears and purple grapes along the lane; inn after inn proffer you their cups of raw wine; river by river receive your body in the sultry noon. Wherever you went warm valleys and high trees and pleasant villages should compass you about; and light fellowships should take you by the arm, and walk with you an hour upon your way. You may see from afar off what it will come to in the end – the weather-beaten red-nosed vagabond, consumed by a fever of the feet, cut off from all near touch of human sympathy, a waif, an Ishmael, and an outcast. And yet it will seem well – and yet, in the air of the forest, this will seem the best – to break all the network bound about your feet by birth and old companionship and loyal love, and bear your shovelful of phosphates to and fro, in town country, until the hour of the great dissolvent.

Or, perhaps, you will keep to the cover. For the forest is by itself, and forest life owns small kinship with life in the dismal land of labour. Men are so far sophisticated that they cannot take the world as it is given to them by the sight of their eyes. Not only what they see and hear, but what they know to be behind, enter into their notion of a place. If the sea, for instance, lie just across the hills, sea-thoughts will come to them at intervals, and the tenor of their dreams from time to time will suffer a sea-change. And so here, in this forest, a knowledge of its greatness is for much in the effect produced. You reckon up the miles that lie between you and intrusion. You may walk before you all day long, and not fear to touch the barrier of your Eden, or stumble out of fairyland into the land of gin and steam-hammers. And there is an old tale enhances for the imagination the grandeur of the woods of France, and secures you in the thought of your seclusion. When Charles VI[11] hunted in the time of his wild boyhood near Senlis, there was captured an old stag, having a collar of bronze about his neck, and these words engraved on the collar: 'Caesar mihi hoc donavit.' It is no wonder if the minds of men were moved at this occurrence and they stood aghast to find themselves thus touching hands with forgotten ages, and following an antiquity with hound and horn. And even for you, it is scarcely in an idle curiosity that you ponder how many centuries this stag had carried its free antlers through the wood, and how many summers and winters had shone and snowed on the imperial badge. If the extent of solemn wood could thus safeguard a tall stag from the hunter's hounds and houses, might not you also play hide-and-seek, in these groves, with all the pangs and trepidations of man's life, and elude Death, the mighty hunter, for more than the span of human years? Here, also, crash his arrows; here, in the farthest glade, sounds the gallop of the pale horse. But he does not hunt this cover with all his hounds, for the game is thin and small: and if you were but alert and wary, if you lodged ever in the deepest thickets, you too might live on into later generations and astonish men by your stalwart age and the trophies of an immemorial success.

For the forest takes away from you all excuse to die. There is nothing here to cabin or thwart your free desires. Here all the impudencies of the brawling world reach you no more. You may count your hours, like Endymion, by the strokes of the lone woodcutter, or by the progression of the lights and shadows and the sun wheeling his wide circuit through the naked heavens. Here shall you see no enemies but winter and rough weather. And if a pang comes to you at all, it will be a pang of healthful hunger. All the puling sorrows, all the carking repentance, all this talk of duty that is no duty, in the great peace, in the pure daylight of these woods, fall away from you like a garment. And if perchance you come forth upon an eminence, where the wind blows upon you large and fresh, and the pines knock their long stems together, like an ungainly sort of puppets, and see far away over the plain a factory chimney defined against the pale horizon – it is for you, as for the staid and simple peasant when, with his plough, he upturns old arms and harness from the furrow of the glebe. Ay, sure enough, there was a battle there in the old times; and, sure enough, there is a world out yonder where men strive together with a noise of oaths and weeping and clamorous dispute. So much you apprehend by an athletic act of the imagination. A faint far-off rumour as of Merovingian wars; a legend as of some dead religion.

Notes

1. Stevenson's vivid description of the fields beyond Barbizon was inspired by the work of the French painter, Jean-Francois Millet, particularly *The Angelus* (1859). See Nicholas Rankin, *Dead Man's Chest: Travels after Robert Louis Stevenson* (London: Phoenix Press, 2001), p. 91.

2. Jules Michelet (1798–1874), French historian.

3. Translation. 'The Lord of the Manor shuts up his peasants as though there were a door and hinges from the heaven to the ground. Everything is his, the ancient forest, the bird in the air, the fish in the stream, the beast in the thicket, the water which flows, the bell whose sound rolls, into the distance.' See Robert Louis Stevenson, *Travels with a Donkey in the Cévennes and Selected Travel Writings*. Edited with an Introduction by Emma Letley (New York: Oxford University Press, 1992), p. 333.

4. Napoleon Bonaparte (1769–1821), emperor of France.

5. The village of Grez.

6. Siron's Inn. See also 'Fontainebleau' in this volume.

7. Pierre de Ronsard (1524–1585), French poet.

8. Translation. 'There is the water.'

9. Horace (65–8 BC), Roman poet.

10. Pierre-Jean de Beranger (1780–1857), French poet.

11. Charles VI (1368–1422), king of France from 1380 to 1422.

In the Latin Quarter

This excerpt from In the Latin Quarter *originally appeared in the*
London Magazine, *10 and 17 February 1877.*

I. THE BALL AT MR. ELSINARE'S

Mr Elsinare's studio lies in a long, rambling, silent street not a hundred miles
from the Boulevard Mont-Parnasse – a quarter of Paris which is cheap, airy, and
free from the visitation of tourists.[1] The house presents to the thoroughfare a
modest gable, a rickety carriage-gate, and a sort of cottage on the other side of it,
which looks as if it was meant for the porter. The wicket stands open as we arrive,
but there is no sign of life. We venture in, as we might venture after nightfall into
a farm-steading, with a kind of beware-of-the-dog feeling at heart. The court is
long and narrow like a bit of a country lane; the ground descends, the pavement
is of the roughest; and ladies with high heels, on their way to Mr Elsinare's, stumble in the darkness over all manner of heights and hollows, and have to pilot their
drapery through many dangers.

The studio is up several pair of stairs; it has been arranged with much art for
the occasion.[2] The floor is cleaned; Elsinare and his partner, Smiler, have been
rubbing it with candle-ends all the morning, until now it as shiny and as slippery
as heart could wish. Two Chinese lanterns and a couple of bronze lamps illumi-
nate the ballroom from the rafters. There is a piano against the wall, and casts
make a great figure on the shelves.

A door stands open on one side, and gives entrance into a small closet which is
to do duty on the present occasion as a buttery and a lady's cloak-room. Here is a
French *bonne*, lent for the evening by the lady patroness, mixes glasses of syrup
and water and lays out sweet biscuits for distribution. She is surrounded by cloaks
and hats and great-coats, and from time to time examines her own face critically
in the mirror. Even in the cloak-room, the eye is scared by unexpected and inharmonious details. An iron bedstead leaning against the wall strikes rather a homely note for the ante-chambers of a festival. One corner is occupied by a lay figure
with an air of glaring immorality. From another, a death's-head, jauntily accoutred
with a helmet, scowls down upon the syrup and sweet biscuits, and catches the
young ladies; eyes wickedly in the mirror, as it to remind them of the vanity of
balls. Truly, this Egyptian refinement is but little in key with the mild and innocent diversions of the evening. Syrup and water is scarcely the right sort of beverage to quaff among the emblems of mortality.

The company is mixed as to nationality, and varied in attire. The chaperon is an
Austrian Countess, who seems to have had all the Austrian taken out of her by a

prolonged sojourn in New York. There are many Americans, a sprinkling of French, a Swede, and some Britishers. Most of the men are in evening dress, a one or two in costume. Elsinare appears as Hamlet, and makes a very graceful host. Dear Smiler, the best of men, has waxed his moustaches until he is nearly off the face of the earth, and radiates welcome and good happiness as though he had six thousand a year and an island in the Aegean. The floor is just a trifle too much waxed for his free, Californian style of dancing; and, as he goes round in the last figure of the quadrille, he falls into the arms of all the ladies in succession. It makes no difference, however, for they are mostly bigger than he is, and he carries it off with a good humour that is more beautiful than grace. Shaun O'Shaughnessy also bites the dust repeatedly with true Hibernian *aplomb*. George Rowland, dressed as a Yorkshire farmer of the old school, makes his entrance in character, to the unfeigned alarm of all the French. They evidently think the scalping is going to begin. But it is just Rowland's way, and they are reassured by the laughter to the rest. Willie MacIntytre, in the national costume, brings with him a powerful atmosphere of sporran. He does not dance from motives of delicacy, and tries as far as possible to keep the sporran in unfrequented corners. A sporran, like a bag-pipe, is most agreeable in the extreme distance, and in breezy, mountainous places.

Almost all the young ladies are in costume. There are some pretty Italian dresses round the room, to say nothing of their wearers. But Belle Bird[3] is not to be passed over among the rest. She is a Californian girl, and has spent her childhood among Bret Harte's stories, petted by miners, and gamblers, and trappers, and ranche-men, and all the *dramatis personae* of the new romance;[4] and, I must say, they seem to spoil people in the right direction, for Belle is frank and simple and not at all like an American miss. She looks like a Russian – a South Russian, I mean. The pleasant gentlemen, old and young, who make it their business to accost ladies on the streets of Paris, had a favourite phrase by way of endeavouring to open a friendly understanding with her: – '*Quelle jolie, gentile petite Russe!*' they would remark. Belle says it was by mistake she hit one of these intelligent young men over the mouth last winter; but, of course, we all have our own ideas; I am glad, at least, it was the intelligent young man who got the buffet, instead of you or me. For a young lady of sixteen, to employ her own idiom, you bet your sweet life she'd fetch him! Tonight she is dressed in gilt, like a stage fairy, and her hair is full of gold powder; her dark face is flushed, and her eyes shine with happiness. She and Smiler are quite the features of the evening; Smiler looks so gratified with everybody else, and she looks so pleased with herself. Upon my word, it is impossible to say which is the more becoming sentiment. You cannot set eyes on either of them without solid satisfaction. Your heart gives a bounce and a thrill; and, like the Ancient Mariner with the watersnakes, you want badly to bless them, I know I keep blessing little Smiler all night long.

George Rowland considers syrup and water an unwholesome, if not an impertinent, beverage. He eyes the tray dejectedly; and so I draw near and begin to conjure up divine drinks before his thirsty imagination. I ask him what he would think of a pint of stout? 'I should look upon it with a very friendly eye,' answers George, in a tragic voice. 'Or a bottle of the Cluny Pommard?' I go on, referring to the crack café of the Quarter. George passes his hand waterily over his mouth, and his eyes wink and look suffused. 'Or even one of Laverne's Fleury?' He begs me to stop, and we drink to each other dispiritedly in syrup and water.

Willie MacIntyre is only a passing visitor in town. He has the eccentricity to remain all winter at one of those artistic villages, which are the Brighton and Scarborough of the Latin Quarter. Hence he is an object of interest; and old frequenters of G_____ draw near the sporran gingerly to hear the news. The landlord's daughter has been unwell; the captain of the *pompiers* has been exceptionally drunk. MacIntyre, being a man of means, is going to build a studio at the back of the inn, entering out of the room Reake Yetton had last summer. It is to be more of a menagerie than a studio, as is to be expected from the man in question; and he has come up to town to buy pigeons, a cat, a monkey, and another dog – Taureau, his bull terrier, having succumbed to natural laws on a diet of absinthe, vermouth, coffee, champagne, and mutton cutlets.

There is another topic of interest. Shaun O'Shaughnessy, MacIntyre, and another Scotchman, happily absent from Paris and still ignorant of his misfortune, are in a fair way to lose all their furniture for another man's debts, owing to some infamous chink in the French Code. MacIntyre looks stiff and smiles evilly when the subject is broached. Rowland offers burlesque counsel in a graveyard tone of voice, and relapses into his character part of the Yorkshire farmer fitfully and rather feebly; for the syrup has done its work. Shaun comes into the corner between the dances, and denunciates the whole French nation in a sweeping organ-roll of brogue.

It is strange to think that almost all these good folk are daubers of canvas; even Belle has a maul-stick with which she will break your head if you are impolite; and yet, while they all diligently paint and paint by the month together, and wash their brushes with quite as knowing an air as any RA, in England, and send really quite a considerable extent of canvas into different exhibitions – there is not one painter that ever you heard of in the party; they are all as unknown as if they were dead, and the most of them have never sold a pennyworth of their productions. You may hear of them some day for all that; and, in the meantime, I am sure they enjoy their evening rarely.

Notes

1. An ironic observation on Stevenson's part given the later influx of Americans, English, and other nationalities to this part of Paris during the so-called Lost Generation era of the 1920s.
2. Stevenson came to Paris to visit his cousin, Robert Alan Mowry 'Bob' Stevenson, who was

studying painting at Carolus-Duran's nearby studio, and set up living quarters at 81 Boulevard de Montparnasse. The American painter, John Singer Sargent, was also a pupil at the studio. See Nicholas Rankin, *Dead Man's Chest: Travels after Robert Louis Stevenson* (London: Phoenix Press, 2001), p. 87.

3. Isobel ('Belle') Osbourne, Fanny Osbourne's daughter.

4. Bret Harte (1836–1902), American writer, best known for 'The Outcasts of Poker Flat' (1869) and other stories of frontier life in California.

FROM *An Inland Voyage*

An Inland Voyage was Stevenson's first published book (1878). An account of a picaresque canoe trip that he made in 1876 in Belgium and northern France with his loyal friend Sir Walter Grindlay Simpson, it is an enjoyable and often humorous read. Stevenson called his French cedar canoe Arethusa; *Simpson his English oak canoe* Cigarette *(they also referred to themselves by the names of their crafts). The voyage began in Antwerp on 25 August 1876 and ended at Pontoise, just north of Paris, in mid-September – a distance of some 200 miles. It was a disaster from the start: the weather did not cooperate and Stevenson – although, significantly, not the dapper Simpson – was often mistaken for a peddler and a spy.*

ANTWERP TO BOOM

WE made a great stir in Antwerp Docks. A stevedore and a lot of dock porters took up the two canoes, and ran with them for the slip. A crowd of children followed cheering. The *Cigarette* went off in a splash and a bubble of small breaking water. Next moment the *Arethusa* was after her. A steamer was coming down, men on the paddle-box shouted hoarse warnings, the stevedore and his porters were bawling from the quay. But in a stroke or two the canoes were away out in the middle of the Scheldt, and all steamers, and stevedores, and other 'long-shore' vanities were left behind.

The sun shone brightly; the tide was making – four jolly miles an hour; the wind blew steadily, with occasional squalls. For my part, I had never been in a canoe under sail in my life; and my first experiment out in the middle of this big river was not made without some trepidation. What would happen when the wind first caught my little canvas? I suppose it was almost as trying a venture into the regions of the unknown as to publish a first book, or to marry. But my doubts were not of long duration; and in five minutes you will not be surprised to learn that I had tied my sheet.

I own I was a little struck by this circumstance myself; of course, in company with the rest of my fellow-men, I had always tied the sheet in a sailing-boat; but in so little and crank a concern as a canoe, and with these charging squalls, I was not prepared to find myself follow the same principle; and it inspired me with some contemptuous views of our regard for life. It is certainly easier to smoke with the sheet fastened; but I had never before weighed a comfortable pipe of tobacco against an obvious risk, and gravely elected for the comfortable pipe. It is a commonplace that we cannot answer for ourselves before we have been tried. But it is not so common a reflection, and surely more consoling, that we usually find ourselves a great deal braver and better than we thought. I believe this is every one's experience: but an apprehension that they may belie themselves in the future prevents mankind from trumpeting this cheerful sentiment abroad. I wish sincerely, for it would have saved me much trouble, there had been some one to put me in a good heart about life when I was younger; to tell me how dangers are most portentous on a distant sight; and how the good in a man's spirit will not suffer itself to be overlaid, and rarely or never deserts him in the hour of need. But we are all for tootling on the sentimental flute in literature; and not a man among us will go to the head of the march to sound the heady drums.

It was agreeable upon the river. A barge or two went past laden with hay. Reeds and willows bordered the stream; and cattle and grey venerable horses came and hung their mild heads over the embankment. Here and there was a pleasant village among trees, with a noisy shipping-yard; here and there a villa in a lawn. The wind served us well up the Scheldt and thereafter up the Rupel; and we were running pretty free when we began to sight the brickyards of Boom, lying for a long way on the right bank of the river. The left bank was still green and pastoral, with alleys of trees along the embankment, and here and there a flight of steps to serve a ferry, where perhaps there sat a woman with her elbows on her knees, or an old gentleman with a staff and silver spectacles. But Boom and its brickyards grew smokier and shabbier with every minute; until a great church with a clock, and a wooden bridge over the river, indicated the central quarters of the town.

Boom is not a nice place, and is only remarkable for one thing: that the majority of the inhabitants have a private opinion that they can speak English, which is not justified by fact. This gave a kind of haziness to our intercourse. As for the Hotel de la Navigation, I think it is the worst feature of the place. It boasts of a sanded parlour, with a bar at one end, looking on the street; and another sanded parlour, darker and colder, with an empty bird-cage and a tricolour subscription box by way of sole adornment, where we made shift to dine in the company of three uncommunicative engineer apprentices and a silent bagman. The food, as usual in Belgium, was of a nondescript occasional character; indeed I have never been able to detect anything in the nature of a meal among this pleasing people; they seem to peck and trifle with viands all day long in an amateur spirit: tentatively French, truly German, and somehow falling between the two.

The empty bird-cage, swept and garnished, and with no trace of the old piping favourite, save where two wires had been pushed apart to hold its lump of sugar, carried with it a sort of graveyard cheer. The engineer apprentices would have nothing to say to us, nor indeed to the bagman; but talked low and sparingly to one another, or raked us in the gaslight with a gleam of spectacles. For though handsome lads, they were all (in the Scots phrase) barnacled …

ON THE WILLEBROEK CANAL

NEXT morning, when we set forth on the Willebroek Canal, the rain began heavy and chill. The water of the canal stood at about the drinking temperature of tea; and under this cold aspersion, the surface was covered with steam. The exhilaration of departure, and the easy motion of the boats under each stroke of the paddles, supported us through this misfortune while it lasted; and when the cloud passed and the sun came out again, our spirits went up above the range of stay-at-home humours. A good breeze rustled and shivered in the rows of trees that bordered the canal. The leaves flickered in and out of the light in tumultuous masses. It seemed sailing weather to eye and ear; but down between the banks, the wind reached us only in faint and desultory puffs. There was hardly enough to steer by. Progress was intermittent and unsatisfactory. A jocular person, of marine antecedents, hailed us from the tow-path with a *'C'est vite, mais c'est long.'*

The canal was busy enough. Every now and then we met or overtook a long string of boats, with great green tillers; high sterns with a window on either side of the rudder, and perhaps a jug or a flower-pot in one of the windows; a dinghy following behind; a woman busied about the day's dinner, and a handful of children. These barges were all tied one behind the other with tow ropes, to the number of twenty-five or thirty; and the line was headed and kept in motion by a steamer of strange construction. It had neither paddle-wheel nor screw; but by some gear not rightly comprehensible to the unmechanical mind, it fetched up over its bow a small bright chain which lay along the bottom of the canal, and paying it out again over the stern, dragged itself forward, link by link, with its whole retinue of loaded skows. Until one had found out the key to the enigma, there was something solemn and uncomfortable in the progress of one of these trains, as it moved gently along the water with nothing to mark its advance but an eddy alongside dying away into the wake.

Of all the creatures of commercial enterprise, a canal barge is by far the most delightful to consider. It may spread its sails, and then you see it sailing high above the tree-tops and the windmill, sailing on the aqueduct, sailing through the green corn-lands: the most picturesque of things amphibious. Or the horse plods along at a foot-pace as if there were no such thing as business in the world; and the man dreaming at the tiller sees the same spire on the horizon all day long. It is a mystery how things ever get to their destination at this rate; and to see the barges waiting their turn at a lock, affords a fine lesson of how easily the world may be taken. There should be many contented spirits on board, for such a life is both to travel and to stay at home.

The chimney smokes for dinner as you go along; the banks of the canal slowly unroll their scenery to contemplative eyes; the barge floats by great forests and through great cities with their public buildings and their lamps at night; and for the bargee, in his floating home, 'travelling abed', it is merely as if he were listening to another man's story or turning the leaves of a picture-book in which he had no concern. He may take his afternoon walk in some foreign country on the banks of the canal, and then come home to dinner at his own fireside.

There is not enough exercise in such a life for any high measure of health; but a high measure of health is only necessary for unhealthy people. The slug of a fellow, who is never ill nor well, has a quiet time of it in life, and dies all the easier.

I am sure I would rather be a bargee than occupy any position under heaven that required attendance at an office. There are few callings, I should say, where a man gives up less of his liberty in return for regular meals. The bargee is on shipboard – he is master in his own ship – he can land whenever he will – he can never be kept beating off a lee-shore a whole frosty night when the sheets are as hard as iron; and so far as I can make out, time stands as nearly still with him as is compatible with the return of bed-time or the dinner-hour. It is not easy to see why a bargee should ever die.

Half-way between Willebroek and Villevorde, in a beautiful reach of canal like a squire's avenue, we went ashore to lunch. There were two eggs, a junk of bread, and a bottle of wine on board the *Arethusa*; and two eggs and an Etna cooking apparatus on board the *Cigarette*. The master of the latter boat smashed one of the eggs in the course of disembarkation; but observing pleasantly that it might still be cooked *à la papier*, he dropped it into the Etna, in its covering of Flemish newspaper. We landed in a blink of fine weather; but we had not been two minutes ashore before the wind freshened into half a gale, and the rain began to patter on our shoulders. We sat as close about the Etna as we could. The spirits burned with great ostentation; the grass caught flame every minute or two, and had to be trodden out; and before long, there were several burnt fingers of the party. But the solid quantity of cookery accomplished was out of proportion with so much display; and when we desisted, after two applications of the fire, the sound egg was little more than loo-warm; and as for *à la papier*, it was a cold and sordid *fricassée* of printer's ink and broken egg-shell. We made shift to roast the other two, by putting them close to the burning spirits; and that with better success. And then we uncorked the bottle of wine, and sat down in a ditch with our canoe aprons over our knees. It rained smartly. Discomfort, when it is honestly uncomfortable and makes no nauseous pretensions to the contrary, is a vastly humorous business; and people well steeped and stupefied in the open air are in a good vein for laughter. From this point of view, even egg *à la papier* offered by way of food may pass muster as a sort of accessory to the fun. But this manner of jest, although it may be taken in good part, does not invite repetition; and from that time forward, the Etna voyaged like a gentleman in the locker of the *Cigarette*.

It is almost unnecessary to mention that when lunch was over and we got aboard again and made sail, the wind promptly died away. The rest of the journey to Villevorde, we still spread our canvas to the unfavouring air; and with now and then a puff, and now and then a spell of paddling, drifted along from lock to lock, between the orderly trees.

It was a fine, green, fat landscape; or rather a mere green water-lane, going on from village to village. Things had a settled look, as in places long lived in. Crop-headed children spat upon us from the bridges as we went below, with a true conservative feeling. But even more conservative were the fishermen, intent upon their floats, who let us go by without one glance. They perched upon sterlings and buttresses and along the slope of the embankment, gently occupied. They were indifferent, like pieces of dead nature. They did not move any more than if they had been fishing in an old Dutch print. The leaves fluttered, the water lapped, but they continued in one stay like so many churches established by law. You might have trepanned every one of their innocent heads, and found no more than so much coiled fishing-line below their skulls. I do not care for your stalwart fellows in india-rubber stockings breasting up mountain torrents with a salmon rod; but I do dearly love the class of man who plies his unfruitful art, for ever and a day, by still and depopulated waters.

At the last lock, just beyond Villevorde, there was a lock-mistress who spoke French comprehensibly, and told us we were still a couple of leagues from Brussels. At the same place, the rain began again. It fell in straight, parallel lines; and the surface of the canal was thrown up into an infinity of little crystal fountains. There were no beds to be had in the neighbourhood. Nothing for it but to lay the sails aside and address ourselves to steady paddling in the rain.

Beautiful country houses, with clocks and long lines of shuttered windows, and fine old trees standing in groves and avenues, gave a rich and sombre aspect in the rain and the deepening dusk to the shores of the canal. I seem to have seen something of the same effect in engravings: opulent landscapes, deserted and overhung with the passage of storm. And throughout we had the escort of a hooded cart, which trotted shabbily along the tow-path, and kept at an almost uniform distance in our wake.

LA FÈRE OF CURSED MEMORY

WE lingered in Moy a good part of the day, for we were fond of being philosophical, and scorned long journeys and early starts on principle. The place, moreover, invited to repose. People in elaborate shooting costumes sallied from the chateau with guns and game-bags; and this was a pleasure in itself, to remain behind while these elegant pleasure-seekers took the first of the morning. In this way, all the world may be an aristocrat, and play the duke among marquises, and the reigning monarch among dukes, if he will only outvie them in tranquillity. An imperturbable demeanour comes from perfect patience. Quiet minds cannot be perplexed or frightened, but go on in fortune or misfortune at their own private pace, like a clock during a thunderstorm.

We made a very short day of it to La Fère; but the dusk was falling, and a small rain had begun before we stowed the boats. La Fère is a fortified town in a plain, and has two belts of rampart. Between the first and the second extends a region of waste land and cultivated patches. Here and there along the wayside were posters forbidding trespass in the name of military engineering. At last, a second gateway admitted us to the town itself. Lighted windows looked gladsome, whiffs of comfortable cookery came abroad upon the air. The town was full of the military reserve, out for the French Autumn Manoeuvres, and the reservists walked speedily and wore their formidable great-coats. It was a fine night to be within doors over dinner, and hear the rain upon the windows.

The *Cigarette* and I could not sufficiently congratulate each other on the prospect, for we had been told there was a capital inn at La Fère. Such a dinner as we were going to eat! such beds as we were to sleep in! – and all the while the rain raining on houseless folk over all the poplared countryside! It made our mouths water. The inn bore the name of some woodland animal, stag, or hart, or hind, I forget which. But I shall never forget how spacious and how eminently habitable it looked as we drew near. The carriage entry was lighted up, not by intention, but from the mere superfluity of fire and candle in the house. A rattle of many dishes came to our ears; we sighted a great field of table-cloth; the kitchen glowed like a forge and smelt like a garden of things to eat.

Into this, the inmost shrine and physiological heart of a hostelry, with all its furnaces in action, and all its dressers charged with viands, you are now to suppose us making our triumphal entry, a pair of damp rag-and-bone men, each with a limp india-rubber bag upon his arm. I do not believe I have a sound view of that kitchen; I saw it through a sort of glory: but it seemed to me crowded with the snowy caps of cookmen, who all turned round from their saucepans and looked at us with surprise. There was no doubt about the landlady, however: there she was, heading her army, a flushed, angry woman, full of affairs. Her I asked politely – too politely, thinks the *Cigarette* – if we could have beds: she surveying us coldly from head to foot.

'You will find beds in the suburb,' she remarked. 'We are too busy for the like of you.'

If we could make an entrance, change our clothes, and order a bottle of wine, I felt sure we could put things right; so said I: 'If we cannot sleep, we may at least dine,' – and was for depositing my bag.

What a terrible convulsion of nature was that which followed in the landlady's face! She made a run at us, and stamped her foot.

'Out with you – out of the door!' she screeched. '*Sortez! sortez! sortez par la porte!*'

I do not know how it happened, but next moment we were out in the rain and darkness, and I was cursing before the carriage entry like a disappointed mendicant. Where were the boating men of Belgium? where the Judge and his good wines? and where the graces of Origny? Black, black was the night after the fire-lit kitchen; but what was that to the blackness in our heart? This was not the first time that I have been refused a lodging. Often and often have I planned what I should do if such a misadventure happened to me again. And nothing is easier to plan. But to put in execution, with the heart boiling at the indignity? Try it; try it only once; and tell me what you did.

It is all very fine to talk about tramps and morality. Six hours of police surveillance (such as I have had), or one brutal rejection from an inn-door, change your views upon the subject like a course of lectures. As long as you keep in the upper regions, with all the world bowing to you as you go, social arrangements have a very handsome air; but once get under the wheels, and you wish society were at the devil. I will give most respectable men a fortnight of such a life, and then I will offer them twopence for what remains of their morality.

For my part, when I was turned out of the Stag, or the Hind, or whatever it was, I would have set the temple of Diana on fire, if it had been handy. There was no crime complete enough to express my disapproval of human institutions. As for the *Cigarette*, I never knew a man so altered. 'We have been taken for pedlars again,' said he. 'Good God, what it must be to be a pedlar in reality!' He particularised a complaint for every joint in the landlady's body. Timon was a philanthropist alongside of him. And then, when he was at the top of his maledictory bent, he would suddenly break away and begin whimperingly to commiserate the poor. 'I hope to God,' he said, – and I trust the prayer was answered, – 'that I shall never be uncivil to a pedlar.' Was this the imperturbable *Cigarette*? This, this was he. O change beyond report, thought, or belief!

Meantime the heaven wept upon our heads; and the windows grew brighter as the night increased in darkness. We trudged in and out of La Fère streets; we saw shops, and private houses where people were copiously dining; we saw stables where carters' nags had plenty of fodder and clean straw; we saw no end of reservists, who were very sorry for themselves this wet night, I doubt not, and yearned for their country homes; but had they not each man his place in La Fère barracks? And we, what had we?

There seemed to be no other inn in the whole town. People gave us directions, which we followed as best we could, generally with the effect of bringing us out again upon the scene of our disgrace. We were very sad people indeed by the time we had gone all over La Fère; and the *Cigarette* had already made up his mind to lie under a poplar and sup off a loaf of bread. But right at the other end, the house next the town-gate was full of light and bustle. *'Bazin, aubergiste, loge à pied,'* was the sign. *'A la Croix de Malte.'* There were we received.

The room was full of noisy reservists drinking and smoking; and we were very glad indeed when the drums and bugles began to go about the streets, and one and all had to snatch shakoes and be off for the barracks.

Bazin was a tall man, running to fat: soft-spoken, with a delicate, gentle face. We asked him to share our wine; but he excused himself, having pledged reservists all day long. This was a very different type of the workman-innkeeper from the bawling disputatious fellow at Origny. He also loved Paris, where he had worked as a decorative painter in his youth. There were such opportunities for self-instruction there, he said. And if any one has read Zola's description of the workman's marriage-party visiting the Louvre, they would do well to have heard Bazin by way of antidote. He had delighted in the museums in his youth. 'One sees there little miracles of work,' he said; 'that is what makes a good workman; it kindles a spark.' We asked him how he managed in La Fère. 'I am married,' he said, 'and I have my pretty children. But frankly, it is no life at all. From morning to night I pledge a pack of good enough fellows who know nothing.'

It faired as the night went on, and the moon came out of the clouds. We sat in front of the door, talking softly with Bazin. At the guard-house opposite, the guard was being for ever turned out, as trains of field artillery kept clanking in out of the night, or patrols of horsemen trotted by in their cloaks. Madame Bazin came out after a while; she was tired with her day's work, I suppose; and she nestled up to her husband and laid her head upon his breast. He had his arm about her, and kept gently patting her on the shoulder. I think Bazin was right, and he was really married. Of how few people can the same be said!

Little did the Bazins know how much they served us. We were charged for candles, for food and drink, and for the beds we slept in. But there was nothing in the bill for the husband's pleasant talk; nor for the pretty spectacle of their married life. And there was yet another item unchanged. For these people's politeness really set us up again in our own esteem. We had a thirst for consideration; the sense of insult was still hot in our spirits; and civil usage seemed to restore us to our position in the world.

How little we pay our way in life! Although we have our purses continually in our hand, the better part of service goes still unrewarded. But I like to fancy that a grateful spirit gives as good as it gets. Perhaps the Bazins knew how much I liked them? perhaps they also were healed of some slights by the thanks that I gave them in my manner?

EPILOGUE:
THE LOING VALLEY CHÂTILLON
AND LA BUSSIÈRE

The following epilogue of An Inland Voyage *was not included in the first edition. It did, however, appear in* Scribner's Magazine *in August 1888 and was published in* Across the Plains *in 1892. The selection is memorable for two incidents: one in which the village postal carrier mistakes the portraits in Stevenson's knapsack for pornography and, more seriously, when Stevenson, temporarily separated from his companion Walter Simpson, is stopped by local French police and placed under arrest when it is discovered he has no 'papers' on him and is mistaken for a German spy. It is classic Stevenson.*

THE country where they journeyed, that green, breezy valley of the Loing, is one very attractive to cheerful and solitary people. The weather was superb; all night it thundered and lightened, and the rain fell in sheets; by day, the heavens were cloudless, the sun fervent, the air vigorous and pure. They walked separate: the *Cigarette* plodding behind with some philosophy, the lean *Arethusa* posting on ahead. Thus each enjoyed his own reflections by the way; each had perhaps time to tire of them before he met his comrade at the designated inn; and the pleasures of society and solitude combined to fill the day. The *Arethusa* carried in his knapsack the works of Charles of Orleans,[1] and employed some of the hours of travel in the concoction of English roundels. In this path, he must thus have preceded Mr. Lang, Mr. Dobson, Mr. Henley, and all contemporary roundeleers; but for good reasons, he will be the last to publish the result. The *Cigarette* walked burthened with a volume of Michelet. And both these books, it will be seen, played a part in the subsequent adventure.

The *Arethusa* was unwisely dressed. He is no precisian in attire; but by all accounts, he was never so ill-inspired as on that tramp; having set forth indeed, upon a moment's notice, from the most unfashionable spot in Europe, Barbizon. On his head he wore a smoking-cap of Indian work, the gold lace pitifully frayed and tarnished. A flannel shirt of an agreeable dark hue, which the satirical called black; a light tweed coat made by a good English tailor; ready-made cheap linen trousers and leathern gaiters completed his array. In person, he is exceptionally lean; and his face is not, like those of happier mortals, a certificate. For years he could not pass a frontier or visit a bank without suspicion; the police everywhere, but in his native city, looked askance upon him; and (though I am sure it will not be credited) he is actually denied admittance to the casino of Monte Carlo. If you will imagine him, dressed as above, stooping under his knapsack, walking nearly five miles an hour with the folds of the ready-made trousers fluttering about his spindle shanks, and still looking eagerly round him as if in terror of pursuit – the figure, when realised, is far from reassuring. When Villon[2] journeyed (perhaps by the same pleasant valley) to his exile at Roussillon, I wonder if he had not something of the same appearance. Something of the same preoccupation he had beyond a doubt, for he too must have tinkered verses as he walked, with more success than his successor. And if he had anything like the same inspiring weather, the same nights of uproar, men in armour rolling and resounding down the stairs of heaven, the rain hissing on the village streets, the wild bull's-eye of the storm flashing all night long into the bare inn-chamber – the same sweet return of day, the same unfathomable blue of noon, the same high-coloured, halcyon eves – and above all, if he had anything like as good a comrade, anything like as keen a relish for what he saw, and what he ate, and the rivers that he bathed in, and the rubbish that he wrote, I would exchange estates to-day with the poor exile, and count myself a gainer.

But there was another point of similarity between the two journeys, for which the *Arethusa* was to pay dear: both were gone upon in days of incomplete security. It was not long after the Franco-Prussian war. Swiftly as men forget, that country-side was still alive with tales of *uhlans*, and outlying sentries, and hairbreadth 'scapes from the ignominious cord, and pleasant momentary friendships between invader and invaded. A year, at the most two years later, you might have tramped all that country over and not heard one anecdote. And a year or two later, you would – if you were a rather ill-looking young man in nondescript array – have gone your rounds in greater safety; for along with more interesting matter, the Prussian spy would have somewhat faded from men's imaginations.

For all that, our voyager had got beyond Château Renard before he was conscious of arousing wonder. On the road between that place and Châtillon-sur-Loing, however, he encountered a rural postman; they fell together in talk, and spoke of a variety of subjects; but through one and all, the postman was still visibly preoccupied, and his eyes were faithful to the *Arethusa*'s knapsack. At last, with mysterious roguishness, he inquired what it contained, and on being answered, shook his head with kindly incredulity. '*non*,' said he, '*non, vous avez des portraits.*' And then with a languishing appeal, '*voyons*, show me the portraits!' It was some little while before the *Arethusa*, with a shout of laughter, recognised his drift. By portraits he meant indecent photographs; and in the *Arethusa*, an austere and rising author, he thought to have identified a pornographic *colporteur.* When countryfolk in France have made up their minds as to a person's calling, argument is fruitless. Along all the rest of the way, the postman piped and fluted meltingly to get a sight of the collection; now he would upbraid, now he would reason – '*voyons*, I will tell nobody'; then he tried corruption, and insisted on paying for a glass of wine; and, at last when their ways separated – '*non*,' said he, '*ce n'est pas bien de votre part. O non, ce n'est pas bien.*' And shaking his head with quite a sentimental sense of injury, he departed unrefreshed.

On certain little difficulties encountered by the *Arethusa* at Châtillon-sur-Loing, I have not space to dwell; another Châtillon, of grislier memory, looms too near at hand. But the next day, in a certain hamlet called La Jussiere, he stopped to drink a glass of syrup in a very poor, bare drinking shop. The hostess, a comely woman, suckling a child, examined the traveller with kindly and pitying eyes.

'You are not of this department?' she asked.

The *Arethusa* told her he was English.[3] 'Ah!' she said, surprised. 'We have no English. We have many Italians, however, and they do very well; they do not complain of the people hereabouts. An Englishman may do very well also; it will be something new.' Here was a dark saying, over which the *Arethusa* pondered as he drank his grenadine; but when he rose and asked what was to pay, the light came upon him in a flash. *'oh, pour vous,'* replied the landlady, 'a halfpenny!' *pour vous?* By heaven, she took him for a beggar! He paid his halfpenny, feeling that it were ungracious to correct her. But when he was forth again upon the road, he became vexed in spirit. The conscience is no gentleman, he is a rabbinical fellow; and his conscience told him he had stolen the syrup.

THE UPPER LOIRE CHÂTILLON
AND THE COMMISSARY

That night the travellers slept in Gien; the next day they passed the river and set forth (severally, as their custom was) on a short stage through the green plain upon the Berry side, to Châtillon-sur-Loire. It was the first day of the shooting; and the air rang with the report of firearms and the admiring cries of sportsmen. Overhead the birds were in consternation, wheeling in clouds, settling and re-arising. And yet with all this bustle on either hand, the road itself lay solitary. The *Arethusa* smoked a pipe beside a milestone, and I remember he laid down very exactly all he was to do at Châtillon: how he was to enjoy a cold plunge, to change his shirt, and to await the *Cigarette's* arrival, in sublime inaction, by the margin of the Loire. Fired by these ideas, he pushed the more rapidly forward, and came, early in the afternoon and in a breathing heat, to the entering-in of that ill-fated town. Childe Roland to the dark tower came.

A polite gendarme threw his shadow on the path.

'Monsieur est voyageur?' he asked.

And the *Arethusa*, strong in his innocence, forgetful of his vile attire, replied – I had almost said with gaiety: 'So it would appear.'

'His papers are in order?' said the gendarme. And when the *Arethusa*, with a slight change of voice, admitted he had none, he was informed (politely enough) that he must appear before the Commissary.

The Commissary sat at a table in his bedroom, stripped to the shirt and trousers, but still copiously perspiring; and when he turned upon the prisoner a large meaningless countenance, that was (like Bardolph's) 'all whelks and bubuckles,' the dullest might have been prepared for grief. Here was a stupid man, sleepy with the heat and fretful at the interruption, whom neither appeal nor argument could reach.

THE COMMISSARY. You have no papers?

THE ARETHUSA. Not here.

THE COMMISSARY. Why?

THE ARETHUSA. I have left them behind in my valise.

THE COMMISSARY. You know, however, that it is forbidden to circulate without papers?

THE ARETHUSA. Pardon me: I am convinced of the contrary. I am here on my rights as an English subject by international treaty.

THE COMMISSARY (*with scorn*). You call yourself an Englishman?

THE ARETHUSA. I do.

THE COMMISSARY. Humph. – What is your trade?

THE ARETHUSA. I am a Scotch advocate.

THE COMMISSARY (*with singular annoyance*). A Scotch advocate! Do you then pretend to support yourself by that in this department?

The *Arethusa* modestly disclaimed the pretension. The Commissary had scored a point.

THE COMMISSARY. Why, then, do you travel?

THE ARETHUSA. I travel for pleasure.

THE COMMISSARY (*pointing to the knapsack, and with sublime incredulity*). *Avec ça? Voyez-vous, je suis un homme intelligent!* (With that? Look here, I am a person of intelligence!)

The culprit remaining silent under this home thrust, the Commissary relished his triumph for a while, and then demanded (like the postman, but with what different expectations!) to see the contents of the knapsack. And here the *Arethusa*, not yet sufficiently awake to his position, fell into a grave mistake. There was little or no furniture in the room except the Commissary's chair and table; and to facilitate matters, the *Arethusa* (with all the innocence on earth) leant the knapsack on a corner of the bed. The Commissary fairly bounded from his seat; his face and neck flushed past purple, almost into blue; and he screamed to lay the desecrating object on the floor.

The knapsack proved to contain a change of shirts, of shoes, of socks, and of linen trousers, a small dressing-case, a piece of soap in one of the shoes, two volumes of the *Collection Jannet* lettered *Poésies de Charles d'Orléans*, a map, and a version book containing diverse notes in prose and the remarkable English roundels of the voyager, still to this day unpublished: the Commissary of Châtillon is the only living man who has clapped an eye on these artistic trifles. He turned the assortment over with a contumelious finger; it was plain from his daintiness that he regarded the *Arethusa* and all his belongings as the very temple of infection. Still there was nothing suspicious about the map, nothing really criminal except the roundels; as for Charles of Orléans, to the ignorant mind of the prisoner, he seemed as good as a certificate; and it was supposed the farce was nearly over.

The inquisitor resumed his seat.

THE COMMISSARY (after a pause). *Eh bien, je vais vous dire ce que vous êtes. Vous êtes allemand et vous venez chanter à la foire.* (Well, then, I will tell you what you are. You are a German and have come to sing at the fair.)

THE ARETHUSA. Would you like to hear me sing? I believe I could convince you of the contrary.

THE COMMISSARY. *Pas de plaisanterie, monsieur!*

THE ARETHUSA. Well, sir, oblige me at least by looking at this book. Here, I open it with my eyes shut. Read one of these songs – read this one – and tell me, you who are a man of intelligence, if it would be possible to sing it at a fair?

THE COMMISSARY (*critically*). *Mais oui. Très bien.*

THE ARETHUSA. *Comment, monsieur!* What! But do you not observe it is antique. It is difficult to understand, even for you and me; but for the audience at a fair, it would be meaningless.

THE COMMISSARY (*taking a pen*). *Enfin, il faui en finir.* What is your name?

THE ARETHUSA (*speaking with the swallowing vivacity of the English*). Robert-Louis-Stev'ns'n.

THE COMMISSARY (*aghast*). *Hé! Quoi?*

THE ARETHUSA (*perceiving and improving his advantage*). Rob'rt-Lou's-Stev'ns'n.

THE COMMISSARY (*after several conflicts with his pen*). *Eh bien, il faut se passer du nom. Ça ne s'écrit pas.* (Well, we must do without the name: it is unspellable.)

The above is a rough summary of this momentous conversation, in which I have been chiefly careful to preserve the plums of the Commissary; but the remainder of the scene, perhaps because of his rising anger, has left but little definite in the memory of the *Arethusa*. The Commissary was not, I think, a practised literary man; no sooner, at least, had he taken pen in hand and embarked on the composition of the *procès-verbal*, than he became distinctly more uncivil and began to show a predilection for that simplest of all forms of repartee: 'You lie!' Several times the *Arethusa* let it pass, and then suddenly flared up, refused to accept more insults or to answer further questions, defied the Commissary to do his worst, and promised him, if he did, that he should bitterly repent it. Perhaps if he had worn this proud front from the first, instead of beginning with a sense of entertainment and then going on to argue, the thing might have turned otherwise; for even at this eleventh hour the Commissary was visibly staggered. But it was too late; he had been challenged the *procès-verbal* was begun; and he again squared his elbows over his writing, and the *Arethusa* was led forth a prisoner.

A step or two down the hot road stood the gendarmerie. Thither was our unfortunate conducted, and there he was bidden to empty forth the contents of his pockets. A handkerchief, a pen, a pencil, a pipe and tobacco, matches, and some ten francs of change: that was all. Not a file, not a cipher, not a scrap of writing whether to identify or to condemn. The very gendarme was appalled before such destitution.

'I regret,' he said, 'that I arrested you, for I see that you are no *voyou*.' And he promised him every indulgence.

The *Arethusa*, thus encouraged, asked for his pipe. That he was told was impossible, but if he chewed, he might have some tobacco. He did not chew, however, and asked instead to have his handkerchief.

'*Non*,' said the gendarme. '*Nous avons eu des histoires de gens qui se sont pendus.*' (No, we have had histories of people who hanged themselves.)

'What,' cried the *Arethusa*. 'And is it for that you refuse me my handkerchief? But see how much more easily I could hang myself in my trousers!'

The man was struck by the novelty of the idea; but he stuck to his colours, and only continued to repeat vague offers of service.

'At least,' said the *Arethusa*, 'be sure that you arrest my comrade; he will follow me ere long on the same road, and you can tell him by the sack upon his shoulders.' This promised, the prisoner was led round into the back court of the building, a cellar door was opened, he was motioned down the stair, and bolts grated and chains clanged behind his descending person.

The philosophic and still more the imaginative mind is apt to suppose itself prepared for any mortal accident. Prison, among other ills, was one that had been often faced by the undaunted *Arethusa*. Even as he went down the stairs, he was telling himself that here was a famous occasion for a roundel, and that like the committed linnets of the tuneful cavalier, he too would make his prison musical. I will tell the truth at once: the roundel was never written, or it should be printed in this place, to raise a smile. Two reasons interfered: the first moral, the second physical.

It is one of the curiosities of human nature, that although all men are liars, they can none of them bear to be told so of themselves. To get and take the lie with equanimity is a stretch beyond the stoic; and the *Arethusa*, who had been surfeited upon that insult, was blazing inwardly with a white heat of smothered wrath. But the physical had also its part. The cellar in which he was confined was some feet underground, and it was only lighted by an unglazed, narrow aperture high up in the wall and smothered in the leaves of a green vine. The walls were of naked masonry, the floor of bare earth; by way of furniture there was an earth-enware basin, a water-jug, and a wooden bedstead with a blue-gray cloak for bedding. To be taken from the hot air of a summer's afternoon, the reverberation of the road and the stir of rapid exercise, and plunged into the gloom and damp of this receptacle for vagabonds, struck an instant chill upon the *Arethusa*'s blood. Now see in how small a matter a hardship may consist: the floor was exceedingly uneven underfoot, with the very spade-marks, I suppose, of the labourers who dug the foundations of the barrack; and what with the poor twilight and the irregular surface, walking was impossible. The caged author resisted for a good while; but the chill of the place struck deeper and deeper; and at length, with such reluctance as you may fancy, he was driven to climb upon the bed and wrap himself in the public covering. There, then, he lay upon the verge of shivering, plunged in semi-darkness, wound in a garment whose touch he dreaded like the plague, and (in a spirit far removed from resignation) telling the roll of the insults he had just received. These are not circumstances favourable to the muse.

Meantime (to look at the upper surface where the sun was still shining and the guns of sportsmen were still noisy through the tufted plain) the *Cigarette* was drawing near at his more philosophic pace. In those days of liberty and health he was the constant partner of the *Arethusa*, and had ample opportunity to share in that gentleman's disfavour with the police. Many a bitter bowl had he partaken of with that disastrous comrade. He was himself a man born to float easily through life, his face and manner artfully recommending him to all. There was but one suspicious circumstance he could not carry off, and that was his companion. He will not readily forget the Commissary in what is ironically called the free town of Frankfort-on-the-Main; nor the Franco-Belgian frontier; nor the inn at La Fère; last, but not least, he is pretty certain to remember Châtillon-sur-Loire.

At the town entry, the gendarme culled him like a wayside flower; and a moment later, two persons, in a high state of surprise, were confronted in the Commissary's office. For if the *Cigarette* was surprised to be arrested, the Commissary was no less taken aback by the appearance and appointments of his captive. Here was a man about whom there could be no mistake: a man of an unquestionable and unassailable manner, in apple-pie order, dressed not with neatness merely but elegance, ready with his passport, at a word, and well supplied with money: a man the Commissary would have doffed his hat to on chance upon the highway; and this *beau cavalier* unblushingly claimed the *Arethusa* for his comrade! The conclusion of the interview was foregone; of its humours, I remember only one. 'Baronet?' demanded the magistrate, glancing up from the passport. *'alors, monsieur, vous êtes le fils d'un baron?'* And when the *Cigarette* (his one mistake throughout the interview) denied the soft impeachment, *'alors,'* from the Commissary, *'ce n'est pas votre passeport!'* But these were ineffectual thunders; he never dreamed of laying hands upon the *Cigarette*; presently he fell into a mood of unrestrained admiration, gloating over the contents of the knap-sack, commending our friend's tailor. Ah, what an honoured guest was the Commissary entertaining! what suitable clothes he wore for the warm weather! what beautiful maps, what an attractive work of history he carried in his knapsack! You are to understand there was now but one point of difference between them: what was to be done with the *Arethusa?* the *Cigarette* demanding his release, the Commissary still claiming him as the dungeon's own. Now it chanced that the *Cigarette* had passed some years of his life in Egypt, where he had made acquain-tance with two very bad things, cholera morbus and pashas; and in the eye of the Commissary, as he fingered the volume of Michelet, it seemed to our traveller there was something Turkish. I pass over this lightly; it is highly possible there was some misunderstanding, highly possible that the Commissary (charmed with his visitor) supposed the attraction to be mutual and took for an act of growing friend-ship what the *Cigarette* himself regarded as a bribe. And at any rate, was there ever a bribe more singular than an odd volume of Michelet's history? The work was promised him for the morrow, before our departure; and presently after, either because he had his price, or to show that he was not the man to be behind in friendly offices – *'eh bien,'* he said, *'je suppose qu'il faut lâcher voire camarade.'* And he tore up that feast of humour, the unfinished *procès-verbal.* Ah, if he had only torn up instead the *Arethusa's* roundels! There were many works burnt at Alexandria, there are many treasured in the British Museum, that I could better spare than the *procès-verbal* of Châtillon. Poor bubuckled Commissary! I begin to be sorry that he never had his Michelet: perceiving in him fine human traits, a broad-based stupidity, a gusto in his magisterial functions, a taste for letters, a ready admiration for the admirable. And if he did not admire the *Arethusa*, he was not alone in that.

To the imprisoned one, shivering under the public covering, there came sud-denly a noise of bolts and chains. He sprang to his feet, ready to welcome a com-panion in calamity; and instead of that, the door was flung wide, the friendly gendarme appeared above in the strong daylight, and with a magnificent gesture (being probably a student of the drama) – *'vous êtes libre!'* he said. None too soon for the *Arethusa*. I doubt if he had been half-an-hour imprisoned; but by the watch in a man's brain (which was the only watch he carried) he should have been eight times longer; and he passed forth with ecstasy up the cellar stairs into the healing warmth of the afternoon sun; and the breath of the earth came as sweet as a cow's into his nostril; and he heard again (and could have laughed for pleas-ure) the concord of delicate noises that we call the hum of life.

And here it might be thought that my history ended; but not so, this was an act-drop and not the curtain. Upon what followed in front of the barrack, since there was a lady in the case, I scruple to expatiate. The wife of the Maréchal-des-logis was a handsome woman, and yet the *Arethusa* was not sorry to be gone from her society. Something of her image, cool as a peach on that hot afternoon, still lingers in his memory: yet more of her conversation. 'You have there a very fine parlour,' said the poor gentleman. – 'Ah,' said Madame la Maréchale (des-logis), 'you are very well acquainted with such parlours!' And you should have seen with what a hard and scornful eye she measured the vagabond before her! I do not think he ever hated the Commissary; but before that interview was at an end, he hated Madame la Maréchale. His passion (as I am led to understand by one who was present) stood confessed in a burning eye, a pale cheek, and a trembling utterance; Madame meanwhile tasting the joys of the matador, goading him with barbed words and staring him coldly down.

It was certainly good to be away from this lady, and better still to sit down to an excellent dinner in the inn. Here, too, the despised travellers scraped acquaintance with their next neighbour, a gentleman of these parts, returned from the day's sport, who had the good taste to find pleasure in their society. The dinner at an end, the gentleman proposed the acquaintance should be ripened in the *café*.

The *café* was crowded with sportsmen conclamantly explaining to each other and the world the smallness of their bags. About the centre of the room, the *Cigarette* and the *Arethusa* sat with their new acquaintance; a trio very well pleased, for the travellers (after their late experience) were greedy of consideration, and their sportsman rejoiced in a pair of patient listeners. Suddenly the glass door flew open with a crash; the Maréchal-des-logis appeared in the interval, gorgeously belted and befrogged, entered without salutation, strode up the room with a clang of spurs and weapons, and disappeared through a door at the far end. Close at his heels followed the *Arethusa's* gendarme of the afternoon, imitating, with a nice shade of difference, the imperial bearing of his chief; only, as he passed, he struck lightly with his open hand on the shoulder of his late captive, and with that ringing, dramatic utterance of which he had the secret – *'suivez!'* said he.

The arrest of the members, the oath of the Tennis Court, the signing of the Declaration of Independence, Mark Antony's oration, all the brave scenes of history, I conceive as having been not unlike that evening in the *café* at Châtillon. Terror breathed upon the assembly. A moment later, when the *Arethusa* had followed his recaptors into the farther part of the house, the *Cigarette* found himself alone with his coffee in a ring of empty chairs and tables, all the lusty sportsmen huddled into corners, all their clamorous voices hushed in whispering, all their eyes shooting at him furtively as at a leper.

And the *Arethusa*? Well, he had a long, sometimes a trying, interview in the back kitchen. The Maréchal-des-logis, who was a very handsome man, and I believe both intelligent and honest, had no clear opinion on the case. He thought the Commissary had done wrong, but he did not wish to get his subordinates into trouble; and he proposed this, that, and the other, to all of which the *Arethusa* (with a growing sense of his position) demurred.

'In short,' suggested the *Arethusa*, 'you want to wash your hands of further responsibility? Well, then, let me go to Paris.'

The Maréchal-des-logis looked at his watch.

'You may leave,' said he, 'by the ten o'clock train for Paris.'

And at noon the next day the travellers were telling their misadventure in the dining-room at Siron's.

Notes

1. Charles of Orleans (1391–1465), French poet.
2. Francois Villon (1431–1463), French poet.
3. Perhaps Stevenson did not have the energy to explain he was a Scotsman. Writes Nicholas Rankin, 'For the first and last time, he is posing as 'an Englishman'.' Nicholas Rankin, *Dead Man's Chest: Travels after Robert Louis Stevenson* (London: Phoenix Press, 201), p. 100.

FROM *Travels with a Donkey in the Cévennes*

Travels with a Donkey in the Cévannes (1879), his memoir of a twelve-day walking tour through central France in 1878, was Stevenson's second travel narrative (and third book). By this time, he had met and fallen in love with the Indiana-born Fanny Osbourne, the estranged wife of a Kentucky lawyer, at an arts colony in France. Despondent over Fanny's return to America, Stevenson began his journey, a 120-mile trek between Le Monastier-sur-Gazeille and St-Jean-du-Gard, alone. Although ostensibly written as an easy way to make some fast money, Travels with a Donkey *is now considered a classic of travel writing and Modestine – the stubbornly slow, dim-witted donkey – one of its most memorable characters.*

THE DONKEY, THE PACK, AND THE PACK-SADDLE

IN a little place called Le Monastier, in a pleasant highland valley fifteen miles from Le Puy, I spent about a month of fine days. Monastier is notable for the making of lace, for drunkenness, for freedom of language, and for unparalleled political dissension.[1] There are adherents of each of the four French parties – Legitimists, Orleanists, Imperialists, and Republicans – in this little mountain-town; and they all hate, loathe, decry, and calumniate each other. Except for business purposes, or to give each other the lie in a tavern brawl, they have laid aside even the civility of speech. 'Tis a mere mountain Poland. In the midst of this Babylon I found myself a rallying-point; every one was anxious to be kind and helpful to the stranger. This was not merely from the natural hospitality of mountain people, nor even from the surprise with which I was regarded as a man living of his own free will in Le Monastier, when he might just as well have lived anywhere else in this big world; it arose a good deal from my projected excursion southward through the Cévennes. A traveller of my sort was a thing hitherto unheard of in that district. I was looked upon with contempt, like a man who should project a journey to the moon, but yet with a respectful interest, like one setting forth for the inclement Pole. All were ready to help in my preparations; a crowd of sympathisers supported me at the critical moment of a bargain; not a step was taken but was heralded by glasses round and celebrated by a dinner or a breakfast.

It was already hard upon October before I was ready to set forth, and at the high altitudes over which my road lay there was no Indian summer to be looked for. I was determined, if not to camp out, at least to have the means of camping out in my possession; for there is nothing more harassing to an easy mind than the necessity of reaching shelter by dusk, and the hospitality of a village inn is not always to be reckoned sure by those who trudge on foot. A tent, above all for a solitary traveller, is troublesome to pitch, and troublesome to strike again; and even on the march it forms a conspicuous feature in your baggage. A sleeping-sack, on the other hand, is always ready – you have only to get into it; it serves a double purpose – a bed by night, a portmanteau by day; and it does not advertise your intention of camping out to every curious passer-by. This is a huge point. If a camp is not secret, it is but a troubled resting-place; you become a public character; the convivial rustic visits your bedside after an early supper; and you must sleep with one eye open, and be up before the day. I decided on a sleeping-sack; and after repeated visits to Le Puy, and a deal of high living for myself and my advisers, a sleeping-sack was designed, constructed, and triumphantly brought home.

This child of my invention was nearly six feet square, exclusive of two triangular flaps to serve as a pillow by night and as the top and bottom of the sack by day. I call it 'the sack,' but it was never a sack by more than courtesy: only a sort of long roll or sausage, green waterproof cart-cloth without and blue sheep's fur within. It was commodious as a valise, warm and dry for a bed. There was luxurious turning room for one; and at a pinch the thing might serve for two. I could bury myself in it up to the neck; for my head I trusted to a fur cap, with a hood to fold down over my ears and a band to pass under my nose like a respirator; and in case of heavy rain I proposed to make myself a little tent, or tentlet, with my waterproof coat, three stones, and a bent branch.

It will readily be conceived that I could not carry this huge package on my own, merely human, shoulders. It remained to choose a beast of burden. Now, a horse is a fine lady among animals, flighty, timid, delicate in eating, of tender health; he is too valuable and too restive to be left alone, so that you are chained to your brute as to a fellow galley-slave; a dangerous road puts him out of his wits; in short, he's an uncertain and exacting ally, and adds thirty-fold to the troubles of the voyager. What I required was something cheap and small and hardy, and of a stolid and peaceful temper; and all these requisites pointed to a donkey.

There dwelt an old man in Monastier, of rather unsound intellect according to some, much followed by street-boys, and known to fame as Father Adam. Father Adam had a cart, and to draw the cart a diminutive she-ass, not much bigger than a dog, the colour of a mouse, with a kindly eye and a determined under-jaw. There was something neat and high-bred, a quakerish elegance, about the rogue that hit my fancy on the spot. Our first interview was in Monastier market-place. To prove her good temper, one child after another was set upon her back to ride, and one after another went head over heels into the air; until a want of confidence began to reign in youthful bosoms, and the experiment was discontinued from a dearth of subjects. I was already backed by a deputation of my friends; but as if this were not enough, all the buyers and sellers came round and helped me in the bargain; and the ass and I and Father Adam were the centre of a hubbub for near half an hour. At length she passed into my service for the consideration of sixty-five francs and a glass of brandy. The sack had already cost eighty francs and two glasses of beer; so that Modestine,[2] as I instantly baptised her, was upon all accounts the cheaper article. Indeed, that was as it should be; for she was only an appurtenance of my mattress, or self-acting bedstead on four castors.

I had a last interview with Father Adam in a billiard-room at the witching hour of dawn, when I administered the brandy. He professed himself greatly touched by the separation, and declared he had often bought white bread for the donkey when he had been content with black bread for himself; but this, according to the best authorities, must have been a flight of fancy. He had a name in the village for brutally misusing the ass; yet it is certain that he shed a tear, and the tear made a clean mark down one cheek.

By the advice of a fallacious local saddler, a leather pad was made for me with rings to fasten on my bundle; and I thoughtfully completed my kit and arranged my toilette. By way of armoury and utensils, I took a revolver, a little spirit-lamp and pan, a lantern and some halfpenny candles, a jack-knife and a large leather flask. The main cargo consisted of two entire changes of warm clothing – besides my travelling wear of country velveteen, pilot-coat, and knitted spencer – some books, and my railway-rug, which, being also in the form of a bag, made me a double castle for cold nights. The permanent larder was represented by cakes of chocolate and tins of Bologna sausage. All this, except what I carried about my person, was easily stowed into the sheepskin bag; and by good fortune I threw in my empty knapsack, rather for convenience of carriage than from any thought that I should want it on my journey. For more immediate needs I took a leg of cold mutton, a bottle of Beaujolais, an empty bottle to carry milk, an egg-beater, and a considerable quantity of black bread and white, like Father Adam, for myself and donkey, only in my scheme of things the destinations were reversed.

Monastrians, of all shades of thought in politics, had agreed in threatening me with many ludicrous misadventures, and with sudden death in many surprising forms. Cold, wolves, robbers, above all the nocturnal practical joker, were daily and eloquently forced on my attention. Yet in these vaticinations, the true, patent danger was left out. Like Christian, it was from my pack I suffered by the way. Before telling my own mishaps, let me in two words relate the lesson of my experience. If the pack is well strapped at the ends, and hung at full length – not doubled, for your life – across the pack-saddle, the traveller is safe. The saddle will certainly not fit, such is the imperfection of our transitory life; it will assuredly topple and tend to overset; but there are stones on every roadside, and a man soon learns the art of correcting any tendency to overbalance with a well-adjusted stone.

On the day of my departure I was up a little after five; by six, we began to load the donkey; and ten minutes after, my hopes were in the dust. The pad would not stay on Modestine's back for half a moment. I returned it to its maker, with whom I had so contumelious a passage that the street outside was crowded from wall to wall with gossips looking on and listening. The pad changed hands with much vivacity; perhaps it would be more descriptive to say that we threw it at each other's heads; and, at any rate, we were very warm and unfriendly, and spoke with a deal of freedom.

I had a common donkey pack-saddle – a *barde*, as they call it – fitted upon Modestine; and once more loaded her with my effects. The doubled sack, my pilot-coat (for it was warm, and I was to walk in my waistcoat), a great bar of black bread, and an open basket containing the white bread, the mutton, and the bottles, were all corded together in a very elaborate system of knots, and I looked on the result with fatuous content. In such a monstrous deck-cargo, all poised above the donkey's shoulders, with nothing below to balance, on a brand-new pack-saddle that had not yet been worn to fit the animal, and fastened with brand-new girths that might be expected to stretch and slacken by the way, even a very careless traveller should have seen disaster brewing. That elaborate system of knots, again, was the work of too many sympathisers to be very artfully designed. It is true they tightened the cords with a will; as many as three at a time would have a foot against Modestine's quarters, and be hauling with clenched teeth; but I learned afterwards that one thoughtful person, without any exercise of force, can make a more solid job than half-a-dozen heated and enthusiastic grooms. I was then but a novice; even after the misadventure of the pad nothing could disturb my security, and I went forth from the stable door as an ox goeth to the slaughter.

Stevenson, the son of devout Presbyterian parents, continues his journey and eventually finds himself outside the doors of a Trappist monastery.

FATHER APOLLINARIS

NEXT morning (Thursday, 20th September) I took the road in a new order. The sack was no longer doubled, but hung at full length across the saddle, a green sausage six feet long with a tuft of blue wool hanging out of either end. It was more picturesque, it spared the donkey, and, as I began to see, it would ensure stability, blow high, blow low. But it was not without a pang that I had so decided. For although I had purchased a new cord, and made all as fast as I was able, I was yet jealously uneasy lest the flaps should tumble out and scatter my effects along the line of march.

My way lay up the bald valley of the river, along the march of Vivarais and Gevaudan. The hills of Gevaudan on the right were a little more naked, if anything, than those of Vivarais upon the left, and the former had a monopoly of a low dotty underwood that grew thickly in the gorges and died out in solitary burrs upon the shoulders and the summits. Black bricks of fir-wood were plastered here and there upon both sides, and here and there were cultivated fields. A railway ran beside the river; the only bit of railway in Gevaudan, although there are many proposals afoot and surveys being made, and even, as they tell me, a station standing ready built in Mende. A year or two hence and this may be another world. The desert is beleaguered. Now may some Languedocian Wordsworth turn the sonnet into patois: 'Mountains and vales and floods, heard YE that whistle?'

At a place called La Bastide I was directed to leave the river, and follow a road that mounted on the left among the hills of Vivarais, the modern Ardeche; for I was now come within a little way of my strange destination, the Trappist monastery of Our Lady of the Snows.³ The sun came out as I left the shelter of a pine-wood, and I beheld suddenly a fine wild landscape to the south. High rocky hills, as blue as sapphire, closed the view, and between these lay ridge upon ridge, heathery, craggy, the sun glittering on veins of rock, the underwood clambering in the hollows, as rude as God made them at the first. There was not a sign of man's hand in all the prospect; and indeed not a trace of his passage, save where generation after generation had walked in twisted footpaths, in and out among the beeches, and up and down upon the channelled slopes. The mists, which had hitherto beset me, were now broken into clouds, and fled swiftly and shone brightly in the sun. I drew a long breath. It was grateful to come, after so long, upon a scene of some attraction for the human heart. I own I like definite form in what my eyes are to rest upon; and if landscapes were sold, like the sheets of characters of my boyhood, one penny plain and twopence coloured, I should go the length of twopence every day of my life.

But if things had grown better to the south, it was still desolate and inclement near at hand. A spidery cross on every hill-top marked the neighbourhood of a religious house; and a quarter of a mile beyond, the outlook southward opening out and growing bolder with every step, a white statue of the Virgin at the corner of a young plantation directed the traveller to Our Lady of the Snows. Here, then, I struck leftward, and pursued my way, driving my secular donkey before me, and creaking in my secular boots and gaiters, towards the asylum of silence.

I had not gone very far ere the wind brought to me the clanging of a bell, and somehow, I can scarce tell why, my heart sank within me at the sound. I have rarely approached anything with more unaffected terror than the monastery of Our Lady of the Snows. This it is to have had a Protestant education. And suddenly, on turning a corner, fear took hold on me from head to foot – slavish, superstitious fear; and though I did not stop in my advance, yet I went on slowly, like a man who should have passed a bourne unnoticed, and strayed into the country of the dead. For there, upon the narrow new-made road, between the stripling pines, was a mediaeval friar, fighting with a barrowful of turfs. Every Sunday of my childhood I used to study the Hermits of Marco Sadeler – enchanting prints, full of wood and field and mediaeval landscapes, as large as a county, for the imagination to go a-travelling in; and here, sure enough, was one of Marco Sadeler's heroes. He was robed in white like any spectre, and the hood falling back, in the instancy of his contention with the barrow, disclosed a pate as bald and yellow as a skull. He might have been buried any time these thousand years, and all the lively parts of him resolved into earth and broken up with the farmer's harrow.

I was troubled besides in my mind as to etiquette. Durst I address a person who was under a vow of silence? Clearly not. But drawing near, I doffed my cap to him with a far-away superstitious reverence. He nodded back, and cheerfully addressed me. Was I going to the monastery? Who was I? An Englishman? Ah, an Irishman, then?

'No,' I said, 'a Scotsman.'

A Scotsman? Ah, he had never seen a Scotsman before. And he looked me all over, his good, honest, brawny countenance shining with interest, as a boy might look upon a lion or an alligator. From him I learned with disgust that I could not be received at Our Lady of the Snows; I might get a meal, perhaps, but that was all. And then, as our talk ran on, and it turned out that I was not a pedlar, but a literary man, who drew landscapes and was going to write a book, he changed his manner of thinking as to my reception (for I fear they respect persons even in a Trappist monastery), and told me I must be sure to ask for the Father Prior, and state my case to him in full. On second thoughts he determined to go down with me himself; he thought he could manage for me better. Might he say that I was a geographer?

No; I thought, in the interests of truth, he positively might not.

'Very well, then' (with disappointment), 'an author.'

It appeared he had been in a seminary with six young Irishmen, all priests long since, who had received newspapers and kept him informed of the state of ecclesiastical affairs in England. And he asked me eagerly after Dr. Pusey, for whose conversion the good man had continued ever since to pray night and morning.

'I thought he was very near the truth,' he said; 'and he will reach it yet; there is so much virtue in prayer.'

He must be a stiff, ungodly Protestant who can take anything but pleasure in this kind and hopeful story. While he was thus near the subject, the good father asked me if I were a Christian; and when he found I was not, or not after his way, he glossed it over with great good-will.

The road which we were following, and which this stalwart father had made with his own two hands within the space of a year, came to a corner, and showed us some white buildings a little farther on beyond the wood. At the same time, the bell once more sounded abroad. We were hard upon the monastery. Father Apollinaris (for that was my companion's name) stopped me.

'I must not speak to you down there,' he said. 'Ask for the Brother Porter, and all will be well. But try to see me as you go out again through the wood, where I may speak to you. I am charmed to have made your acquaintance.'

And then suddenly raising his arms, flapping his fingers, and crying out twice, 'I must not speak, I must not speak!' he ran away in front of me, and disappeared into the monastery door.

I own this somewhat ghastly eccentricity went a good way to revive my terrors. But where one was so good and simple, why should not all be alike? I took heart of grace, and went forward to the gate as fast as Modestine, who seemed to have a disaffection for monasteries, would permit. It was the first door, in my acquaintance of her, which she had not shown an indecent haste to enter. I summoned the place in form, though with a quaking heart. Father Michael, the Father Hospitaller, and a pair of brown-robed brothers came to the gate and spoke with me a while. I think my sack was the great attraction; it had already beguiled the heart of poor Apollinaris, who had charged me on my life to show it to the Father Prior, But whether it was my address, or the sack, or the idea speedily published among that part of the brotherhood who attend on strangers that I was not a ped-lar after all, I found no difficulty as to my reception. Modestine was led away by a layman to the stables, and I and my pack were received into Our Lady of the Snows.

A NIGHT AMONG THE PINES

FROM Bleymard after dinner, although it was already late, I set out to scale a portion of the Lozere. An ill-marked stony drove-road guided me forward; and I met nearly half-a-dozen bullock-carts descending from the woods, each laden with a whole pine-tree for the winter's firing. At the top of the woods, which do not climb very high upon this cold ridge, I struck leftward by a path among the pines, until I hit on a dell of green turf, where a streamlet made a little spout over some stones to serve me for a water-tap. 'In a more sacred or sequestered bower … nor nymph nor faunus haunted.' The trees were not old, but they grew thick-ly round the glade: there was no outlook, except north-eastward upon distant hill-tops, or straight upward to the sky; and the encampment felt secure and private like a room. By the time I had made my arrangements and fed Modestine, the day was already beginning to decline. I buckled myself to the knees into my sack and made a hearty meal; and as soon as the sun went down, I pulled my cap over my eyes and fell asleep.

Night is a dead monotonous period under a roof; but in the open world it passes lightly, with its stars and dews and perfumes, and the hours are marked by changes in the face of Nature. What seems a kind of temporal death to people choked between walls and curtains, is only a light and living slumber to the man who sleeps afield. All night long he can hear Nature breathing deeply and freely; even as she takes her rest, she turns and smiles; and there is one stirring hour unknown to those who dwell in houses, when a wakeful influence goes abroad over the sleeping hemisphere, and all the outdoor world are on their feet. It is then that the cock first crows, not this time to announce the dawn, but like a cheerful watchman speeding the course of night. Cattle awake on the meadows; sheep break their fast on dewy hillsides, and change to a new lair among the ferns; and houseless men, who have lain down with the fowls, open their dim eyes and behold the beauty of the night.

At what inaudible summons, at what gentle touch of Nature, are all these sleepers thus recalled in the same hour to life? Do the stars rain down an influence, or do we share some thrill of mother earth below our resting bodies? Even shepherds and old country-folk, who are the deepest read in these arcana, have not a guess as to the means or purpose of this nightly resurrection. Towards two in the morning they declare the thing takes place; and neither know nor inquire further. And at least it is a pleasant incident. We are disturbed in our slumber only, like the luxurious Montaigne,[4] 'that we may the better and more sensibly relish it.' We have a moment to look upon the stars. And there is a special pleasure for some minds in the reflection that we share the impulse with all outdoor creatures in our neighbourhood, that we have escaped out of the Bastille of civilisation, and are become, for the time being, a mere kindly animal and a sheep of Nature's flock.

When that hour came to me among the pines, I wakened thirsty. My tin was standing by me half full of water. I emptied it at a draught; and feeling broad awake after this internal cold aspersion, sat upright to make a cigarette. The stars were clear, coloured, and jewel–like, but not frosty. A faint silvery vapour stood for the Milky Way. All around me the black fir-points stood upright and stock-still. By the whiteness of the pack-saddle, I could see Modestine walking round and round at the length of her tether; I could hear her steadily munching at the sward; but there was not another sound, save the indescribable quiet talk of the runnel over the stones. I lay lazily smoking and studying the colour of the sky, as we call the void of space, from where it showed a reddish grey behind the pines to where it showed a glossy blue-black between the stars. As if to be more like a pedlar, I wear a silver ring. This I could see faintly shining as I raised or lowered the cigarette; and at each whiff the inside of my hand was illuminated, and became for a second the highest light in the landscape.

A faint wind, more like a moving coolness than a stream of air, passed down the glade from time to time; so that even in my great chamber the air was being renewed all night long. I thought with horror of the inn at Chasserades and the congregated nightcaps; with horror of the nocturnal prowesses of clerks and students, of hot theatres and pass–keys and close rooms. I have not often enjoyed a more serene possession of myself, nor felt more independent of material aids. The outer world, from which we cower into our houses, seemed after all a gentle habitable place; and night after night a man's bed, it seemed, was laid and waiting for him in the fields, where God keeps an open house. I thought I had rediscovered one of those truths which are revealed to savages and hid from political economists: at the least, I had discovered a new pleasure for myself. And yet even while I was exulting in my solitude I became aware of a strange lack. I wished a companion to lie near me in the starlight, silent and not moving, but ever within touch. For there is a fellowship more quiet even than solitude, and which, rightly understood, is solitude made perfect. And to live out of doors with the woman a man loves is of all lives the most complete and free.

As I thus lay, between content and longing, a faint noise stole towards me through the pines. I thought, at first, it was the crowing of cocks or the barking of dogs at some very distant farm; but steadily and gradually it took articulate shape in my ears, until I became aware that a passenger was going by upon the highroad in the valley, and singing loudly as he went. There was more of good-will than grace in his performance; but he trolled with ample lungs; and the sound of his voice took hold upon the hillside and set the air shaking in the leafy glens. I have heard people passing by night in sleeping cities; some of them sang; one, I remember, played loudly on the bagpipes. I have heard the rattle of a cart or carriage spring up suddenly after hours of stillness, and pass, for some minutes, within the range of my hearing as I lay abed. There is a romance about all who are abroad in the black hours, and with something of a thrill we try to guess their business. But here the romance was double: first, this glad passenger, lit internally with wine, who sent up his voice in music through the night; and then I, on the other hand, buckled into my sack, and smoking alone in the pine-woods between four and five thousand feet towards the stars.

When I awoke again (Sunday, 29th September), many of the stars had disappeared; only the stronger companions of the night still burned visibly overhead; and away towards the east I saw a faint haze of light upon the horizon, such as had been the Milky Way when I was last awake. Day was at hand. I lit my lantern, and by its glow-worm light put on my boots and gaiters; then I broke up some bread for Modestine, filled my can at the water-tap, and lit my spirit-lamp to boil myself some chocolate. The blue darkness lay long in the glade where I had so sweetly slumbered; but soon there was a broad streak of orange melting into gold along the mountain-tops of Vivarais. A solemn glee possessed my mind at this gradual and lovely coming in of day. I heard the runnel with delight; I looked round me for something beautiful and unexpected; but the still black pine-trees, the hollow glade, the munching ass, remained unchanged in figure. Nothing had altered but the light, and that, indeed, shed over all a spirit of life and of breathing peace, and moved me to a strange exhilaration.

I drank my water-chocolate, which was hot if it was not rich, and strolled here and there, and up and down about the glade. While I was thus delaying, a gush of steady wind, as long as a heavy sigh, poured direct out of the quarter of the morning. It was cold, and set me sneezing. The trees near at hand tossed their black plumes in its passage; and I could see the thin distant spires of pine along the edge of the hill rock slightly to and fro against the golden east. Ten minutes after, the sunlight spread at a gallop along the hillside, scattering shadows and sparkles, and the day had come completely.

I hastened to prepare my pack, and tackle the steep ascent that lay before me; but I had something on my mind. It was only a fancy; yet a fancy will sometimes be importunate. I had been most hospitably received and punctually served in my green caravanserai. The room was airy, the water excellent, and the dawn had called me to a moment. I say nothing of the tapestries or the inimitable ceiling, nor yet of the view which I commanded from the windows; but I felt I was in some one's debt for all this liberal entertainment. And so it pleased me, in a half-laughing way, to leave pieces of money on the turf as I went along, until I had left enough for my night's lodging. I trust they did not fall to some rich and churlish drover.

IN THE VALLEY OF THE TARN

A NEW road leads from Pont de Montvert to Florac by the valley of the Tarn; a smooth sandy ledge, it runs about half-way between the summit of the cliffs and the river in the bottom of the valley; and I went in and out, as I followed it, from bays of shadow into promontories of afternoon sun. This was a pass like that of Killiecrankie;[5] a deep turning gully in the hills, with the Tarn making a wonderful hoarse uproar far below, and craggy summits standing in the sunshine high above. A thin fringe of ash-trees ran about the hill-tops, like ivy on a ruin; but on the lower slopes, and far up every glen, the Spanish chestnut-trees stood each four-square to heaven under its tented foliage. Some were planted, each on its own terrace no larger than a bed; some, trusting in their roots, found strength to grow and prosper and be straight and large upon the rapid slopes of the valley; others, where there was a margin to the river, stood marshalled in a line and mighty like cedars of Lebanon. Yet even where they grew most thickly they were not to be thought of as a wood, but as a herd of stalwart individuals; and the dome of each tree stood forth separate and large, and as it were a little hill, from among the domes of its companions. They gave forth a faint sweet perfume which pervaded the air of the afternoon; autumn had put tints of gold and tarnish in the green; and the sun so shone through and kindled the broad foliage, that each chestnut was relieved against another, not in shadow, but in light. A humble sketcher here laid down his pencil in despair.

I wish I could convey a notion of the growth of these noble trees; of how they strike out boughs like the oak, and trail sprays of drooping foliage like the willow; of how they stand on upright fluted columns like the pillars of a church; or like the olive, from the most shattered bole can put out smooth and youthful shoots, and begin a new life upon the ruins of the old. Thus they partake of the nature of many different trees; and even their prickly top-knots, seen near at hand against the sky, have a certain palm-like air that impresses the imagination. But their individuality, although compounded of so many elements, is but the richer and the more original. And to look down upon a level filled with these knolls of foliage, or to see a clan of old unconquerable chestnuts cluster 'like herded elephants' upon the spur of a mountain, is to rise to higher thoughts of the powers that are in Nature.

Between Modestine's laggard humour and the beauty of the scene, we made little progress all that afternoon; and at last finding the sun, although still far from setting, was already beginning to desert the narrow valley of the Tarn, I began to cast about for a place to camp in. This was not easy to find; the terraces were too narrow, and the ground, where it was unterraced, was usually too steep for a man to lie upon. I should have slipped all night, and awakened towards morning with my feet or my head in the river.

After perhaps a mile, I saw, some sixty feet above the road, a little plateau large enough to hold my sack, and securely parapeted by the trunk of an aged and enormous chestnut. Thither, with infinite trouble, I goaded and kicked the reluctant Modestine, and there I hastened to unload her. There was only room for myself upon the plateau, and I had to go nearly as high again before I found so much as standing-room for the ass. It was on a heap of rolling stones, on an artificial terrace, certainly not five feet square in all. Here I tied her to a chestnut, and having given her corn and bread and made a pile of chestnut-leaves, of which I found her greedy, I descended once more to my own encampment.

The position was unpleasantly exposed. One or two carts went by upon the road; and as long as daylight lasted I concealed myself, for all the world like a hunted Camisard,[6] behind my fortification of vast chestnut trunk; for I was passionately afraid of discovery and the visit of jocular persons in the night. Moreover, I saw that I must be early awake; for these chestnut gardens had been the scene of industry no further gone than on the day before. The slope was strewn with lopped branches, and here and there a great package of leaves was propped against a trunk; for even the leaves are serviceable, and the peasants use them in winter by way of fodder for their animals. I picked a meal in fear and trembling, half lying down to hide myself from the road; and I daresay I was as much concerned as if I had been a scout from Joani's band above upon the

Lozere, or from Salomon's across the Tarn, in the old times of psalm-singing and blood. Or, indeed, perhaps more; for the Camisards had a remarkable confidence in God; and a tale comes back into my memory of how the Count of Gevaudan, riding with a party of dragoons and a notary at his saddlebow to enforce the oath of fidelity in all the country hamlets, entered a valley in the woods, and found Cavalier and his men at dinner, gaily seated on the grass, and their hats crowned with box-tree garlands, while fifteen women washed their linen in the stream. Such was a field festival in 1703; at that date Antony Watteau[7] would be painting similar subjects.

This was a very different camp from that of the night before in the cool and silent pine-woods. It was warm and even stifling in the valley. The shrill song of frogs, like the tremolo note of a whistle with a pea in it, rang up from the river-side before the sun was down. In the growing dusk, faint rustlings began to run to and fro among the fallen leaves; from time to time a faint chirping or cheeping noise would fall upon my ear; and from time to time I thought I could see the movement of something swift and indistinct between the chestnuts. A profusion of large ants swarmed upon the ground; bats whisked by, and mosquitoes droned overhead. The long boughs with their bunches of leaves hung against the sky like garlands; and those immediately above and around me had somewhat the air of a trellis which should have been wrecked and half overthrown in a gale of wind.

Sleep for a long time fled my eyelids; and just as I was beginning to feel quiet stealing over my limbs, and settling densely on my mind, a noise at my head startled me broad awake again, and, I will frankly confess it, brought my heart into my mouth.

It was such a noise as a person would make scratching loudly with a finger-nail; it came from under the knapsack which served me for a pillow, and it was thrice repeated before I had time to sit up and turn about. Nothing was to be seen, nothing more was to be heard, but a few of these mysterious rustlings far and near, and the ceaseless accompaniment of the river and the frogs. I learned next day that the chestnut gardens are infested by rats; rustling, chirping, and scraping were probably all due to these; but the puzzle, for the moment, was insoluble, and I had to compose myself for sleep, as best I could, in wondering uncertainty about my neighbours.

I was wakened in the grey of the morning (Monday, 30th September) by the sound of foot-steps not far off upon the stones, and opening my eyes, I beheld a peasant going by among the chestnuts by a footpath that I had not hitherto observed. He turned his head neither to the right nor to the left, and disappeared in a few strides among the foliage. Here was an escape! But it was plainly more than time to be moving. The peasantry were abroad; scarce less terrible to me in my nondescript position than the soldiers of Captain Poul to an undaunted Camisard. I fed Modestine with what haste I could; but as I was returning to my sack, I saw a man and a boy come down the hillside in a direction crossing mine. They unintelligibly hailed me, and I replied with inarticulate but cheerful sounds, and hurried forward to get into my gaiters.

The pair, who seemed to be father and son, came slowly up to the plateau, and stood close beside me for some time in silence. The bed was open, and I saw with regret my revolver lying patently disclosed on the blue wool. At last, after they had looked me all over, and the silence had grown laughably embarrassing, the man demanded in what seemed unfriendly tones:

'You have slept here?'

'Yes,' said I. 'As you see.'

'Why?' he asked.

'My faith,' I answered lightly, 'I was tired.'

He next inquired where I was going and what I had had for dinner; and then, without the least transition, '*C'est bien,*' he added, 'come along.' And he and his son, without another word, turned off to the next chestnut-tree but one, which they set to pruning. The thing had passed of more simply than I hoped. He was a grave, respectable man; and his unfriendly voice did not imply that he thought he was speaking to a criminal, but merely to an inferior.

I was soon on the road, nibbling a cake of chocolate and seriously occupied with a case of conscience. Was I to pay for my night's lodging? I had slept ill, the bed was full of fleas in the shape of ants, there was no water in the room, the very dawn had neglected to call me in the morning. I might have missed a train, had there been any in the neighbourhood to catch. Clearly, I was dissatisfied with my entertainment; and I decided I should not pay unless I met a beggar.

The valley looked even lovelier by morning; and soon the road descended to the level of the river. Here, in a place where many straight and prosperous chestnuts stood together, making an aisle upon a swarded terrace, I made my morning toilette in the water of the Tarn. It was marvellously clear, thrillingly cool; the soap-suds disappeared as if by magic in the swift current, and the white boulders gave one a model for cleanliness. To wash in one of God's rivers in the open air seems to me a sort of cheerful solemnity or semi-pagan act of worship. To dabble among dishes in a bedroom may perhaps make clean the body; but the imagination takes no share in such a cleansing. I went on with a light and peaceful heart, and sang psalms to the spiritual ear as I advanced.

Suddenly up came an old woman, who point-blank demanded alms.

'Good,' thought I; 'here comes the waiter with the bill.'

And I paid for my night's lodging on the spot. Take it how you please, but this was the first and the last beggar that I met with during all my tour.

A step or two farther I was overtaken by an old man in a brown nightcap, clear-eyed, weather-beaten, with a faint excited smile. A little girl followed him, driving two sheep and a goat; but she kept in our wake, while the old man walked beside me and talked about the morning and the valley. It was not much past six; and for healthy people who have slept enough, that is an hour of expansion and of open and trustful talk.

'*Connaissez-vous le Seigneur?*' he said at length.

I asked him what Seigneur he meant; but he only repeated the question with more emphasis and a look in his eyes denoting hope and interest.

'Ah,' said I, pointing upwards, 'I understand you now. Yes, I know Him; He is the best of acquaintances.'

The old man said he was delighted. 'Hold,' he added, striking his bosom; 'it makes me happy here.' There were a few who knew the Lord in these valleys, he went on to tell me; not many, but a few. 'Many are called,' he quoted, 'and few chosen.'[8]

'My father,' said I, 'it is not easy to say who know the Lord; and it is none of our business. Protestants and Catholics, and even those who worship stones, may know Him and be known by Him; for He has made all.'

I did not know I was so good a preacher.

The old man assured me he thought as I did, and repeated his expressions of pleasure at meeting me. 'We are so few,' he said. 'They call us Moravians here; but down in the Department of Gard, where there are also a good number, they are called Derbists, after an English pastor.'

I began to understand that I was figuring, in questionable taste, as a member of some sect to me unknown; but I was more pleased with the pleasure of my companion than embarrassed by my own equivocal position. Indeed, I can see no dishonesty in not avowing a difference; and especially in these high matters, where we have all a sufficient assurance that, whoever may be in the wrong, we ourselves are not completely in the right. The truth is much talked about; but this old man in a brown nightcap showed himself so simple, sweet, and friendly, that I am not unwilling to profess myself his convert. He was, as a matter of fact, a Plymouth Brother. Of what that involves in the way of doctrine I have no idea nor the time to inform myself; but I know right well that we are all embarked upon a troublesome world, the children of one Father, striving in many essential points to do and to become the same. And although it was somewhat in a mistake that he shook hands with me so often and showed himself so ready to receive my words, that was a mistake of the truth-finding sort. For charity begins blindfold; and only through a series of similar misapprehensions rises at length into a settled principle of love and patience, and a firm belief in all our fellow-men. If I deceived this good old man, in the like manner I would willingly go on to deceive others. And if ever at length, out of our separate and sad ways, we should all come together into one common house, I have a hope, to which I cling dearly, that my mountain Plymouth Brother will hasten to shake hands with me again.

Thus, talking like Christian and Faithful by the way, he and I came down upon a hamlet by the Tarn. It was but a humble place, called La Vernede, with less than a dozen houses, and a Protestant chapel on a knoll. Here he dwelt; and here, at the inn, I ordered my breakfast. The inn was kept by an agreeable young man, a stone-breaker on the road, and his sister, a pretty and engaging girl. The village schoolmaster dropped in to speak with the stranger. And these were all Protestant – a fact which pleased me more than I should have expected; and, what pleased me still more, they seemed all upright and simple people. The Plymouth Brother hung round me with a sort of yearning interest, and returned at least thrice to make sure I was enjoying my meal. His behaviour touched me deeply at the time, and even now moves me in recollection. He feared to intrude, but he would not willingly forego one moment of my society; and he seemed never weary of shaking me by the hand.

When all the rest had drifted off to their day's work, I sat for near half an hour with the young mistress of the house, who talked pleasantly over her seam of the chestnut harvest, and the beauties of the Tarn, and old family affections, broken up when young folk go from home, yet still subsisting. Hers, I am sure, was a sweet nature, with a country plainness and much delicacy underneath; and he who takes her to his heart will doubtless be a fortunate young man.

The valley below La Vernede pleased me more and more as I went forward. Now the hills approached from either hand, naked and crumbling, and walled in the river between cliffs; and now the valley widened and became green. The road led me past the old castle of Miral on a steep; past a battlemented monastery, long since broken up and turned into a church and parsonage; and past a cluster of black roofs, the village of Cocures, sitting among vineyards, and meadows, and orchards thick with red apples, and where, along the highway, they were knocking down walnuts from the roadside trees, and gathering them in sacks and baskets. The hills, however much the vale might open, were still tall and bare, with cliffy battlements and here and there a pointed summit; and the Tarn still rattled through the stones with a mountain noise. I had been led, by bagmen of a picturesque turn of mind, to expect a horrific country after the heart of Byron;[9] but to my Scottish eyes it seemed smiling and plentiful, as the weather still gave an impression of high summer to my Scottish body; although the chestnuts were already picked out by the autumn, and the poplars, that here began to mingle with them, had turned into pale gold against the approach of winter.

There was something in this landscape, smiling although wild, that explained to me the spirit of the Southern Covenanters. Those who took to the hills for conscience' sake in Scotland had all gloomy and bedevilled thoughts; for once that they received God's comfort they would be twice engaged with Satan; but the Camisards had only bright and supporting visions. They dealt much more in blood, both given and taken; yet I find no obsession of the Evil One in their records. With a light conscience, they pursued their life in these rough times and circumstances. The soul of Seguier, let us not forget, was like a garden. They knew they were on God's side, with a knowledge that has no parallel among the Scots; for the Scots, although they might be certain of the cause, could never rest confident of the person.

'We flew,' says one old Camisard, 'when we heard the sound of psalm-singing, we flew as if with wings. We felt within us an animating ardour, a transporting desire. The feeling cannot be expressed in words. It is a thing that must have been experienced to be understood. However weary we might be, we thought no more of our weariness, and grew light so soon as the psalms fell upon our ears.'

The valley of the Tarn and the people whom I met at La Vernede not only explain to me this passage, but the twenty years of suffering which those, who were so stiff and so bloody when once they betook themselves to war, endured with the meekness of children and the constancy of saints and peasants.

FAREWELL, MODESTINE

ON examination, on the morning of 4th October, Modestine was pronounced unfit for travel. She would need at least two days' repose, according to the ostler; but I now eager to reach Alais for my letters; and, being in a civilised country of stage-coaches, I determined to sell my lady friend and be off by the diligence that afternoon. Our yesterday's march, with the testimony of the driver who had pursued us up the long hill of St. Pierre, spread a favourable notion of my donkey's capabilities. Intending purchases were aware of an unrivalled opportunity. Before ten I had an offer of twenty-five francs; and before noon, after a desperate engagement, I sold her, saddle and all, for five-and-thirty. The pecuniary gain is not obvious, but I had bought freedom into the bargain.

St. Jean du Gard is a large place, and largely Protestant. The maire, a Protestant, asked me to help him in a small matter which is itself characteristic of the country. The young women of the Cévennes profit by the common religion and the difference of the language to go largely as governesses into England; and here was one, a native of Mialet, struggling with English circulars from two different agencies in London. I gave what help I could; and volunteered some advice, which struck me as being excellent.

One thing more I note. The phylloxera has ravaged the vineyards in this neighbourhood; and in the early morning, under some chestnuts by the river, I found a party of men working with a cider-press. I could not at first make out what they were after, and asked one fellow to explain.

'Making cider,' he said. '*Oui, c'est comme ca. Comme dans le nord!*'

There was a ring of sarcasm in his voice: the country was going to the devil.

It was not until I was fairly seated by the driver, and rattling through a rocky valley with dwarf olives, that I became aware of my bereavement. I had lost Modestine. Up to that moment I had thought I hated her; but now she was gone,

And oh!

The difference to me!

For twelve days we had been fast companions; we had travelled upwards of a hundred and twenty miles, crossed several respectable ridges, and jogged along with our six legs by many a rocky and many a boggy by-road. After the first day, although sometimes I was hurt and distant in manner, I still kept my patience; and as for her, poor soul! she had come to regard me as a god. She loved to eat out of my hand. She was patient, elegant in form, the colour of an ideal mouse, and inimitably small. Her faults were those of her race and sex; her virtues were her own. Farewell, and if for ever –

Father Adam wept when he sold her to me; after I had sold her in my turn, I was tempted to follow his example; and being alone with a stage-driver and four or five agreeable young men, I did not hesitate to yield to my emotion.[10]

Notes

1. Hunter Davies follows in Stevenson's footsteps in his entertaining travelogue, *The Teller of Tales: In Search of Robert Louis Stevenson* (New York: Interlink Books, 1996). The townspeople of contemporary Monastier 'acknowledge you here,' he writes. 'There's a plaque on a stone slab outside the post office, put there by an American, stating that this is where you started your journey, and the local museum has a 'Salle Robert Louis Stevenson,' which sounds impressive but is very disappointing. It does consist of a whole room, but most if it is bare wall and some dried flowers. The RLS memorabilia amount to a few faded cuttings and photographs, badly framed.' See Davies, p. 82.

2. On the centenary of Stevenson's trip, *The Cévennes Journal: Notes on a Journey through the French Highlands* was published (Edinburgh: Mainstream; New York: Taplinger, 1979), the first publication of the complete manuscript notebook kept by Stevenson on his journey. It featured Stevenson's original notes, in which he admits, among other things, how cruel he had to be to Modestine to get the beast moving at a regular pace.

3. Our Lady of the Snows, a Trappist monastery visited by Stevenson. Located about a 1/4 mile northeast of La Bastide, it is not open to the public but it does host spiritual retreats. (Tel.: 04-66-46-59-00).

4. Michel Eyquem Montaigne (1533–1592), French essayist.

5. Located in Perthshire, in the Scottish Highlands. Site of a famous battle associated with the defeat of John Graham of Claverhouse, the 'Bonny Dundee' of legend, against the Covenanters. See note 6 below.

6. French Protestants. In 1589, Henri IV issued the Edict of Nantes, granting religious freedom to France's Protestant subjects. In 1685, however, Louis XIV revoked it; in essence, denying the Protestants the right to practice their faith. Those Protestants who lived in the Cévennes decided to resist. The Camisard rebellion lasted until the 1790s. Stevenson found much in common between the Scottish Covenanters and the French Camisards.

7. Antoine Watteau (1684–1721), French painter.

8. Matthew 12:14.

9. Lord Byron (1788–1824), Anglo-Scottish poet.

10. Over the years, many travellers have followed Stevenson's footsteps in the Cévennes or have been inspired in other ways. The title of John Steinbeck's *Travels with Charley*, an account of the author's bittersweet journey across America in 1960 with his French poodle Charley, is a case in point. Stevenson's *Travels with a Donkey* was 'one of Steinbeck's favorite books.' See John Steinbeck, *Travels with Charley: In Search of America*. Introduction by Jay Parini (New York: Penguin Books, 1997), p. xvii. Interest has not subsided. In 1994, the Stevenson Trail, also known as the GR70, was created during the centenary year of RLS's French sojourn. Several companies continue to organise hikes along the trail. Donkey hires are also available. Based in Le Pont-de-Montvert, France, the Association Sur le Chemin de RL Stevenson 48220 promotes the Stevenson Trail. (Tel/fax: 04 66 45 86 31; www.chemin-stevenson.org).

Fontainebleau

VILLAGE COMMUNITIES OF PAINTERS

Fontainebleau originally appeared in the Magazine of Art
in May and June 1884.

I

THE charm of Fontainebleau is a thing apart.[1] It is a place that people love even more than they admire. The vigorous forest air, the silence, the majestic avenues of highway, the wilderness of tumbled boulders, the great age and dignity of certain groves – these are but ingredients, they are not the secret of the philtre. The place is sanative; the air, the light, the perfumes, and the shapes of things concord in happy harmony. The artist may be idle and not fear the 'blues.' He may dally with his life. Mirth, lyric mirth, and a vivacious classical contentment are of the very essence of the better kind of art; and these, in that most smiling forest, he has the chance to learn or to remember. Even on the plain of Biere, where the Angelus of Millet still tolls upon the ear of fancy, a larger air, a higher heaven, something ancient and healthy in the face of nature, purify the mind alike from dulness and hysteria. There is no place where the young are more gladly conscious of their youth, or the old better contented with their age.

The fact of its great and special beauty further recommends this country to the artist. The field was chosen by men in whose blood there still raced some of the gleeful or solemn exultation of great art – Millet who loved dignity like Michelangelo, Rousseau whose modern brush was dipped in the glamour of the ancients.[2] It was chosen before the day of that strange turn in the history of art, of which we now perceive the culmination in impressionistic tales and pictures – that voluntary aversion of the eye from all speciously strong and beautiful effects – that disinterested love of dulness which has set so many Peter Bells to paint the river-side primrose. It was then chosen for its proximity to Paris. And for the same cause, and by the force of tradition, the painter of to-day continues to inhabit and to paint it. There is in France scenery incomparable for romance and harmony. Provence, and the valley of the Rhone from Vienne to Tarascon, are one succession of masterpieces waiting for the brush. The beauty is not merely beauty; it tells, besides, a tale to the imagination, and surprises while it charms. Here you shall see castellated towns that would befit the scenery of dreamland; streets that glow with colour like cathedral windows; hills of the most exquisite proportions; flowers of every precious colour, growing thick like grass. All these, by the grace of railway travel, are brought to the very door of the modern painter; yet he does not seek them; he remains faithful to Fontainebleau, to the eternal bridge of Gretz, to the watering-pot cascade in Cernay valley. Even Fontainebleau was chosen for him; even in Fontainebleau he shrinks from what is sharply charactered. But one thing, at least, is certain, whatever he may choose to paint and in whatever manner, it is good for the artist to dwell among graceful shapes. Fontainebleau, if it be but quiet scenery, is classically graceful; and though the student may look for different qualities, this quality, silently present, will educate his hand and eye.

But, before all its other advantages – charm, loveliness, or proximity to Paris – comes the great fact that it is already colonised.[3] The institution of a painters' colony is a work of time and tact. The population must be conquered. The innkeeper has to be taught, and he soon learns, the lesson of unlimited credit; he must be taught to welcome as a favoured guest a young gentleman in a very greasy coat, and with little baggage beyond a box of colours and a canvas; and he must learn to preserve his faith in customers who will eat heartily and drink of the best, borrow money to buy tobacco, and perhaps not pay a stiver for a year.[4] A colour merchant has next to be attracted. A certain vogue must be given to the place, lest the painter, most gregarious of animals, should find himself alone. And no sooner are these first difficulties overcome, than fresh perils spring up upon the other side; and the bourgeois and the tourist are knocking at the gate. This is the crucial moment for the colony. If these intruders gain a footing, they not only banish freedom and amenity; pretty soon, by means of their long purses, they will have undone the education of the innkeeper; prices will rise and credit shorten; and the poor painter must fare farther on and find another hamlet. 'Not here, O Apollo!' will become his song. Thus Trouville and, the other day, St. Raphael were lost to the arts. Curious and not always edifying are the shifts that the French student uses to defend his lair; like the cuttlefish, he must sometimes blacken the waters of his chosen pool; but at such a time and for so practical a purpose Mrs. Grundy must allow him licence. Where his own purse and credit are not threatened, he will do the honours of his village generously. Any artist is made welcome, through whatever medium he may seek expression; science is respected; even the idler, if he prove, as he so rarely does, a gentleman, will soon begin to find himself at home. And when that essentially modern creature, the English or American girl-student, began to walk calmly into his favourite inns as if into a drawing-room at home, the French painter owned himself defenceless; he submitted or he fled. His French respectability, quite as precise as ours, though covering different provinces of life, recoiled aghast before the innovation. But the girls were painters; there was nothing to be done; and Barbizon, when I last saw it and for the time at least, was practically ceded to the fair invader. Paterfamilias, on the other hand, the common tourist, the holiday shopman, and the cheap young gentleman upon the spree, he hounded from his villages with every circumstance of contumely.

This purely artistic society is excellent for the young artist. The lads are mostly fools; they hold the latest orthodoxy in its crudeness; they are at that stage of education, for the most part, when a man is too much occupied with style to be aware of the necessity for any matter; and this, above all for the Englishman, is excellent. To work grossly at the trade, to forget sentiment, to think of his material and nothing else, is, for awhile at least, the king's highway of progress. Here, in England, too many painters and writers dwell dispersed, unshielded, among the intelligent bourgeois. These, when they are not merely indifferent, prate to him about the lofty aims and moral influence of art. And this is the lad's ruin. For art is, first of all and last of all, a trade. The love of words and not a desire to publish new discoveries, the love of form and not a novel reading of historical events, mark the vocation of the writer and the painter. The arabesque, properly speaking, and even in literature, is the first fancy of the artist; he first plays with his material as a child plays with a kaleidoscope; and he is already in a second stage when he begins to use his pretty counters for the end of representation. In that, he must pause long and toil faithfully; that is his apprenticeship; and it is only the few who will really grow beyond it, and go forward, fully equipped, to do the business of real art – to give life to abstractions and significance and charm to facts. In the meanwhile, let him dwell much among his fellow-craftsmen. They alone can take a serious interest in the childish tasks and pitiful successes of these years. They alone can behold with equanimity this fingering of the dumb keyboard, this polishing of empty sentences, this dull and literal painting of dull and insignificant subjects. Outsiders will spur him on. They will say, 'Why do you not write a great book? paint a great picture?' If his guardian angel fail him, they may even persuade him to the attempt, and, ten to one, his hand is coarsened and his style falsified for life.

And this brings me to a warning. The life of the apprentice to any art is both unstrained and pleasing; it is strewn with small successes in the midst of a career of failure, patiently supported; the heaviest scholar is conscious of a certain progress; and if he come not appreciably nearer to the art of Shakespeare, grows letter-perfect in the domain of A-B, ab. But the time comes when a man should cease prelusory gymnastic, stand up, put a violence upon his will, and, for better or worse, begin the business of creation. This evil day there is a tendency continually to postpone: above all with painters. They have made so many studies that it has become a habit; they make more, the walls of exhibitions blush with them; and death finds these aged students still busy with their horn-book. This class of man finds a congenial home in artist villages; in the slang of the English colony at Barbizon we used to call them 'Snoozers.' Continual returns to the city, the society of men farther advanced, the study of great works, a sense of humour or, if such a thing is to be had, a little religion or philosophy, are the means of treatment. It will be time enough to think of curing the malady after it has been caught; for to catch it is the very thing for which you seek that dream-land of the painters' village. 'Snoozing' is a part of the artistic education; and the rudiments must be learned stupidly, all else being forgotten, as if they were an object in themselves.

Lastly, there is something, or there seems to be something, in the very air of France that communicates the love of style.[5] Precision, clarity, the cleanly and crafty employment of material, a grace in the handling, apart from any value in the thought, seem to be acquired by the mere residence; or if not acquired, become at least the more appreciated. The air of Paris is alive with this technical inspiration. And to leave that airy city and awake next day upon the borders of the forest is but to change externals. The same spirit of dexterity and finish breathes from the long alleys and the lofty groves, from the wildernesses that are still pretty in their confusion, and the great plain that contrives to be decorative in its emptiness.

II

In spite of its really considerable extent, the forest of Fontainebleau is hardly anywhere tedious. I know the whole western side of it with what, I suppose, I may call thoroughness; well enough at least to testify that there is no square mile without some special character and charm. Such quarters, for instance, as the Long Rocher, the Bas-Breau, and the Reine Blanche, might be a hundred miles apart; they have scarce a point in common beyond the silence of the birds. The two last are really conterminous; and in both are tall and ancient trees that have outlived a thousand political vicissitudes. But in the one the great oaks prosper placidly upon an even floor; they beshadow a great field; and the air and the light are very free below their stretching boughs. In the other the trees find difficult footing; castles of white rock lie tumbled one upon another, the foot slips, the crooked viper slumbers, the moss clings in the crevice; and above it all the great beech goes spiring and casting forth her arms, and, with a grace beyond church architecture, canopies this rugged chaos. Meanwhile, dividing the two cantons, the broad white causeway of the Paris road runs in an avenue: a road conceived for pageantry and for triumphal marches, an avenue for an army; but, its days of glory over, it now lies grilling in the sun between cool groves, and only at intervals the vehicle of the cruising tourist is seen far away and faintly audible along its ample sweep. A little upon one side, and you find a district of sand and birch and boulder; a little upon the other lies the valley of Apremont, all juniper and heather; and close beyond that you may walk into a zone of pine trees. So artfully are the ingredients mingled. Nor must it be forgotten that, in all this part, you come continually forth upon a hill-top, and behold the plain, northward and westward, like an unrefulgent sea; nor that all day long the shadows keep changing; and at last, to the red fires of sunset, night succeeds, and with the night a new forest, full of whisper, gloom, and fragrance. There are few things more renovating than to leave Paris, the lamplit arches of the Carrousel, and the long alignment of the glittering streets, and to bathe the senses in this fragrant darkness of the wood.

In this continual variety the mind is kept vividly alive. It is a changeful place to paint, a stirring place to live in. As fast as your foot carries you, you pass from scene to scene, each vigorously painted in the colours of the sun, each endeared by that hereditary spell of forests on the mind of man who still remembers and salutes the ancient refuge of his race.

And yet the forest has been civilised throughout. The most savage corners bear a name, and have been cherished like antiquities; in the most remote, Nature has prepared and balanced her effects as if with conscious art; and man, with his guiding arrows of blue paint, has countersigned the picture. After your farthest wandering, you are never surprised to come forth upon the vast avenue of highway, to strike the centre point of branching alleys, or to find the aqueduct trailing, thousand-footed, through the brush. It is not a wilderness; it is rather a preserve. And, fitly enough, the centre of the maze is not a hermit's cavern. In the midst, a little mirthful town lies sunlit, humming with the business of pleasure; and the palace, breathing distinction and peopled by historic names, stands smokeless among gardens.

Perhaps the last attempt at savage life was that of the harmless humbug who called himself the hermit. In a great tree, close by the highroad, he had built himself a little cabin after the manner of the Swiss Family Robinson; thither he mounted at night, by the romantic aid of a rope ladder; and if dirt be any proof of sincerity, the man was savage as a Sioux. I had the pleasure of his acquaintance; he appeared grossly stupid, not in his perfect wits, and interested in nothing but small change; for that he had a great avidity. In the course of time he proved to be a chicken-stealer, and vanished from his perch; and perhaps from the first he was no true votary of forest freedom, but an ingenious, theatrically-minded beggar, and his cabin in the tree was only stock-in-trade to beg withal. The choice of his position would seem to indicate so much; for if in the forest there are no places still to be discovered, there are many that have been forgotten, and that lie unvisited. There, to be sure, are the blue arrows waiting to reconduct you, now blazed upon a tree, now posted in the corner of a rock. But your security from interruption is complete; you might camp for weeks, if there were only water, and not a soul suspect your presence; and if I may suppose the reader to have committed some great crime and come to me for aid, I think I could still find my way to a small cavern, fitted with a hearth and chimney, where he might lie perfectly concealed. A confederate landscape-painter might daily supply him with food; for water, he would have to make a nightly tramp as far as to the nearest pond; and at last, when the hue and cry began to blow over, he might get gently on the train at some side station, work round by a series of junctions, and be quietly captured at the frontier.

Thus Fontainebleau, although it is truly but a pleasure-ground, and although, in favourable weather, and in the more celebrated quarters, it literally buzzes with the tourist, yet has some of the immunities and offers some of the repose of natural forests. And the solitary, although he must return at night to his frequented inn, may yet pass the day with his own thoughts in the companionable silence of the trees. The demands of the imagination vary; some can be alone in a back garden looked upon by windows; others, like the ostrich, are content with a solitude that meets the eye; and others, again, expand in fancy to the very borders of their desert, and are irritably conscious of a hunter's camp in an adjacent county. To these last, of course, Fontainebleau will seem but an extended tea-garden: a Rosherville on a by-day. But to the plain man it offers solitude: an excellent thing in itself, and a good whet for company.

III

I was for some time a consistent Barbizonian; *et ego in Arcadia vixi*, it was a pleasant season; and that noiseless hamlet lying close among the borders of the wood is for me, as for so many others, a green spot in memory. The great Millet was just dead, the green shutters of his modest house were closed; his daughters were in mourning. The date of my first visit was thus an epoch in the history of art: in a lesser way, it was an epoch in the history of the Latin Quarter. *The Petit Cenacle*[6] was dead and buried; Murger and his crew of sponging vagabonds were all at rest from their expedients; the tradition of their real life was nearly lost; and the petrified legend of the *Vie de Boheme* had become a sort of gospel, and still gave the cue to zealous imitators.[7] But if the book be written in rose-water, the imitation was still farther expurgated; honesty was the rule; the innkeepers gave, as I have said, almost unlimited credit; they suffered the seediest painter to depart, to take all his belongings, and to leave his bill unpaid; and if they sometimes lost, it was by English and Americans alone. At the same time, the great influx of Anglo-Saxons had begun to affect the life of the studious. There had been disputes; and, in one instance at least, the English and the Americans had made common cause to prevent a cruel pleasantry. It would be well if nations and races could communicate their qualities; but in practice when they look upon each other, they have an eye to nothing but defects. The Anglo-Saxon is essentially dishonest; the French is devoid by nature of the principle that we call 'Fair Play.' The Frenchman marvelled at the scruples of his guest, and, when that defender of innocence retired over-seas and left his bills unpaid, he marvelled once again; the good and evil were, in his eyes, part and parcel of the same eccentricity; a shrug expressed his judgment upon both.

At Barbizon there was no master, no pontiff in the arts. Palizzi bore rule at Gretz – urbane, superior rule – his memory rich in anecdotes of the great men of yore, his mind fertile in theories; sceptical, composed, and venerable to the eye; and yet beneath these outworks, all twittering with Italian superstition, his eye scouting for omens, and the whole fabric of his manners giving way on the appearance of a hunchback. Cernay had Pelouse, the admirable, placid Pelouse, smilingly critical of youth, who, when a full-blown commercial traveller, suddenly threw down his samples, bought a colour-box, and became the master whom we have all admired. Marlotte, for a central figure, boasted Olivier de Penne. Only Barbizon, since the death of Millet, was a headless commonwealth.[8] Even its secondary lights, and those who in my day made the stranger welcome, have since deserted it. The good Lachevre has departed, carrying his household gods; and long before that Gaston Lafenestre was taken from our midst by an untimely death. He died before he had deserved success; it may be, he would never have deserved it; but his kind, comely, modest countenance still haunts the memory of all who knew him. Another – whom I will not name – has moved farther on, pursuing the strange Odyssey of his decadence. His days of royal favour had departed even then; but he still retained, in his narrower life at Barbizon, a certain stamp of conscious importance, hearty, friendly, filling the room, the occupant of several chairs; nor had he yet ceased his losing battle, still labouring upon great canvases that none would buy, still waiting the return of fortune. But these days also were too good to last; and the former favourite of two sovereigns fled, if I heard the truth, by night. There was a time when he was counted a great man, and Millet but a dauber; behold, how the whirligig of time brings in his revenges! To pity Millet is a piece of arrogance; if life be hard for such resolute and pious spirits, it is harder still for us, had we the wit to understand it; but we may pity his unhappier rival, who, for no apparent merit, was raised to opulence and momentary fame, and, through no apparent fault was suffered step by step to sink again to nothing. No misfortune can exceed the bitterness of such back-foremost progress, even bravely supported as it was; but to those also who were taken early from the easel, a regret is due. From all the young men of this period, one stood out by the vigour of his promise; he was in the age of fermentation, enamoured of eccentricities. 'Il faut faire de la peinture nouvelle,' was his watchword; but if time and experience had continued his education, if he had been granted health to return from these excursions to the steady and the central, I must believe that the name of Hills had become famous.

Siron's inn, that excellent artists' barrack, was managed upon easy principles. At any hour of the night, when you returned from wandering in the forest, you went to the billiard-room and helped yourself to liquors, or descended to the cellar and returned laden with beer or wine. The Sirons were all locked in slumber; there was none to check your inroads; only at the week's end a computation was made, the gross sum was divided, and a varying share set down to every lodger's name under the rubric: *estrats*. Upon the more long-suffering the larger tax was levied; and your bill lengthened in a direct proportion to the easiness of your disposition. At any hour of the morning, again, you could get your coffee or cold milk, and set forth into the forest. The doves had perhaps wakened you, fluttering into your chamber; and on the threshold of the inn you were met by the aroma of the forest. Close by were the great aisles, the mossy boulders, the interminable field of forest shadow. There you were free to dream and wander. And at noon, and again at six o'clock, a good meal awaited you on Siron's table. The whole of your accommodation, set aside that varying item of the *estrats*, cost you five francs a day; your bill was never offered you until you asked it; and if you were out of luck's way, you might depart for where you pleased and leave it pending.

IV

Theoretically, the house was open to all corners; practically, it was a kind of club. The guests protected themselves, and, in so doing, they protected Siron. Formal manners being laid aside, essential courtesy was the more rigidly exacted; the new arrival had to feel the pulse of the society; and a breach of its undefined observances was promptly punished. A man might be as plain, as dull, as slovenly, as free of speech as he desired; but to a touch of presumption or a word of hectoring these free Barbizonians were as sensitive as a tea-party of maiden ladies. I have seen people driven forth from Barbizon; it would be difficult to say in words what they had done, but they deserved their fate. They had shown themselves unworthy to enjoy these corporate freedoms; they had pushed themselves; they had 'made their head'; they wanted tact to appreciate the 'fine shades' of Barbizonian etiquette. And once they were condemned, the process of extrusion was ruthless in its cruelty; after one evening with the formidable Bodmer, the Baily of our commonwealth, the erring stranger was beheld no more; he rose exceedingly early the next day, and the first coach conveyed him from the scene of his discomfiture. These sentences of banishment were never, in my knowledge, delivered against an artist; such would, I believe, have been illegal; but the odd and pleasant fact is this, that they were never needed. Painters, sculptors, writers, singers, I have seen all of these in Barbizon; and some were sulky, and some blatant and inane; but one and all entered at once into the spirit of the association. This singular society is purely French, a creature of French virtues, and possibly of French defects. It cannot be imitated by the English. The roughness, the impatience, the more obvious selfishness, and even the more ardent friendships of the Anglo-Saxon, speedily dismember such a commonwealth. But this random gathering of young French painters, with neither apparatus nor parade of government, yet kept the life of the place upon a certain footing, insensibly imposed their etiquette upon the docile, and by caustic speech enforced their edicts against the unwelcome. To think of it is to wonder the more at the strange failure of their race upon the larger theatre. This inbred civility – to use the word in its completest meaning – this natural and facile adjustment of contending liberties, seems all that is required to make a governable nation and a just and prosperous country.

Our society, thus purged and guarded, was full of high spirits, of laughter, and of the initiative of youth. The few elder men who joined us were still young at heart, and took the key from their companions. We returned from long stations in the fortifying air, our blood renewed by the sunshine, our spirits refreshed by the silence of the forest; the Babel of loud voices sounded good; we fell to eat and play like the natural man; and in the high inn chamber, panelled with indifferent pictures and lit by candles guttering in the night air, the talk and laughter sounded far into the night. It was a good place and a good life for any naturally-minded youth; better yet for the student of painting, and perhaps best of all for the student of letters. He, too, was saturated in this atmosphere of style; he was shut out from the disturbing currents of the world, he might forget that there existed other and more pressing interests than that of art. But, in such a place, it was hardly possible to write; he could not drug his conscience, like the painter, by the production of listless studies; he saw himself idle among many who were apparently, and some who were really, employed; and what with the impulse of increasing health and the continual provocation of romantic scenes, he became tormented with the desire to work. He enjoyed a strenuous idleness full of visions, hearty meals, long, sweltering walks, mirth among companions; and still floating like music through his brain, foresights of great works that Shakespeare might be proud to have conceived, headless epics, glorious torsos of dramas, and words that were alive with import. So in youth, like Moses from the mountain, we have sights of that House Beautiful of art which we shall never enter. They are dreams and unsubstantial; visions of style that repose upon no base of human meaning; the last heart-throbs of that excited amateur who has to die in all of us before the artist can be born. But they come to us in such a rainbow of glory that all subsequent achievement appears dull and earthly in comparison. We were all artists; almost all in the age of illusion, cultivating an imaginary genius, and walking to the strains of some deceiving Ariel; small wonder, indeed, if we were happy! But art, of whatever nature, is a kind mistress; and though these dreams of youth fall by their own baselessness, others succeed, graver and more substantial; the symptoms change, the amiable malady endures; and still, at an equal distance, the House Beautiful shines upon its hill-top.

V

Grez lies out of the forest, down by the bright river.[9] It boasts a mill, an ancient church, a castle, and a bridge of many sterlings. And the bridge is a piece of public property; anonymously famous; beaming on the incurious dilettante from the walls of a hundred exhibitions. I have seen it in the Salon; I have seen it in the Academy; I have seen it in the last French Exposition, excellently done by Bloomer; in a black-and-white by Mr. A Henley, it once adorned this essay in the pages of the *Magazine of Art*. Long-suffering bridge! And if you visit Grez to-morrow, you shall find another generation, camped at the bottom of Chevillon's garden under their white umbrellas, and doggedly painting it again.

The bridge taken for granted, Grez is a less inspiring place than Barbizon. I give it the palm over Cernay. There is something ghastly in the great empty village square of Cernay, with the inn tables standing in one corner, as though the stage were set for rustic opera, and in the early morning all the painters breaking their fast upon white wine under the windows of the villagers. It is vastly different to awake in Grez, to go down the green inn-garden, to find the river streaming through the bridge, and to see the dawn begin across the poplared level. The meals are laid in the cool arbour, under fluttering leaves. The splash of oars and bathers, the bathing costumes out to dry, the trim canoes beside the jetty, tell of a society that has an eye to pleasure. There is 'something to do' at Grez. Perhaps, for that very reason, I can recall no such enduring ardours, no such glories of exhilaration, as among the solemn groves and uneventful hours of Barbizon. This 'something to do' is a great enemy to joy; it is a way out of it; you wreak your high spirits on some cut-and-dry employment, and behold them gone! But Grez is a merry place after its kind: pretty to see, merry to inhabit. The course of its pellucid river, whether up or down, is full of gentle attractions for the navigator: islanded reed-mazes where, in autumn, the red berries cluster; the mirrored and inverted images of trees, lilies, and mills, and the foam and thunder of weirs. And of all noble sweeps of roadway, none is nobler, on a windy dusk, than the highroad to Nemours between its lines of talking poplar.

But even Grez is changed. The old inn, long shored and trussed and buttressed, fell at length under the mere weight of years, and the place as it was is but a fading image in the memory of former guests. They, indeed, recall the ancient wooden stair; they recall the rainy evening, the wide hearth, the blaze of the twig fire, and the company that gathered round the pillar in the kitchen. But the material fabric is now dust; soon, with the last of its inhabitants, its very memory shall follow; and they, in their turn, shall suffer the same law, and, both in name and lineament, vanish from the world of men. 'For remembrance of the old house' sake,' as Pepys[10] once quaintly put it, let me tell one story. When the tide of invasion swept over France, two foreign painters were left stranded and penniless in Grez;

and there, until the war was over, the Chevillons ungrudgingly harboured them. It was difficult to obtain supplies; but the two waifs were still welcome to the best, sat down daily with the family to table, and at the due intervals were supplied with clean napkins, which they scrupled to employ. Madame Chevillon observed the fact and reprimanded them. But they stood firm; eat they must, but having no money they would soil no napkins.

VI

Nemours and Moret, for all they are so picturesque, have been little visited by painters. They are, indeed, too populous; they have manners of their own, and might resist the drastic process of colonisation. Montigny has been somewhat strangely neglected, I never knew it inhabited but once, when Will H Low[11] installed himself there with a barrel of *piquette*, and entertained his friends in a leafy trellis above the weir, in sight of the green country and to the music of the falling water. It was a most airy, quaint, and pleasant place of residence, just too rustic to be stagey; and from my memories of the place in general, and that garden trellis in particular – at morning, visited by birds, or at night, when the dew fell and the stars were of the party – I am inclined to think perhaps too favourably of the future of Montigny. Chailly-en-Biere has outlived all things, and lies dustily slumbering in the plain – the cemetery of itself. The great road remains to testify of its former bustle of postilions and carriage bells; and, like memorial tablets, there still hang in the inn room the paintings of a former generation, dead or decorated long ago. In my time, one man only, greatly daring, dwelt there. From time to time he would walk over to Barbizon like a shade revisiting the glimpses of the moon, and after some communication with flesh and blood return to his austere hermitage. But even he, when I last revisited the forest, had come to Barbizon for good, and closed the roll of Chaillyites. It may revive – but I much doubt it. Acheres and Recloses still wait a pioneer; Bourron is out of the question, being merely Grez over again, without the river, the bridge, or the beauty; and of all the possible places on the western side, Marlotte alone remains to be discussed. I scarcely know Marlotte, and, very likely for that reason, am not much in love with it. It seems a glaring and unsightly hamlet. The inn of Mother Antonie is unattractive; and its more reputable rival, though comfortable enough, is commonplace. Marlotte has a name; it is famous; if I were the young painter I would leave it alone in its glory.

VII

These are the words of an old stager; and though time is a good conservative in forest places, much may be untrue to-day. Many of us have passed Arcadian days there and moved on, but yet left a portion of our souls behind us buried in the woods. I would not dig for these reliquiae; they are incommunicable treasures that will not enrich the finder; and yet there may lie, interred below great oaks or scattered along forest paths, stores of youth's dynamite and dear remembrances. And as one generation passes on and renovates the field of tillage for the next, I entertain a fancy that when the young men of to-day go forth into the forest they shall find the air still vitalised by the spirits of their predecessors, and, like those 'unheard melodies' that are the sweetest of all, the memory of our laughter shall still haunt the field of trees. Those merry voices that in woods call the wanderer farther, those thrilling silences and whispers of the groves, surely in Fontainebleau they must be vocal of me and my companions? We are not content to pass away entirely from the scenes of our delight; we would leave, if but in gratitude, a pillar and a legend.

One generation after another fall like honey-bees upon this memorable forest, rifle its sweets, pack themselves with vital memories, and when the theft is consummated depart again into life richer, but poorer also. The forest, indeed, they have possessed, from that day forward it is theirs indissolubly, and they will return to walk in it at night in the fondest of their dreams, and use it for ever in their books and pictures. Yet when they made their packets, and put up their notes and sketches, something, it should seem, had been forgotten. A projection of themselves shall appear to haunt unfriended these scenes of happiness, a natural child of fancy, begotten and forgotten unawares. Over the whole field of our wanderings such fetches are still travelling like indefatigable bagmen; but the imps of Fontainebleau, as of all beloved spots, are very long of life, and memory is piously unwilling to forget their orphanage. If anywhere about that wood you meet my airy bantling, greet him with tenderness. He was a pleasant lad, though now abandoned. And when it comes to your own turn to quit the forest, may you leave behind you such another; no Antony or Werther, let us hope, no tearful whipster, but, as becomes this not uncheerful and most active age in which we figure, the child of happy hours.

No art, it may be said, was ever perfect, and not many noble, that has not been mirthfully conceived. And no man, it may be added, was ever anything but a wet blanket and a cross to his companions who boasted not a copious spirit of enjoyment. Whether as man or artist let the youth make haste to Fontainebleau, and once there let him address himself to the spirit of the place; he will learn more from exercise than from studies, although both are necessary; and if he can get into his heart the gaiety and inspiration of the woods he will have gone far to undo the evil of his sketches. A spirit once well strung up to the concert-pitch of the primeval out-of-doors will hardly dare to finish a study and magniloquently ticket it a picture. The incommunicable thrill of things, that is the tuning-fork by which we test the flatness of our art. Here it is that Nature teaches and condemns, and still spurs up to further effort and new failure. Thus it is that she sets us blushing at our ignorant and tepid works; and the more we find of these inspiring shocks the less shall we be apt to love the literal in our productions. In all sciences and senses the letter kills; and to-day, when cackling human geese express their ignorant condemnation of all studio pictures, it is a lesson most useful to be learnt. Let the young painter go to Fontainebleau, and while he stupefies himself with studies that teach him the mechanical side of his trade, let him walk in the great air, and be a servant of mirth, and not pick and botanise, but wait upon the moods of nature. So he will learn – or learn not to forget – the poetry of life and earth, which, when he has acquired his track, will save him from joyless reproduction.

Notes

1. The Barbizon School was an artists' colony located at the edge of the forest of Fontainebleau. By the time Stevenson and his cousin, Bob, were there, it was in decline: ' ... the great painters associated with it no longer active. Rousseau was dead, Millet about to die.' See Philip Callow, *Louis: A Life of Robert Louis Stevenson* (Chicago: Ivan R Dee, 2001), p. 70.

2. Both French painters. Jean-Francais Millet (1814–1975) was best known for *The Angelus* (1857–59) and *The Gleaners* (1857), Theodore Rousseau (1812–1867) for *The Forest of Fontainebleau, Morning* (1850).

3. Stevenson savoured the community of artists – and the camaraderie of spirit – that flourished at Fontainebleau.

4. Siron's Inn in Barbizon was such a place. 'Here all artists entered into a communal spirit and were welcomed as comrades, no matter how personally unprepossessing they were.' See Frank McLynn, *Robert Louis Stevenson: A Biography* (New York: Random House, 1993), p. 95.

5. 'His love affair with France was deeper than recreational bohemianism and more passionate than the fashion of the day allowed. France's manners, mores, and habits of studied enjoyment struck chords in him during every visit. He was tied to Scotland ... but he found in France a sense of freedom that touched every part of his life and art.' See Ian Bell, *Dreams of Exile – Robert Louis Stevenson: A Biography* (New York: Henry Holt, 1992), p. 91.

6. Stevenson is referring here to a group of French Romantics, led by Petrus Borel (1809–1859).

7. Henri Murger (1822–1861), author of the wildly popular *Scenes de la vie de Boheme*, the inspiration of Puccini's opera *La Boheme* and, more recently, the Broadway sensation, *Rent*.

8. 'By 1875 there was no single commanding figure at Barbizon; at Grez there was Palizzi, at Cernay, Pelouse and at Marlotte, Olivier de Peune, and although Stevenson visited all these places in turn, it was Barbizon he particularly liked, because there was no 'king'.' McLynn, *Robert Louis Stevenson*, p. 95.

9. Grez was a particular favourite of Parisian artists.

10. Samuel Pepys (1633–1703), English diarist.

11. Will Hicok Low (1853–1932), American artist who studied in France in the 1870s. He wrote about his friendship with Stevenson in *A Chronicle of Friendships, 1873–1900* (London, 1908).

America

FROM *The Amateur Emigrant*

Partly written in Monterey and San Francisco, The Amateur Emigrant *was posthumously published in a shortened version in 1895. The full version did not appear until 1966 under the title of* From Scotland to Silverado, *edited by James D Hart (The Belknap Press of Harvard University Press). Since then, there have been various editions. In the introduction to the Hogarth edition (1984) noted travel writer Jonathan Raban called* The Amateur Emigrant *' the best account ever written of the great European adventure in the nineteenth century, the passage to America ... [It] has a richness of detail and feeling that is unmatched in American literature ...' The Amateur Emigrant, he wrote, is 'the best book [Stevenson] ever wrote – a marvellous piece of writing ... a genuine original.'*

THE SECOND CABIN

I first encountered my fellow-passengers on the Broomielaw in Glasgow.[1] Thence we descended the Clyde in no familiar spirit, but looking askance on each other as on possible enemies. A few Scandinavians, who had already grown acquainted on the North Sea, were friendly and voluble over their long pipes; but among English speakers distance and suspicion reigned supreme. The sun was soon overclouded, the wind freshened and grew sharp as we continued to descend the widening estuary; and with the falling temperature the gloom among the passengers increased. Two of the women wept. Any one who had come aboard might have supposed we were all absconding from the law. There was scarce a word interchanged, and no common sentiment but that of cold united us, until at length, having touched at Greenock,[2] a pointing arm and a rush to the starboard now announced that our ocean steamer was in sight. There she lay in mid-river, at the Tail of the Bank, her sea-signal flying: a wall of bulwark, a street of white deck-houses, an aspiring forest of spars, larger than a church, and soon to be as populous as many an incorporated town in the land to which she was to bear us.

I was not, in truth, a steerage passenger. Although anxious to see the worst of emigrant life, I had some work to finish on the voyage, and was advised to go by the second cabin, where at least I should have a table at command. The advice was excellent; but to understand the choice, and what I gained, some outline of the internal disposition of the ship will first be necessary. In her very nose is Steerage No. 1, down two pair of stairs. A little abaft, another companion, labelled Steerage No. 2 and 3, gives admission to three galleries, two running forward towards Steerage No. 1, and the third aft towards the engines. The starboard forward gallery is the second cabin. Away abaft the engines and below the officers' cabins, to complete our survey of the vessel, there is yet a third nest of steerages, labelled 4 and 5. The second cabin, to return, is thus a modified oasis in the very heart of the steerages. Through the thin partition you can hear the steerage passengers being sick, the rattle of tin dishes as they sit at meals, the varied accents in which they converse, the crying of their children terrified by this new experience, or the clean flat smack of the parental hand in chastisement.

There are, however, many advantages for the inhabitant of this strip. He does not require to bring his own bedding or dishes, but finds berths and a table completely if somewhat roughly furnished. He enjoys a distinct superiority in diet; but this, strange to say, differs not only on different ships, but on the same ship according as her head is to the east or west. In my own experience, the principal difference between our table and that of the true steerage passenger was the table itself, and the crockery plates from which we ate. But lest I should show myself ungrateful, let me recapitulate every advantage. At breakfast we had a choice between tea and coffee for beverage; a choice not easy to make, the two were so surprisingly alike. I found that I could sleep after the coffee and lay awake after the tea, which is proof conclusive of some chemical disparity; and even by the palate I could distinguish a smack of snuff in the former from a flavour of boiling and dish-cloths in the second. As a matter of fact, I have seen passengers, after many sips, still doubting which had been supplied them. In the way of eatables at the same meal we were gloriously favoured; for in addition to porridge, which was common to all, we had Irish stew, sometimes a bit of fish, and sometimes rissoles. The dinner of soup, roast fresh beef, boiled salt junk, and potatoes, was, I believe, exactly common to the steerage and the second cabin; only I have heard it rumoured that our potatoes were of a superior brand; and twice a week, on pudding-days, instead of duff, we had a saddle-bag filled with currants under the name of a plum-pudding. At tea we were served with some broken meat from the saloon; sometimes in the comparatively elegant form of spare patties or rissoles; but as a general thing mere chicken-bones and flakes of fish, neither hot nor cold. If these were not the scrapings of plates their looks belied them sorely; yet we were all too hungry to be proud, and fell to these leavings greedily. These, the bread, which was excellent, and the soup and porridge which were both good, formed my whole diet throughout the voyage; so that except for the broken meat and the convenience of a table I might as well have been in the steerage outright. Had they given me porridge again in the evening, I should have been perfectly contented with the fare. As it was, with a few biscuits and some whisky and water before turning in, I kept my body going and my spirits up to the mark.

The last particular in which the second cabin passenger remarkably stands ahead of his brother of the steerage is one altogether of sentiment. In the steerage there are males and females; in the second cabin ladies and gentlemen. For some time after I came aboard I thought I was only a male; but in the course of a voyage of discovery between decks, I came on a brass plate, and learned that I was still a gentleman. Nobody knew it, of course. I was lost in the crowd of males and females, and rigorously confined to the same quarter of the deck. Who could tell whether I housed on the port or starboard side of steerage No. 2 and 3? And it was only there that my superiority became practical; everywhere else I was incognito, moving among my inferiors with simplicity, not so much as a swagger to indicate that I was a gentleman after all, and had broken meat to tea. Still, I was like one with a patent of nobility in a drawer at home; and when I felt out of spirits I could go down and refresh myself with a look of that brass plate.

For all these advantages I paid but two guineas. Six guineas is the steerage fare; eight that by the second cabin; and when you remember that the steerage passenger must supply bedding and dishes, and, in five cases out of ten, either brings some dainties with him, or privately pays the steward for extra rations, the difference in price becomes almost nominal. Air comparatively fit to breathe, food comparatively varied, and the satisfaction of being still privately a gentleman, may thus be had almost for the asking. Two of my fellow-passengers in the second cabin had already made the passage by the cheaper fare, and declared it was an experiment not to be repeated. As I go on to tell about my steerage friends, the reader will perceive that they were not alone in their opinion. Out of ten with whom I was more or less intimate, I am sure not fewer than five vowed, if they returned, to travel second cabin; and all who had left their wives behind them assured me they would go without the comfort of their presence until they could afford to bring them by saloon.

Our party in the second cabin was not perhaps the most interesting on board. Perhaps even in the saloon there was as much good-will and character. Yet it had some elements of curiosity. There was a mixed group of Swedes, Danes, and Norsemen, one of whom, generally known by the name of 'Johnny', in spite of his own protests, greatly diverted us by his clever, cross-country efforts to speak English, and became on the strength of that an universal favourite – it takes so little in this world of shipboard to create a popularity. There was, besides, a Scots mason, known from his favourite dish as 'Irish Stew', three or four nondescript Scots, a fine young Irishman, O'Reilly, and a pair of young men who deserve a special word of condemnation. One of them was Scots; the other claimed to be American; admitted, after some fencing, that he was born in England; and ultimately proved to be an Irishman born and nurtured, but ashamed to own his country. He had a sister on board, whom he faithfully neglected throughout the voyage, though she was not only sick, but much his senior, and had nursed and cared for him in childhood. In appearance he was like an imbecile Henry the Third of France. The Scotsman, though perhaps as big an ass, was not so dead of heart; and I have only bracketed them together because they were fast friends, and disgraced themselves equally by their conduct at the table.

Next, to turn to topics more agreeable, we had a newly-married couple, devoted to each other, with a pleasant story of how they had first seen each other years ago at a preparatory school, and that very afternoon he had carried her books home for her. I do not know if this story will be plain to southern readers; but to me it recalls many a school idyll, with wrathful swains of eight and nine confronting each other stride-legs, flushed with jealousy; for to carry home a young lady's books was both a delicate attention and a privilege.

Then there was an old lady, or indeed I am not sure that she was as much old as antiquated and strangely out of place, who had left her husband, and was travelling all the way to Kansas by herself. We had to take her own word that she was married; for it was sorely contradicted by the testimony of her appearance. Nature seemed to have sanctified her for the single state; even the colour of her hair was incompatible with matrimony, and her husband, I thought, should be a man of saintly spirit and phantasmal bodily presence. She was ill, poor thing; her soul turned from the viands; the dirty tablecloth shocked her like an impropriety; and the whole strength of her endeavour was bent upon keeping her watch true to Glasgow time till she should reach New York. They had heard reports, her husband and she, of some unwarrantable disparity of hours between these two cities; and with a spirit commendably scientific, had seized on this occasion to put them to the proof. It was a good thing for the old lady; for she passed much leisure time in studying the watch. Once, when prostrated by sickness, she let it run down. It was inscribed on her harmless mind in letters of adamant that the hands of a watch must never be turned backwards; and so it behoved her to lie in wait for the exact moment ere she started it again. When she imagined this was about due, she sought out one of the young second-cabin Scotsmen, who was embarked on the same experiment as herself and had hitherto been less neglectful. She was in quest of two o'clock; and when she learned it was already seven on the shores of Clyde, she lifted up her voice and cried 'Gravy!' I had not heard this innocent expletive since I was a young child; and I suppose it must have been the same with the other Scotsmen present, for we all laughed our fill.

Last but not least, I come to my excellent friend Mr. Jones. It would be difficult to say whether I was his right-hand man, or he mine, during the voyage. Thus at table I carved, while he only scooped gravy; but at our concerts, of which more anon, he was the president who called up performers to sing, and I but his messenger who ran his errands and pleaded privately with the over-modest. I knew I liked Mr. Jones from the moment I saw him. I thought him by his face to be Scottish; nor could his accent undeceive me. For as there is a *lingua franca* of many tongues on the moles and in the feluccas of the Mediterranean, so there is a free or common accent among English-speaking men who follow the sea. They catch a twang in a New England Port; from a cockney skipper, even a Scotsman sometimes learns to drop an H; a word of a dialect is picked up from another band in the forecastle; until often the result is undecipherable, and you have to ask for the man's place of birth. So it was with Mr. Jones. I thought him a Scotsman who had been long to sea; and yet he was from Wales, and had been most of his life a blacksmith at an inland forge; a few years in America and half a score of ocean voyages having sufficed to modify his speech into the common pattern. By his own account he was both strong and skilful in his trade. A few years back, he had been married and after a fashion a rich man; now the wife was dead and the money gone. But his was the nature that looks forward, and goes on from one year to another and through all the extremities of fortune undismayed; and if the sky were to fall to-morrow, I should look to see Jones, the day following, perched on a step-ladder and getting things to rights. He was always hovering round inventions like a bee over a flower, and lived in a dream of patents. He had with him a patent medicine, for instance, the composition of which he had bought years ago for five dollars from an American pedlar, and sold the other day for a hundred pounds (I think it was) to an English apothecary. It was called Golden Oil, cured all maladies without exception; and I am bound to say that I partook of it myself with good results. It is a character of the man that he was not only perpetually dosing himself with Golden Oil, but wherever there was a head aching or a finger cut, there would be Jones with his bottle.

If he had one taste more strongly than another, it was to study character. Many an hour have we two walked upon the deck dissecting our neighbours in a spirit that was too purely scientific to be called unkind; whenever a quaint or human trait slipped out in conversation, you might have seen Jones and me exchanging glances; and we could hardly go to bed in comfort till we had exchanged notes and discussed the day's experience. We were then like a couple of anglers comparing a day's kill. But the fish we angled for were of a metaphysical species, and we angled as often as not in one another's baskets. Once, in the midst of a serious talk, each found there was a scrutinising eye upon himself; I own I paused in embarrassment at this double detection; but Jones, with a better civility, broke into a peal of unaffected laughter, and declared, what was the truth, that there was a pair of us indeed.

EARLY IMPRESSIONS

We steamed out of the Clyde on Thursday night, and early on the Friday forenoon we took in our last batch of emigrants at Lough Foyle, in Ireland, and said farewell to Europe. The company was now complete, and began to draw together, by inscrutable magnetisms, upon the decks. There were Scots and Irish in plenty, a few English, a few Americans, a good handful of Scandinavians, a German or two, and one Russian; all now belonging for ten days to one small iron country on the deep.

As I walked the deck and looked round upon my fellow-passengers, thus curiously assorted from all northern Europe, I began for the first time to understand the nature of emigration. Day by day throughout the passage, and thenceforward across all the States, and on to the shores of the Pacific, this knowledge grew more clear and melancholy. Emigration, from a word of the most cheerful import, came to sound most dismally in my ear. There is nothing more agreeable to picture and nothing more pathetic to behold. The abstract idea, as conceived at home, is hopeful and adventurous. A young man, you fancy, scorning restraints and helpers, issues forth into life, that great battle, to fight for his own hand. The most pleasant stories of ambition, of difficulties overcome, and of ultimate success, are but as episodes to this great epic of self-help. The epic is composed of individual heroisms; it stands to them as the victorious war which subdued an empire stands to the personal act of bravery which spiked a single cannon and was adequately rewarded with a medal. For in emigration the young men enter direct and by the shipload on their heritage of work; empty continents swarm, as at the bo's'un's whistle, with industrious hands, and whole new empires are domesticated to the service of man.

This is the closet picture, and is found, on trial, to consist mostly of embellishments. The more I saw of my fellow-passengers, the less I was tempted to the lyric note. Comparatively few of the men were below thirty; many were married, and encumbered with families; not a few were already up in years; and this itself was out of tune with my imaginations, for the ideal emigrant should certainly be young. Again, I thought he should offer to the eye some bold type of humanity, with bluff or hawk-like features, and the stamp of an eager and pushing disposition. Now those around me were for the most part quiet, orderly, obedient citizens, family men broken by adversity, elderly youths who had failed to place themselves in life, and people who had seen better days. Mildness was the prevailing character; mild mirth and mild endurance. In a word, I was not taking part in an impetuous and conquering sally, such as swept over Mexico or Siberia, but found myself, like Marmion, 'in the lost battle, borne down by the flying.'

Labouring mankind had in the last years, and throughout Great Britain, sustained a prolonged and crushing series of defeats. I had heard vaguely of these reverses; of whole streets of houses standing deserted by the Tyne, the cellar-doors broken and removed for firewood; of homeless men loitering at the street-corners of Glasgow with their chests beside them; of closed factories, useless strikes, and starving girls. But I had never taken them home to me or represented these distresses livingly to my imagination.

A turn of the market may be a calamity as disastrous as the French retreat from Moscow; but it hardly lends itself to lively treatment, and makes a trifling figure in the morning papers. We may struggle as we please, we are not born economists. The individual is more affecting than the mass. It is by the scenic accidents, and the appeal to the carnal eye, that for the most part we grasp the significance of tragedies. Thus it was only now, when I found myself involved in the rout, that I began to appreciate how sharp had been the battle. We were a company of the rejected; the drunken, the incompetent, the weak, the prodigal, all who had been unable to prevail against circumstances in the one land, were now fleeing pitiful-ly to another; and though one or two might still succeed, all had already failed. We were a shipful of failures, the broken men of England. Yet it must not be sup-posed that these people exhibited depression. The scene, on the contrary, was cheerful. Not a tear was shed on board the vessel. All were full of hope for the future, and showed an inclination to innocent gaiety. Some were heard to sing, and all began to scrape acquaintance with small jests and ready laughter.

The children found each other out like dogs, and ran about the decks scraping acquaintance after their fashion also. 'What do you call your mither?' I heard one ask. 'Mawmaw,' was the reply, indicating, I fancy, a shade of difference in the social scale. When people pass each other on the high seas of life at so early an age, the contact is but slight, and the relation more like what we may imagine to be the friendship of flies than that of men; it is so quickly joined, so easily dis-solved, so open in its communications and so devoid of deeper human qualities. The children, I observed, were all in a band, and as thick as thieves at a fair, while their elders were still ceremoniously manoeuvring on the outskirts of acquain-tance. The sea, the ship, and the seamen were soon as familiar as home to these half-conscious little ones. It was odd to hear them, throughout the voyage, employ shore words to designate portions of the vessel. 'Go 'way doon to yon dyke,' I heard one say, probably meaning the bulwark. I often had my heart in my mouth, watching them climb into the shrouds or on the rails, while the ship went swing-ing through the waves; and I admired and envied the courage of their mothers, who sat by in the sun and looked on with composure at these perilous feats. 'He'll maybe be a sailor,' I heard one remark; 'now's the time to learn.' I had been on the point of running forward to interfere, but stood back at that, reproved. Very few in the more delicate classes have the nerve to look upon the peril of one dear to them; but the life of poorer folk, where necessity is so much more immediate and imperious, braces even a mother to this extreme of endurance. And perhaps, after all, it is better that the lad should break his neck than that you should break his spirit.

And since I am here on the chapter of the children, I must mention one little fellow, whose family belonged to Steerage No. 4 and 5, and who, wherever he went, was like a strain of music round the ship. He was an ugly, merry, unbreeched child of three, his lint-white hair in a tangle, his face smeared with suet and treacle; but he ran to and fro with so natural a step, and fell and picked himself up again with such grace and good-humour, that he might fairly be called beautiful when he was in motion. To meet him, crowing with laughter and beat-ing an accompaniment to his own mirth with a tin spoon upon a tin cup, was to meet a little triumph of the human species. Even when his mother and the rest of his family lay sick and prostrate around him, he sat upright in their midst and sang aloud in the pleasant heartlessness of infancy.

Throughout the Friday, intimacy among us men made but a few advances. We discussed the probable duration of the voyage, we exchanged pieces of information, naming our trades, what we hoped to find in the new world, or what we were fleeing from in the old; and, above all, we condoled together over the food and the vileness of the steerage. One or two had been so near famine that you may say they had run into the ship with the devil at their heels; and to these all seemed for the best in the best of possible steamers. But the majority were hugely contented. Coming as they did from a country in so low a state as Great Britain, many of them from Glasgow, which commercially speaking was as good as dead, and many having long been out of work, I was surprised to find them so dainty in their notions. I myself lived almost exclusively on bread, porridge, and soup, precisely as it was supplied to them, and found it, if not luxurious, at least sufficient. But these working men were loud in their outcries. It was not 'food for human beings', it was 'only fit for pigs', it was 'a disgrace.' Many of them lived almost entirely upon biscuit, others on their own private supplies, and some paid extra for better rations from the ship. This marvellously changed my notion of the degree of luxury habitual to the artisan. I was prepared to hear him grumble, for grumbling is the traveller's pastime; but I was not prepared to find him turn away from a diet which was palatable to myself. Words I should have disregarded, or taken with a liberal allowance; but when a man prefers dry biscuit there can be no question of the sincerity of his disgust.

With one of their complaints I could most heartily sympathise. A single night of the steerage had filled them with horror. I had myself suffered, even in my decent-second-cabin berth, from the lack of air; and as the night promised to be fine and quiet, I determined to sleep on deck, and advised all who complained of their quarters to follow my example. I dare say a dozen of others agreed to do so, and I thought we should have been quite a party. Yet, when I brought up my rug about seven bells, there was no one to be seen but the watch. That chimerical terror of good night-air, which makes men close their windows, list their doors, and seal themselves up with their own poisonous exhalations, had sent all these healthy workmen down below. One would think we had been brought up in a fever country; yet in England the most malarious districts are in the bedchambers.

I felt saddened at this defection, and yet half-pleased to have the night so quietly to myself. The wind had hauled a little ahead on the starboard bow, and was dry but chilly. I found a shelter near the fire-hole, and made myself snug for the night.

The ship moved over the uneven sea with a gentle and cradling movement. The ponderous, organic labours of the engine in her bowels occupied the mind, and prepared it for slumber. From time to time a heavier lurch would disturb me as I lay, and recall me to the obscure borders of consciousness; or I heard, as it were through a veil, the clear note of the clapper on the brass and the beautiful sea-cry, 'All's well!' I know nothing, whether for poetry or music, that can surpass the effect of these two syllables in the darkness of a night at sea.

The day dawned fairly enough, and during the early part we had some pleasant hours to improve acquaintance in the open air; but towards nightfall the wind freshened, the rain began to fall, and the sea rose so high that it was difficult to keep ones footing on the deck. I have spoken of our concerts. We were indeed a musical ship's company, and cheered our way into exile with the fiddle, the accordion, and the songs of all nations. Good, bad, or indifferent – Scottish, English, Irish, Russian, German or Norse, – the songs were received with generous applause. Once or twice, a recitation, very spiritedly rendered in a powerful Scottish accent, varied the proceedings; and once we sought in vain to dance a quadrille, eight men of us together, to the music of the violin. The performers were all humorous, frisky fellows, who loved to cut capers in private life; but as soon as they were arranged for the dance, they conducted themselves like so many mutes at a funeral. I have never seen decorum pushed so far; and as this was not expected, the quadrille was soon whistled down, and the dancers departed under a cloud. Eight Frenchmen, even eight Englishmen from another rank of society, would have dared to make some fun for themselves and the spectators; but the working man, when sober, takes an extreme and even melancholy view of personal deportment. A fifth-form schoolboy is not more careful of dignity. He dares not be comical; his fun must escape from him unprepared, and above all, it must be unaccompanied by any physical demonstration. I like his society under most circumstances, but let me never again join with him in public gambols.

But the impulse to sing was strong, and triumphed over modesty and even the inclemencies of sea and sky. On this rough Saturday night, we got together by the main deck-house, in a place sheltered from the wind and rain. Some clinging to a ladder which led to the hurricane deck, and the rest knitting arms or taking hands, we made a ring to support the women in the violent lurching of the ship; and when we were thus disposed, sang to our hearts' content. Some of the songs were appropriate to the scene; others strikingly the reverse. Bastard doggrel of the music-hall, such as, 'Around her splendid form, I weaved the magic circle,' sounded bald, bleak, and pitifully silly. 'We don't want to fight, but, by Jingo, if we do,' was in some measure saved by the vigour and unanimity with which the chorus was thrown forth into the night. I observed a Platt-Deutsch mason, entirely innocent of English, adding heartily to the general effect. And perhaps the German mason is but a fair example of the sincerity with which the song was rendered; for nearly all with whom I conversed upon the subject were bitterly opposed to war, and attributed their own misfortunes, and frequently their own taste for whisky, to the campaigns in Zululand and Afghanistan.

Every now and again, however, some song that touched the pathos of our situation was given forth; and you could hear by the voices that took up the burden how the sentiment came home to each, 'The Anchor's Weighed' was true for us. We were indeed 'Rocked on the bosom of the stormy deep.' How many of us could say with the singer, 'I'm lonely to-night, love, without you,' or, 'Go, some one, and tell them from me, to write me a letter from home'! And when was there a more appropriate moment for 'Auld Lang Syne' than now, when the land, the friends, and the affections of that mingled but beloved time were fading and fleeing behind us in the vessel's wake? It pointed forward to the hour when these labours should be overpast, to the return voyage, and to many a meeting in the sanded inn, when those who had parted in the spring of youth should again drink a cup of kindness in their age. Had not Burns contemplated emigration, I scarce believe he would have found that note. All Sunday the weather remained wild and cloudy; many were prostrated by sickness; only five sat down to tea in the second cabin, and two of these departed abruptly ere the meal was at an end. The Sabbath was observed strictly by the majority of the emigrants. I heard an old woman express her surprise that 'the ship didna gae doon,' as she saw some one pass her with a chess-board on the holy day. Some sang Scottish psalms. Many went to service, and in true Scottish fashion came back ill pleased with their divine. 'I didna think he was an experienced preacher,' said one girl to me.

It was a bleak, uncomfortable day; but at night, by six bells, although the wind had not yet moderated, the clouds were all wrecked and blown away behind the rim of the horizon, and the stars came out thickly overhead. I saw Venus burning as steadily and sweetly across this hurly-burly of the winds and waters as ever at home upon the summer woods. The engine pounded, the screw tossed out of the water with a roar, and shook the ship from end to end; the bows battled with loud reports against the billows: and as I stood in the lee-scuppers and looked up to where the funnel leaned out, over my head, vomiting smoke, and the black and monstrous top-sails blotted, at each lurch, a different crop of stars, it seemed as if all this trouble were a thing of small account, and that just above the mast reigned peace unbroken and eternal.

Notes

1. The Broomielaw is the site of Glasgow's harbour, on the north bank of the River Clyde. According to Joe Fisher, its name means 'gorse or broom-covered slope'. See Joe Fisher, *The Glasgow Encyclopedia* (Edinburgh: Mainstream Publishing, 1994).
2. Greenock is an important industrial town on the Clyde Estuary. It has been an embarkation point for many emigrants over the centuries.

Across the Plains

Part of this account was originally published in Longman's Magazine *in 1883, but it did not appear as a separate volume until nearly a decade later when it was published as the title piece of Stevenson's 1892 essay collection of the same name. Several years later, portions of* The Amateur Emigrant *and* Across the Plains *were posthumously published together as* The Amateur Emigrant: From the Clyde to Sandy Hook *in 1895.*

NEW YORK

As we drew near to New York I was at first amused, and then somewhat staggered, by the cautious and the grisly tales that went the round. You would have thought we were to land upon a cannibal island. You must speak to no one in the streets, as they would not leave you till you were rooked and beaten. You must enter a hotel with military precautions; for the least you had to apprehend was to awake next morning without money or baggage, or necessary raiment, a lone forked radish in a bed; and if the worst befell, you would instantly and mysteriously disappear from the ranks of mankind.

I have usually found such stories correspond to the least modicum of fact. Thus I was warned, I remember, against the roadside inns of the Cévennes, and that by a learned professor; and when I reached Pradelles the warning was explained – it was but the far-away rumour and reduplication of a single terrifying story already half a century old, and half forgotten in the theatre of the events. So I was tempted to make light of these reports against America. But we had on board with us a man whose evidence it would not do to put aside. He had come near these perils in the body; he had visited a robber inn. The public has an old and well-grounded favour for this class of incident, and shall be gratified to the best of my power.

My fellow-passenger, whom we shall call M'Naughten, had come from New York to Boston with a comrade, seeking work. They were a pair of rattling blades; and, leaving their baggage at the station, passed the day in beer saloons, and with congenial spirits, until midnight struck. Then they applied themselves to find a lodging, and walked the streets till two, knocking at houses of entertainment and being refused admittance, or themselves declining the terms. By two the inspiration of their liquor had begun to wear off; they were weary and humble, and after a great circuit found themselves in the same street where they had begun their search, and in front of a French hotel where they had already sought accommodation. Seeing the house still open, they returned to the charge. A man in a white cap sat in an office by the door. He seemed to welcome them more warmly than when they had first presented themselves, and the charge for the night had somewhat unaccountably fallen from a dollar to a quarter. They thought him ill-looking, but paid their quarter apiece, and were shown upstairs to the top of the house. There, in a small room, the man in the white cap wished them pleasant slumbers.

It was furnished with a bed, a chair, and some conveniences. The door did not lock on the inside; and the only sign of adornment was a couple of framed pictures, one close above the head of the bed, and the other opposite the foot, and both curtained, as we may sometimes see valuable water-colours, or the portraits of the dead, or works of art more than usually skittish in the subject. It was perhaps in the hope of finding something of this last description that M'Naughten's comrade pulled aside the curtain of the first. He was startlingly disappointed. There was no picture. The frame surrounded, and the curtain was designed to hide, an oblong aperture in the partition, through which they looked forth into the dark corridor. A person standing without could easily take a purse from under the pillow, or even strangle a sleeper as he lay abed. M'Naughten and his comrade stared at each other like Vasco's seamen, 'with a wild surmise'; and then the latter, catching up the lamp, ran to the other frame and roughly raised the curtain. There he stood, petrified; and M'Naughten, who had followed, grasped him by the wrist in terror. They could see into another room, larger in size than that which they occupied, where three men sat crouching and silent in the dark. For a second or so these five persons looked each other in the eyes, then the curtain was dropped, and M'Naughten and his friend made but one bolt of it out of the room and downstairs. The man in the white cap said nothing as they passed him; and they were so pleased to be once more in the open night that they gave up all notion of a bed, and walked the streets of Boston till the morning.

No one seemed much cast down by these stories, but all inquired after the address of a respectable hotel; and I, for my part, put myself under the conduct of Mr. Jones. Before noon of the second Sunday we sighted the low shores outside of New York harbour; the steerage passengers must remain on board to pass through Castle Garden[1] on the following morning; but we of the second cabin made our escape along with the lords of the saloon; and by six o'clock Jones and I issued into West Street, sitting on some straw in the bottom of an open baggage-wagon. It rained miraculously; and from that moment till on the following night I left New York, there was scarce a lull, and no cessation of the downpour. The roadways were flooded; a loud strident noise of falling water filled the air; the restaurants smelt heavily of wet people and wet clothing.

It took us but a few minutes, though it cost us a good deal of money, to be rattled along West Street to our destination: 'Reunion House, No. 10 West Street, one minutes walk from Castle Garden; convenient to Castle Garden, the Steamboat Landings, California Steamers and Liverpool Ships; Board and Lodging per day 1 dollar, single meals 25 cents, lodging per night 25 cents; private rooms for families; no charge for storage or baggage; satisfaction guaranteed to all persons; Michael Mitchell, Proprietor.' Reunion House was, I may go the length of saying, a humble hostelry. You entered through a long bar-room, thence passed into a little dining-room, and thence into a still smaller kitchen. The furniture was of the plainest; but the bar was hung in the American taste, with encouraging and hospitable mottoes.

Jones was well known; we were received warmly; and two minutes afterwards I had refused a drink from the proprietor, and was going on, in my plain European fashion, to refuse a cigar, when Mr. Mitchell sternly interposed, and explained the situation. He was offering to treat me, it appeared, whenever an American bar-keeper proposes anything, it must be borne in mind that he is offering to treat; and if I did not want a drink, I must at least take the cigar. I took it bashfully, feeling I had begun my American career on the wrong foot. I did not enjoy that cigar; but this may have been from a variety of reasons, even the best cigar often failing to please if you smoke three-quarters of it in a drenching rain.

For many years America was to me a sort of promised land; 'westward the march of empire holds its way'; the race is for the moment to the young; what has been and what is we imperfectly and obscurely know; what is to be yet lies beyond the flight of our imaginations. Greece, Rome, and Judaea are gone by forever, leaving to generations the legacy of their accomplished work; China still endures, an old-inhabited house in the brand-new city of nations; England has already declined, since she has lost the States; and to these States, therefore, yet unde-veloped, full of dark possibilities, and grown, like another Eve, from one rib out of the side of their own old land, the minds of young men in England turn natu-rally at a certain hopeful period of their age. It will be hard for an American to understand the spirit. But let him imagine a young man, who shall have grown up in an old and rigid circle, following bygone fashions and taught to distrust his own fresh instincts, and who now suddenly hears of a family of cousins, all about his own age, who keep house together by themselves and live far from restraint and tradition; let him imagine this, and he will have some imperfect notion of the sen-timent with which spirited English youths turn to the thought of the American Republic. It seems to them as if, out west, the war of life was still conducted in the open air, and on free barbaric terms; as if it had not yet been narrowed into parlours, nor begun to be conducted, like some unjust and dreary arbitration, by compromise, costume forms of procedure, and sad, senseless self-denial. Which of these two he prefers, a man with any youth still left in him will decide rightly for himself. He would rather be houseless than denied a pass-key; rather go with-out food than partake of stalled ox in stiff, respectable society; rather be shot out of hand than direct his life according to the dictates of the world.

He knows or thinks nothing of the Maine Laws, the Puritan sourness, the fierce, sordid appetite for dollars, or the dreary existence of country towns. A few wild story-books which delighted his childhood form the imaginative basis of his picture of America. In course of time, there is added to this a great crowd of stimulating details – vast cities that grow up as by enchantment; the birds, that have gone south in autumn, returning with the spring to find thousands camped upon their marshes, and the lamps burning far and near along populous streets; forests that disappear like snow; countries larger than Britain that are cleared and settled, one man running forth with his household goods before another, while the bear and the Indian are yet scarce aware of their approach; oil that gushes from the earth; gold that is washed or quarried in the brooks or glens of the Sierras; and all that bustle, courage, action, and constant kaleidoscopic change that Walt Whitman has seized and set forth in his vigorous, cheerful, and loquacious verses.

Here I was at last in America, and was soon out upon New York streets, spying for things foreign. The place had to me an air of Liverpool; but such was the rain that not Paradise itself would have looked inviting. We were a party of four, under two umbrellas; Jones and I and two Scots lads, recent immigrants, and not indisposed to welcome a compatriot. They had been six weeks in New York, and neither of them had yet found a single job or earned a single halfpenny. Up to the present they were exactly out of pocket by the amount of the fare.

The lads soon left us. Now I had sworn by all my gods to have such a dinner as would rouse the dead; there was scarce any expense at which I should have hesitated; the devil was in it, but Jones and I should dine like heathen emperors. I set to work, asking after a restaurant; and I chose the wealthiest and most gastronomical-looking passers-by to ask from. Yet, although I had told them I was willing to pay anything in reason, one and all sent me off to cheap, fixed-price houses, where I would not have eaten that night for the cost of twenty dinners. I do not know if this were characteristic of New York, or whether it was only Jones and I who looked un-dinerly and discouraged enterprising suggestions. But at length, by our own sagacity, we found a French restaurant, where there was a French waiter, some fair French cooking, some so-called French wine, and French coffee to conclude the whole. I never entered into the feelings of Jack on land so completely as when I tasted that coffee.

I suppose we had one of the 'private rooms for families' at Reunion House. It was very small, furnished with a bed, a chair, and some clothes-pegs; and it derived all that was necessary for the life of the human animal through two borrowed lights; one looking into the passage, and the second opening, without sash, into another apartment, where three men fitfully snored, or in intervals of wakefulness, drearily mumbled to each other all night long. It will be observed that this was almost exactly the disposition of the room in M'Naughten's story. Jones had the bed; I pitched my camp upon the floor; he did not sleep until near morning, and I, for my part, never closed an eye.

At sunrise I heard a cannon fired; and shortly afterwards the men in the next room gave over snoring for good, and began to rustle over their toilettes. The sound of their voices as they talked was low and like that of people watching by the sick. Jones, who had at last begun to doze, tumbled and murmured, and every now and then opened unconscious eyes upon me where I lay. I found myself growing eerier and eerier, for I dare say I was a little fevered by my restless night, and hurried to dress and get downstairs.

You had to pass through the rain, which still fell thick and resonant, to reach a lavatory on the other side of the court. There were three basin-stands, and a few crumpled towels and pieces of wet soap, white and slippery like fish; nor should I forget a looking- glass and a pair of questionable combs. Another Scots lad was here, scrubbing his face with a good will. He had been three months in New York and had not yet found a single job nor earned a single halfpenny. Up to the present, he also was exactly out of pocket by the amount of the fare. I began to grow sick at heart for my fellow-emigrants.

Of my nightmare wanderings in New York I spare to tell. I had a thousand and one things to do; only the day to do them in, and a journey across the continent before me in the evening. It rained with patient fury; every now and then I had to get under cover for a while in order, so to speak, to give my mackintosh a rest; for under this continued drenching it began to grow damp on the inside. I went to banks, post-offices, railway-offices, restaurants, publishers, booksellers, money-changers, and wherever I went a pool would gather about my feet, and those who were careful of their floors would look on with an unfriendly eye. Wherever I went, too, the same traits struck me: the people were all surprisingly rude and surprisingly kind. The money-changer cross-questioned me like a French commissary, asking my age, my business, my average income, and my destination, beating down my attempts at evasion, and receiving my answers in silence; and yet when all was over, he shook hands with me up to the elbows, and sent his lad nearly a quarter of a mile in the rain to get me books at a reduction. Again, in a very large publishing and bookselling establishment, a man, who seemed to be the manager, received me as I had certainly never before been received in any human shop, indicated squarely that he put no faith in my honesty, and refused to look up the names of books or give me the slightest help or information, on the ground, like the steward, that it was none of his business. I lost my temper at last, said I was a stranger in America and not learned in their etiquette; but I would assure him, if he went to any bookseller in England, of more handsome usage. The boast was perhaps exaggerated; but like many a long shot, it struck the gold. The manager passed at once from one extreme to the other; I may say that from that moment he loaded me with kindness; he gave me all sorts of good advice, wrote me down addresses, and came bareheaded into the rain to point me out a restaurant, where I might lunch, nor even then did he seem to think that he had done enough. These are (it is as well to be bold in statement) the manners of America. It is this same opposition that has most struck me in people of almost all classes and from east to west. By the time a man had about strung me up to be the death of him by his insulting behaviour, he himself would be just upon the point of melting into confidence and serviceable attentions. Yet I suspect, although I have met with the like in so many parts, that this must be the character of some particular state or group of states, for in America, and this again in all classes, you will find some of the softest-mannered gentlemen in the world.

I was so wet when I got back to Mitchell's toward the evening, that I had simply to divest myself of my shoes, socks, and trousers, and leave them behind for the benefit of New York city. No fire could have dried them ere I had to start; and to pack them in their present condition was to spread ruin among my other possessions. With a heavy heart I said farewell to them as they lay a pulp in the middle of a pool upon the floor of Mitchell's kitchen. I wonder if they are dry by now. Mitchell hired a man to carry my baggage to the station, which was hard by, accompanied me thither himself, and recommended me to the particular attention of the officials. No one could have been kinder. Those who are out of pocket may go safely to Reunion House, where they will get decent meals and find an honest and obliging landlord. I owed him this word of thanks, before I enter fairly on the second and far less agreeable chapter of my emigrant experience.

NOTES BY THE WAY TO COUNCIL BLUFFS

MONDAY. – It was, if I remember rightly, five o'clock when we were all signalled to be present at the Ferry Depot of the railroad. An emigrant ship had arrived at New York on the Saturday night, another on the Sunday morning, our own on Sunday afternoon, a fourth early on Monday; and as there is no emigrant train on Sunday a great part of the passengers from these four ships was concentrated on the train by which I was to travel. There was a babel of bewildered men, women, and children. The wretched little booking-office, and the baggage-room, which was not much larger, were crowded thick with emigrants, and were heavy and rank with the atmosphere of dripping clothes. Open carts full of bedding stood by the half-hour in the rain. The officials loaded each other with recriminations. A bearded, mildewed little man, whom I take to have been an emigrant agent, was all over the place, his mouth full of brimstone, blustering and interfering. It was plain that the whole system, if system there was, had utterly broken down under the strain of so many passengers.

My own ticket was given me at once, and an oldish man, who preserved his head in the midst of this turmoil, got my baggage registered, and counselled me to stay quietly where I was till he should give me the word to move. I had taken along with me a small valise, a knapsack, which I carried on my shoulders, and in the bag of my railway rug the whole of *Bancroft's History of the United States*, in six fat volumes. It was as much as I could carry with convenience even for short distances, but it insured me plenty of clothing, and the valise was at that moment, and often after, useful for a stool. I am sure I sat for an hour in the baggage-room, and wretched enough it was; yet, when at last the word was passed to me and I picked up my bundles and got under way, it was only to exchange discomfort for downright misery and danger.

I followed the porters into a long shed reaching downhill from West Street to the river. It was dark, the wind blew clean through it from end to end; and here I found a great block of passengers and baggage, hundreds of one and tons of the other. I feel I shall have a difficulty to make myself believed; and certainly the scene must have been exceptional, for it was too dangerous for daily repetition. It was a tight jam; there was no fair way through the mingled mass of brute and living obstruction. Into the upper skirts of the crowd porters, infuriated by hurry and overwork, clove their way with shouts. I may say that we stood like sheep, and that the porters charged among us like so many maddened sheep-dogs; and I believe these men were no longer answerable for their acts. It mattered not what they were carrying, they drove straight into the press, and when they could get no farther, blindly discharged their barrowful. With my own hand, for instance, I saved the life of a child as it sat upon its mother's knee, she sitting on a box; and since I heard of no accident, I must suppose that there were many similar interpositions in the course of the evening. It will give some idea of the state of mind to which we were reduced if I tell you that neither the porter nor the mother of the child paid the least attention to my act. It was not till some time after that I understood what I had done myself, for to ward off heavy boxes seemed at the moment a natural incident of human life. Cold, wet, clamour, dead opposition to progress, such as one encounters in an evil dream, had utterly daunted the spirits. We had accepted this purgatory as a child accepts the conditions of the world. For my part, I shivered a little, and my back ached wearily; but I believe I had neither a hope nor a fear, and all the activities of my nature had become tributary to one massive sensation of discomfort.

At length, and after how long an interval I hesitate to guess, the crowd began to move, heavily straining through itself. About the same time some lamps were lighted, and threw a sudden flare over the shed. We were being filtered out into the river boat for Jersey City. You may imagine how slowly this filtering proceeded, through the dense, choking crush, every one overladen with packages or children, and yet under the necessity of fishing out his ticket by the way; but it ended at length for me, and I found myself on deck under a flimsy awning and with a trifle of elbow-room to stretch and breathe in. This was on the starboard; for the bulk of the emigrants stuck hopelessly on the port side, by which we had entered. In vain the seamen shouted to them to move on, and threatened them with shipwreck. These poor people were under a spell of stupor, and did not stir a foot. It rained as heavily as ever, but the wind now came in sudden claps and capfuls, not without danger to a boat so badly ballasted as ours; and we crept over the river in the darkness, trailing one paddle in the water like a wounded duck, and passed ever and again by huge, illuminated steamers running many knots, and heralding their approach by strains of music. The contrast between these pleasure embarkations and our own grim vessel, with her list to port and her freight of wet and silent emigrants, was of that glaring description which we count too obvious for the purposes of art.

The landing at Jersey City was done in a stampede. I had a fixed sense of calamity, and to judge by conduct, the same persuasion was common to us all. A panic selfishness, like that produced by fear, presided over the disorder of our landing. People pushed, and elbowed, and ran, their families following how they could. Children fell, and were picked up to be rewarded by a blow. One child, who had lost her parents, screamed steadily and with increasing shrillness, as though verging towards a fit; an official kept her by him, but no one else seemed so much as to remark her distress; and I am ashamed to say that I ran among the rest. I was so weary that I had twice to make a halt and set down my bundles in the hundred yards or so between the pier and the railway station, so that I was quite wet by the time that I got under cover. There was no waiting-room, no refreshment room; the cars were locked; and for at least another hour, or so it seemed, we had to camp upon the draughty, gaslit platform. I sat on my valise, too crushed to observe my neighbours; but as they were all cold, and wet, and weary, and driven stupidly crazy by the mismanagement to which we had been subjected, I believe they can have been no happier than myself. I bought half-a-dozen oranges from a boy, for oranges and nuts were the only refection to be had. As only two of them had even a pretence of juice, I threw the other four under the cars, and beheld, as in a dream, grown people and children groping on the track after my leavings.

At last we were admitted into the cars, utterly dejected, and far from dry. For my own part, I got out a clothes-brush, and brushed my trousers as hard as I could till I had dried them and warmed my blood into the bargain; but no one else, except my next neighbour to whom I lent the brush, appeared to take the least precaution. As they were, they composed themselves to sleep. I had seen the lights of Philadelphia, and been twice ordered to change carriages and twice countermanded, before I allowed myself to follow their example.

TUESDAY. – When I awoke, it was already day; the train was standing idle; I was in the last carriage, and, seeing some others strolling to and fro about the lines, I opened the door and stepped forth, as from a caravan by the wayside. We were near no station, nor even, as far as I could see, within reach of any signal. A green, open, undulating country stretched away upon all sides. Locust trees and a single field of Indian corn gave it a foreign grace and interest; but the contours

190

of the land were soft and English. It was not quite England, neither was it quite France; yet like enough either to seem natural in my eyes. And it was in the sky, and not upon the earth, that I was surprised to find a change. Explain it how you may, and for my part I cannot explain it at all, the sun rises with a different splendour in America and Europe. There is more clear gold and scarlet in our old country mornings; more purple, brown, and smoky orange in those of the new. It may be from habit, but to me the coming of day is less fresh and inspiriting in the latter; it has a duskier glory, and more nearly resembles sunset; it seems to fit some subsequential, evening epoch of the world, as though America were in fact, and not merely in fancy, farther from the orient of Aurora and the springs of day. I thought so then, by the railroad side in Pennsylvania, and I have thought so a dozen times since in far distant parts of the continent. If it be an illusion it is one very deeply rooted, and in which my eyesight is accomplice.

Soon after a train whisked by, announcing and accompanying its passage by the swift beating of a sort of chapel bell upon the engine; and as it was for this we had been waiting, we were summoned by the cry of 'All aboard!' and went on again upon our way. The whole line, it appeared, was topsy-turvy; an accident at midnight having thrown all the traffic hours into arrear. We paid for this in the flesh, for we had no meals all that day. Fruit we could buy upon the cars; and now and then we had a few minutes at some station with a meagre show of rolls and sandwiches for sale; but we were so many and so ravenous that, though I tried at every opportunity, the coffee was always exhausted before I could elbow my way to the counter.

Our American sunrise had ushered in a noble summer's day. There was not a cloud; the sunshine was baking; yet in the woody river valleys among which we wound our way, the atmosphere preserved a sparkling freshness till late in the afternoon. It had an inland sweetness and variety to one newly from the sea; it smelt of woods, rivers, and the delved earth. These, though in so far a country, were airs from home. I stood on the platform by the hour; and as I saw, one after another, pleasant villages, carts upon the highway and fishers by the stream, and heard cockcrows and cheery voices in the distance, and beheld the sun, no longer shining blankly on the plains of ocean, but striking among shapely hills and his light dispersed and coloured by a thousand accidents of form and surface, I began to exult with myself upon this rise in life like a man who had come into a rich estate. And when I had asked the name of a river from the brakesman, and heard that it was called the Susquehanna, the beauty of the name seemed to be part and parcel of the beauty of the land. As when Adam with divine fitness named the creatures, so this word Susquehanna was at once accepted by the fancy. That was the name, as no other could be, for that shining river and desirable valley.

None can care for literature in itself who do not take a special pleasure in the sound of names; and there is no part of the world where nomenclature is so rich, poetical, humorous, and picturesque as the United States of America. All times, races, and languages have brought their contribution. Pekin is in the same State with Euclid, with Bellefontaine, and with Sandusky. Chelsea, with its London associations of red brick, Sloane Square, and the King's Road, is own suburb to stately and primeval Memphis; there they have their seat, translated names of cities, where the Mississippi runs by Tennessee and Arkansas; and both, while I was crossing the continent, lay, watched by armed men, in the horror and isolation of a plague. Old, red Manhattan lies, like an Indian arrowhead under a steam factory, below anglified New York. The names of the States and Territories themselves form a chorus of sweet and most romantic vocables: Delaware, Ohio, Indiana, Florida, Dakota, Iowa, Wyoming, Minnesota, and the Carolinas; there are few poems with a nobler music for the ear: a songful, tuneful land; and if the new Homer shall arise from the Western continent, his verse will be enriched, his pages sing spontaneously, with the names of states and cities that would strike the fancy in a business circular.

Late in the evening we were landed in a waiting-room at Pittsburg. I had now under my charge a young and sprightly Dutch widow with her children; these I was to watch over providentially for a certain distance farther on the way; but as I found she was furnished with a basket of eatables, I left her in the waiting-room to seek a dinner for myself. I mention this meal, not only because it was the first of which I had partaken for about thirty hours, but because it was the means of my first introduction to a coloured gentleman. He did me the honour to wait upon me after a fashion, while I was eating; and with every word, look, and gesture marched me farther into the country of surprise. He was indeed strikingly unlike the negroes of Mrs. Beecher Stowe, or the Christy Minstrels[2] of my youth. Imagine a gentleman, certainly somewhat dark, but of a pleasant warm hue, speaking English with a slight and rather odd foreign accent, every inch a man of the world, and armed with manners so patronisingly superior that I am at a loss to name their parallel in England. A butler perhaps rides as high over the unbut-lered, but then he sets you right with a reserve and a sort of sighing patience which one is often moved to admire. And again, the abstract butler never stoops to familiarity. But the coloured gentleman will pass you a wink at a time; he is familiar like an upper form boy to a fag; he unbends to you like Prince Hal with Poins and Falstaff. He makes himself at home and welcome. Indeed, I may say, this waiter behaved himself to me throughout that supper much as, with us, a young, free, and not very self-respecting master might behave to a good-looking chambermaid. I had come prepared to pity the poor negro, to put him at his ease, to prove in a thousand condescensions that I was no sharer in the prejudice of race; but I assure you I put my patronage away for another occasion, and had the grace to be pleased with that result.

Seeing he was a very honest fellow, I consulted him upon a point of etiquette:

if one should offer to tip the American waiter? Certainly not, he told me. Never. It would not do. They considered themselves too highly to accept. They would even resent the offer. As for him and me, we had enjoyed a very pleasant conversation; he, in particular, had found much pleasure in my society; I was a stranger; this was exactly one of those rare conjunctures.... Without being very clear seeing, I can still perceive the sun at noonday; and the coloured gentleman deftly pocketed a quarter.

WEDNESDAY. – A little after midnight I convoyed my widow and orphans on board the train; and morning found us far into Ohio. This had early been a favourite home of my imagination; I have played at being in Ohio by the week, and enjoyed some capital sport there with a dummy gun, my person being still unbreeched. My preference was founded on a work which appeared in *Cassell's Family Paper*, and was read aloud to me by my nurse. It narrated the doings of one Custaloga, an Indian brave, who, in the last chapter, very obligingly washed the paint off his face and became Sir Reginald Somebody-or-other; a trick I never forgave him. The idea of a man being an Indian brave, and then giving that up to be a baronet, was one which my mind rejected. It offended verisimilitude, like the pretended anxiety of Robinson Crusoe and others to escape from uninhabited islands.

But Ohio was not at all as I had pictured it. We were now on those great plains which stretch unbroken to the Rocky Mountains. The country was flat like Holland, but far from being dull. All through Ohio, Indiana, Illinois, and Iowa, or for as much as I saw of them from the train and in my waking moments, it was rich and various, and breathed an elegance peculiar to itself. The tall corn pleased the eye; the trees were graceful in themselves, and framed the plain into long, aerial vistas; and the clean, bright, gardened townships spoke of country fare and pleasant summer evenings on the stoop. It was a sort of flat paradise; but, I am afraid, not unfrequented by the devil. That morning dawned with such a freezing chill as I have rarely felt; a chill that was not perhaps so measurable by instrument, as it struck home upon the heart and seemed to travel with the blood. Day came in with a shudder. White mists lay thinly over the surface of the plain, as we see them more often on a lake; and though the sun had soon dispersed and drunk them up, leaving an atmosphere of fever heat and crystal pureness from horizon to horizon, the mists had still been there, and we knew that this paradise was haunted by killing damps and foul malaria. The fences along the line bore but two descriptions of advertisement; one to recommend tobaccos, and the other to vaunt remedies against the ague. At the point of day, and while we were all in the grasp of that first chill, a native of the state, who had got in at some way station, pronounced it, with a doctoral air, 'a fever and ague morning.'

The Dutch widow was a person of some character. She had conceived at first sight a great aversion for the present writer, which she was at no pains to conceal.

But being a woman of a practical spirit, she made no difficulty about accepting my attentions, and encouraged me to buy her children fruits and candies, to carry all her parcels, and even to sleep upon the floor that she might profit by my empty seat. Nay, she was such a rattle by nature, and, so powerfully moved to autobiographical talk, that she was forced, for want of a better, to take me into confidence and tell me the story of her life. I heard about her late husband, who seemed to have made his chief impression by taking her out pleasuring on Sundays. I could tell you her prospects, her hopes, the amount of her fortune, the cost of her housekeeping by the week, and a variety of particular matters that are not usually disclosed except to friends. At one station, she shook up her children to look at a man on the platform and say if he were not like Mr. Z.; while to me she explained how she had been keeping company with this Mr. Z., how far matters had proceeded, and how it was because of his desistance that she was now travelling to the West. Then, when I was thus put in possession of the facts, she asked my judgment on that type of manly beauty. I admired it to her heart's content. She was not, I think, remarkably veracious in talk, but broidered as fancy prompted, and built castles in the air out of her past; yet she had that sort of candour, to keep me, in spite of all these confidences, steadily aware of her aversion. Her parting words were ingeniously honest. 'I am sure,' said she, 'we all OUGHT to be very much obliged to you.' I cannot pretend that she put me at my ease; but I had a certain respect for such a genuine dislike. A poor nature would have slipped, in the course of these familiarities, into a sort of worthless toleration for me.

We reached Chicago in the evening. I was turned out of the cars, bundled into an omnibus, and driven off through the streets to the station of a different railroad. Chicago seemed a great and gloomy city. I remember having subscribed, let us say sixpence, towards its restoration at the period of the fire;[3] and now when I beheld street after street of ponderous houses and crowds of comfortable burghers, I thought it would be a graceful act for the corporation to refund that sixpence, or, at the least, to entertain me to a cheerful dinner. But there was no word of restitution. I was that city's benefactor, yet I was received in a third-class waiting-room, and the best dinner I could get was a dish of ham and eggs at my own expense.

I can safely say, I have never been so dog-tired as that night in Chicago. When it was time to start, I descended the platform like a man in a dream. It was a long train, lighted from end to end; and car after car, as I came up with it, was not only filled but overflowing. My valise, my knapsack, my rug, with those six ponderous tomes of Bancroft, weighed me double; I was hot, feverish, painfully athirst; and there was a great darkness over me, an internal darkness, not to be dispelled by gas. When at last I found an empty bench, I sank into it like a bundle of rags, the world seemed to swim away into the distance, and my consciousness dwindled within me to a mere pin's head, like a taper on a foggy night.

When I came a little more to myself, I found that there had sat down beside me a very cheerful, rosy little German gentleman, somewhat gone in drink, who was talking away to me, nineteen to the dozen, as they say. I did my best to keep up the conversation; for it seemed to me dimly as if something depended upon that. I heard him relate, among many other things, that there were pickpockets on the train, who had already robbed a man of forty dollars and a return ticket; but though I caught the words, I do not think I properly understood the sense until next morning; and I believe I replied at the time that I was very glad to hear it. What else he talked about I have no guess; I remember a gabbling sound of words, his profuse gesticulation, and his smile, which was highly explanatory: but no more. And I suppose I must have shown my confusion very plainly; for, first, I saw him knit his brows at me like one who has conceived a doubt; next, he tried me in German, supposing perhaps that I was unfamiliar with the English tongue; and finally, in despair, he rose and left me. I felt chagrined; but my fatigue was too crushing for delay, and, stretching myself as far as that was possible upon the bench, I was received at once into a dreamless stupor.

The little German gentleman was only going a little way into the suburbs after a DINER FIN, and was bent on entertainment while the journey lasted. Having failed with me, he pitched next upon another emigrant, who had come through from Canada, and was not one jot less weary than myself. Nay, even in a natural state, as I found next morning when we scraped acquaintance, he was a heavy, uncommunicative man. After trying him on different topics, it appears that the little German gentleman flounced into a temper, swore an oath or two, and departed from that car in quest of livelier society. Poor little gentleman! I suppose he thought an emigrant should be a rollicking, free-hearted blade, with a flask of foreign brandy and a long, comical story to beguile the moments of digestion.

THURSDAY. – I suppose there must be a cycle in the fatigue of travelling, for when I awoke next morning, I was entirely renewed in spirits and ate a hearty breakfast of porridge, with sweet milk, and coffee and hot cakes, at Burlington upon the Mississippi. Another long day's ride followed, with but one feature worthy of remark. At a place called Creston, a drunken man got in. He was aggressively friendly, but, according to English notions, not at all unpresentable upon a train. For one stage he eluded the notice of the officials; but just as we were beginning to move out of the next station, Cromwell by name, by came the conductor. There was a word or two of talk; and then the official had the man by the shoulders, twitched him from his seat, marched him through the car, and sent him flying on to the track. It was done in three motions, as exact as a piece of drill. The train was still moving slowly, although beginning to mend her pace, and the drunkard got his feet without a fall. He carried a red bundle, though not so red as his cheeks; and he shook this menacingly in the air with one hand, while the other stole behind him to the region of the kidneys. It was the first indication that I had come among revolvers, and I observed it with some emotion. The conductor stood on the steps with one hand on his hip, looking back at him; and perhaps this attitude imposed upon the creature, for he turned without further ado, and went off staggering along the track towards Cromwell followed by a peal of laughter from the cars. They were speaking English all about me, but I knew I was in a foreign land.

Twenty minutes before nine that night, we were deposited at the Pacific Transfer Station near Council Bluffs, on the eastern bank of the Missouri river. Here we were to stay the night at a kind of caravanserai, set apart for emigrants. But I gave way to a thirst for luxury, separated myself from my companions, and marched with my effects into the Union Pacific Hotel. A white clerk and a coloured gentleman whom, in my plain European way, I should call the boots, were installed behind a counter like bank tellers. They took my name, assigned me a number, and proceeded to deal with my packages. And here came the tug of war. I wished to give up my packages into safe keeping; but I did not wish to go to bed. And this, it appeared, was impossible in an American hotel.

It was, of course, some inane misunderstanding, and sprang from my unfamiliarity with the language. For although two nations use the same words and read the same books, intercourse is not conducted by the dictionary. The business of life is not carried on by words, but in set phrases, each with a special and almost a slang signification. Some international obscurity prevailed between me and the coloured gentleman at Council Bluffs; so that what I was asking, which seemed very natural to me, appeared to him a monstrous exigency. He refused, and that with the plainness of the West. This American manner of conducting matters of business is, at first, highly unpalatable to the European. When we approach a man in the way of his calling, and for those services by which he earns his bread, we consider him for the time being our hired servant. But in the American opinion, two gentlemen meet and have a friendly talk with a view to exchanging favours if they shall agree to please. I know not which is the more convenient, nor even which is the more truly courteous. The English stiffness unfortunately tends to be continued after the particular transaction is at an end, and thus favours class separations. But on the other hand, these equalitarian plainnesses leave an open field for the insolence of Jack-in-office.

I was nettled by the coloured gentleman's refusal, and unbuttoned my wrath under the similitude of ironical submission. I knew nothing, I said, of the ways of American hotels; but I had no desire to give trouble. If there was nothing for it but to get to bed immediately, let him say the word, and though it was not my habit, I should cheerfully obey.

He burst into a shout of laughter. 'Ah!' said he, 'you do not know about America. They are fine people in America. Oh! you will like them very well. But you mustn't get mad. I know what you want. You come along with me.'

And issuing from behind the counter, and taking me by the arm like an old acquaintance, he led me to the bar of the hotel.

'There,' said he, pushing me from him by the shoulder, 'go and have a drink!'

THE EMIGRANT TRAIN

All this while I had been travelling by mixed trains, where I might meet with Dutch widows and little German gentry fresh from table. I had been but a latent emigrant; now I was to be branded once more, and put apart with my fellows. It was about two in the afternoon of Friday that I found myself in front of the Emigrant House, with more than a hundred others, to be sorted and boxed for the journey. A white-haired official, with a stick under one arm, and a list in the other hand, stood apart in front of us, and called name after name in the tone of a command. At each name you would see a family gather up its brats and bundles and run for the hindmost of the three cars that stood awaiting us, and I soon concluded that this was to be set apart for the women and children. The second or central car, it turned out, was devoted to men travelling alone, and the third to the Chinese. The official was easily moved to anger at the least delay; but the emigrants were both quick at answering their names, and speedy in getting themselves and their effects on board.

The families once housed, we men carried the second car without ceremony by simultaneous assault. I suppose the reader has some notion of an American railroad-car, that long, narrow wooden box, like a flat-roofed Noah's ark, with a stove and a convenience, one at either end, a passage down the middle, and transverse benches upon either hand. Those destined for emigrants on the Union Pacific are only remarkable for their extreme plainness, nothing but wood entering in any part into their constitution, and for the usual inefficacy of the lamps, which often went out and shed but a dying glimmer even while they burned. The benches are too short for anything but a young child. Where there is scarce elbow-room for two to sit, there will not be space enough for one to lie. Hence the company, or rather, as it appears from certain bills about the Transfer Station, the company's servants, have conceived a plan for the better accommodation of travellers. They prevail on every two to chum together. To each of the chums they sell a board and three square cushions stuffed with straw, and covered with thin cotton. The benches can be made to face each other in pairs, for the backs are reversible. On the approach of night the boards are laid from bench to bench, making a couch wide enough for two, and long enough for a man of the middle height; and the chums lie down side by side upon the cushions with the head to the conductor's van and the feet to the engine. When the train is full, of course this plan is impossible, for there must not be more than one to every bench, neither can it be carried out unless the chums agree. It was to bring about this last condition that our white-haired official now bestirred himself. He made a most active master of ceremonies, introducing likely couples, and even guaranteeing the amiability and honesty of each. The greater the number of happy couples the better for his pocket, for it was he who sold the raw material of the beds. His price for one board and three straw cushions began with two dollars and a half; but before the train left, and, I am sorry to say, long after I had purchased mine, it had fallen to one dollar and a half.

The match-maker had a difficulty with me; perhaps, like some ladies, I showed myself too eager for union at any price; but certainly the first who was picked out to be my bedfellow, declined the honour without thanks. He was an old, heavy, slow-spoken man, I think from Yankeeland, looked me all over with great timidity, and then began to excuse himself in broken phrases. He didn't know the young man, he said. The young man might be very honest, but how was he to know that? There was another young man whom he had met already in the train; he guessed he was honest, and would prefer to chum with him upon the whole. All this without any sort of excuse, as though I had been inanimate or absent. I began to tremble lest every one should refuse my company, and I be left rejected. But the next in turn was a tall, strapping, long-limbed, small-headed, curly-haired Pennsylvania Dutchman, with a soldierly smartness in his manner. To be exact, he had acquired it in the navy. But that was all one; he had at least been trained to desperate resolves, so he accepted the match, and the white-haired swindler pronounced the connubial benediction, and pocketed his fees.

The rest of the afternoon was spent in making up the train. I am afraid to say how many baggage-waggons followed the engine, certainly a score; then came the Chinese, then we, then the families, and the rear was brought up by the conductor in what, if I have it rightly, is called his caboose. The class to which I belonged was of course far the largest, and we ran over, so to speak, to both sides; so that there were some Caucasians among the Chinamen, and some bachelors among the families. But our own car was pure from admixture, save for one little boy of eight or nine who had the whooping-cough. At last, about six, the long train crawled out of the Transfer Station and across the wide Missouri river to Omaha, westward bound.

It was a troubled uncomfortable evening in the cars. There was thunder in the air, which helped to keep us restless. A man played many airs upon the cornet, and none of them were much attended to, until he came to 'Home, sweet home.' It was truly strange to note how the talk ceased at that, and the faces began to lengthen. I have no idea whether musically this air is to be considered good or bad; but it belongs to that class of art which may be best described as a brutal assault upon the feelings. Pathos must be relieved by dignity of treatment. If you wallow naked in the pathetic, like the author of 'Home, sweet home', you make your hearers weep in an unmanly fashion; and even while yet they are moved, they despise themselves and hate the occasion of their weakness. It did not come to tears that night, for the experiment was interrupted. An elderly, hard-looking man, with a goatee beard and about as much appearance of sentiment as you would expect from a retired slaver, turned with a start and bade the performer stop that 'damned thing'. 'I've heard about enough of that,' he added; 'give us something about the good country we're going to.' A murmur of adhesion ran round the car; the performer took the instrument from his lips, laughed and nodded, and then struck into a dancing measure; and, like a new Timotheus, stilled immediately the emotion he had raised.

The day faded; the lamps were lit; a party of wild young men, who got off next evening at North Platte, stood together on the stern platform, singing 'The Sweet By-and-bye' with very tuneful voices; the chums began to put up their beds; and it seemed as if the business of the day were at an end. But it was not so; for, the train stopping at some station, the cars were instantly thronged with the natives, wives and fathers, young men and maidens, some of them in little more than nightgear, some with stable lanterns, and all offering beds for sale. Their charge began with twenty-five cents a cushion, but fell, before the train went on again, to fifteen, with the bed-board gratis, or less than one-fifth of what I had paid for mine at the Transfer. This is my contribution to the economy of future emigrants.

A great personage on an American train is the newsboy. He sells books (such books!), papers, fruit, lollipops, and cigars; and on emigrant journeys, soap, towels, tin washing dishes, tin coffee pitchers, coffee, tea, sugar, and tinned eatables, mostly hash or beans and bacon. Early next morning the newsboy went around the cars, and chumming on a more extended principle became the order of the hour. It requires but a copartnery of two to manage beds; but washing and eating can be carried on most economically by a syndicate of three. I myself entered a little after sunrise into articles of agreement, and became one of the firm of Pennsylvania, Shakespeare, and Dubuque. Shakespeare was my own nickname on the cars; Pennsylvania that of my bedfellow; and Dubuque, the name of a place in the State of Iowa, that of an amiable young fellow going west to cure an asthma, and retarding his recovery by incessantly chewing or smoking, and sometimes chewing and smoking together. I have never seen tobacco so sillily abused. Shakespeare bought a tin washing-dish, Dubuque a towel, and Pennsylvania a brick of soap. The partners used these instruments, one after another, according to the order of their first awaking; and when the firm had finished there was no want of borrowers. Each filled the tin dish at the water filter opposite the stove, and retired with the whole stock in trade to the platform of the car. There he knelt down, supporting himself by a shoulder against the woodwork or one elbow crooked about the railing, and made a shift to wash his face and neck and hands; a cold, an insufficient, and, if the train is moving rapidly, a somewhat dangerous toilet.

On a similar division of expense, the firm of Pennsylvania, Shakespeare, and Dubuque supplied themselves with coffee, sugar, and necessary vessels; and their operations are a type of what went on through all the cars. Before the sun was up the stove would be brightly burning; at the first station the natives would come on board with milk and eggs and coffee cakes; and soon from end to end the car would be filled with little parties breakfasting upon the bed-boards. It was the pleasantest hour of the day.

There were meals to be had, however, by the wayside: a breakfast in the morning, a dinner somewhere between eleven and two, and supper from five to eight or nine at night. We had rarely less than twenty minutes for each; and if we had not spent many another twenty minutes waiting for some express upon a side track among miles of desert, we might have taken an hour to each repast and arrived at San Francisco up to time. For haste is not the foible of an emigrant train. It gets through on sufferance, running the gauntlet among its more considerable brethren; should there be a block, it is unhesitatingly sacrificed; and they cannot, in consequence, predict the length of the passage within a day or so. Civility is the main comfort that you miss. Equality, though conceived very largely in America, does not extend so low down as to an emigrant. Thus in all other trains, a warning cry of 'All aboard!' recalls the passengers to take their seats; but as soon as I was alone with emigrants, and from the Transfer all the way to San Francisco, I found this ceremony was pretermitted; the train stole from the station without note of warning, and you had to keep an eye upon it even while you ate. The annoyance is considerable, and the disrespect both wanton and petty.

Many conductors, again, will hold no communication with an emigrant. I asked a conductor one day at what time the train would stop for dinner; as he made no answer I repeated the question, with a like result; a third time I returned to the charge, and then Jack-in-office looked me coolly in the face for several seconds and turned ostentatiously away. I believe he was half ashamed of his brutality; for when another person made the same inquiry, although he still refused the information, he condescended to answer, and even to justify his reticence in a voice loud enough for me to hear. It was, he said, his principle not to tell people where they were to dine; for one answer led to many other questions, as what o'clock it was? or, how soon should we be there? and he could not afford to be eternally worried.

As you are thus cut off from the superior authorities, a great deal of your comfort depends on the character of the newsboy. He has it in his power indefinitely to better and brighten the emigrant's lot. The newsboy with whom we started from the Transfer was a dark, bullying, contemptuous, insolent scoundrel, who treated us like dogs. Indeed, in his case, matters came nearly to a fight. It happened thus: he was going his rounds through the cars with some commodities for sale, and coming to a party who were at SEVEN-UP or CASCINO (our two games), upon a bed-board, slung down a cigar-box in the middle of the cards, knocking one man's hand to the floor. It was the last straw. In a moment the whole party were upon their feet, the cigars were upset, and he was ordered to 'get out of that directly, or he would get more than he reckoned for.' The fellow grumbled and muttered, but ended by making off, and was less openly insulting in the future. On the other hand, the lad who rode with us in this capacity from Ogden to Sacramento made himself the friend of all, and helped us with information, attention, assistance, and a kind countenance. He told us where and when we should have our meals, and how long the train would stop; kept seats at table for those who were delayed, and watched that we should neither be left behind nor yet unnecessarily hurried. You, who live at home at ease, can hardly realise the greatness of this service, even had it stood alone. When I think of that lad coming and going, train after train, with his bright face and civil words, I see how easily a good man may become the benefactor of his kind. Perhaps he is discontented with himself, perhaps troubled with ambitions; why, if he but knew it, he is a hero of the old Greek stamp; and while he thinks he is only earning a profit of a few cents, and that perhaps exorbitant, he is doing a man's work, and bettering the world.

I must tell here an experience of mine with another newsboy. I tell it because it gives so good an example of that uncivil kindness of the American, which is perhaps their most bewildering character to one newly landed. It was immediately after I had left the emigrant train; and I am told I looked like a man at death's door, so much had this long journey shaken me. I sat at the end of a car, and the catch being broken, and myself feverish and sick, I had to hold the door open with my foot for the sake of air. In this attitude my leg debarred the newsboy from his box of merchandise. I made haste to let him pass when I observed that he was coming; but I was busy with a book, and so once or twice he came upon me unawares. On these occasions he most rudely struck my foot aside; and though I myself apologised, as if to show him the way, he answered me never a word. I chafed furiously, and I fear the next time it would have come to words. But suddenly I felt a touch upon my shoulder, and a large juicy pear was put into my hand. It was the newsboy, who had observed that I was looking ill, and so made me this present out of a tender heart. For the rest of the journey I was petted like a sick child; he lent me newspapers, thus depriving himself of his legitimate profit on their sale, and came repeatedly to sit by me and cheer me up.

THE PLAINS OF NEBRASKA

It had thundered on the Friday night, but the sun rose on Saturday without a cloud. We were at sea – there is no other adequate expression – on the plains of Nebraska. I made my observatory on the top of a fruit-waggon, and sat by the hour upon that perch to spy about me, and to spy in vain for something new. It was a world almost without a feature; an empty sky, an empty earth; front and back, the line of railway stretched from horizon to horizon, like a cue across a billiard-board; on either hand, the green plain ran till it touched the skirts of heaven. Along the track innumerable wild sunflowers, no bigger than a crown-piece, bloomed in a continuous flower-bed; grazing beasts were seen upon the prairie at all degrees of distance and diminution; and now and again we might perceive a few dots beside the railroad which grew more and more distinct as we drew nearer till they turned into wooden cabins, and then dwindled and dwindled in our wake until they melted into their surroundings, and we were once more alone upon the billiard-board. The train toiled over this infinity like a snail; and being the one thing moving, it was wonderful what huge proportions it began to assume in our regard. It seemed miles in length, and either end of it within but a step of the horizon. Even my own body or my own head seemed a great thing in that emptiness. I note the feeling the more readily as it is the contrary of what I have read of in the experience of others. Day and night, above the roar of the train, our ears were kept busy with the incessant chirp of grasshoppers – a noise like the winding up of countless clocks and watches, which began after a while to seem proper to that land.

To one hurrying through by steam there was a certain exhilaration in this spacious vacancy, this greatness of the air, this discovery of the whole arch of heaven, this straight, unbroken, prison-line of the horizon. Yet one could not but reflect upon the weariness of those who passed by there in old days, at the foot's pace of oxen, painfully urging their teams, and with no landmark but that unattainable evening sun for which they steered, and which daily fled them by an equal stride. They had nothing, it would seem, to overtake; nothing by which to reckon their advance; no sight for repose or for encouragement; but stage after stage, only the dead green waste under foot, and the mocking, fugitive horizon. But the eye, as I have been told, found differences even here; and at the worst the emigrant came, by perseverance, to the end of his toil. It is the settlers, after all, at whom we have a right to marvel. Our consciousness, by which we live, is itself but the creature of variety. Upon what food does it subsist in such a land? What livelihood can repay a human creature for a life spent in this huge sameness? He is cut off from books, from news, from company, from all that can relieve existence but the prosecution of his affairs. A sky full of stars is the most varied spectacle that he can hope. He may walk five miles and see nothing; ten, and it is as though he had not moved; twenty, and still he is in the midst of the same great level, and has approached no nearer to the one object within view, the flat horizon which keeps pace with his advance. We are full at home of the question of agreeable wall-papers, and wise people are of opinion that the temper may be quieted by sedative surroundings. But what is to be said of the Nebraskan settler? His is a wall-paper with a vengeance – one quarter of the universe laid bare in all its gauntness.

His eye must embrace at every glance the whole seeming concave of the visible world; it quails before so vast an outlook, it is tortured by distance; yet there is no rest or shelter till the man runs into his cabin, and can repose his sight upon things near at hand. Hence, I am told, a sickness of the vision peculiar to these empty plains.

Yet perhaps with sunflowers and cicadae, summer and winter, cattle, wife and family, the settler may create a full and various existence. One person at least I saw upon the plains who seemed in every way superior to her lot. This was a woman who boarded us at a way station, selling milk. She was largely formed; her features were more than comely; she had that great rarity – a fine complexion which became her; and her eyes were kind, dark, and steady. She sold milk with patriarchal grace. There was not a line in her countenance, not a note in her soft and sleepy voice, but spoke of an entire contentment with her life. It would have been fatuous arrogance to pity such a woman. Yet the place where she lived was to me almost ghastly. Less than a dozen wooden houses, all of a shape and all nearly of a size, stood planted along the railway lines. Each stood apart in its own lot. Each opened direct off the billiard-board, as if it were a billiard-board indeed, and these only models that had been set down upon it ready made. Her own, into which I looked, was clean but very empty, and showed nothing homelike but the burning fire. This extreme newness, above all in so naked and flat a country, gives a strong impression of artificiality. With none of the litter and discoloration of human life; with the paths unworn, and the houses still sweating from the axe, such a settlement as this seems purely scenic. The mind is loth to accept it for a piece of reality; and it seems incredible that life can go on with so few properties, or the great child, man, find entertainment in so bare a playroom.

And truly it is as yet an incomplete society in some points; or at least it contained, as I passed through, one person incompletely civilised. At North Platte, where we supped that evening, one man asked another to pass the milk-jug. This other was well-dressed and of what we should call a respectable appearance; a darkish man, high spoken, eating as though he had some usage of society; but he turned upon the first speaker with extraordinary vehemence of tone –

'There's a waiter here!' he cried.

'I only asked you to pass the milk,' explained the first.

Here is the retort verbatim –

'Pass! Hell! I'm not paid for that business; the waiter's paid for it. You should use civility at table, and, by God, I'll show you how!'

The other man very wisely made no answer, and the bully went on with his supper as though nothing had occurred. It pleases me to think that some day soon he will meet with one of his own kidney; and that perhaps both may fall.

THE DESERT OF WYOMING

To cross such a plain is to grow homesick for the mountains. I longed for the Black Hills of Wyoming, which I knew we were soon to enter, like an ice-bound whaler for the spring. Alas! and it was a worse country than the other. All Sunday and Monday we travelled through these sad mountains, or over the main ridge of the Rockies, which is a fair match to them for misery of aspect. Hour after hour it was the same unhomely and unkindly world about our onward path; tumbled boulders, cliffs that drearily imitate the shape of monuments and fortifications – how drearily, how tamely, none can tell who has not seen them; not a tree, not a patch of sward, not one shapely or commanding mountain form; sage-brush, eternal sage-brush; over all, the same weariful and gloomy colouring, grays warming into brown, grays darkening towards black; and for sole sign of life, here and there a few fleeing antelopes; here and there, but at incredible intervals, a creek running in a canon. The plains have a grandeur of their own; but here there is nothing but a contorted smallness. Except for the air, which was light and stimulating, there was not one good circumstance in that God-forsaken land.

I had been suffering in my health a good deal all the way; and at last, whether I was exhausted by my complaint or poisoned in some wayside eating-house, the evening we left Laramie, I fell sick outright.[4] That was a night which I shall not readily forget. The lamps did not go out; each made a faint shining in its own neighbourhood, and the shadows were confounded together in the long, hollow box of the car. The sleepers lay in uneasy attitudes; here two chums alongside, flat upon their backs like dead folk; there a man sprawling on the floor, with his face upon his arm; there another half seated with his head and shoulders on the bench. The most passive were continually and roughly shaken by the movement of the train; others stirred, turned, or stretched out their arms like children; it was surprising how many groaned and murmured in their sleep; and as I passed to and fro, stepping across the prostrate, and caught now a snore, now a gasp, now a half-formed word, it gave me a measure of the worthlessness of rest in that unresting vehicle. Although it was chill, I was obliged to open my window, for the degradation of the air soon became intolerable to one who was awake and using the full supply of life. Outside, in a glimmering night, I saw the black, amorphous hills shoot by unweariedly into our wake. They that long for morning have never longed for it more earnestly than I.

And yet when day came, it was to shine upon the same broken and unsightly quarter of the world. Mile upon mile, and not a tree, a bird, or a river. Only down the long, sterile canons, the train shot hooting and awoke the resting echo. That train was the one piece of life in all the deadly land; it was the one actor, the one spectacle fit to be observed in this paralysis of man and nature. And when I think how the railroad has been pushed through this unwatered wilderness and haunt of savage tribes, and now will bear an emigrant for some 12 pounds from the Atlantic to the Golden Gates [*sic*]; how at each stage of the construction, roaring, impromptu cities, full of gold and lust and death, sprang up and then died away again, and are now but wayside stations in the desert; how in these uncouth places pig-tailed Chinese pirates worked side by side with border ruffians and broken men from Europe, talking together in a mixed dialect, mostly oaths, gambling, drinking, quarrelling and murdering like wolves; how the plumed hereditary lord of all America heard, in this last fastness, the scream of the 'bad medicine wag-gon' charioting his foes; and then when I go on to remember that all this epical turmoil was conducted by gentlemen in frock coats, and with a view to nothing more extraordinary than a fortune and a subsequent visit to Paris, it seems to me, I own, as if this railway were the one typical achievement of the age in which we live, as if it brought together into one plot all the ends of the world and all the degrees of social rank, and offered to some great writer the busiest, the most extended, and the most varied subject for an enduring literary work. If it be romance, if it be contrast, if it be heroism that we require, what was Troy town to this? But, alas! it is not these things that are necessary – it is only Homer ...

FELLOW-PASSENGERS

At Ogden we changed cars from the Union Pacific to the Central Pacific line of railroad. The change was doubly welcome; for, first, we had better cars on the new line; and, second, those in which we had been cooped for more than ninety hours had begun to stink abominably. Several yards away, as we returned, let us say from dinner, our nostrils were assailed by rancid air. I have stood on a platform while the whole train was shunting; and as the dwelling-cars drew near, there would come a whiff of pure menagerie, only a little sourer, as from men instead of mon-keys. I think we are human only in virtue of open windows. Without fresh air, you only require a bad heart, and a remarkable command of the Queen's English, to become such another as Dean Swift;[5] a kind of leering, human goat, leaping and wagging your scut on mountains of offence. I do my best to keep my head the other way, and look for the human rather than the bestial in this Yahoo-like busi-ness of the emigrant train. But one thing I must say, the car of the Chinese was notably the least offensive.

The cars on the Central Pacific were nearly twice as high, and so proportional-ly airier; they were freshly varnished, which gave us all a sense of cleanliness as though we had bathed; the seats drew out and joined in the centre, so that there was no more need for bed boards; and there was an upper tier of berths which could be closed by day and opened at night.

I had by this time some opportunity of seeing the people whom I was among. They were in rather marked contrast to the emigrants I had met on board ship while crossing the Atlantic. They were mostly lumpish fellows, silent and noisy, a common combination; somewhat sad, I should say, with an extraordinary poor taste in humour, and little interest in their fellow-creatures beyond that of a cheap and merely external curiosity. If they heard a man's name and business, they seemed to think they had the heart of that mystery; but they were as eager to know that much as they were indifferent to the rest. Some of them were on nettles till they learned your name was Dickson and you a journeyman baker; but beyond that, whether you were Catholic or Mormon, dull or clever, fierce or friendly, was all one to them. Others who were not so stupid, gossiped a little, and, I am bound to say, unkindly. A favourite witticism was for some lout to raise the alarm of 'All aboard!' while the rest of us were dining, thus contributing his mite to the general discomfort. Such a one was always much applauded for his high spirits. When I was ill coming through Wyoming, I was astonished – fresh from the eager humanity on board ship – to meet with little but laughter. One of the young men even amused himself by incommoding me, as was then very easy; and that not from ill-nature, but mere clodlike incapacity to think, for he expected me to join the laugh. I did so, but it was phantom merriment. Later on, a man from Kansas had three violent epileptic fits, and though, of course, there were not wanting some to help him, it was rather superstitious terror than sympathy that his case evoked among his fellow-passengers. 'Oh, I hope he's not going to die!' cried a woman; 'it would be terrible to have a dead body!' And there was a very general movement to leave the man behind at the next station. This, by good fortune, the conductor negatived.

There was a good deal of story-telling in some quarters; in others, little but silence. In this society, more than any other that ever I was in, it was the narrator alone who seemed to enjoy the narrative. It was rarely that any one listened for the listening. If he lent an ear to another man's story, it was because he was in immediate want of a hearer for one of his own. Food and the progress of the train were the subjects most generally treated; many joined to discuss these who otherwise would hold their tongues. One small knot had no better occupation than to worm out of me my name; and the more they tried, the more obstinately fixed I grew to baffle them. They assailed me with artful questions and insidious offers of correspondence in the future; but I was perpetually on my guard, and parried their assaults with inward laughter. I am sure Dubuque would have given me ten dollars for the secret. He owed me far more, had he understood life, for thus preserving him a lively interest throughout the journey. I met one of my fellow-passengers months after, driving a street tramway car in San Francisco; and, as the joke was now out of season, told him my name without subterfuge. You never saw a man more chapfallen. But had my name been Demogorgon, after so prolonged a mystery he had still been disappointed.

There were no emigrants direct from Europe – save one German family and a knot of Cornish miners who kept grimly by themselves, one reading the New Testament all day long through steel spectacles, the rest discussing privately the secrets of their old-world, mysterious race. Lady Hester Stanhope believed she could make something great of the Cornish; for my part, I can make nothing of them at all. A division of races, older and more original than that of Babel, keeps this close, esoteric family apart from neighbouring Englishmen. Not even a Red Indian seems more foreign in my eyes. This is one of the lessons of travel – that some of the strangest races dwell next door to you at home.

The rest were all American born, but they came from almost every quarter of that Continent. All the States of the North had sent out a fugitive to cross the plains with me. From Virginia, from Pennsylvania, from New York, from far western Iowa and Kansas, from Maine that borders on the Canadas, and from the Canadas themselves – some one or two were fleeing in quest of a better land and better wages. The talk in the train, like the talk I heard on the steamer, ran upon hard times, short commons, and hope that moves ever westward. I thought of my shipful from Great Britain with a feeling of despair. They had come 3000 miles, and yet not far enough. Hard times bowed them out of the Clyde, and stood to welcome them at Sandy Hook. Where were they to go? Pennsylvania, Maine, Iowa, Kansas? These were not places for immigration, but for emigration, it appeared; not one of them, but I knew a man who had lifted up his heel and left it for an ungrateful country. And it was still westward that they ran. Hunger, you would have thought, came out of the east like the sun, and the evening was made of edible gold. And, meantime, in the car in front of me, were there not half a hundred emigrants from the opposite quarter? Hungry Europe and hungry China, each pouring from their gates in search of provender, had here come face to face. The two waves had met; east and west had alike failed; the whole round world had been prospected and condemned; there was no El Dorado anywhere; and till one could emigrate to the moon, it seemed as well to stay patiently at home. Nor was there wanting another sign, at once more picturesque and more disheartening; for, as we continued to steam westward toward the land of gold, we were continually passing other emigrant trains upon the journey east; and these were as crowded as our own. Had all these return voyagers made a fortune in the mines? Were they all bound for Paris, and to be in Rome by Easter? It would seem not, for, whenever we met them, the passengers ran on the platform and cried to us through the windows, in a kind of wailing chorus, to 'come back.' On the plains of Nebraska, in the mountains of Wyoming, it was still the same cry, and dismal to my heart, 'Come back!' That was what we heard by the way 'about the good country we were going to.' And at that very hour the Sand-lot of San Francisco was crowded with the unemployed, and the echo from the other side of Market Street was repeating the rant of demagogues.

If, in truth, it were only for the sake of wages that men emigrate, how many

thousands would regret the bargain! But wages, indeed, are only one consideration out of many; for we are a race of gipsies, and love change and travel for themselves.

TO THE GOLDEN GATES

A little corner of Utah is soon traversed, and leaves no particular impressions on
the mind. By an early hour on Wednesday morning we stopped to breakfast at
Toano, a little station on a bleak, high-lying plateau in Nevada. The man who kept
the station eating-house was a Scot, and learning that I was the same, he grew
very friendly, and gave me some advice on the country I was now entering. 'You
see,' said he, 'I tell you this, because I come from your country.' Hail, brither
Scots! ...

From Toano we travelled all day through deserts of alkali and sand, horrible to
man, and bare sage-brush country that seemed little kindlier, and came by sup-
per-time to Elko. As we were standing, after our manner, outside the station, I saw
two men whip suddenly from underneath the cars, and take to their heels across
country. They were tramps, it appeared, who had been riding on the beams since
eleven of the night before; and several of my fellow- passengers had already seen
and conversed with them while we broke our fast at Toano. These land stowaways
play a great part over here in America, and I should have liked dearly to become
acquainted with them.

At Elko an odd circumstance befell me. I was coming out from supper, when I
was stopped by a small, stout, ruddy man, followed by two others taller and ruddier than himself.

'Excuse me, sir,' he said, 'but do you happen to be going on?'

I said I was, whereupon he said he hoped to persuade me to desist from that
intention. He had a situation to offer me, and if we could come to terms, why,
good and well. 'You see,' he continued, 'I'm running a theatre here, and we're a
little short in the orchestra. You're a musician, I guess?'

I assured him that, beyond a rudimentary acquaintance with 'Auld Lang Syne'
and 'The Wearing of the Green', I had no pretension whatever to that style. He
seemed much put out of countenance; and one of his taller companions asked
him, on the nail, for five dollars.

'You see, sir,' added the latter to me, 'he bet you were a musician; I bet you
weren't. No offence, I hope?'

'None whatever,' I said, and the two withdrew to the bar, where I presume the
debt was liquidated.

This little adventure woke bright hopes in my fellow-travellers, who thought
they had now come to a country where situations went a-begging. But I am not so
sure that the offer was in good faith. Indeed, I am more than half persuaded it

was but a feeler to decide the bet.

Of all the next day I will tell you nothing, for the best of all reasons, that I remember no more than that we continued through desolate and desert scenes, fiery hot and deadly weary. But some time after I had fallen asleep that night, I was awakened by one of my companions. It was in vain that I resisted. A fire of enthusiasm and whisky burned in his eyes; and he declared we were in a new country, and I must come forth upon the platform and see with my own eyes. The train was then, in its patient way, standing halted in a by-track. It was a clear, moonlit night; but the valley was too narrow to admit the moonshine direct, and only a diffused glimmer whitened the tall rocks and relieved the blackness of the pines. A hoarse clamour filled the air; it was the continuous plunge of a cascade somewhere near at hand among the mountains. The air struck chill, but tasted good and vigorous in the nostrils – a fine, dry, old mountain atmosphere. I was dead sleepy, but I returned to roost with a grateful mountain feeling at my heart.

When I awoke next morning, I was puzzled for a while to know if it were day or night, for the illumination was unusual. I sat up at last, and found we were grading slowly downward through a long snowshed; and suddenly we shot into an open; and before we were swallowed into the next length of wooden tunnel, I had one glimpse of a huge pine-forested ravine upon my left, a foaming river, and a sky already coloured with the fires of dawn. I am usually very calm over the displays of nature; but you will scarce believe how my heart leaped at this. It was like meeting one's wife. I had come home again – home from unsightly deserts to the green and habitable corners of the earth. Every spire of pine along the hill-top, every trouty pool along that mountain river, was more dear to me than a blood relation. Few people have praised God more happily than I did. And thenceforward, down by Blue Canon, Alta, Dutch Flat, and all the old mining camps, through a sea of mountain forests, dropping thousands of feet toward the far sea-level as we went, not I only, but all the passengers on board, threw off their sense of dirt and heat and weariness, and bawled like schoolboys, and thronged with shining eyes upon the platform and became new creatures within and without. The sun no longer oppressed us with heat, it only shone laughingly along the mountain-side, until we were fain to laugh ourselves for glee. At every turn we could see farther into the land and our own happy futures. At every town the cocks were tossing their clear notes into the golden air, and crowing for the new day and the new country. For this was indeed our destination; this was 'the good country' we had been going to so long.

By afternoon we were at Sacramento, the city of gardens in a plain of corn; and the next day before the dawn we were lying to upon the Oakland side of San Francisco Bay. The day was breaking as we crossed the ferry; the fog was rising over the citied hills of San Francisco; the bay was perfect – not a ripple, scarce a stain, upon its blue expanse; everything was waiting, breathless, for the sun. A spot of cloudy gold lit first upon the head of Tamalpais,[6] and then widened downward on its shapely shoulder; the air seemed to awaken, and began to sparkle; and suddenly

'The tall hills Titan discovered,'

and the city of San Francisco, and the bay of gold and corn, were lit from end to end with summer daylight.

Notes

1. Originally built as a fortress against the British during the War of 1812, Castle Garden served as a concert hall. In Stevenson's day, it was an emigration centre, the precursor of Ellis Island.

2. Harriet Beecher Stowe (1811–1896), American writer, whose best-known work is *Uncle Tom's Cabin* (1852).

3. The Great Chicago Fire started on October 8, 1871, destroyed more than 17,000 buildings and left 300 dead and nearly 100,000 people homeless.

4. 'My illness is a subject of great mirth to some of my fellow travellers, and I smile rather sickly at their jests,' Stevenson confessed in a letter dated 25 August 1879 to WE Henley. See *Selected Letters of Robert Louis Stevenson*. Edited by Ernest Mehew (New Haven: Yale University Press, 2001), p. 150.

5. Jonathan Swift (1667–1745), Anglo-Irish satirist and Dean of St. Patrick's Cathedral in Dublin.

6. Mount Tamalpais, a 2,604- foot summit northwest of San Francisco.

The Old Pacific Capital

The Old Pacific Capital appeared in *Fraser's Magazine in 1880 and later was reprinted in* Across the Plains. *It also appears in* From Scotland to Silverado *edited by James D Hart (Cambridge, Mass.: Belknap Press of Harvard University Press, 1966) and* From the Clyde to California: Robert Louis Stevenson's Emigrant Journey *edited by Andrew Noble (Aberdeen: University of Aberdeen Press, 1985).*

THE WOODS AND THE PACIFIC

THE Bay of Monterey has been compared by no less a person than General Sherman to a bent fishing-hook; and the comparison, if less important than the march through Georgia, still shows the eye of a soldier for topography.[1] Santa Cruz sits exposed at the shank; the mouth of the Salinas River is at the middle of the bend; and Monterey itself is cosily ensconced beside the barb. Thus the ancient capital of California faces across the bay, while the Pacific Ocean, though hidden by low hills and forest, bombards her left flank and rear with never-dying surf. In front of the town, the long line of sea-beach trends north and north-west, and then westward to enclose the bay. The waves which lap so quietly about the jetties of Monterey grow louder and larger in the distance; you can see the breakers leaping high and white by day; at night, the outline of the shore is traced in transparent silver by the moonlight and the flying foam; and from all round, even in quiet weather, the distant, thrilling roar of the Pacific hangs over the coast and the adjacent country like smoke above a battle.

These long beaches are enticing to the idle man. It would be hard to find a walk more solitary and at the same time more exciting to the mind. Crowds of ducks and sea-gulls hover over the sea. Sandpipers trot in and out by troops after the retiring waves, trilling together in a chorus of infinitesimal song. Strange sea-tangles, new to the European eye, the bones of whales, or sometimes a whole whale's carcase, white with carrion-gulls and poisoning the wind, lie scattered here and there along the sands. The waves come in slowly, vast and green, curve their translucent necks, and burst with a surprising uproar, that runs, waxing and waning, up and down the long key-board of the beach. The foam of these great ruins mounts in an instant to the ridge of the sand glacis, swiftly fleets back again, and is met and buried by the next breaker. The interest is perpetually fresh. On no other coast that I know shall you enjoy, in calm, sunny weather, such a spectacle of Ocean's greatness, such beauty of changing colour, or such degrees of thunder in the sound. The very air is more than usually salt by this Homeric deep.

Inshore, a tract of sand-hills borders on the beach. Here and there a lagoon, more

211

or less brackish, attracts the birds and hunters. A rough, undergrowth partially conceals the sand. The crouching, hardy live-oaks flourish singly or in thickets – the kind of wood for murderers to crawl among – and here and there the skirts of the forest extend downward from the hills with a floor of turf and long aisles of pine-trees hung with Spaniard's Beard. Through this quaint desert the railway cars drew near to Monterey from the junction at Salinas City – though that and so many other things are now for ever altered – and it was from here that you had the first view of the old township lying in the sands, its white windmills bickering in the chill, perpetual wind, and the first fogs of the evening drawing drearily around it from the sea.

The one common note of all this country is the haunting presence of the ocean. A great faint sound of breakers follows you high up into the inland canons; the roar of water dwells in the clean, empty rooms of Monterey as in a shell upon the chimney; go where you will, you have but to pause and listen to hear the voice of the Pacific. You pass out of the town to the south-west, and mount the hill among pine-woods. Glade, thicket, and grove surround you. You follow winding sandy tracks that lead nowhither. You see a deer; a multitude of quail arises. But the sound of the sea still follows you as you advance, like that of wind among the trees, only harsher and stranger to the ear; and when at length you gain the summit, out breaks on every hand and with freshened vigour that same unending, distant, whispering rumble of the ocean; for now you are on the top of Monterey peninsula, and the noise no longer only mounts to you from behind along the beach towards Santa Cruz, but from your right also, round by Chinatown and Pinos lighthouse, and from down before you to the mouth of the Carmello river. The whole woodland is begirt with thundering surges. The silence that immediately surrounds you where you stand is not so much broken as it is haunted by this distant, circling rumour. It sets your senses upon edge; you strain your attention; you are clearly and unusually conscious of small sounds near at hand; you walk listening like an Indian hunter; and that voice of the Pacific is a sort of disquieting company to you in your walk.

When once I was in these woods I found it difficult to turn homeward. All woods lure a rambler onward; but in those of Monterey it was the surf that particularly invited me to prolong my walks. I would push straight for the shore where I thought it to be nearest. Indeed, there was scarce a direction that would not, sooner or later, have brought me forth on the Pacific. The emptiness of the woods gave me a sense of freedom and discovery in these excursions. I never in all my visits met but one man. He was a Mexican, very dark of hue, but smiling and fat, and he carried an axe, though his true business at that moment was to seek for straying cattle. I asked him what o'clock it was, but he seemed neither to know nor care; and when he in his turn asked me for news of his cattle, I showed myself equally indifferent. We stood and smiled upon each other for a few seconds, and then turned without a word and took our several ways across the forest.

One day – I shall never forget it – I had taken a trail that was new to me. After a while the woods began to open, the sea to sound nearer hand. I came upon a road, and, to my surprise, a stile. A step or two farther, and, without leaving the woods, I found myself among trim houses. I walked through street after street, parallel and at right angles, paved with sward and dotted with trees, but still undeniable streets, and each with its name posted at the corner, as in a real town. Facing down the main thoroughfare – 'Central Avenue', as it was ticketed – I saw an open-air temple, with benches and sounding-board, as though for an orchestra. The houses were all tightly shuttered; there was no smoke, no sound but of the waves, no moving thing. I have never been in any place that seemed so dreamlike. Pompeii is all in a bustle with visitors, and its antiquity and strangeness deceive the imagination; but this town had plainly not been built above a year or two, and perhaps had been deserted overnight. Indeed, it was not so much like a deserted town as like a scene upon the stage by daylight, and with no one on the boards. The barking of a dog led me at last to the only house still occupied, where a Scotch pastor and his wife pass the winter alone in this empty theatre. The place was 'The Pacific Camp Grounds, the Christian Seaside Resort'. Thither, in the warm season, crowds come to enjoy a life of teetotalism, religion, and flirtation, which I am willing to think blameless and agreeable. The neighbourhood at least is well selected. The Pacific booms in front. Westward is Point Pinos, with the lighthouse in a wilderness of sand, where you will find the lightkeeper playing the piano, making models and bows and arrows, studying dawn and sunrise in amateur oil-painting, and with a dozen other elegant pursuits and interests to surprise his brave, old-country rivals. To the east, and still nearer, you will come upon a space of open down, a hamlet, a haven among rocks, a world of surge and screaming sea-gulls. Such scenes are very similar in different climates; they appear homely to the eyes of all; to me this was like a dozen spots in Scotland. And yet the boats that ride in the haven are of strange outlandish design; and, if you walk into the hamlet, you will behold costumes and faces and hear a tongue that are unfamiliar to the memory. The joss-stick burns, the opium pipe is smoked, the floors are strewn with slips of coloured paper – prayers, you would say, that had somehow missed their destination – and a man guiding his upright pencil from right to left across the sheet, writes home the news of Monterey to the Celestial Empire.

The woods and the Pacific rule between them the climate of this seaboard region. On the streets of Monterey, when the air does not smell salt from the one, it will be blowing perfumed from the resinous tree-tops of the other. For days together a hot, dry air will overhang the town, close as from an oven, yet healthful and aromatic in the nostrils. The cause is not far to seek, for the woods are afire, and the hot wind is blowing from the hills. These fires are one of the great dangers of California. I have seen from Monterey as many as three at the same time, by day a cloud of smoke, by night a red coal of conflagration in the distance.

A little thing will start them, and, if the wind be favourable, they gallop over miles of country faster than a horse. The inhabitants must turn out and work like demons, for it is not only the pleasant groves that are destroyed; the climate and the soil are equally at stake, and these fires prevent the rains of the next winter and dry up perennial fountains. California has been a land of promise in its time, like Palestine; but if the woods continue so swiftly to perish, it may become, like Palestine, a land of desolation.

To visit the woods while they are languidly burning is a strange piece of experience. The fire passes through the underbrush at a run. Every here and there a tree flares up instantaneously from root to summit, scattering tufts of flame, and is quenched, it seems, as quickly. But this last is only in semblance. For after this first squib-like conflagration of the dry moss and twigs, there remains behind a deep-rooted and consuming fire in the very entrails of the tree. The resin of the pitch-pine is principally condensed at the base of the bole and in the spreading roots. Thus, after the light, showy, skirmishing flames, which are only as the match to the explosion, have already scampered down the wind into the distance, the true harm is but beginning for this giant of the woods. You may approach the tree from one side, and see it scorched indeed from top to bottom, but apparently survivor of the peril. Make the circuit, and there, on the other side of the column, is a clear mass of living coal, spreading like an ulcer; while underground, to their most extended fibre, the roots are being eaten out by fire, and the smoke is rising through the fissures to the surface. A little while, and, without a nod of warning, the huge pine-tree snaps off short across the ground and falls prostrate with a crash. Meanwhile the fire continues its silent business; the roots are reduced to a fine ash; and long afterwards, if you pass by, you will find the earth pierced with radiating galleries, and preserving the design of all these subterranean spurs, as though it were the mould for a new tree instead of the print of an old one. These pitch-pines of Monterey are, with the single exception of the Monterey cypress, the most fantastic of forest trees. No words can give an idea of the contortion of their growth; they might figure without change in a circle of the nether hell as Dante pictured it; and at the rate at which trees grow, and at which forest fires spring up and gallop through the hills of California, we may look forward to a time when there will not be one of them left standing in that land of their nativity. At least they have not so much to fear from the axe, but perish by what may be called a natural although a violent death; while it is man in his short-sighted greed that robs the country of the nobler redwood. Yet a little while and perhaps all the hills of seaboard California may be as bald as Tamalpais.

I have an interest of my own in these forest fires, for I came so near to lynching on one occasion, that a braver man might have retained a thrill from the experience. I wished to be certain whether it was the moss, that quaint funereal ornament of Californian forests, which blazed up so rapidly when the flame first touched the tree. I suppose I must have been under the influence of Satan, for instead of plucking off a piece for my experiment what should I do but walk up to a great pine-tree in a portion of the wood which had escaped so much as scorching, strike a match, and apply the flame gingerly to one of the tassels. The tree went off simply like a rocket; in three seconds it was a roaring pillar of fire. Close by I could hear the shouts of those who were at work combating the original conflagration. I could see the waggon that had brought them tied to a live oak in a piece of open; I could even catch the flash of an axe as it swung up through the underwood into the sunlight. Had any one observed the result of my experiment my neck was literally not worth a pinch of snuff; after a few minutes of passionate expostulation I should have been run up to convenient bough.

To die for faction is a common evil;
But to be hanged for nonsense is the devil.

I have run repeatedly, but never as I ran that day. At night I went out of town, and there was my own particular fire, quite distinct from the other, and burning as I thought with even greater vigour.[2]

But it is the Pacific that exercises the most direct and obvious power upon the climate.[3] At sunset, for months together, vast, wet, melancholy fogs arise and come shoreward from the ocean. From the hill-top above Monterey the scene is often noble, although it is always sad. The upper air is still bright with sunlight; a glow still rests upon the Gabelano Peak; but the fogs are in possession of the lower levels; they crawl in scarves among the sandhills; they float, a little higher, in clouds of a gigantic size and often of a wild configuration; to the south, where they have struck the seaward shoulder of the mountains of Santa Lucia, they double back and spire up skyward like smoke. Where their shadow touches, colour dies out of the world. The air grows chill and deadly as they advance. The trade-wind freshens, the trees begin to sigh, and all the windmills in Monterey are whirling and creaking and filling their cisterns with the brackish water of the sands. It takes but a little while till the invasion is complete. The sea, in its lighter order, has submerged the earth. Monterey is curtained in for the night in thick, wet, salt, and frigid clouds, so to remain till day returns; and before the sun's rays they slowly disperse and retreat in broken squadrons to the bosom of the sea. And yet often when the fog is thickest and most chill, a few steps out of the town and up the slope, the night will be dry and warm and full of inland perfume.

MEXICANS, AMERICANS, AND INDIANS

The history of Monterey has yet to be written. Founded by Catholic missionaries, a place of wise beneficence to Indians, a place of arms, a Mexican capital continually wrested by one faction from another, an American capital when the first House of Representatives held its deliberations, and then falling lower and lower from the capital of the State to the capital of a county, and from that again, by the loss of its charter and town lands, to a mere bankrupt village, its rise and decline is typical of that of all Mexican institutions and even Mexican families in California.

Nothing is stranger in that strange State than the rapidity with which the soil has changed hands. The Mexicans, you may say, are all poor and landless, like their former capital; and yet both it and they hold themselves apart and preserve their ancient customs and something of their ancient air.

The town, when I was there, was a place of two or three streets, economically paved with sea-sand, and two or three lanes, which were watercourses in the rainy season, and were, at all times, rent up by fissures four or five feet deep. There were no street lights. Short sections of wooden sidewalk only added to the dangers of the night, for they were often high above the level of the roadway, and no one could tell where they would be likely to begin or end. The houses were, for the most part, built of unbaked adobe brick, many of them old for so new a country, some of very elegant proportions, with low, spacious, shapely rooms, and walls so thick that the heat of summer never dried them to the heart. At the approach of the rainy season a deathly chill and a graveyard smell began to hang about the lower floors; and diseases of the chest are common and fatal among house-keeping people of either sex.

There was no activity but in and around the saloons, where people sat almost all day long playing cards. The smallest excursion was made on horseback. You would scarcely ever see the main street without a horse or two tied to posts, and making a fine figure with their Mexican housings. It struck me oddly to come across some of the *Cornhill* illustrations to Mr. Blackmore's *Erema*, and see all the characters astride on English saddles. As a matter of fact, an English saddle is a rarity even in San Francisco, and, you may say, a thing unknown in all the rest of California. In a place so exclusively Mexican as Monterey, you saw not only Mexican saddles but true Vaquero riding – men always at the hand-gallop up hill and down dale, and round the sharpest corner, urging their horses with cries and gesticulations and cruel rotatory spurs, checking them dead with a touch, or wheeling them right-about-face in a square yard. The type of face and character of bearing are surprisingly un-American. The first ranged from something like the pure Spanish, to something, in its sad fixity, not unlike the pure Indian, although I do not suppose there was one pure blood of either race in all the country. As for the second, it was a matter of perpetual surprise to find, in that world of absolutely mannerless Americans, a people full of deportment, solemnly courteous, and doing all things with grace and decorum. In dress they ran to colour and bright sashes. Not even the most Americanised could always resist the temptation to stick a red rose into his hat-band. Not even the most Americanised would descend to wear the vile dress hat of civilisation. Spanish was the language of the streets. It was difficult to get along without a word or two of that language for an occasion. The only communications in which the population joined were with a view to amusement. A weekly public ball took place with great etiquette, in addition to the numerous fandangoes in private houses. There was a really fair amateur brass band. Night after night serenaders would be going about the street, sometimes in a company and with several instruments and voice together, sometimes severally, each guitar before a different window. It was a strange thing to lie awake in nineteenth-century America, and hear the guitar accompany, and one of these old, heart-breaking Spanish love-songs mount into the night air, perhaps in a deep baritone, perhaps in that high-pitched, pathetic, womanish alto which is so common among Mexican men, and which strikes on the unaccustomed ear as something not entirely human but altogether sad.

The town, then, was essentially and wholly Mexican; and yet almost all the land in the neighbourhood was held by Americans, and it was from the same class, numerically so small, that the principal officials were selected. This Mexican and that Mexican would describe to you his old family estates, not one rood of which remained to him. You would ask him how that came about, and elicit some tangled story back-foremost, from which you gathered that the Americans had been greedy like designing men, and the Mexicans greedy like children, but no other certain fact. Their merits and their faults contributed alike to the ruin of the former landholders. It is true they were improvident, and easily dazzled with the sight of ready money; but they were gentlefolk besides, and that in a way which curiously unfitted them to combat Yankee craft. Suppose they have a paper to sign, they would think it a reflection on the other party to examine the terms with any great minuteness; nay, suppose them to observe some doubtful clause, it is ten to one they would refuse from delicacy to object to it. I know I am speaking within the mark, for I have seen such a case occur, and the Mexican, in spite of the advice of his lawyer, has signed the imperfect paper like a lamb. To have spoken in the matter, he said, above all to have let the other party guess that he had seen a lawyer, would have 'been like doubting his word'. The scruple sounds oddly to one of ourselves, who have been brought up to understand all business as a competition in fraud, and honesty itself to be a virtue which regards the carrying out but not the creation of agreements. This single unworldly trait will account for much of that revolution of which we are speaking. The Mexicans have the name of being great swindlers, but certainly the accusation cuts both ways. In a contest of this sort, the entire booty would scarcely have passed into the hands of the more scrupulous race.

Physically the Americans have triumphed; but it is not entirely seen how far they have themselves been morally conquered. This is, of course, but a part of a part of an extraordinary problem now in the course of being solved in the various States of the American Union. I am reminded of an anecdote. Some years ago, at a great sale of wine, all the odd lots were purchased by a grocer in a small way in the old town of Edinburgh. The agent had the curiosity to visit him some time after and inquire what possible use he could have for such material. He was shown, by way of answer, a huge vat where all the liquors, from humble Gladstone to imperial Tokay, were fermenting together. 'And what,' he asked, 'do you propose to call this?' 'I'm no very sure,' replied the grocer, 'but I think it's going to turn out port.' In the older Eastern States, I think we may say that this hotchpotch of races is going to turn out English, or thereabout. But the problem is indefinitely varied in other zones. The elements are differently mingled in the south, in what we may call the Territorial belt and in the group of States on the Pacific coast. Above all, in these last, we may look to see some monstrous hybrid – Whether good or evil, who shall forecast? but certainly original and all their own. In my little restaurant at Monterey,[4] we have sat down to table day after day, a Frenchman, two Portuguese, an Italian, a Mexican, and a Scotchman: we had for common visitors an American from Illinois, a nearly pure blood Indian woman, and a naturalised Chinese; and from time to time a Switzer and a German came down from country ranches for the night. No wonder that the Pacific coast is a foreign land to visitors from the Eastern States, for each race contributes something of its own. Even the despised Chinese have taught the youth of California, none indeed of their virtues, but the debasing use of opium. And chief among these influences is that of the Mexicans.

The Mexicans although in the State are out of it. They still preserve a sort of international independence, and keep their affairs snug to themselves. Only four or five years ago Vasquez, the bandit,[5] his troops being dispersed and the hunt too hot for him in other parts of California, returned to his native Monterey, and was seen publicly in her streets and saloons, fearing no man. The year that I was there, there occurred two reputed murders. As the Montereyans are exceptionally vile speakers of each other and of every one behind his back, it is not possible for me to judge how much truth there may have been in these reports; but in the one case everyone believed, and in the other some suspected, that there had been foul play; and nobody dreamed for an instant of taking the authorities into their counsel. Now this is, of course, characteristic enough of the Mexicans; but it is a noteworthy feature that all the Americans in Monterey acquiesced without a word in this inaction. Even when I spoke to them upon the subject, they seemed not to understand my surprise; they had forgotten the traditions of their own race and upbringing, and become, in a word, wholly Mexicanised.

Again, the Mexicans, having no ready money to speak of, rely almost entirely in their business transactions upon each other's worthless paper. Pedro the penniless pays you with an IOU from the equally penniless Miguel. It is a sort of local currency by courtesy. Credit in these parts has passed into a superstition. I have seen a strong, violent man struggling for months to recover a debt, and getting nothing but an exchange of waste paper. The very storekeepers are averse to asking for cash payments, and are more surprised than pleased when they are offered. They fear there must be something under it, and that you mean to withdraw your custom from them. I have seen the enterprising chemist and stationer begging me with fervour to let my account run on, although I had my purse open in my hand; and partly from the commonness of the case, partly from some remains of that generous old Mexican tradition which made all men welcome to their tables, a person may be notoriously both unwilling and unable to pay, and still find credit for the necessaries of life in the stores of Monterey. Now this villainous habit of living upon 'tick' has grown into Californian nature. I do not mean that the American and European storekeepers of Monterey are as lax as Mexicans; I mean that American farmers in many parts of the State expect unlimited credit, and profit by it in the meanwhile, without a thought for consequences. Jew storekeepers have already learned the advantage to be gained from this; they lead on the farmer into irretrievable indebtedness, and keep him ever after as their bond-slave hopelessly grinding in the mill. So the whirligig of time brings in its revenges, and except that the Jew knows better than to foreclose, you may see Americans bound in the same chains with which they themselves had formerly bound the Mexican. It seems as if certain sorts of follies, like certain sorts of grain, were natural to the soil rather than to the race that holds and tills it for the moment.

In the meantime, however, the Americans rule in Monterey County. The new county seat, Salinas City, in the bald, corn-bearing plain under the Gabelano Peak, is a town of a purely American character. The land is held, for the most part, in those enormous tracts which are another legacy of Mexican days, and form the present chief danger and disgrace of California; and the holders are mostly of American or British birth. We have here in England no idea of the troubles and inconveniences which flow from the existence of these large landholders – land-thieves, land-sharks, or land-grabbers, they are more commonly and plainly called. Thus the townlands of Monterey are all in the hands of a single man. How they came there is an obscure, vexatious question, and, rightly or wrongly, the man is hated with a great hatred. His life has been repeatedly in danger. Not very long ago, I was told, the stage was stopped and examined three evenings in succession by disguised horsemen thirsting for his blood. A certain house on the Salinas road, they say, he always passes in his buggy at full speed, for the squatter sent him warning long ago. But a year since he was publicly pointed out for death by no less a man than Mr. Dennis Kearney. Kearney is a man too well known in California, but a word of explanation is required for English readers. Originally an Irish dray-man, he rose, by his command of bad language, to almost dictatorial authority in the State; throned it there for six months or so, his mouth full of oaths, gallowses, and conflagrations; was first snuffed out last winter by Mr. Coleman, backed by his San Francisco Vigilantes and three gatling guns; completed his own ruin by throwing in his lot with the grotesque Green-backer party; and had at last to be rescued by his old enemies, the police, out of the hands of his rebellious followers. It was while he was at the top of his fortune that Kearney visited Monterey with his battle-cry against Chinese labour, the railroad monopolists, and the land-thieves; and his one articulate counsel to the Montereyans was to 'hang David Jacks.' Had the town been American, in my private opinion, this would have been done years ago. Land is a subject on which there is no jesting in the West, and I have seen my friend the lawyer drive out of Monterey to adjust a competition of titles with the face of a captain going into battle and his Smith-and-Wesson convenient to his hand.

On the ranch of another of these landholders you may find our old friend, the truck system, in full operation. Men live there, year in year out, to cut timber for a nominal wage, which is all consumed in supplies. The longer they remain in this desirable service the deeper they will fall in debt – a burlesque injustice in a new country, where labour should be precious, and one of those typical instances which explains the prevailing discontent and the success of the demagogue Kearney.

In a comparison between what was and what is in California, the praisers of times past will fix upon the Indians of Carmel. The valley drained by the river so named is a true Californian valley, bare, dotted with chaparal, overlooked by quaint, unfinished hills. The Carmel runs by many pleasant farms, a clear and shallow river, loved by wading kine; and at last, as it is falling towards a quicksand and the great Pacific, passes a ruined mission on a hill. From the mission church the eye embraces a great field of ocean, and the ear is filled with a continuous sound of distant breakers on the shore. But the day of the Jesuit has gone by, the day of the Yankee has succeeded, and there is no one left to care for the converted savage. The church is roofless and ruinous, sea-breezes and sea-fogs, and the alternation of the rain and sunshine, daily widening the breaches and casting the crockets from the wall.[6] As an antiquity in this new land, a quaint specimen of missionary architecture, and a memorial of good deeds, it had a triple claim to preservation from all thinking people; but neglect and abuse have been its portion. There is no sign of American interference, save where a headboard has been torn from a grave to be a mark for pistol bullets. So it is with the Indians for whom it was erected. Their lands, I was told, are being yearly encroached upon by the neighbouring American proprietor, and with that exception no man troubles his head for the Indians of Carmel. Only one day in the year, the day before our Guy Fawkes, the *padre* drives over the hill from Monterey; the little sacristy, which is the only covered portion of the church, is filled with seats and decorated for the service; the Indians troop together, their bright dresses contrasting with their dark and melancholy faces; and there, among a crowd of somewhat unsympathetic holiday-makers, you may hear God served with perhaps more touching circumstances than in any other temple under heaven. An Indian, stone-blind and about eighty years of age, conducts the singing; other Indians compose the choir; yet they have the Gregorian music at their finger ends, and pronounce the Latin so correctly that I could follow the meaning as they sang. The pronunciation was odd and nasal, the singing hurried and staccato. 'In saecula saeculoho-horum,' they went, with a vigorous aspirate to every additional syllable. I have never seen faces more vividly lit up with joy than the faces of these Indian singers. It was to them not only the worship of God, nor an act by which they recalled and commemorated better days, but was besides an exercise of culture, where all they knew of art and letters was united and expressed. And it made a man's heart sorry for the good fathers of yore who had taught them to dig and to reap, to read and to sing, who had given them European mass-books which they still preserve and study in their cottages, and who had now passed away from all authority and influence in that land – to be succeeded by greedy land-thieves and sacrilegious pistol-shots. So ugly a thing may our Anglo-Saxon Protestantism appear beside the doings of the Society of Jesus.

But revolution in this world succeeds to revolution. All that I say in this paper is in a paulo-past tense. The Monterey of last year exists no longer. A huge hotel has sprung up in the desert by the railway.[7] Three sets of diners sit down successively to table. Invaluable toilettes figure along the beach and between the live oaks; and Monterey is advertised in the newspapers, and posted in the waiting-rooms at railway stations, as a resort for wealth and fashion. Alas for the little town! it is not strong enough to resist the influence of the flaunting caravanserai, and the poor, quaint, penniless native gentlemen of Monterey must perish, like a lower race, before the millionaire vulgarians of the Big Bonanza.

Notes

1. Philip Sheridan (1831–1888), American Civil War general.
2. In a letter to WE Henley, Stevenson describes his little 'experiment': 'Yesterday I set fire to the forest, for which, had I been caught, I should have been hung out of hand to the nearest tree; Judge Lynch being an active person hereaway. You should have seen my retreat (which was entirely for strategical purposes). I ran like hell.' See *Selected Letters of Robert Louis Stevenson*. Edited by Ernest Mehew (New Haven, Conn.: Yale University Press, 2001), p. 153.
3. 'This is a lovely place, which I am growing to love. The Pacific licks all other oceans out of hand; there is no place but the Pacific Coast to hear eternal roaring surf. When I get to the top of the woods behind Monterey, I can hear the seas breaking all round over ten or twelve miles of coast from near Carmel on my left, out to Point Pinos in front and away to the right along the sands of Monterey to Castroville and the mouth of the Salinas.' Letter from Stevenson to WE Henley, late October/early November 1879. See Mehew, *Selected Letters of Robert Louis Stevenson*, ibid.
4. Simoneau's was run by French immigrant Jules Simoneau (1821–1908), who Stevenson described in a letter to WE Henley as 'a most pleasant old boy with whom I discuss the universe and play chess

daily.' See Mehew, *Selected Letters of Robert Louis Stevenson*, p. 152. See also Robert Louis Stevenson, *A Friendship: Robert Louis Stevenson, Jules Simoneau* (San Francisco: Taylor, Nash, & Taylor, 1911) and Josephine Mildred Blanch, *The Story of a Friendship: Robert Louis Stevenson, Jules Simoneau. A California Reminiscence of Stevenson* (San Francisco, c.1921). Both books are in the Huntington Library, California.

5. Tiburcio Vasquez, a Mexican Robin Hood, was hanged in 1875. See *From the Clyde to California: Robert Louis Stevenson's Emigrant Journey*. Edited and Introduced by Andrew Noble (Aberdeen: Aberdeen University Press, 1985), p. 172.

6. Restoration of the Carmel Mission (full name: Mission Basilica San Carlos Borromeo del Rio Carmelo) began in the 1930s. California's second mission, it was established in the early 1770s. It is located west of Highway 1 at 3080 Rio Road and is open for self-guided tours. Admission is free. Stevenson's adventures in the Carmel area were not always pleasant. Distraught over what he considered his uncertain future with Fanny Osbourne, Stevenson, already in a weakened state from the long overland cross-country journey, went hiking in the Carmel hills – with an 'itch and a broken heart' – when he collapsed, some eighteen miles south of Monterey along the San Clemente Creek. Discovered by Sarah and Dolly Wright, two local girls, he was taken to their father Jonathan Wright's nearby angora goat ranch and nursed back to health by Wright's partner, seventy-two year old Mexican War veteran and ex-bear hunter Captain Anson Smith, and his Indian comrade Tom.

7. The Hotel Del Monte opened in 1880. It is now the site of the Naval Postgraduate School.

Simoneau's at Monterey

Simoneau's at Monterey *was written during 1880–1881 and was first published in full in James D Hart's* From Scotland to Silverado *(1966). It also appears in* Andrew Noble's From the Clyde to California *(1985).*

A place does not clearly exist for the imagination, till we have moved elsewhere. The tenor of our experience, one day melting into another, unifies into a single picture; out of many sunsets, many dawns, and many starry rambles, we compound a *tertium quid*, a glorified quintessence; the honey of honey, the cream of cream; a classical landscape, artificially composed and far more lively, winning and veracious than the scene it represents. For single glances may, indeed, be memorable; but they are the traits of which we afterwards compose our fancy likeness; but the eye cannot embrace a panorama; the eye, like the etcher's needle, cannot elaborate from nature; and literature, which is the language of our thoughts, must be gently elaborated in the course of time. Hence it is that a palace grows upon our fancy after we have left it, taking more and more the colour of our predilections, growing, like our childhood, daily more beautiful through the cunning excisions of oblivion; until it means at last, for that inward eye of which the poet tells us, something at once familiar and express, like the remembered countenance of a friend. We know what the eyes are to the face; the inn where we dined is similarly all in this memorial picture of a neighbourhood. It was the centre of our explorations, to which we still returned; it was the first highlight of an evening when we re-entered, blinking, from a woodland ramble; it was there we went to eat when we were hungry, to be warmed when we were cold, to talk when our spirits mounted; and it was there, over the digestive coffee, that we reviewed at night the toils and pleasures of the inn. On the chart of his terrigenous pilgrimage, he beholds his airy effigy arriving about sundown at one inn after another in every quarter of the world; there he unslings his knapsack, there he descends ungainly from his omnibus; there they dined by the chimney where the snowwind was hooting, there he breakfasted, with an open shirt, in the green trellis at the garden end; but it was always from an inn that he departed, and towards an inn that he fared farther forth.

Out of all my private recollections of remembered inns and restaurants – and I believe it, other things equal, to be unrivalled – one particular house of entertainment stands forth alone. I am grateful, indeed, to many a swinging signboard, to many a rusty wine-bush; but not with the same kind of gratitude. Some were beautifully situated, some had an admirable table, some were the gathering-places if excellent companions; but take them for all in all, not one can be compared with Simoneau's at Monterey.[1]

To the front, it was part barber's shop, part bar; to the back, there was a kitchen and a sale-a-manger. The intending diner found himself in a little, chilly, bare, adobe room, furnished with chairs and tables, and adorned with some oil sketches roughly brushed upon the wall in the manner of Barbizon and Cernay.[2] The table, at whatever hour you entered, was already laid with a not spotless napkin and, by way of epergne, with a dish of green peppers and tomatoes, pleasing alike to eye and palate. If you stayed there to meditate before a meal, you would hear Simoneau all about kitchen, now rattling among the dishes, now clearing a semi-military chest with a 'hroum-hroum', a drumming of his fists, and a snatch of music. Out of the single window, you beheld a court, with a well, and hens and chickens and stacks of empty bottles, and on the other side, a very massive and crumbling outhouse of adobe. It was a storied outhouse, one of the oldest buildings on the Pacific coast: the prison of Monterey, where many a poor soul has slept his last night, and Padres, long since dead themselves, have wrestled by the hour with those about to die. I have sat out there in the court, long times together, among the bottles or beside the well, for the sake of the warm sunshine; and, strange as it may seem, I never had the smallest visiting of inspirations from the neighbourhood of that grim relic. I forget to what trivial use it had then fallen; but it looked placid like a browsing cow.

There were two set meals a day; and there it was that our polyglot society assembled.[3] There were rarely more than two of the same race together; though we were rich in pairs with two Frenchmen, two Portuguese and two Ligurians. Among Spanish, English and French, the sound of our talk was a little like Babel. But whatever tongue might be the speaker's fancy for the moment, the oaths that shone among his sentences were always English. By survival of the fittest, English oaths are destined to an immortality of service. Nothing in French, and only 'carrajo' in Spanish, can struggle long for their existence in the company of our rugged, fierce and pithy execrations. And again, in whatever the language the sentence might be couched, the western expletive 'you bet' would be thrown out hoarsely in the midst. This friendly synthesis of tongues put everyone at home. We spoke neither English, Spanish or French; we spoke Simoneaudean, the language of our common country.

Francois the baker filled the chair of presidence, his light eyes shining clearly under his rugged brows, his halting Provencal tongue sometimes wandering back upon old days in Chili or Brazil, sometimes uttering projects for the future of his joyous return to France and his family as that American Uncle, dear to playwrights. Our supper was Francois's breakfast, and our breakfast his supper; at which last, after his long, sweltering night's work and perhaps a glass of absinthe, I am bound to own he shone like the red sunrise among our starlight morning faces.

Frank the Italian Fisherman – though he usually took his meals among his fellow fishers, in a wooden house on stilts at the pier's end, redolent of nets and fish and apples and country wine on the tap – yet when things went well and the 'take' was large, would join our company in the adobe parlour. He had served on the Lakes in Garibaldian days; and Garibaldi was always 'my old man' with him, each of the three words rolled out with rough Italian gusto. He was the most polit-ically-minded man I ever knew. Unredeemed Italy was his pillowthought, and he waded after his nets at sunrise with the concerns of an ambassador. Foreign pol-itics, as the matter of a prolonged talk, ranks among the dullest; but Frank had a way of personifying European nations – Mr Rooshia, Mr Prooshia and Mr Owstria – which made the subject wonderfully lively. Finding that I could pronounce Italian, he would bring Italian journals up to papa Simoneau's, and set me read-ing aloud, while he, with a cigarette in his big fingers, and a perfect fire of inter-est in his eye, sat drinking as a reader usually delivers things of which he understands about a third. It was only the other day that the reason of this mania flashed across my mind. Frank, the critic of Mr Prooshia, had been denied the benefits of an education.

Frank had a younger man who came with him, a Ligurian, Dutra, notable for little beyond pleasant looks. The elder Dutra was a regular boarder, principally distinguished for singing Mexican serenades and trying vainly to teach me Mexican courtesy; I could never so much as learn to lend my cigarette with the proper and, I must add, sensible and graceful manoeuvre. Don A – I have forgot his name – a solemn gentleman, who had squandered a fortune, I was led to understand, in the pursuit of gallantry – was equally unsuccessful in his attempts to teach me Spanish; but he made a very grave figure at the board and gave our gatherings a flavour or respectability. The Captain of the Carmel whalers, a fierce, sensible Portuguese, joined us from time to time when he was in town on busi-ness. Once or twice, there came a melancholy example of a French savant, after beetles or plants, a man so filled with his own superiority that he could not address a fellow creature without offering or at least implying insult: a compound of the arrogance of science with the manners of the bagman, such as in fits of spleen, I suppose Haeckel to be like, poor man. And once only in my time – once was enough – there came down from his ranch upon the mountains, an incredi-ble Swiss boy in the best spirits, I suppose, that ever were enjoyed by man. He broke dishes, he bawled, he told us stories of his wife (and he was newly married), he sang, he played on various instruments, most of which he broke; and in short, by the time I took my way homeward, the neighbourhood of the Monterey prison house echoed like a Bedlam, and the next morning the whole company was pale and taciturn. As for the Swiss, if I am not misled, he took home with him to his mountain bride a notable headache and an empty purse. It is true he had been living for three months exclusively on tea and slapjacks.

The editor of the paper, Crevole Bronson[4], my patron as I shall proceed to show, was not frequently a diner, but he was a hanger on of our society, attracted by the character of our mirth which, for Monterey, was intellectual. Bronson, and his attendant youth, slept in the office of the journal in an atmosphere of printer's ink; the youth set up the exchanges, while Bronson, composing stick in hand, poured forth the leading articles. He had a disinterested love for polysyllables, and knew a great many. I can see him still, a very stout, large-faced, brown man with handsome eyes, leaning slightly forward against the case, the composing stick balanced in his hand, his spirit placidly pursuing longer words. His delight in the material of the art shows a rudimentary faculty; I cannot say that Bronson could write, but he wished to write, and he had an ideal of style. The Monterey paper was a losing business; its principal revenue was paid in kind by advertising shop-keepers; and one after another the editors wrestled for awhile, and then sold the paper, press and all, for something less than they had paid for it. Nor was it even amusing to conduct: the greater part of its columns were devoted to the exchanges and the advertisements by which it lived; and the only original matter which awoke much interest was in the form of personals. These take, in such a journal, one of two classical forms: As thus: 'Jack Smith came over Tuesday, from Tres Pinos where he is doing a great hardware business. He was looking splendid, and left a bottle of whiskey at our office. Call again, Jack!' Or again as thus: 'It is not true that Alexandro Gomez lost his way going home from the Fandango.' The first ministers to the vanity of Jack; the second to the mirth of Alexandar's friends. But to a man of dumb literary aspirations, the field is somewhat narrow; and Bronson chafed against his boundaries, like Bonaparte in Elba. He never men-tioned the word ambition; but he scarcely concealed his disappointment. He hurled polysyllables, somewhat vaguely, at the Monterey public …

All this time I have said nothing of papa Simoneau himself; always in his waist-coat and shirt sleeves, upright as a boy, with a rough, trooper-like smartness, vaunting his dishes if they were good, himself the first to condemn if they were unsuccessful; now red hot in a discussion, now playing his flute with antique graces, now shamelessly hurrying off the other boarders that he might sit down to chess with me: a man who had been most things from a man in business to a navvy, and kept his spirit and his kind heart through all.

I ask myself if I shall ever again sit down nightly with a pleasanter society; or if any human speech will ever sound more familiarly in my ears than the babel in that room beside the prison. And I am very sure, for one thing, I shall never find another landlord like my papa Simoneau. I was the spoiled child of the house; when my appetite failed, he broke his heart to find me dainties; if there was any-thing delicate in Monterey, papa Simoneau was sure to have some of it laid by for his favourite boarder. And then the talks that we had upon all subjects divine and human; the studies that we made in chess, Cunningham's gambit and what not; the long pleasant evenings in the corner by the stove! Once when I was three days confined to bed, I was wakened daily before sunrise by the cheery voice of Simoneau – I can hear it still – hailing me in the grey morning from the street, '*Stevenson – comment ca va?*' O mon bon Simoneau!, and the candles are blown out, and the shadows fall early round the prison, and we are all scattered to the four winds of heaven, and you yourself, as they write to me, are gone somewhere vaguely into the south, among the sand and the tarantulas, and I cannot even send you this word that your kindnesses are still remembered! ...

Notes
1. Jules Simoneau, a native of Nantes, France, who ran the popular establishment in Monterey.
2. Stevenson had spent some time in these French art colonies.
3. Stevenson had his own daily routine while staying at Monterey. 'I go to the PO for my mail... I call at Hadsell's for my paper; at length behold us installed in Simoneau's little white-washed back room, round a dirty tablecloth ... Then home to my great airy rooms with five windows opening on a balcony ... ' The latter refers to the 'French House' – now the Stevenson House museum, but then a meetinghouse run by Manuela Girardin. See Ernest Mehew, ed. *Selected Letters of Robert Louis Stevenson* (New Haven, Conn.: Yale University Press, 1997), p. 154. In 1932 the Literary Anniversary Club placed a bronze plaque on what is now referred to as the Stevenson House; in 1949 it was dedicated a state historic monument.
4. Crevole Bronson was the owner and editor of the *Monterey Californian*.

San Francisco

Stevenson lived in San Francisco[1] from mid-December 1879 until his marriage there on 19 May 1880.[2] Stevenson scholars believe he began writing the essay during the spring of 1882. It originally was published in The Magazine of Art *(May 1883) under the title of* A Modern Cosmopolis. *It also appears in Andrew Noble's* From the Clyde to California: Robert Louis Stevenson's Emigrant Journey *(Aberdeen: Aberdeen University Press, 1985).*

THE PACIFIC coast of the United States, as you may see by the map, and still better in that admirable book, *Two Years before the Mast*, by Dana,[3] is one of the most exposed and shelterless on earth. The trade-wind blows fresh; the huge Pacific swell booms along degree after degree of an unbroken line of coast. South of the joint firth of the Columbia and Williamette, there flows in no considerable river; south of Puget Sound there is no protected inlet of ocean. Along the whole seaboard of California there are but two unexceptionable anchorages – the bight of the Bay of Monterey, and the inland sea that takes its name from San Francisco.

Whether or not it was here that Drake put in in 1597, we cannot tell.[4] There is no other place so suitable; and yet the narrative of Francis Pretty scarcely seems to suit the features of the scene. Viewed from seaward, the Golden Gates should give no very English impression to justify the name of a new Albion. On the west, the deep lies open; nothing near but the still vexed Farallones. The coast is rough and barren. Tamalpais, a mountain of a memorable figure, spring direct from the sea-level, over-plumbs the narrow entrance from the north. On the south, the loud music of the Pacific sounds along beaches and cliffs, and among broken reefs, the sporting-place of the sea-lion. Dismal, shifting sandhills, wrinkled by the wind, appear behind. Perhaps, too, in the days of Drake, Tamalpais would be clothed to its peak with the majestic redwoods.

Within the memory of persons not yet old, a mariner might have steered into these narrows – not yet the Golden Gates [*sic*] – opened out the surface of the bay – here girt with hills, there lying broad to the horizon – and beheld a scene as empty of the presence, as pure from the handiwork, of man, as in the days of our old sea-commander. A Spanish mission, fort, and church took the place of those 'houses of the people of the country' which were seen by Pretty, 'close to the water-side'. All else would be unchanged. Now, a generation later, a great city covers the sandhills on the west, a growing town lies along the muddy shallows of the east; steamboats pant continually between them from before sunrise till the small hours of the morning; lines of great seagoing ships lie ranged at anchor; colours fly upon the islands; and from all around the hum of corporate life, of beaten bells, and steam, and running carriages, goes cheerily abroad in the sunshine. Choose a place on one of the huge throbbing ferry-boats, and, when you are mid-way between the city and the suburb, look around. The air is fresh and salt as if you were at sea. On the one hand is Oakland, gleaming white among its gardens. On the other, to seaward, hill after hill is crowded and crowned with the palaces west, across the sparkling picture; a forest of masts bristles like bulrushes about its feet; nothing remains of the days of Drake but the faithful tradewind scatter-ing the smoke, the fogs that will begin to muster about sundown, and the fine bulk of Tamalpais looking down on San Francisco, like Arthur's seat on Edinburgh.

Thus, in the course of a generation only, this city and its suburb have arisen. Men are alive by the score who have hunted all over the foundations in a dreary waste. I have dined, near the 'punctual centre' of San Francisco, with a gentleman (then newly married), who told me of his former pleasures, wading with his fowl-ing-piece in sand and scrub, on the site of the house where we were dining. In this busy, moving generation, we have all known cities to cover our boyish play-ground, we have all started for a country walk and stumbled on a new suburb; but I wonder what enchantment of the *Arabian Nights* can have equaled this evoca-tion of a roaring city, in a few years of a man's life, from the marshes and the blow-ing sand. Such swiftness of increase, as with an overgrown youth, suggests a corresponding swiftness of destruction. The sandy peninsula of San Francisco, mirroring itself on one side in the bay, beaten on the other by the surge of the Pacific, and shaken to the heart by frequent earthquakes, seems in itself no very durable foundation. According to Indian tales, perhaps older than the name of California, it once rose out of the sea in a moment, and sometime or other shall, in a moment, sink again. No Indian, they say, cares to linger on that doubtful land. 'The earth hath bubbles as the water has, and this is of them.' Here, indeed, all is new, nature as well as towns. The very hills of California have an unfinished look; the rains and the streams have not yet carved them to their perfect shape. The forests spring like mushrooms from the unexhausted soil; and they are mown down yearly by the forest fires. We are in early geological epochs, changeful and insecure; and we feel, as with a sculptor's model, that the author may yet grow weary of and shatter the rough sketch.

Fancy apart, San Francisco is a city beleaguered with alarms. The lower parts, along the bay side, sit on piles; old wrecks decaying, fish dwelling unsunned, beneath the populous houses; and a trifling subsidence might drown the business quarters in an hour. Earthquakes are not only common, they are sometimes threatening in their violence; the fear of them grows yearly on a resident; he begins with indifference, ends in sheer panic; and no one feels safe in any but a wooden house. Hence it comes that, in that rainless clime, the whole city is built of timber – a woodyard of unusual extent and complication; that fires spring up readily, and served by the unwearying trade-wind, swiftly spread; that all over the city there are fire-signal boxes; that the sound of the bell, telling the number of the threatened ward, is soon familiar to the ear; and that nowhere else in the world is the art of the fireman carried to so nice a point.

Next, perhaps, in order of strangeness to the rapidity of its appearance, is the mingling of the races that combine to people it. The town is essentially not Anglo-Saxon; still more essentially not American. The Yankee and the Englishman find themselves alike in a strange country. There are none of these touches – not of nature, and I dare scarcely say of art – by which the Anglo-Saxon feels himself at home in so great a diversity of lands. Here, on the contrary, are airs of Marseilles and of Pekin. The shops along the street are like the consulates of different nations. The passers-by vary in feature like the slides of a magic-lantern. For we are here in that city of gold to which adventurers congregated out of all the winds of heaven; we are in a land that the sea that laves the piers of San Francisco is the ocean of the East and of the isles of summer. There goes the Mexican, unmistakable; there the blue-clad Chinaman with his white slippers; there the soft-spoken, brown Kanaka, or perhaps a waif from far-away Malaya. You hear French, German, Italian, Spanish, and English indifferently. You taste the food of all nations in the various restaurants; passing from a French *prix-fixe* where every one is French, to a roaring German ordinary where every one is German; ending, perhaps, in a cool and silent Chinese tea-house. For every man, for every race and nation, that city is a foreign city; humming with foreign tongues and customs; and yet each and all have made themselves at home. The Germans have a German theatre and innumerable beer-gardens. The French Fall of the Bastille is celebrated with squibs and banners, and marching patriots, as noisily as the American Fourth of July. The Italians have their dear domestic quarter, with Italian caricatures in the windows, Chianti and polenta in the taverns. The Chinese are settled as in China. The goods they offer for sale are as foreign as the lettering on the signboards of the shop: dried fish from the China seas; pale cakes and sweetmeats – the like, perhaps, once eaten by Babroubadour; nuts of unfriendly shape; ambiguous outlandish vegetables, misshapen, lean, or bulbous – telling of a country where the trees are not as our trees, and the very back-garden is a cabinet of curiosities. The joss-house is hard by, heavy with incense, packed with quaint carvings and the paraphernalia of a foreign ceremonial. All these you behold, crowded together in the narrower arteries of the city, cool, sunless, a little mouldy, with the unfamiliar faces at your elbow, and the high, musical sing-song of that alien language in your ears. Yet the houses are of Occidental build; the lines of a hundred telegraph pass, thick as a ship's rigging, overhead, a kite hanging among them, perhaps, or perhaps two, one European, one Chinese, in shape and colour; mercantile Jack, the Italian fisher, the Dutch merchant, the Mexican vaquero, go hustling by; at the sunny end of the street, a thoroughfare roars with European traffic; and meanwhile, high and clear, out breaks perhaps the San

Francisco fire-alarm, and people pause to count the strokes, and in the stations of the double fire-service you know that the electric bells are ringing, the traps opening, and clapping to, and the engine, manned and harnessed, being whisked into the seat, before the sound of the alarm has ceased to vibrate on your ear. Of all romantic places for a boy to loiter in, that Chinese quarter is the most romantic. There, on a half-holiday, three doors from home, he may visit an actual foreign land, foreign in people, language, things and customs. The very barber of the *Arabian Nights* shall be at work before him, shaving heads; he shall see Alladin playing on the streets; who knows but among those namesless vegetables the fruit of the nosetree itself may be exposed for sale? And the interest is heightened with a chill of horror. Below, you hear, the cellars are alive with mystery; opium dens, where the smokers lie one above another, shelf above shelf, close-packed and groveling in deadly stupor; the seats of unknown vices and cruelties, the prisons of unacknowledged slaves and secret lazarettos of disease.

With all this mass of nationalities, crime is common. There are rough quarters where it is dangerous o' nights; cellars of public entertainment which the wary pleasure-seeker chooses to avoid. Concealed weapons are unlawful, but the law is continually broken. One editor was shot dead while I was there; another walked the streets accompanied by a bravo, his guardian angel. I have been quietly eating a dish of oysters in a restaurant, where, not more than ten minutes after I had left, shots were exchanged and took effect; and one night about ten o'clock, I saw a man standing watchfully at a streetcorner with a long Smith-and-Wesson glittering in his hand behind his back. Somebody had done something he should not, and was being looked for with a vengeance. It is odd, too, that the seat of the last vigilance committee I know of – a mediaeval *Vehmgericht* – was none other than the Palace Hotel, the world's greatest caravanserai, served by lifts and lit with electricity; where, in the great glazed court, a band nightly discourses music from a grove of palms. So do extremes meet in this city of contrasts: extremes of wealth and poverty, apathy and excitement, the conveniences of civilisation and the red justice of Judge Lynch.

The streets lie straight up and down the hills, and straight across at right angles, these in sun, those in shadow, a trenchant pattern of gloom and glare; and what with the crisp illumination, the sea-air singing in your ears, the chill and glitter, the changing aspects both of things and people, the fresh sights at every corner of your walk – sights of the bay, of Tamalpais, of steep, descending streets, of the outspread city – whiffs of alien speech, sailors singing on shipboard. Chinese coolies toiling on the shore, crowds brawling all day in the street before the Stock Exchange – one brief impression follows and obliterates another, and the city leaves upon the mind no general and stable picture, but a profusion of airy and incongruous images, of the sea and shore, the east and west, the summer and the winter.

In the better parts of the most interesting city there is apt to be a touch of the commonplace. It is in the slums and suburbs that the city dilettante finds his game. And there is nothing more characteristic and original than the outlying quarters of San Francisco. The Chinese district is the most famous;[5] but it is far from the only truffle in the pie. There is many another dingy corner, many a young antiquity, many a *terrain vague* with that stamp of quaintness that the city lover seeks and dwells on; and the indefinite prolongation of its streets, up hill and down dale, makes San Francisco a place apart. The same street in its career visits and unites so many different classes of society, here echoing with drays, there lying decorously silent between the mansions of Bonanza millionaires, to founder at last among the drifting sands beside Lone Mountain cemetery, or die out among the sheds and lumber of the north. Thus you may be struck with a spot, set it down for the most romantic of the city, and, glancing at the name-plate, find it is the same street that you yourself inhabit in another quarter of the town.

The great net of straight thoroughfares lying at right angles, east and west and north and south, over the shoulders of Nob Hill, the hill of palaces, must certainly be counted the best part of San Francisco. It is there that the millionaires are gathered together vying with each other in display. From thence, looking down over the business wards of the city, we can descry a building with a little belfry, and that is the Stock Exchange, the heart of San Francisco: a great pump we might call it, continually pumping up the savings of the lower quarters into the pockets of the millionaires upon the hill. But these same thoroughfares that enjoy for awhile so elegant a destiny have their lines prolonged into more unpleasant places. Some meet their fate in the sands; some must take a cruise in the ill-famed China quarters; some run into the sea; some perish unwept among pig-sties and rubbish-heaps.

Nob Hill comes, of right, in the place of honour; but the two other hills of San Francisco are more entertaining to explore. On both there is a world of old wooden houses snoozing together all forgotten. Some are of the quaintest design, others only romantic by neglect and age. Some have been almost undermined by new thoroughfares, and sit high up on the margin of the sandy cutting, only to be reached by stairs. Some are curiously painted, and I have seen one at least with ancient carvings panelled in its wall. Surely they are not of Californian building, but far voyagers from round the stormy Horn, like those who sent for them and dwelt in them at first. Brought to be the favourites of the wealthy, they have sunk into these poor, forgotten districts, where, like old town toasts, they keep each other silently in countenance. Telegraph Hill and Rincon Hill, these are the two dozing quarters that I recommend to the city dilettante. There stand these forgotten houses, enjoying the unbroken sun and quiet. There, if there were such an author, would the San Francisco Fortune de Boisgobey pitch the first chapter of his mystery. But the first is the quainter of the two, and commands, moreover, a noble view. As it stands at the turn of the bay, its skirts are all waterside, and round from North Reach to the Bay Front you can follow doubtful paths from one quaint corner to another. Everywhere the same tumble-down decay and sloppy progress, new things yet unmade, old things tottering to their fall; everywhere the same out-at-elbows, many-nationed loungers at dim, irregular grog-shops; everywhere the same sea-air and isleted sea-prospect; and for a last and more romantic note, you have on the one hand Tamalpais standing high in the blue air, and on the other the tail of that long alignment of three-masted, full-rigged, deep-sea ships that make a forest of spars along the eastern front of San Francisco. In no other port is such a navy congregated. For the coast trade is so trifling, and the ocean trade from round the Horn so large, that the smaller ships are swallowed up, and can do nothing to confuse the majestic order of these merchant princes. In an age when the ship-of-the-line is already a thing of the past, and we can never again hope to go coasting in a cock-boat between the 'wooden walls' of a squadron at anchor, there is perhaps no place on earth where the power and beauty of sea architecture can be so perfectly enjoyed as in this bay.

Notes

1. Stevenson lived at 608 Bush Street, a boarding house run by an Irish landlady named Mary Carson. He settled in and quickly started a routine. Between eight and half past nine in the morning 'a slender gentleman in an ulster' would leave his residence and descend Powell Street 'with an active step'. He then went to the Pine Street Coffee House on Sixth Street and ordered a cup of coffee, roll, and a pat of butter for 10 cents. For three to four hours in the afternoon, he returned to his room to work, and then in the evening enjoyed a meal at Donnadieu's at 425 Bush Street. See *Selected Letters of Robert Louis Stevenson*. Edited by Ernest Mehew (New Haven, Conn.: Yale University Press, 2001), p. 158–59.

2. Fanny Osbourne obtained her divorce on 15 December 1879. The couple was married on 19 May 1880 by the Reverend Dr William Anderson Scott (1813–1885), a Scots Presbyterian minister and president of the local chapter of the St. Andrews Society, at his home at 521 Post Street. The witnesses were Dora Williams, a friend of the Stevensons; the minister's wife; and a cat. 'After the service, the Stevensons took Dora to dine with them in a good restaurant, the Viennese Bakery, then went to the Palace Hotel to stay for two or three nights.' See Joan Parry Dutton, *They Left Their Mark: Famous Passages through the Wine Country* (Calistoga, Calif.: Sharpsteen Museum Association, 1998), p. 25.

3. Richard Henry Dana (1815–1882), American lawyer and author.

4. Sir Frances Drake (1543?–1596), English navigator and buccaneer.

5. Stevenson spent many hours sitting in Portsmouth Plaza in Chinatown. A memorial to RLS was unveiled on 17 October 1897 by the RLS Fellowship.

FROM *The Silverado Squatters*

The Silverado Squatters was first serialised in the Century Illustrated Monthly Magazine in November and December 1883. The American edition of the book was published by Roberts Brothers of Boston late in 1883 and simultaneously in London by Chatto and Windus. It remains one of Stevenson's most popular works of nonfiction.

IN THE VALLEY

CALISTOGA

IT is difficult for a European to imagine Calistoga, the whole place is so new, and of such an accidental pattern; the very name, I hear, was invented at a supper-party by the man who found the springs.[1]

The railroad and the highway come up the valley about parallel to one another. The street of Calistoga joins the perpendicular to both – a wide street, with bright, clean, low houses, here and there a verandah over the sidewalk, here and there a horse-post, here and there lounging townsfolk. Other streets are marked out, and most likely named; for these towns in the New World begin with a firm resolve to grow larger, Washington and Broadway, and then First and Second, and so forth, being boldly plotted out as soon as the community indulges in a plan. But, in the meanwhile, all the life and most of the houses of Calistoga are concentrated upon that street between the railway station and the road. I never heard it called by any name, but I will hazard a guess that it is either Washington or Broadway. Here are the blacksmith's, the chemist's, the general merchant's, and Kong Sam Kee, the Chinese laundryman's; here, probably, is the office of the local paper (for the place has a paper – they all have papers); and here certainly is one of the hotels, Cheeseborough's,[2] whence the daring Foss,[3] a man dear to legend, starts his horses for the Geysers.

It must be remembered that we are here in a land of stage-drivers and highwaymen: a land, in that sense, like England a hundred years ago. The highway robber – road-agent, he is quaintly called – is still busy in these parts. The fame of Vasquez is still young. Only a few years ago, the Lakeport stage was robbed a mile or two from Calistoga. In 1879, the dentist of Mendocino City, fifty miles away upon the coast, suddenly threw off the garments of his trade, like Grindoff, in *The Miller and His Men*, and flamed forth in his second dress as a captain of banditti. A great robbery was followed by a long chase, a chase of days if not of weeks, among the intricate hill-country; and the chase was followed by much desultory fighting, in which several – and the dentist, I believe, amongst the number – bit the dust. The grass was springing for the first time, nourished upon their blood, when I arrived in Calistoga. I am reminded of another highwayman of that same year. 'He had been unwell,' so ran his humorous defence, 'and the doctor told him to take something, so he took the express-box.'

The cultus of the stage-coachman always flourishes highest where there are thieves on the road, and where the guard travels armed, and the stage is not only a link between country and city, and the vehicle of news, but has a faint warfaring aroma, like a man who should be brother to a soldier. California boasts her famous stage-drivers, and among the famous Foss is not forgotten. Along the unfenced, abominable mountain roads, he launches his team with small regard to human life or the doctrine of probabilities. Flinching travellers, who behold themselves coasting eternity at every corner, look with natural admiration at their driver's huge, impassive, fleshy countenance. He has the very face for the driver in Sam Weller's anecdote, who upset the election party at the required point. Wonderful tales are current of his readiness and skill. One in particular, of how one of his horses fell at a ticklish passage of the road, and how Foss let slip the reins, and, driving over the fallen animal, arrived at the next stage with only three. This I relate as I heard it, without guarantee.

I only saw Foss once, though, strange as it may sound, I have twice talked with him. He lives out of Calistoga, at a ranch called Fossville. One evening, after he was long gone home, I dropped into Cheeseborough's, and was asked if I should like to speak with Mr. Foss. Supposing that the interview was impossible, and that I was merely called upon to subscribe the general sentiment, I boldly answered 'Yes.' Next moment, I had one instrument at my ear, another at my mouth and found myself, with nothing in the world to say, conversing with a man several miles off among desolate hills. Foss rapidly and somewhat plaintively brought the conversation to an end; and he returned to his night's grog at Fossville, while I strolled forth again on Calistoga high street. But it was an odd thing that here, on what we are accustomed to consider the very skirts of civilisation, I should have used the telephone for the first time in my civilised career. So it goes in these young countries; telephones, and telegraphs, and newspapers, and advertisements running far ahead among the Indians and the grizzly bears.

Alone, on the other side of the railway, stands the Springs Hotel, with its attendant cottages. The floor of the valley is extremely level to the very roots of the hills; only here and there a hillock, crowned with pines, rises like the barrow of some chieftain famed in war; and right against one of these hillocks is the Springs Hotel – is or was; for since I was there the place has been destroyed by fire, and has risen again from its ashes. A lawn runs about the house, and the lawn is in its turn surrounded by a system of little five-roomed cottages, each with a verandah and a weedy palm before the door. Some of the cottages are let to residents, and these are wreathed in flowers. The rest are occupied by ordinary visitors to the

Hotel; and a very pleasant way this is, by which you have a little country cottage of your own, without domestic burthens, and by the day or week.

The whole neighbourhood of Mount Saint Helena⁴ is full of sulphur and of boiling springs. The Geysers are famous; they were the great health resort of the Indians before the coming of the whites. Lake County is dotted with spas; Hot Springs and White Sulphur Springs are the names of two stations on the Napa Valley railroad; and Calistoga itself seems to repose on a mere film above a boiling, subterranean lake. At one end of the hotel enclosure are the springs from which it takes its name, hot enough to scald a child seriously while I was there. At the other end, the tenant of a cottage sank a well, and there also the water came up boiling. It keeps this end of the valley as warm as a toast. I have gone across to the hotel a little after five in the morning, when a sea fog from the Pacific was hanging thick and gray, and dark and dirty overhead, and found the thermometer had been up before me, and had already climbed among the nineties; and in the stress of the day it was sometimes too hot to move about.

But in spite of this heat from above and below, doing one on both sides, Calistoga was a pleasant place to dwell in; beautifully green, for it was then that favoured moment in the Californian year, when the rains are over and the dusty summer has not yet set in; often visited by fresh airs, now from the mountain, now across Sonoma from the sea; very quiet, very idle, very silent but for the breezes and the cattle bells afield. And there was something satisfactory in the sight of that great mountain that enclosed us to the north: whether it stood, robed in sunshine, quaking to its topmost pinnacle with the heat and brightness of the day; or whether it set itself to weaving vapours, wisp after wisp growing, trembling, fleeting, and fading in the blue.

The tangled, woody, and almost trackless foot-hills that enclose the valley, shutting it off from Sonoma on the west, and from Yolo on the east – rough as they were in outline, dug out by winter streams, crowned by cliffy bluffs and nodding pine trees – wore dwarfed into satellites by the bulk and bearing of Mount Saint Helena. She over-towered them by two-thirds of her own stature. She excelled them by the boldness of her profile. Her great bald summit, clear of trees and pasture, a cairn of quartz and cinnabar, rejected kinship with the dark and shaggy wilderness of lesser hill-tops.

NAPA WINE

I was interested in Californian wine. Indeed, I am interested in all wines, and have been all my life, from the raisin wine that a schoolfellow kept secreted in his play-box up to my last discovery, those notable Valtellines, that once shone upon the board of Caesar.

Some of us, kind old Pagans, watch with dread the shadows falling on the age:

how the unconquerable worm invades the sunny terraces of France, and Bordeaux is no more, and the Rhone a mere Arabia Petraea. Chateau Neuf is dead, and I have never tasted it; Hermitage – a hermitage indeed from all life's sorrows – lies expiring by the river. And in the place of imperial elixirs, beautiful to every sense, gem-hued, flower-scented, dream-compellers: – behold upon the quays at Cette the chemicals arrayed; behold the analyst at Marseilles, raising hands in obsecration, attesting god Lyceus, and the vats staved in, and the dishonest wines poured forth among the sea. It is not Pan only: Bacchus, too, is dead.

If wine is to withdraw its most poetic countenance, the sun of the white dinner-cloth, a deity to be invoked by two or three, all fervent, hushing their talk, degusting tenderly, and storing reminiscences – for a bottle of good wine, like a good act, shines ever in the retrospect – if wine is to desert us, go thy ways, old Jack! Now we begin to have compunctions, and look back at the brave bottles squandered upon dinner-parties, where the guests drank grossly, discussing politics the while, and even the schoolboy 'took his whack,' like liquorice water. And at the same time, we look timidly forward, with a spark of hope, to where the new lands, already wearing of producing gold, begin to green with vineyards. A nice point in human history falls to be decided by Californian and Australian wines.

Wine in California is still in the experimental stage; and when you taste a vintage, grave economical questions are involved.[5] The beginning of vine-planting is like the beginning of mining for the precious metals: the wine-grower also 'prospects.' One corner of land after another is tried with one kind of grape after another. This is a failure; that is better; a third best. So, bit by bit, they grope about for their Clos Vougeot and Lafite. Those lodes and pockets of earth, more precious than the precious ores, that yield inimitable fragrance and soft fire; those virtuous Bonanzas, where the soil has subliminated under sun and stars to something finer, and the wine is bottled poetry: these still lie undiscovered; chaparral conceals, thicket embowers them; the miner chips the rock and wanders farther, and the grizzly muses undisturbed. But there they bide their hour, awaiting their Columbus; and nature nurses and prepares them. The smack of Californian earth shall linger on the palate of your grandson.

Meanwhile the wine is simply a good wine; the best that I have tasted better than a Beaujolais, and not unlike. But the trade is poor; it lives from hand to mouth, putting its all into experiments, and forced to sell its vintages. To find one properly matured, and bearing its own name, it to be fortune's favourite.

Bearing its own name, I say, and dwell upon the innuendo.

'You want to know why California wine is not drunk in the States?' a San Francisco wine merchant said to me, after he had shown me through his premises. 'Well, here's the reason.'

And opening a large cupboard, fitted with many little drawers, he proceeded to shower me all over with a great variety of gorgeously tinted labels, blue, red, or yellow, stamped with crown or coronet, and hailing down from such a profusion of *clos* and *chateaux*, that a single department could scarce have furnished forth the names. But it was strange that all looked unfamiliar.

'Chateau X_____?' said I. 'I never heard of that.'

'I dare say not,' said he, 'I had been reading one of X_____'s novels.'

They were all castles in Spain! But that sure enough is the reason why California wine is not drunk in the States.

Napa Valley has been long a seat of the wine-growing industry.[6] It did not here begin, as it does too often, in the low valley lands along the river, but took at once to the rough foot-hills, where alone it can expect to prosper. A basking inclination, and stones, to be a reservoir of the day's heat, seem necessary to the soil for wine; the grossness of the earth must be evaporated, its marrow daily melted and refined for ages; until at length these clods that break below our footing, and to the eye appear but common earth, are truly and to the perceiving mind, a masterpiece of nature. The dust of Richebourg, which the wind carries away, what an apotheosis of the dust! Not man himself can seem a stranger child of that brown, friable powder, than the blood and sun in that old flask behind the faggots.

A Californian vineyard, one of the man's outposts in the wilderness, has features of its own. There is nothing here to remind you of the Rhine or Rhone, of the low *cote d'or*, or the infamous and scabby deserts of Champagne; but all is green, solitary, covert. We visited two of them, Mr. Schram's and Mr. M'Eckron's, sharing the same glen.[7]

Some way down the valley below Calistoga, we turned sharply to the south and plunged into the thick of the wood. A rude trail rapidly mounting; a little stream tinkling by on the one hand, big enough perhaps after the rains, but already yielding up its life; overhead and on all sides a bower of green and tangled thicket, still fragrant, and still flower-bespangled by the early season, where thimble-berry played the part of our English hawthorn, and the buck-eyes were putting forth their twisted horns of blossom: through all this, we struggled toughly upwards, canted to and fro by the roughness of the trail, and continually switched across the face by sprays of leaf or bottom. The last is of no great inconvenience at home; but here in California it is a matter of some moment. For in all woods and by every wayside there prospers an abominable shrub or weed, called poison-oak, whose very neighbourhood is venomous to some, and whose actual touch is avoided by the most impervious.

The two houses, with their vineyards, stood each in a green niche of its own in this steep and narrow forest dell. Though they were so near, there was already a good difference in level; and Mr. M'Eckron's head must be a long way under the feet of Mr. Schram. No more had been cleared than was necessary for cultivation; close around each oasis ran the tangled wood; the glen unfolds them; there they lie basking in sun and silence, concealed from all but the clouds and the mountain birds.

Mr. M'Eckron's is a bachelor establishment; a little bit of a wooden house, a small

cellar hard by in the hillside, and a patch of vines planted and tended single-handed by himself. He had but recently begun; his vines were young, his business young
also; but I thought he had the look of the man who succeeds. He hailed from
Greenock: he remembered his father putting him inside Mons Meg,[8] and that
touched me home; and we exchanged a word or two of Scotch, which pleased me
more than you would fancy.

Mr. Schram's, on the other hand, is the oldest vineyard in the valley, eighteen
years old, I think; yet he began a penniless barber, and even after he had broken
ground up here with his black malvoisies, continued for long to tramp the valley
with his razor.[9] Now, his place is the picture of prosperity: stuffed birds in the verandah, cellars far dug into the hillside, and resting on pillars like a bandit's cave: – all
trimness, varnish, flowers, and sunshine, among the tangled wildwood. Stout, smiling Mrs. Schram, who has been to Europe and apparently all about the States for
pleasure, entertained Fanny in the verandah, while I was tasting wines in the cellar.
To Mr. Schram this was a solemn office; his serious gusto warmed my heart; prosperity had not yet wholly banished a certain neophyte and girlish trepidation, and
he followed every sip and read my face with proud anxiety. I tasted all. I tasted every
variety and shade of Schramberger, red and white Schramberger, Burgundy
Schramberger, Schramberger Hock, Schramberger Golden Chasselas, the latter
with a notable bouquet, and I fear to think how many more. Much of it goes to
London – most, I think; and Mr. Schram has a great notion of the English taste.

In this wild spot, I did not feel the sacredness of ancient cultivation. It was still
raw, it was no Marathon, and no Johannisberg; yet the stirring sunlight, and the
growing vines, and the vats and bottles in the cavern, made a pleasant music for the
mind. Here, also, earth's cream was being skimmed and garnered; and the London
customers can taste, such as it is, the tang of the earth in this green valley. So local,
so quintessential is a wine, that it seems the very birds in the verandah might communicate a flavour, and that romantic cellar influence the bottle next to be
uncorked in Pimlico,[10] and the smile of jolly Mr. Schram might mantle in the glass.

But these are but experiments. All things in this new land are moving farther on:
the wine-vats and the miner's blasting tools but picket for a night, like Bedouin
pavilions; and tomorrow to fresh woods! This stir of change and these perpetual
echoes of the moving footfall, haunt the land. Men move eternally, still chasing
Fortune; and Fortune found, still wander. As we drove back to Calistoga, the road
lay empty of mere passengers, but its green side was dotted with the camps of travelling families: one cumbered with a great waggonful of household stuff, settlers
going to occupy a ranch they had taken up in Mendocino, or perhaps Tehama
County; another, a party in dust coats, men and women, whom we found camped
in a grove on the roadside, all on pleasure bent, with a Chinaman to cook for them,
and who waved their hands to us as we drove by.

THE SCOT ABROAD

A FEW pages back, I wrote that a man belonged, in these days, to a variety of countries; but the old land is still the true love, the others are but pleasant infidelities. Scotland is indefinable; it has no unity except upon the map. Two languages, many dialects, innumerable forms of piety, and countless local patriotisms and prejudices, part us among ourselves more widely than the extreme east and west of that great continent of America. When I am at home, I feel a man from Glasgow to be something like a rival, a man from Barra to be more than half a foreigner. Yet let us meet in some far country, and, whether we hail from the braes of Manor or the braes of Mar, some ready-made affection joins us on the instant. It is not race. Look at us. One is Norse, one Celtic, and another Saxon. It is not community of tongue. We have it not among ourselves; and we have it almost to perfection, with English, or Irish, or American. It is no tie of faith, for we detest each other's errors. And yet somewhere, deep down in the heart of each one of us, something yearns for the old land, and the old kindly people.

Of all mysteries of the human heart, this is perhaps the most inscrutable. There is no special loveliness in that gray country, with its rainy, sea-beat archipelago; its fields of dark mountains; its unsightly places, black with coal; its treeless, sour, unfriendly looking corn-lands; its quaint, gray, castled city, where the bells clash of a Sunday, and the wind squalls, and the salt showers fly and beat. I do not even know if I desire to live there; but let me hear, in some far land, a kindred voice sing out, 'Oh, why left I my hame?' and it seems at once as if no beauty under the kind heavens, and no society of the wise and good, can repay me for my absence from my country. And though I think I would rather die elsewhere, yet in my heart of hearts I long to be buried among good Scots clods.[11] I will say it fairly, it grows on me with every year: there are no stars so lovely as Edinburgh streetlamps. When I forget thee, auld Reekie, may my right hand forget its cunning!

The happiest lot on earth is to be born a Scotchman. You must pay for it in many ways, as for all other advantages on earth. You have to learn the paraphrases and the shorter catechism; you generally take to drink; your youth, as far as I can find out, is a time of louder war against society, of more outcry and tears and turmoil, than if you had been born, for instance, in England. But somehow life is warmer and closer; the hearth burns more redly; the lights of home shine softer on the rainy street; the very names, endeared in verse and music, cling nearer round our hearts. An Englishman may meet an Englishman to-morrow, upon Chimborazo, and neither of them care; but when the Scotch wine-grower told me of Mons Meg, it was like magic.

'From the dim shieling on the misty island Mountains divide us, and a world of seas; Yet still our hearts are true, our hearts are Highland, And we, in dreams, behold the Hebrides.'[12]

And, Highland and Lowland, all our hearts are Scotch.

Only a few days after I had seen M'Eckron, a message reached me in my cottage. It was a Scotchman who had come down a long way from the hills to market. He had heard there was a countryman in Calistoga, and came round to the hotel to see him. We said a few words to each other; we had not much to say – should never have seen each other had we stayed at home, separated alike in space and in society; and then we shook hands, and he went his way again to his ranch among the hills, and that was all.

Another Scotchman there was, a resident, who for the more love of the common country, douce, serious, religious man, drove me all about the valley, and took as much interest in me as if I had been his son: more, perhaps; for the son has faults too keenly felt, while the abstract countryman is perfect – like a whiff of peats.

And there was yet another. Upon him I came suddenly, as he was calmly entering my cottage, his mind quite evidently bent on plunder: a man of about fifty, filthy, ragged, roguish, with a chimney-pot hat and a tail coat, and a pursing of his mouth that might have been envied by an elder of the kirk. He had just such a face as I have seen a dozen times behind the plate.

'Hullo, sir!' I cried. 'Where are you going?'

He turned round without a quiver.

'You're a Scotchman, sir?' he said gravely. 'So am I; I come from Aberdeen. This is my card,' presenting me with a piece of pasteboard which he had raked out of some gutter in the period of the rains. 'I was just examining this palm,' he continued, indicating the misbegotten plant before our door, 'which is the largest specimen I have yet observed in Califoarnia.'

There were four or five larger within sight. But where was the use of argument? He produced a tape-line, made me help him to measure the tree at the level of the ground, and entered the figures in a large and filthy pocket-book, all with the gravity of Solomon. He then thanked me profusely, remarking that such little services were due between countrymen; shook hands with me, 'for auld lang syne,' as he said; and took himself solemnly away, radiating dirt and humbug as he went.

A month or two after this encounter of mine, there came a Scot to Sacramento – perhaps from Aberdeen. Anyway, there never was any one more Scotch in this wide world. He could sing and dance, and drink, I presume; and he played the pipes with vigour and success. All the Scotch in Sacramento became infatuated with him, and spent their spare time and money, driving him about in an open cab, between drinks, while he blew himself scarlet at the pipes. This is a very sad story. After he had borrowed money from every one, he and his pipes suddenly disappeared from Sacramento, and when I last heard, the police were looking for him.

I cannot say how this story amused me, when I felt myself so thoroughly ripe on both sides to be duped in the same way.

It is at least a curious thing, to conclude, that the races which wander widest, Jews and Scotch, should be the most clannish in the world. But perhaps these two are cause and effect: 'For ye were strangers in the land of Egypt.'

THE FIRST IMPRESSIONS OF SILVERADO

THE ACT OF SQUATTING

THERE were four of us squatters[13] – myself and my wife, the King and Queen of Silverado; Sam, the Crown Prince; and Chuchu, the Grand Duke. Chuchu, a setter crossed with spaniel, was the most unsuited for a rough life. He had been nurtured tenderly in the society of ladies; his heart was large and soft; he regarded the sofa-cushion as a bed-rook necessary of existence. Though about the size of a sheep, he loved to sit in ladies' laps; he never said a bad word in all his blameless days; and if he had seen a flute, I am sure he could have played upon it by nature. It may seem hard to say it of a dog, but Chuchu was a tame cat.

The king and queen, the grand duke, and a basket of cold provender for immediate use, set forth from Calistoga in a double buggy; the crown prince, on horseback, led the way like an outrider. Bags and boxes and a second-hand stove were to follow close upon our heels by [Rufe] Hanson's team.

It was a beautiful still day; the sky was one field of azure. Not a leaf moved, not a speck appeared in heaven. Only from the summit of the mountain one little snowy wisp of cloud after another kept detaching itself, like smoke from a volcano, and blowing southward in some high stream of air: Mount Saint Helena still at her interminable task, making the weather, like a Lapland witch.

By noon we had come in sight of the mill: a great brown building, half-way up the hill, big as a factory, two stories high, and with tanks and ladders along the roof; which, as a pendicle of Silverado mine, we held to be an outlying province of our own. Thither, then, we went, crossing the valley by a grassy trail; and there lunched out of the basket, sitting in a kind of portico, and wondering, while we ate, at this great bulk of useless building. Through a chink we could look far down into the interior, and see sunbeams floating in the dust and striking on tier after tier of silent, rusty machinery. It cost six thousand dollars, twelve hundred English sovereigns; and now, here it stands deserted, like the temple of a forgotten religion, the busy millers toiling somewhere else. All the time we were there, mill and mill town showed no sign of life; that part of the mountain-side, which is very open and green, was tenanted by no living creature but ourselves and the insects; and nothing stirred but the cloud manufactory upon the mountain summit. It was odd to compare this with the former days, when the engine was in fall blast, the mill palpitating to its strokes, and the carts came rattling down from Silverado, charged with ore.[14]

By two we had been landed at the mine, the buggy was gone again, and we were left to our own reflections and the basket of cold provender, until Hanson should arrive. Hot as it was by the sun, there was something chill in such a home-coming, in that world of wreck and rust, splinter and rolling gravel, where for so many years no fire had smoked.

Silverado platform filled the whole width of the canyon. Above, as I have said, this was a wild, red, stony gully in the mountains; but below it was a wooded dingle. And through this, I was told, there had gone a path between the mine and the Toll House – our natural north-west passage to civilisation. I found and followed it, clearing my way as I went through fallen branches and dead trees. It went straight down that steep canyon, till it brought you out abruptly over the roofs of the hotel. There was nowhere any break in the descent. It almost seemed as if, were you to drop a stone down the old iron chute at our platform, it would never rest until it hopped upon the Toll House shingles. Signs were not wanting of the ancient greatness of Silverado. The footpath was well marked, and had been well trodden in the old clays by thirsty miners. And far down, buried in foliage, deep out of sight of Silverado, I came on a last outpost of the mine – a mound of gravel, some wreck of wooden aqueduct, and the mouth of a tunnel, like a treasure grotto in a fairy story. A stream of water, fed by the invisible leakage from our shaft, and dyed red with cinnabar or iron, ran trippingly forth out of the bowels of the cave; and, looking far under the arch, I could see something like an iron lantern fastened on the rocky wall. It was a promising spot for the imagination. No boy could have left it unexplored.

The stream thenceforward stole along the bottom of the dingle, and made, for that dry land, a pleasant warbling in the leaves. Once, I suppose, it ran splashing down the whole length of the canyon, but now its head waters had been tapped by the shaft at Silverado, and for a great part of its course it wandered sunless among the joints of the mountain. No wonder that it should better its pace when it sees, far before it, daylight whitening in the arch, or that it should come trotting forth into the sunlight with a song.

The two stages had gone by when I got down, and the Toll House stood, dozing in sun and dust and silence, like a place enchanted.[15] My mission was after hay for bedding, and that I was readily promised. But when I mentioned that we were waiting for Rufe, the people shook their heads. Rufe was not a regular man any way, it seemed; and if he got playing poker – Well, poker was too many for Rufe. I had not yet heard them bracketted together; but it seemed a natural conjunction, and commended itself swiftly to my fears; and as soon as I returned to Silverado and had told my story, we practically gave Hanson up, and set ourselves to do what we could find do-able in our desert-island state.

The lower room had been the assayer's office.[16] The floor was thick with debris – part human, from the former occupants; part natural, sifted in by mountain winds. In a sea of red dust there swam or floated sticks, boards, hay, straw, stones, and paper; ancient newspapers, above all – for the newspaper, especially when torn, soon becomes an antiquity – and bills of the Silverado boarding-house, some dated Silverado, some Calistoga Mine. Here is one, verbatim; and if any one can calculate the scale of charges, he has my envious admiration.

Calistoga Mine, May 3rd, 1875. John Stanley To S. Chapman, Cr. To board from April 1st, to April 30 $25 75 ' ' ' May lst, to 3rd ... 2 00 27 75

Where is John Stanley mining now? Where is S. Chapman, within whose hospitable walls we were to lodge? The date was but five years old, but in that time the world had changed for Silverado; like Palmyra in the desert, it had outlived its people and its purpose; we camped, like Layard, amid ruins, and these names spoke to us of prehistoric time. A boot-jack, a pair of boots, a dog-hutch, and these bills of Mr. Chapman's were the only speaking relics that we disinterred from all that vast Silverado rubbish-heap; but what would I not have given to unearth a letter, a pocket- book, a diary, only a ledger, or a roll of names, to take me back, in a more personal manner, to the past? It pleases me, besides, to fancy that Stanley or Chapman, or one of their companions, may light upon this chronicle, and be struck by the name, and read some news of their anterior home, coming, as it were, out of a subsequent epoch of history in that quarter of the world ...

So much for the lower room. We scraped some of the rougher dirt off the floor, and left it. That was our sitting-room and kitchen, though there was nothing to sit upon but the table, and no provision for a fire except a hole in the roof of the room above, which had once contained the chimney of a stove.

To that upper room we now proceeded. There were the eighteen bunks in a double tier, nine on either hand, where from eighteen to thirty-six miners had once snored together all night long, John Stanley, perhaps, snoring loudest. There was the roof, with a hole in it through which the sun now shot an arrow. There was the floor, in much the same state as the one below, though, perhaps, there was more hay, and certainly there was the added ingredient of broken glass, the man who stole the window-frames having apparently made a miscarriage with this one. Without a broom, without hay or bedding, we could but look about us with a beginning of despair. The one bright arrow of day, in that gaunt and shattered barrack, made the rest look dirtier and darker, and the sight drove us at last into the open.

Here, also, the handiwork of man lay ruined: but the plants were all alive and thriving; the view below was fresh with the colours of nature; and we had exchanged a dim, human garret for a corner, even although it were untidy, of the blue hall of heaven. Not a bird, not a beast, not a reptile. There was no noise in that part of the world, save when we passed beside the staging, and heard the water musically falling in the shaft.

We wandered to and fro. We searched among that drift of lumber-wood and iron, nails and rails, and sleepers and the wheels of tracks. We gazed up the cleft into the bosom of the mountain. We sat by the margin of the dump and saw, far below us, the green treetops standing still in the clear air. Beautiful perfumes, breaths of bay, resin, and nutmeg, came to us more often and grew sweeter and sharper as the afternoon declined. But still there was no word of Hanson.

I set to with pick and shovel, and deepened the pool behind the shaft, till we were sure of sufficient water for the morning; and by the time I had finished, the sun had begun to go down behind the mountain shoulder, the platform was plunged in quiet shadow, and a chill descended from the sky. Night began early in our cleft. Before us, over the margin of the dump, we could see the sun still striking aslant into the wooded nick below, and on the battlemented, pine-bescattered ridges on the farther side.

There was no stove, of course, and no hearth in our lodging, so we betook ourselves to the blacksmith's forge across the platform. If the platform be taken as a stage, and the out-curving margin of the dump to represent the line of the footlights, then our house would be the first wing on the actor's left, and this blacksmith's forge, although no match for it in size, the foremost on the right. It was a low, brown cottage, planted close against the hill, and overhung by the foliage and peeling boughs of a madrona thicket. Within it was full of dead leaves and mountain dust, and rubbish from the mine. But we soon had a good fire brightly blazing, and sat close about it on impromptu seats. Chuchu, the slave of sofa-cushions, whimpered for a softer bed; but the rest of us were greatly revived and comforted by that good creature-fire, which gives us warmth and light and companionable sounds, and colours up the emptiest building with better than frescoes. For a while it was even pleasant in the forge, with the blaze in the midst, and a look over our shoulders on the woods and mountains where the day was dying like a dolphin.

It was between seven and eight before Hanson arrived, with a waggonful of our effects and two of his wife's relatives to lend him a hand. The elder showed surprising strength. He would pick up a huge packing-case, full of books of all things, swing it on his shoulder, and away up the two crazy ladders and the breakneck spout of rolling mineral, familiarly termed a path, that led from the cart-track to our house. Even for a man unburthened, the ascent was toilsome and precarious; but Irvine sealed it with a light foot, carrying box after box, as the hero whisks the stage child up the practicable footway beside the waterfall of the fifth act. With so strong a helper, the business was speedily transacted. Soon the assayer's office was thronged with our belongings, piled higgledy-piggledy, and upside down, about the floor. There were our boxes, indeed, but my wife had left her keys in Calistoga. There was the stove, but, alas! our carriers had forgot the chimney, and lost one of the plates along the road. The Silverado problem was scarce solved.

Rufe himself was grave and good-natured over his share of blame; he even, if I remember right, expressed regret. But his crew, to my astonishment and anger, grinned from ear to ear, and laughed aloud at our distress. They thought it 'real funny' about the stove-pipe they had forgotten; 'real funny' that they should have lost a plate. As for hay, the whole party refused to bring us any till they should have supped. See how late they were! Never had there been such a job as coming up that grade! Nor often, I suspect, such a game of poker as that before they started. But about nine, as a particular favour, we should have some hay.

So they took their departure, leaving me still staring, and we resigned ourselves to wait for their return. The fire in the forge had been suffered to go out, and we were one and all too weary to kindle another. We dined, or, not to take that word in vain, we ate after a fashion, in the nightmare disorder of the assayer's office, perched among boxes. A single candle lighted us. It could scarce be called a housewarming; for there was, of course, no fire, and with the two open doors and the open window gaping on the night, like breaches in a fortress, it began to grow rapidly chill. Talk ceased; nobody moved but the unhappy Chuchu, still in quest of sofa-cushions, who tumbled complainingly among the trunks. It required a certain happiness of disposition to look forward hopefully, from so dismal a beginning, across the brief hours of night, to the warm shining of to-morrow's sun.

But the hay arrived at last, and we turned, with our last spark of courage, to the bedroom. We had improved the entrance, but it was still a kind of rope-walking; and it would have been droll to see us mounting, one after another, by candlelight, under the open stars.

The western door – that which looked up the canyon, and through which we entered by our bridge of flying plank – was still entire, a handsome, panelled door, the most finished piece of carpentry in Silverado. And the two lowest bunks next to this we roughly filled with hay for that night's use. Through the opposite, or eastern-looking gable, with its open door and window, a faint, disused starshine came into the room like mist; and when we were once in bed, we lay, awaiting sleep, in a haunted, incomplete obscurity. At first the silence of the night was utter. Then a high wind began in the distance among the tree-tops, and for hours continued to grow higher. It seemed to me much such a wind as we had found on our visit; yet here in our open chamber we were fanned only by gentle and refreshing draughts, so deep was the canyon, so close our house was planted under the overhanging rock …

THE SEA FOGS

A CHANGE in the colour of the light usually called me in the morning. By a certain hour, the long, vertical chinks in our western gable, where the boards had shrunk and separated, flashed suddenly into my eyes as stripes of dazzling blue, at once so dark and splendid that I used to marvel how the qualities could be combined. At an earlier hour, the heavens in that quarter were still quietly coloured, but the shoulder of the mountain which shuts in the canyon already glowed with sunlight in a wonderful compound of gold and rose and green; and this too would kindle, although more mildly and with rainbow tints, the fissures of our crazy gable. If I were sleeping heavily, it was the bold blue that struck me awake; if more lightly, then I would come to myself in that earlier and fairier fight.

One Sunday morning, about five, the first brightness called me. I rose and turned to the east, not for my devotions, but for air. The night had been very still. The little private gale that blew every evening in our canyon, for ten minutes or perhaps a quarter of an hour, had swiftly blown itself out; in the hours that followed not a sigh of wind had shaken the treetops; and our barrack, for all its breaches, was less fresh that morning than of wont. But I had no sooner reached the window than I forgot all else in the sight that met my eyes, and I made but two bounds into my clothes, and down the crazy plank to the platform.

The sun was still concealed below the opposite hilltops, though it was shining already, not twenty feet above my head, on our own mountain slope. But the scene, beyond a few near features, was entirely changed. Napa valley was gone; gone were all the lower slopes and woody foothills of the range; and in their place, not a thousand feet below me, rolled a great level ocean. It was as though I had gone to bed the night before, safe in a nook of inland mountains, and had awakened in a bay upon the coast. I had seen these inundations from below; at Calistoga I had risen and gone abroad in the early morning, coughing and sneezing, under fathoms on fathoms of gray sea vapour, like a cloudy sky – a dull sight for the artist, and a painful experience for the invalid. But to sit aloft one's self in the pure air and under the unclouded dome of heaven, and thus look down on the submergence of the valley, was strangely different and even delightful to the eyes. Far away were hilltops like little islands. Nearer, a smoky surf beat about the foot of precipices and poured into all the coves of these rough mountains. The colour of that fog ocean was a thing never to be forgotten. For an instant, among the Hebrides and just about sundown, I have seen something like it on the sea itself. But the white was not so opaline; nor was there, what surprisingly increased the effect, that breathless, crystal stillness over all. Even in its gentlest moods the salt sea travails, moaning among the weeds or lisping on the sand; but that vast fog ocean lay in a trance of silence, nor did the sweet air of the morning tremble with a sound.

As I continued to sit upon the dump, I began to observe that this sea was not so level as at first sight it appeared to be. Away in the extreme south, a little hill of fog arose against the sky above the general surface, and as it had already caught the sun, it shone on the horizon like the topsails of some giant ship. There were huge waves, stationary, as it seemed, like waves in a frozen sea; and yet, as I looked again, I was not sure but they were moving after all, with a slow and august advance. And while I was yet doubting, a promontory of the some four or five miles away, conspicuous by a bouquet of tall pines, was in a single instant over-taken and swallowed up. It reappeared in a little, with its pines, but this time as an islet, and only to be swallowed up once more and then for good. This set me looking nearer, and I saw that in every cove along the line of mountains the fog was being piled in higher and higher, as though by some wind that was inaudible to me. I could trace its progress, one pine tree first growing hazy and then disap-pearing after another; although sometimes there was none of this fore-running haze, but the whole opaque white ocean gave a start and swallowed a piece of mountain at a gulp. It was to flee these poisonous fogs that I had left the seaboard, and climbed so high among the mountains. And now, behold, here came the fog to besiege me in my chosen altitudes, and yet came so beautifully that my first thought was of welcome.

The sun had now gotten much higher, and through all the gaps of the hills it cast long bars of gold across that white ocean. An eagle, or some other very great bird of the mountain, came wheeling over the nearer pine-tops, and hung, poised and something sideways, as if to look abroad on that unwonted desolation, spying, perhaps with terror, for the eyries of her comrades. Then, with a long cry, she dis-appeared again towards Lake County and the clearer air. At length it seemed to me as if the flood were beginning to subside. The old landmarks, by whose dis-appearance I had measured its advance, here a crag, there a brave pine tree, now began, in the inverse order, to make their reappearance into daylight. I judged all danger of the fog was over. This was not Noah's flood; it was but a morning spring, and would now drift out seaward whence it came. So, mightily relieved, and a good deal exhilarated by the sight, I went into the house to light the fire.

I suppose it was nearly seven when I once more mounted the platform to look abroad. The fog ocean had swelled up enormously since last I saw it; and a few hundred feet below me, in the deep gap where the Toll House stands and the road runs through into Lake County, it had already topped the slope, and was pouring over and down the other side like driving smoke. The wind had climbed along with it; and though I was still in calm air, I could see the trees tossing below me, and their long, strident sighing mounted to me where I stood.

Half an hour later, the fog had surmounted all the ridge on the opposite side of the gap, though a shoulder of the mountain still warded it out of our canyon. Napa valley and its bounding hills were now utterly blotted out. The fog, sunny white in the sunshine, was pouring over into Lake County in a huge, ragged cataract, tossing treetops appearing and disappearing in the spray. The air struck with a lit-tle chill, and set me coughing. It smelt strong of the fog, like the smell of a wash-ing-house, but with a shrewd tang of the sea salt.

Had it not been for two things – the sheltering spur which answered as a dyke, and the great valley on the other side which rapidly engulfed whatever mounted – our own little platform in the canyon must have been already buried a hundred feet in salt and poisonous air. As it was, the interest of the scene entirely occupied our minds. We were set just out of the wind, and but just above the fog; we could listen to the voice of the one as to music on the stage; we could plunge our eyes down into the other, as into some flowing stream from over the parapet of a bridge; thus we looked on upon a strange, impetuous, silent, shifting exhibition of the powers of nature, and saw the familiar landscape changing from moment to moment like figures in a dream.

The imagination loves to trifle with what is not. Had this been indeed the deluge, I should have felt more strongly, but the emotion would have been similar in kind. I played with the idea, as the child flees in delighted terror from the creations of his fancy. The look of the thing helped me. And when at last I began to flee up the mountain, it was indeed partly to escape from the raw air that kept me coughing, but it was also part in play.

As I ascended the mountain-side, I came once more to overlook the upper surface of the fog; but it wore a different appearance from what I had beheld at daybreak. For, first, the sun now fell on it from high overhead, and its surface shone and undulated like a great nor'land moor country, sheeted with untrodden morning snow. And next the new level must have been a thousand or fifteen hundred feet higher than the old, so that only five or six points of all the broken country below me, still stood out. Napa valley was now one with Sonoma on the west. On the hither side, only a thin scattered fringe of bluffs was unsubmerged; and through all the gaps the fog was pouring over, like an ocean, into the blue clear sunny country on the east. There it was soon lost; for it fell instantly into the bottom of the valleys, following the water-shed; and the hilltops in that quarter were still clear cut upon the eastern sky.

Through the Toll House gap and over the near ridges on the other side, the deluge was immense. A spray of thin vapour was thrown high above it, rising and falling, and blown into fantastic shapes. The speed of its course was like a mountain torrent. Here and there a few treetops were discovered and then whelmed again; and for one second, the bough of a dead pine beckoned out of the spray like the arm of a drowning man. But still the imagination was dissatisfied, still the ear waited for something more. Had this indeed been water (as it seemed so, to the eye), with what a plunge of reverberating thunder would it have rolled upon its course, disembowelling mountains and deracinating pines! And yet water it was, and sea-water at that – true Pacific billows, only somewhat rarefied, rolling in mid air among the hilltops.

I climbed still higher, among the red rattling gravel and dwarf underwood of Mount Saint Helena, until I could look right down upon Silverado, and admire the favoured nook in which it lay. The sunny plain of fog was several hundred feet higher; behind the protecting spur a gigantic accumulation of cottony vapour threatened, with every second, to blow over and submerge our homestead; but the vortex setting past the Toll House was too strong; and there lay our little platform, in the arms of the deluge, but still enjoying its unbroken sunshine. About eleven, however, thin spray came flying over the friendly buttress, and I began to think the fog had hunted out its Jonah after all. But it was the last effort. The wind veered while we were at dinner, and began to blow squally from the mountain summit; and by half-past one, all that world of sea-fogs was utterly routed and flying here and there into the south in little rags of cloud. And instead of a lone sea-beach, we found ourselves once more inhabiting a high mountainside, with the clear green country far below us, and the light smoke of Calistoga blowing in the air.

This was the great Russian campaign for that season. Now and then, in the early morning, a little white lakelet of fog would be seen far down in Napa Valley; but the heights were not again assailed, nor was the surrounding world again shut off from Silverado.

TOILS AND PLEASURES

I MUST try to convey some notion of our life, of how the days passed and what pleasure we took in them, of what there was to do and how we set about doing it, in our mountain hermitage. The house, after we[17] had repaired the worst of the damages, and filled in some of the doors and windows with white cotton cloth, became a healthy and a pleasant dwelling-place, always airy and dry, and haunted by the outdoor perfumes of the glen. Within, it had the look of habitation, the human look. You had only to go into the third room, which we did not use, and see its stones, its sifting earth, its tumbled litter; and then return to our lodging, with the beds made, the plates on the rack, the pail of bright water behind the door, the stove crackling in a corner, and perhaps the table roughly laid against a meal, – and man's order, the little clean spots that he creates to dwell in, were at once contrasted with the rich passivity of nature. And yet our house was everywhere so wrecked and shattered, the air came and went so freely, the sun found so many portholes, the golden outdoor glow shone in so many open chinks, that we enjoyed, at the same time, some of the comforts of a roof and much of the gaiety and brightness of al fresco life. A single shower of rain, to be sure, and we should have been drowned out like mice. But ours was a Californian summer, and an earthquake was a far likelier accident than a shower of rain.

Trustful in this fine weather, we kept the house for kitchen and bedroom, and used the platform as our summer parlour. The sense of privacy, as I have said already, was complete. We could look over the clump on miles of forest and rough hilltop; our eyes commanded some of Napa Valley, where the train ran, and the little country townships sat so close together along the line of the rail. But here there was no man to intrude. None but the Hansons were our visitors. Even they came but at long intervals, or twice daily, at a stated hour, with milk. So our days, as they were never interrupted, drew out to the greater length; hour melted insensibly into hour; the household duties, though they were many, and some of them laborious, dwindled into mere islets of business in a sea of sunny day-time; and it appears to me, looking back, as though the far greater part of our life at Silverado had been passed, propped upon an elbow, or seated on a plank, listening to the silence that there is among the hills.

My work, it is true, was over early in the morning. I rose before any one else, lit the stove, put on the water to boil, and strolled forth upon the platform to wait till it was ready. Silverado would then be still in shadow, the sun shining on the mountain higher up. A clean smell of trees, a smell of the earth at morning, hung in the air. Regularly, every day, there was a single bird, not singing, but awkwardly chirruping among the green madronas, and the sound was cheerful, natural, and stirring. It did not hold the attention, nor interrupt the thread of meditation, like a blackbird or a nightingale; it was mere woodland prattle, of which the mind was conscious like a perfume. The freshness of these morning seasons remained with me far on into the day.

As soon as the kettle boiled, I made porridge and coffee; and that, beyond the literal drawing of water, and the preparation of kindling, which it would be hyperbolical to call the hewing of wood, ended my domestic duties for the day.[18] Thenceforth my wife laboured single-handed in the palace, and I lay or wandered on the platform at my own sweet will. The little corner near the forge, where we found a refuge under the madronas from the unsparing early sun, is indeed connected in my mind with some nightmare encounters over Euclid, and the Latin Grammar. These were known as Sam's lessons. He was supposed to be the victim and the sufferer; but here there must have been some misconception, for whereas I generally retired to bed after one of these engagements, he was no sooner set free than he dashed up to the Chinaman's house, where he had installed a printing press, that great element of civilisation, and the sound of his labours would be faintly audible about the canyon half the day.

To walk at all was a laborious business; the foot sank and slid, the boots were cut to pieces, among sharp, uneven, rolling stones. When we crossed the platform in any direction, it was usual to lay a course, following as much as possible the line of waggon rails. Thus, if water were to be drawn, the water-carrier left the house along some tilting planks that we had laid down, and not laid down very well. These carried him to that great highroad, the railway; and the railway served him as far as to the head of the shaft. But from thence to the spring and back again he made the best of his unaided way, staggering among the stones, and wading in low growth of the calcanthus, where the rattlesnakes lay hissing at his passage. Yet I liked to draw water. It was pleasant to dip the gray metal pail into the clean, colourless, cool water; pleasant to carry it back, with the water ripping at the edge, and a broken sunbeam quivering in the midst.

But the extreme roughness of the walking confined us in common practice to the platform, and indeed to those parts of it that were most easily accessible along the line of rails. The rails came straight forward from the shaft, here and there overgrown with little green bushes, but still entire, and still carrying a truck, which it was Sam's delight to trundle to and fro by the hour with various ladings. About midway down the platform, the railroad trended to the right, leaving our house and coasting along the far side within a few yards of the madronas and the forge, and not far of the latter, ended in a sort of platform on the edge of the dump. There, in old days, the trucks were tipped, and their load sent thundering down the chute. There, besides, was the only spot where we could approach the margin of the dump. Anywhere else, you took your life in your right hand when you came within a yard and a half to peer over. For at any moment the dump might begin to slide and carry you down and bury you below its ruins. Indeed, the neighbourhood of an old mine is a place beset with dangers. For as still as Silverado was, at any moment the report of rotten wood might tell us that the plat-form had fallen into the shaft; the dump might begin to pour into the road below; or a wedge slip in the great upright seam, and hundreds of tons of mountain bury the scene of our encampment.

I have already compared the dump to a rampart, built certainly by some rude people, and for prehistoric wars. It was likewise a frontier. All below was green and woodland, the tall pines soaring one above another, each with a firm outline and full spread of bough. All above was arid, rocky, and bald. The great spout of broken mineral, that had dammed the canyon up, was a creature of man's handi-work, its material dug out with a pick and powder, and spread by the service of the tracks. But nature herself, in that upper district, seemed to have had an eye to nothing besides mining; and even the natural hill-side was all sliding gravel and precarious boulder. Close at the margin of the well leaves would decay to skele-tons and mummies, which at length some stronger gust would carry clear of the canyon and scatter in the subjacent woods. Even moisture and decaying vegetable matter could not, with all nature's alchemy, concoct enough soil to nourish a few poor grasses. It is the same, they say, in the neighbourhood of all silver mines; the nature of that precious rock being stubborn with quartz and poisonous with cinnabar. Both were plenty in our Silverado. The stones sparkled white in the sun-shine with quartz; they were all stained red with cinnabar. Here, doubtless, came the Indians of yore to paint their faces for the war-path; and cinnabar, if I remem-ber rightly, was one of the few articles of Indian commerce. Now, Sam had it in his undisturbed possession, to pound down and slake, and paint his rude designs with. But to me it had always a fine flavour of poetry, compounded out of Indian story and Hawthornden's allusion:

'Desire, alas! I desire a Zeuxis new, From Indies borrowing gold, from Eastern skies Most bright cinoper ...'

Yet this is but half the picture; our Silverado platform has another side to it. Though there was no soil, and scarce a blade of grass, yet out of these tumbled gravel-heaps and broken boulders, a flower garden bloomed as at home in a conservatory. Calcanthus crept, like a hardy weed, all over our rough parlour, choking the railway, and pushing forth its rusty, aromatic cones from between two blocks of shattered mineral. Azaleas made a big snow-bed just above the well. The shoulder of the hill waved white with Mediterranean heath. In the crannies of the ledge and about the spurs of the tall pine, a red flowering stone-plant hung in clusters. Even the low, thorny chaparral was thick with pea-like blossom. Close at the foot of our path nutmegs prospered, delightful to the sight and smell. At sunrise, and again late at night, the scent of the sweet bay trees filled the canyon, and the down-blowing night wind must have borne it hundreds of feet into the outer air.

All this vegetation, to be sure, was stunted. The madrona was here no bigger than the manzanita; the bay was but a stripling shrub; the very pines, with four or five exceptions in all our upper canyon, were not so tall as myself, or but a little taller, and the most of them came lower than my waist. For a prosperous forest tree, we must look below, where the glen was crowded with green spires. But for flowers and ravishing perfume, we had none to envy: our heap of road-metal was thick with bloom, like a hawthorn in the front of June; our red, baking angle in the mountain, a laboratory of poignant scents. It was an endless wonder to my mind, as I dreamed about the platform, following the progress of the shadows, where the madrona with its leaves, the azalea and calcanthus with their blossoms, could find moisture to support such thick, wet, waxy growths, or the bay tree collect the ingredients of its perfume. But there they all grew together, healthy, happy, and happy-making, as though rooted in a fathom of black soil ...

The hours of evening, when we were once curtained in the friendly dark, sped lightly. Even as with the crickets, night brought to us a certain spirit of rejoicing. It was good to taste the air; good to mark the dawning of the stars, as they increased their glittering company; good, too, to gather stones, and send them crashing down the chute, a wave of light. It seemed, in some way, the reward and the fulfilment of the day. So it is when men dwell in the open air; it is one of the simple pleasures that we lose by living cribbed and covered in a house, that, though the coming of the day is still the most inspiriting, yet day's departure, also, and the return of night refresh, renew, and quiet us; and in the pastures of the dusk we stand, like cattle, exulting in the absence of the load.

Our nights wore never cold, and they were always still, but for one remarkable exception. Regularly, about nine o'clock, a warm wind sprang up, and blew for ten minutes, or maybe a quarter of an hour, right down the canyon, fanning it well out, airing it as a mother airs the night nursery before the children sleep. As far as I could judge, in the clear darkness of the night, this wind was purely local: perhaps dependant on the configuration of the glen. At least, it was very welcome to the hot and weary squatters; and if we were not abed already, the springing up of this lilliputian valley-wind would often be our signal to retire.

I was the last to go to bed, as I was still the first to rise. Many a night I have strolled about the platform, taking a bath of darkness before I slept. The rest would be in bed, and even from the forge I could hear them talking together from bunk to bunk. A single candle in the neck of a pint bottle was their only illumination; and yet the old cracked house seemed literally bursting with the light. It shone keen as a knife through all the vertical chinks; it struck upward through the broken shingles; and through the eastern door and window, it fell in a great splash upon the thicket and the overhanging rock. You would have said a conflagration, or at the least a roaring forge; and behold, it was but a candle. Or perhaps it was yet more strange to see the procession moving bedwards round the corner of the house, and up the plank that brought us to the bedroom door; under the immense spread of the starry heavens, down in a crevice of the giant mountain these few human shapes, with their unshielded taper, made so disproportionate a figure in the eye and mind. But the more he is alone with nature, the greater man and his doings bulk in the consideration of his fellow-men. Miles and miles away upon the opposite hill-tops, if there were any hunter belated or any traveller who had lost his way, he must have stood, and watched and wondered, from the time the candle issued from the door of the assayer's office till it had mounted the plank and disappeared again into the miners' dormitory.

Notes

1. 'Calistoga' is a combination of California and Saratoga, the health spa in New York State, coined by a brash Irish-American entrepreneur named Sam Brannan, 'a renegade Mormon,' according to Nicholas Rankin, 'who helped found Sacramento and ran California's first newspaper … Grandiosely drunk, he tried to say he would build the Saratoga Springs of California, but what came out was the "Calistoga of Sarafornia".' See Nicholas Rankin, Dead Man's Chest: Travels After Robert Louis Stevenson (London: Phoenix Press, 2001), pp. 177–78.

2. Actually the Magnolia Hotel, which was owned by a JA Chesebro. See Rankin, Dead Man's Chest, p. 179.

3. Clark Foss, local stagecoach-driver, was renowned in the area for his skill in handling horses.

4. After two nights at the Palace Hotel, the Stevensons spent the rest of their honeymoon in an abandoned mine camp called Silverado, on the wooded slopes of Mount Saint Helena in the Napa Valley. They remained there until June of 1880. Robert Louis Stevenson State Park is located on Mount Saint Helena and contains several hundred acres of woodlands. A memorial – in the form of a stone book – marks the site of Stevenson's makeshift shelter.

5. According to a study commissioned in 1999 by the Wine Institute and the California Grape Growers Association, California is responsible for 91 percent of all wine produced in the United States and 72 percent of all wine sold in the USA, making it the leading wine producing state in the

States. Statistics as to the number of wineries in California vary. According to the same study, there are 847 commercial wineries in the state. In April 2002, the San Francisco-based Wine Institute estimated the retail value of all categories of California wine sold in the US at $13.4 billion in 2001.

6. Some 232 of them are located in the Napa Valley.

7. Jacob Schram (1826–1905), a German winegrower, who emigrated to America at 16, settled in California during the Gold Rush, and established the Schramsberg Vineyard in 1862. 'The house in which he entertained the Stevensons was a vine-covered brown cottage with a long veranda,' writes Anne Roller Issler, *Our Mountain Hermitage: Silverado and Robert Louis Stevenson* (Stanford, Calif.: Stanford University Press, 1950), p. 47.

Jamie Davies, president and CEO of Schramsberg, co-founded the present-day Schramsberg Winery in 1965 with her late husband, Jack. She has since restored the Schram's Victorian house and surrounding grounds to the conditions that Stevenson saw on his visit.

Colin T. McEachran, Schram's neighbor, was born in Greenock in 1824. He emigrated to America with his parents at the age of seven. As a youth, he went to sea, eventually becoming a captain before settling in the Napa Valley where he bought and developed Alta Vineyard.

8. A siege cannon dating from the fifteenth century and located at Edinburgh Castle.

9. Schram was trained as a barber in his native Germany and, in the early days of the winery, continued to work at his trade to supplement his income.

10. A fashionable neighbourhood in London.

11. Ironically, Stevenson, this most Scottish of writers, is buried on the top of Mt. Vaea in Samoa.

12. Stevenson's version of the 'Canadian Boat Song,' believed by some to be written by novelist John Galt (1779–1839), a native of Irvine, Ayrshire, who founded the Canadian city of Guelph, Ontario. Galt's best known work remains *Lawrie Todd* (1830). The more popular version reads as thus: 'From the lone shieling of the misty island/Mountains divide us, and the waste of seas – /Yet still the blood is strong, the heart is Highland/And we in dreams behold the Hebrides'

13. The 'squatters' consisted of Stevenson, his wife Fanny – 'the King and Queen of Silverado' – Fanny's son Lloyd Osbourne, and Chuchu, the dog.

14. The town of Silverado was founded on 11 October 1874. During its heyday, it had a population of approximately 1500 and consisted of the Silverado Hotel, a mining office, a grocery, a schoolhouse, a blacksmith shop, and several saloons. See Ken Stanton, *Mount St. Helena & RL Stevenson State Park* (St. Helena, Calif.: Bonnie View Books, 1998), pp. 37, 108.

15. The original two-storey toll house burned to the ground in 1883; a ranch-style replacement was erected in 1884 and demolished in 1953. See Stanton, p. 54.

16. Stanton describes the old cabin as 'a sloppy, two story affair plastered against the hillside ...', Ibid., p. 203. Joan Parry Dutton refers to it as '... a half-derelict brown wooden house that consisted of three rooms.' See Dutton, *They Left Their Mark: Famous Passages through the Wine Country* (Calistoga, Calif.: Sharpsteen Museum Association, 1998, p.28). A replica of the cabin is on display at the Sharpsteen Museum in Calistoga.

17. By this time, the Stevensons had been joined by Joe Strong, the painter and Fanny's son-in-law, and Belle Strong, Fanny's daughter.

18. 'Partly because of his physical debility, partly because he was anyway useless at working with his hands, Fanny had to do all the hard manual labour ... ' See Frank McLynn, *Robert Louis Stevenson: A Biography* (New York: Random House, 1993), p. 177.

Winter

FROM SONGS OF TRAVEL

*Winter was written at Saranac Lake, New York, in 1887,
and appeared in* Songs of Travel *(1895).*

In rigorous hours, when down the iron lane
The redbreast looks in vain
For hips and haws,
Lo, shining flowers upon my window-pane
The silver pencil of the winter draws.

When all the snowy hill
And the bare woods are still;
When snipes are silent in the frozen bogs,
And all the garden garth is whelmed in mire,
Lo, by the hearth, the laughter of the logs –
More fair than roses, lo, the flowers of fire!

Switzerland

Davos in Winter

Davos in Winter *was originally published in the*
Pall Mall Gazette *on February 21, 1881.*

A MOUNTAIN valley has, at the best, a certain prison-like effect on the imagination, but a mountain valley, an Alpine winter, and an invalid's weakness make
up among them a prison of the most effective kind.¹ The roads indeed are cleared,
and at least one footpath dodging up the hill; but to these the health-seeker is
rigidly confined. There are for him no cross-cuts over the field, no following of
streams, no unguided rambles in the wood. His walks are cut and dry. In five or
six different directions he can push as far, and no farther, than his strength per-
mits; never deviating from the line laid down for him and beholding at each repetition the same field of wood and snow from the same corner of the road. This,
of itself, would be a little trying to the patience in the course of months; but to
this is added, by the heaped mantle of the snow, an almost utter absence of detail
and an almost unbroken identity of colour. Snow, it is true, is not merely
white. The sun touches it with roseate and golden lights. Its own crushed infinity
of crystals, its own richness of tiny sculpture, fills it, when regarded near at hand,
with wonderful depths of coloured shadow, and, though wintrily transformed, it is
still water, and has watery tones of blue. But, when all is said, these fields of white
and blots of crude black forest are but a trite and staring substitute for the infinite variety and pleasantness of the earth's face. Even a boulder, whose front is too
precipitous to have retained the snow, seems, if you come upon it in your walk, a
perfect gem of colour, reminds you almost painfully of other places, and brings
into your head the delights of more Arcadian days – the path across the meadow,
the hazel dell, the lilies on the stream, and the scents, the colours, and the whisper of the woods. And scents here are as rare as colours. Unless you get a gust of
kitchen in passing some hotel, you shall smell nothing all day long but the faint
and choking odour of frost. Sounds, too, are absent: not a bird pipes, not a bough
waves, in the dead, windless atmosphere. If a sleigh goes by, the sleigh-bells ring,
and that is all; you work all winter through to no other accompaniment but the
crunching of your steps upon the frozensnow.

It is the curse of the Alpine valleys to be each one village from one end to the
other. Go where you please, houses will still be in sight, before and behind you,
and to the right and left. Climb as high as an invalid is able, and it is only to spy
new habitations nested in the wood. Nor is that all; for about the health resort the
walks are besieged by single people walking rapidly with plaids about their shoulders, by sudden troops of German boys trying to learn to *jodel*, and by German
couples silently and, as you venture to fancy, not quite happily, pursuing love's

young dream. You may perhaps be an invalid who likes to make bad verses as he walks about. Alas! no muse will suffer this imminence of interruption – and at the second stampede of jodellers you find your modest inspiration fled. Or you may only have a taste for solitude; it may try your nerves to have some one always in front whom you are visibly overtaking, and some one always behind who is audibly overtaking you, to say nothing of a score or so who brush past you in an opposite direction. It may annoy you to take your walks and seats in public view. Alas! there is no help for it among the Alps. There are no recesses, as in Gorbio Valley by the oil-mill; no sacred solitude of olive gardens on the Roccabruna-road; no nook upon Saint Martin's Cape, haunted by the voice of breakers, and fragrant with the threefold sweetness of the rosemary and the sea-pines and the sea.

For this publicity there is no cure, and no alleviation; but the storms of which you will complain so bitterly while they endure, chequer and by their contrast brighten the sameness of the fair-weather scenes. When sun and storm contend together – when the thick clouds are broken up and pierced by arrows of golden daylight – there will be startling rearrangements and transfigurations of the mountain summits. A sun-dazzling spire of alp hangs suspended in mid-sky among awful glooms and blackness; or perhaps the edge of some great mountain shoulder will be designed in living gold, and appear for the duration of a glance bright like a constellation, and alone 'in the unapparent'. You may think you know the figure of these hills; but when they are thus revealed, they belong no longer to the things of earth – meteors we should rather call them, appearances of sun and air that endure but for a moment and return no more. Other variations are more lasting, as when, for instance, heavy and wet snow has fallen through some windless hours, and the thin, spiry, mountain pine trees stand each stock-still and loaded with a shining burthen. You may drive through a forest so disguised, the tongue- tied torrent struggling silently in the cleft of the ravine, and all still except the jingle of the sleigh bells, and you shall fancy yourself in some untrodden northern territory – Lapland, Labrador, or Alaska.

Or, possibly, you arise very early in the morning; totter down stairs in a state of somnambulism; take the simulacrum of a meal by the glimmer of one lamp in the deserted coffee-room; and find yourself by seven o'clock outside in a belated moonlight and a freezing chill. The mail sleigh takes you up and carries you on, and you reach the top of the ascent in the first hour of the day. To trace the fires of the sunrise as they pass from peak to peak, to see the unlit tree- tops stand out soberly against the lighted sky, to be for twenty minutes in a wonderland of clear, fading shadows, disappearing vapours, solemn blooms of dawn, hills half glorified already with the day and still half confounded with the greyness of the western heaven – these will seem to repay you for the discomforts of that early start; but as the hour proceeds, and these enchantments vanish, you will find yourself upon the farther side in yet another Alpine valley, snow white and coal black, with such another long-drawn congeries of hamlets and such another senseless watercourse bickering along the foot. You have had your moment; but you have not changed the scene. The mountains are about you like a trap; you cannot foot it up a hill-side and behold the sea as a great plain, but live in holes and corners, and can change only one for another.

Notes
1. In late 1880, Stevenson's doctor recommended that the perennially sick writer spend the winter at Dr. Karl Ruedi's sanatorium at Davos-Platz in eastern Switzerland. The prevailing medical advice of the day for those patients with respiratory ailments was to seek a cold, dry climate.

Health and Mountains

Health and Mountains was part of a series of Swiss essays published between February and March 1881 in the Pall Mall Gazette.

THERE has come a change in medical opinion, and a change has followed in the lives of sick folk. A year or two ago and the wounded soldiery of mankind were all shut up together in some basking angle of the Riviera, walking a dusty promenade or sitting in dusty olive- yards within earshot of the interminable and unchanging surf – idle among spiritless idlers; not perhaps dying, yet hardly living either, and aspiring, sometimes fiercely, after livelier weather and some vivifying change. These were certainly beautiful places to live in, and the climate was wooing in its softness. Yet there was a later shiver in the sunshine; you were not certain whether you were being wooed; and these mild shores would sometimes seem to you to be the shores of death. There was a lack of a manly element; the air was not reactive; you might write bits of poetry and practise resignation, but you did not feel that here was a good spot to repair your tissue or regain your nerve. And it appears, after all, that there was something just in these appreciations. The invalid is now asked to lodge on wintry Alps; a ruder air shall medicine him; the demon of cold is no longer to be fled from, but bearded in his den. For even Winter has his 'dear domestic cave,' and in those places where he may be said to dwell for ever tempers his austerities.

Any one who has travelled westward by the great transcontinental railroad of America must remember the joy with which he perceived, after the tedious prairies of Nebraska and across the vast and dismal moorlands of Wyoming, a few snowy mountain summits alone, the southern sky. It is among these mountains in the new State of Colorado that the sick man may find, not merely an alleviation of his ailments, but the possibility of an active life and an honest livelihood. There, no longer as a lounger in a plaid, but as a working farmer, sweating at his work, he may prolong and begin anew his life. Instead of the bath-chair, the spade; instead of the regulated walk, rough journeys in the forest, and the pure, rare air of the open mountains for the miasma of the sick-room – these are the changes offered him, with what promise of pleasure and of self- respect, with what a revolution in all his hopes and terrors, none but an invalid can know. Resignation, the cowardice that apes a kind of courage and that lives in the very air of health resorts, is cast aside at a breath of such a prospect. The man can open the door; he can be up and doing; he can be a kind of a man after all and not merely an invalid.

But it is a far cry to the Rocky Mountains. We cannot all of us go farming in Colorado; and there is yet a middle term, which combines the medical benefits of the new system with the moral drawbacks of the old. Again the invalid has to lie aside from life and its wholesome duties; again he has to be an idler among idlers; but this time at a great altitude, far among the mountains, with the snow piled before his door and the frost flowers every morning on his window. The mere fact is tonic to his nerves. His choice of a place of wintering has somehow to his own eyes the air of an act of bold contract; and, since he has wilfully sought low temperatures, he is not so apt to shudder at a touch of chill. He came for that, he looked for it, and he throws it from him with the thought.

A long straight reach of valley, wall-like mountains upon either hand that rise higher and higher and shoot up new summits the higher you climb; a few noble peaks seen even from the valley; a village of hotels; a world of black and white – black pine-woods, clinging to the sides of the valley, and white snow flouring it, and papering it between the pine-woods, and covering all the mountains with a dazzling curd; add a few score invalids marching to and fro upon the snowy road, or skating on the ice-rinks, possibly to music, or sitting under sunshades by the door of the hotel – and you have the larger features of a mountain sanatorium. A certain furious river runs curving down the valley; its pace never varies, it has not a pool for as far as you can follow it; and its unchanging, senseless hurry is strangely tedious to witness. It is a river that a man could grow to hate. Day after day breaks with the rarest gold upon the mountain spires, and creeps, growing and glowing, down into the valley. From end to end the snow reverberates the sunshine; from end to end the air tingles with the light, clear and dry like crystal. Only along the course of the river, but high above it, there hangs far into the noon, one waving scarf of vapour. It were hard to fancy a more engaging feature in a landscape; perhaps it is harder to believe that delicate, long-lasting phantom of the atmosphere, a creature of the incontinent stream whose course it follows. By noon the sky is arrayed in an unrivalled pomp of colour – mild and pale and melting in the north, but towards the zenith, dark with an intensity of purple blue. What with this darkness of heaven and the intolerable lustre of the snow, space is reduced again to chaos. An English painter, coming to France late in life, declared with natural anger that 'the values were all wrong.' Had he got among the Alps on a bright day he might have lost his reason. And even to any one who has looked at landscape with any care, and in any way through the spectacles of representative art, the scene has a character of insanity. The distant shining mountain peak is here beside your eye; the neighbouring dull-coloured house in comparison is miles away; the summit, which is all of splendid snow, is close at hand; the nigh slopes, which are black with pine trees, bear it no relation, and might be in another sphere. Here there are none of those delicate gradations, those intimate, misty joinings-on and spreadings-out into the distance, nothing of that art of air and light by which the face of nature explains and veils itself in climes which we may be allowed to think more lovely. A glaring piece of crudity, where everything that is not white is a solecism and defies the judgment of the eyesight; a scene of blinding definition; a parade of daylight, almost scenically vulgar, more than scenically trying, and yet hearty and healthy, making the nerves to tighten and the mouth to smile: such is the winter daytime in the Alps.

With the approach of evening all is changed. A mountain will suddenly intercept the sun; a shadow fall upon the valley; in ten minutes the thermometer will drop as many degrees; the peaks that are no longer shone upon dwindle into ghosts; and meanwhile, overhead, if the weather be rightly characteristic of the place, the sky fades towards night through a surprising key of colours. The latest gold leaps from the last mountain. Soon, perhaps, the moon shall rise, and in her gentler light the valley shall be mellowed and misted, and here and there a wisp of silver cloud upon a hilltop, and here and there a warmly glowing window in a house, between fire and starlight, kind and homely in the fields of snow.

But the valley is not seated so high among the clouds to be eternally exempt from changes. The clouds gather, black as ink; the wind bursts rudely in; day after day the mists drive overhead, the snow- flakes flutter down in blinding disarray; daily the mail comes in later from the top of the pass; people peer through their windows and foresee no end but an entire seclusion from Europe, and death by gradual dry-rot, each in his indifferent inn; and when at last the storm goes, and the sun comes again, behold a world of unpolluted snow, glossy like fur, bright like daylight, a joy to wallowing dogs and cheerful to the souls of men. Or perhaps from across storied and malarious Italy, a wind cunningly winds about the mountains and breaks, warm and unclean, upon our mountain valley. Every nerve is set ajar; the conscience recognises, at a gust, a load of sins and negligences hitherto unknown; and the whole invalid world huddles into its private chambers, and silently recognises the empire of the Fohn.[1]

Notes
1. A hot dry wind from the South.

The Stimulation of the Alps

The Stimulation of the Alps was part of a series of essays on the Swiss Alps published between February and March 1881 in the Pall Mall Gazette.

To any one who should come from a southern sanitarium to the Alps, the row of sun-burned faces round the table would present the first surprise. He would begin by looking for the invalids, and he would lose his pains, for not one out of five of even the bad cases bears the mark of sickness on his face. The plump sunshine from above and its strong reverberation from below colour the skin like an Indian climate; the treatment, which consists mainly of the open air, exposes even the sickliest to tan, and a tableful of invalids comes, in a month or two, to resemble a tableful of hunters. But although he may be thus surprised at the first glance, his astonishment will grow greater, as he experiences the effects of the climate on himself. In many ways it is a trying business to reside upon the Alps: the stomach is exercised, the appetite often languishes; the liver may at times rebel; and because you have come so far from metropolitan advantages, it does not follow that you shall recover. But one thing is undeniable – that in the rare air, clear, cold, and blinding light of Alpine winters, a man takes a certain troubled

delight in his existence which can nowhere else be paralleled. He is perhaps no happier, but he is stingingly alive. It does not, perhaps, come out of him in work or exercise, yet he feels an enthusiasm of the blood unknown in more temperate climates. It may not be health, but it is fun.

There is nothing more difficult to communicate on paper than this baseless ardour, this stimulation of the brain, this sterile joyousness of spirits. You wake every morning, see the gold upon the snow-peaks, become filled with courage, and bless God for your prolonged existence. The valleys are but a stride to you; you cast your shoe over the hilltops; your ears and your heart sing; in the words of an unverified quotation from the Scotch psalms, you feel yourself fit 'on the wings of all the winds' to 'come flying all abroad.' Europe and your mind are too narrow for that flood of energy. Yet it is notable that you are hard to root out of your bed; that you start forth, singing, indeed, on your walk, yet are unusually ready to turn home again; that the best of you is volatile; and that although the restlessness remains till night, the strength is early at an end. With all these heady jollities, you are half conscious of an underlying languor in the body; you prove not to be so well as you had fancied; you weary before you have well begun; and

though you mount at morning with the lark, that is not precisely a song-bird's heart that you bring back with you when you return with aching limbs and peevish temper to your inn. It is hard to say wherein it lies, but this joy of Alpine winters is its own reward. Baseless, in a sense, it is more than worth more permanent improvements. The dream of health is perfect while it lasts; and if, in trying to realise it, you speedily wear out the dear hallucination, still every day, and many times a day, you are conscious of a strength you scarce possess, and a delight in living as merry as it proves to be transient.

The brightness – heaven and earth conspiring to be bright – the levity and quiet of the air; the odd stirring silence – more stirring than a tumult; the snow, the frost, the enchanted landscape: all have their part in the effect and on the memory, 'tous vous tapent sur la tete'; and yet when you have enumerated all, you have gone no nearer to explain or even to qualify the delicate exhilaration that you feel – delicate, you may say, and yet excessive, greater than can be said in prose, almost greater than an invalid can bear. There is a certain wine of France known in England in some gaseous disguise, but when drunk in the land of its nativity still as a pool, clean as river water, and as heady as verse. It is more than probable that in its noble natural condition this was the very wine of Anjou so beloved by Athos in the Musketeers. Now, if the reader has ever washed down a liberal second breakfast with the wine in question, and gone forth, on the back of these dilutions, into a sultry, sparkling noontide, he will have felt an influence almost as genial, although strangely grosser, than this fair titillation of the nerves among the snow and sunshine of the Alps. That also is a mode, we need not say of intoxication, but of insobriety. Thus also a man walks in a strong sunshine of the mind, and follows smiling, insubstantial meditations. And whether he be really so clever or so strong as he supposes, in either case he will enjoy his chimera while it lasts.

The influence of this giddy air displays itself in many secondary ways. A certain sort of laboured pleasantry has already been recognised, and may perhaps have been remarked in these papers, as a sort peculiar to that climate. People utter their judgments with a cannonade of syllables; a big word is as good as a meal to them; and the turn of a phrase goes further than humour or wisdom. By the professional writer many sad vicissitudes have to be undergone. At first he cannot write at all. The heart, it appears, is unequal to the pressure of business, and the brain, left without nourishment, goes into a mild decline. Next, some power of work returns to him, accompanied by jumping headaches. Last, the spring is opened, and there pours at once from his pen a world of blatant, hustling polysyllables, and talk so high as, in the old joke, to be positively offensive in hot weather. He writes it in good faith and with a sense of inspiration; it is only when he comes to read what he has written that surprise and disquiet seize upon his mind. What is he to do, poor man? All his little fishes talk like whales. This yeasty inflation, this stiff and strutting architecture of the sentence has come upon him while he slept; and it is not he, it is the Alps, who are to blame. He is not, perhaps, alone, which somewhat comforts him. Nor is the ill without a remedy. Some day, when the spring returns, he shall go down a little lower in this world, and remember quieter inflections and more modest language. But here, in the meantime, there seems to swim up some outline of a new cerebral hygiene and a good time coming, when experienced advisers shall send a man to the proper measured level for the ode, the biography, or the religious tract; and a nook may be found between the sea and Chimborazo, where Mr. Swinburne shall be able to write more continently, and Mr. Browning somewhat slower.[1]

Is it a return of youth, or is it a congestion of the brain? It is a sort of congestion, perhaps, that leads the invalid, when all goes well, to face the new day with such a bubbling cheerfulness. It is certainly congestion that makes night hideous with visions, all the chambers of a many-storeyed caravanserai, haunted with vociferous nightmares, and many wakeful people come down late for breakfast in the morning. Upon that theory the cynic may explain the whole affair – exhilaration, nightmares, pomp of tongue and all. But, on the other hand, the peculiar blessedness of boyhood may itself be but a symptom of the same complaint, for the two effects are strangely similar; and the frame of mind of the invalid upon the Alps is a sort of intermittent youth, with periods of lassitude. The fountain of Juventus does not play steadily in these parts; but there it plays, and possibly nowhere else.

Notes
1. Algernon Charles Swinburne (1837–1909), English poet; Robert Browning (1812–1889), English poet.

The South Seas

FROM *Travels in Hawaii*

Stevenson spent six months in Hawaii in 1889 and then visited for five weeks in 1893. His Hawaiian writings originally appeared as part of his letters from the South Seas, which ran in the New York Sun *and* Black and White *in England from roughly 6 February to 13 December 1891. However, most of the Hawaiian sketches did not appear in book form until after Stevenson's death, if at all[1]: in several of his collected works but, more conveniently, in* Travels in Hawaii. *Edited and with an Introduction by A Grove Day (Honolulu: University of Hawaii Press, 1973).*

THE KONA COAST

Of the island of Hawaii, though I have passed days becalmed under its lee, and spent a week upon its shores, I have never yet beheld the profile. Dense clouds continued to enshroud it far below its middle; not only the zone of snow and fire, but a great part of the forest region was covered or at least veiled by a perpetual rain. And yet even on my first sight, beholding so little and that through a glass from the deck of the *Casco*,[2] the rude Plutonic structure of the isle was conspicuous. Here was none of the accustomed glitter of the beach, none of the close shoreside forests of the typical high island. All seemed black and barren, and to slope sheer into the sea. Unexpected movements of the land caught vitreosity; black mouths of caves; ranges of low cliffs, vigorously designed a while in sun and shadow, and that sank again into the general declivity of the island glacis. Under its gigantic cowl of cloud the coast frowned upon us with a face of desolation.

On my return I passed from a humming city,[3] with shops and palaces and busy wharfs, plying cabs and tramcars, telephones in operation and a railway in building; mounted a strong and comfortable local steamer; sailed under desolate shores indeed, but guided in the night by sea and harbor lights, and was set down at last in a village uninhabited by any white, the creature of pure native taste – of which, what am I to say but I know no such village in Europe? A well-to-do Western hamlet in the States would be the closest parallel; and it is a moderate prophecy to call it so already.

Ho'okena is its name.[4] It stands on the same coast which I had wondered at before from the tossing *Casco*, the same coast on which the far-voyager Cook ended a noble career not very nobly.[5] That district of Kona where he fell is one illustrious in the history of Hawaii. It was at first the center of the dominion of the great Kamehameha.

There, in an unknown sepulcher, his bones are still hidden; there, too, his reputed treasures, spoils of a buccaneer, lie and are still vainly sought for, in one of the thousand caverns of the lava. There the tabus were first broken, there the missionaries first received; and, but for the new use of ships and the new need of harbors, here might be still the chief city and the organs of the kingdom. Yet a nearer approach confirmed the impression of the distance. It presents to the seaward one immense decline. Streams of lava have followed and submerged each other down this slope, and overflowed into the sea. These cooled and shrank, and were buried under fresh inundations, or dislocated by fresh tremors of the mountain. A multiplicity of caves is the result. The mouths of caves are everywhere; the lava is tunneled with corridors and halls; under houses high on the mountain the sea can be heard throbbing in the bowels of the land, and there is one gallery of miles which has been used by armies as a pass. Streams are thus unknown. The rain falls continually in the highlands; an isle that rises nearly fourteen thousand feet sheer from the sea could never fail of rain, but the treasure is squandered on a sieve, and by sunless conduits returns unseen into the ocean. Corrugated slopes of lava, bristling lava cliffs, sprouts of metallic clinkers, miles of coast without a well or rivulet, scarce anywhere is a beach, nowhere a harbor – here seems a singular land to be contended for in battle as a seat of courts and princes. Yet it possessed in the eyes of the natives one more than countervailing advantage. The windward shores of the isle are beaten by a monstrous surf; there are places where goods and passengers must be hauled up and lowered by a rope; there are coves which even the daring boatmen of Hamaku dread to enter; and men live isolated in their hamlets or communicate by giddy footpaths in the cliff. Upon the side of Kona the tablelike margin of the lava affords almost everywhere a passage by land, and the waves, reduced by the vast breakwater of the island, allow an almost continual communication by way of sea. Yet even here the surf of the Pacific appears formidable to the stranger as he lands, and daily delights him with its beauty as he walks the shore.

The land and sea breezes alternate on the Kona Coast with regularity, and the veil of rain draws up and down the talus of the mountain – now retiring to the zone of forests, now descending to the margin of the sea. It was in one of the latter and rarer moments that I was set on board a whaleboat full of intermingled barrels, passengers, and oarsmen. The rain fell and blotted the crude and somber colors of the scene. The coast rose but a little way; it was then intercepted by the cloud; and, for all that appeared, we might have been landing on an isle of some two hundred feet of elevation. On the immediate foreshore, under a low cliff, there stood some score of houses, trellised and verandated, set in narrow gardens, and painted gaudily in green and white; the whole surrounded and shaded by a grove of coco palms and fruit trees, springing (as by a miracle) from the bare lava. In front, the population of the neighborhood were gathered for the weekly incident, the passage of the steamer, sixty to eighty strong, and attended by a disproportionate allowance of horses, mules, and donkeys; for this land of rock is, singular to say, a land of breeding. The green trees, the painted houses, the gay dresses of the women, were everywhere relieved on the uncompromising black-ness of the lava; and the rain which fell, unheeded by the sightseers, blended and beautified the contrast.

The boat was run in upon a breaker and we passengers ejected on a flat rock, where the next wave submerged us to the knees. There we continued to stand, the rain drenching us from above, the sea from below, like people mesmerised; and as we were all (being travelers) tricked out with the green garlands of depar-ture, we must have offered somewhat the same appearance as a shipwrecked pic-nic. The purser spied and introduced me to my host, ex-Judge Nahinu, who was then deep in business, dispatching and receiving goods. He was dressed in pearl-gray tweed, like any self-respecting Englishman, only the band of his wide-awake was made of peacock's feather.

'House by and by,' said he, his English being limited, and carried me to the shelter of a rather lofty shed. On three sides it was open, on the fourth closed by a house. It was reached from without by five or six wooden steps. On the fourth side a further flight of ten conducted to the balcony of the house. A table spread with goods divided it across, so that I knew it for the village store and (according to the laws that rule in country life) the village lounging place. People sat with dangling feet along the house veranda; they sat on benches on the level of the shed or among the goods upon the counter; they came and went, they talked and waited; they opened, skimmed, and pocketed half-read their letters; they opened the journal, and found a moment, not for the news, but for the current number of the story – methought, I might have been in France, and the paper the *Petit Journal* instead of the *Nupepa Eleele*. On other islands I had been the center of attention; here none observed my presence. One hundred and ten years before the ancestors of these indifferents had looked in the faces of Cook and his seamen with admiration and alarm; called them gods, called them volcanoes; took their clothes for a loose skin, confounded their hats and their heads, and described their pockets as a 'treasure door, through which they plunge their hands into their bodies and bring forth cutlery and necklaces and cloth and nails'; and today the coming of the most attractive stranger (it would appear) to divert them from Miss Porter's *Scottish Chiefs*, for that was the novel of the day – *Na 'Lii O Sekotia* – so ran the title in Hawaii.

My host returned, and led me round the shore among the mules and donkeys to his house. Like all the houses of the hamlet, it was on the European, or to be more descriptive, on the American plan. The parlor was fitted with the usual fur-niture, and ornamented with the portraits of Kamehameha the Third, Lunalilo, Kalakaua, the queen consort of the isles, and Queen Victoria. There was a Bible on the table; other books stood on a shelf. A comfortable bedroom was placed at my service, the welcome afforded me was cordial and unembarrassed, the food good and plentiful. My host, my hostess, his grown daughters, strapping lassies, his young hopefuls, misbehaving at a meal or perfunctorily employed upon their schoolbooks; all that I found in that house, beyond the speech and a few exotic dishes on the table, would have been familiar and exemplary in Europe.

I walked that night beside the sea. The steamer, with its lights and crowd of tourists, was gone by; it had left me alone among these aliens, and I felt no touch of strangeness. The trim, lamplit houses shining quietly, like villas, each in its narrow garden; the gentle sound of speech from within; the room that awaited my return, with the lamp and the books and the spectacled householder studying his Bible – there was nothing changed; it was in such conditions I had myself grown up and played, a child, besides the borders of another sea. And some ten miles from where I walked Cook was adored as a deity; his bones, when he was dead, were cleansed for worship; his entrails devoured in a mistake by rambling children.

THE LAZARETTO

The windward coast of Molokai[6] is gloomy and abrupt. A wall of cliff of from two to three thousand feet in height extends the more part of the length (some forty miles) from east to west. Wood clusters on its front like ivy; and in the wet season streams descend in waterfalls and play below on the surface of the ocean. For in almost the whole of its length the cliff, without the formality of any beach, plunges in the Pacific. Bold water follows the coast; ships may almost everywhere approach within a trifling distance of the towering shore; and immediately in front of Molokai surveyors have found some of the deepest soundings of that ocean. This unusual depth of water, the continuity of the trade and the length of which fetch extends unbroken from the shores of California, magnify the sea. The swell is nursed by the steady wind, it grows in that long distance, it draws near through the deep soundings without combing, and spends itself undiminished on the cliffs of Molokai.

Toward the eastern end a river in a winding glen descends from the interior; the barrier is quite broken here, and a beach is formed and makes a place of call, Wailau. A few miles farther east, the cove of Pelekunu offers a doubtful chance of landing, and is also visited by steamers. The third and last place of approach is at the Lazaretto. A shelf of undercliff here borders the precipice, expanding toward its western end in a blunt promontory, a little more than a mile square. The lee of this precipice offers unusual facilities for landing and, in favorable states of wind and sea, ships may anchor. But these facilities to seaward are more than counterbalanced by the uncompromising character of the barrier behind. The pali (as the precipice is called) in the extent of this strip of undercliff makes three recesses, Waihanau, Waialeia, and Waikolu – as their names imply, three gutters of the mountain. These are clothed in wood; from a distance they show like verdant niches and retreats for lovers; but the face of the rock is so precipitous that only in the first, Waihanau, is there a practicable path. The rains continually destroy it; it must be renewed continually; to ride there is impossible; to mount without frequent falls seems unexpected; and even the descent exhausts a powerful man. The existence of another path more to the westward was affirmed to me by some, denied by others. At the most, therefore, in two points, the cliff is scantily passable upward. Passage coastwise is beyond expectation to any creature without wings. To the west, the strip of undercliff simply discontinues. To the east, the wall itself thrusts forth a huge protrusion, and the way is barred except to fish and seabirds. Here, then, is a prison fortified by nature, a place where thousands may be quartered and a pair of sentinels suffice to watch and hold the only issues.

The undercliff is in itself narrow; it is widened on one hand by the recesses of the cliff, and on the other by the expansion of the foreland; and the last contains (for a guess) two-thirds of the whole territory. It rises in the midst to a low hill enclosing a dead crater, like a quarry hole; the interior sides clothed with trees; at the foot a salt pool, unsoundable, at least unsounded. Hence the land slopes to the sea's edge and upward toward the pali in grassy downs. A single sick pandanus breaks, or broke while I was there, that naked heath; except in man's enclosures, I can recall nowhere else one switch of timber. The foreland is grazed by some fifteen hundred head of stock, seven hundred of them horses, for the patients are continual and furious riders; the rest cows and asses. These all do excellently well. The horrid pest to which the place is sacred spares them, being man's prerogative. It was strange to see those droves of animals feeding and sporting in exuberant health by the sea margin, and to reflect upon their destiny, brought from so far, at so much cost and toil, only to be ridden to and fro upon and eaten by the defeatured and dying.

The shaven down, the scattered boulders, the cry of the wind in the grass, the frequent showers of rain, the bulk of the pali, the beating of the near sea, all the features and conditions strike the mind as northern, and to the northerner the scene is in consequence grateful, like one of his native minor tunes. It is stirring to look eastward and see the huge viridescent mountain front sunder the settlement from the next habitations of clean men at Pelekunu – at its foot, in the sea, two tilted islets. It is pleasant in the early morning to ride by the roots of the pali, when the low sun and the cool breeze are in your face, and from above, in the cliffside forest, falls a perpetual chirruping of birds. It is pleasant, above all, to wander by the margin of the sea. The heath breaks down, like Helicon, in cliffs. A narrow fringe of emerald edges the precipitous shore; close beyond the blue shows the bold soundings; the wanderer stands plainly on a mere buttress of the vast cathedral front of the island, and above and below him, in the air and in the water, the precipice continues. Along the brink, rock architecture and sea music please the senses, and in that tainted place the thought of the cleanness of the antiseptic ocean is welcome to the mind.

Yet this is but one side of the scenery of the Lazaretto: and I received an impression strongly contrasted when I entered the recess of Waialeaia. The sides were niched and channeled with dry tracks of torrents, grass clung on the sheer precipice, forest clustered on the smallest vantage of a shelf. The floor of the amphitheater was piled with shattered rock, detritus of the mountain, with which, in the time of the rains, the torrents had maintained a cannonade. Vigorously black themselves, these were spotted with plants and trees of a vivid green. The day was overcast; clouds ran low about the edges of the basin; and yet the colors glowed as though immersed in sunshine. On the downs the effect is of some bleak, noble coast of Scotland or Scandinavia; here in the recess I felt myself transported to the tropics.

There are two villages, Kalaupapa, on the western shore of the promontory, Kalawao, toward the east upon the strip of undercliff; and along the road which joins them, each reaches forth scattered habitations.

Kalaupapa, the most sheltered in prevailing winds, is the customary landing place. When the run of the sea inclines the other way ships pass far to the eastward near the two islets, and passengers are landed with extreme difficulty, and I was assured, not without danger, on a spur of rock. Kalaupapa, being quite upon the downs, is the more bleak; a long, bare, irregular, ungardened village of unsightly houses. Here are two churches, Protestant and Catholic, and the Bishop Home for Girls.[7] Kalawao is even beautiful; pleasant houses stand in gardens of flowers; the pali rises behind; in front, across the sea, the eye commands the islets and the huge green face of cliff excluding Pelekunu. This is the view from the window of the lay brother, Mr. Dutton, and he assured me he found its beauty far more striking than the deformations of the sick. The passing visitor can scarce attain to such philosophy. Here is Damien's Home for Boys.[8] Close behind is a double graveyard, where some of the dead retain courtesy titles, and figure in their epitaphs as 'Mr.' or as 'Mrs.' The inevitable twin churches complete the village. A fifth church, the church of the Mormons, exists somewhere in the settlement; but I could never find it. On the westward end of Kalawao what we may call the official quarter stretches toward the promontory. The main feature is the enclosure of the hospital and prison, where bad cases and bad characters are kept in surveillance; a green in a stockade with a few papayas and one flowering oleander, surrounded on three sides by low white houses. A little way off, enclosed in walls and hedges, stands the guesthouse of Kalawao, and beyond that again, the quarters of the doctor.

The guesthouse is kept ready for the visits of members of the board. I arrived there early in the day, opened the gate, turned my horse loose, and entered in possession of the vacant house. I wandered through its chambers, visited the

bathroom and the kitchen, and at last, throwing myself upon a bed, I fell asleep.
Not before the hour of dinner, Dr. Swift, returning from his duties, wakened me
and introduced himself. A similar arrival may be read of in the tale of the Three
Bears; and that is well called a guesthouse where there is no host. Singular indeed
is the isolation of the visitor in the Lazaretto. No patient is suffered to approach
his place of residence. His room is tidied out by a clean helper during the day and
while he is abroad. He returns at night to solitary walls. For a while a bell sounds
at intervals from the hospital; silence succeeds, only pointed by the humming of
the surf or the chirp of crickets. He steps to his door; perhaps a light still shines
in the hospital; all else is dark. He returns and sits by his lamp and the crowding
experiences besiege his memory; sights of pain in a land of disease and disfigure-
ment, bright examples of fortitude and kindness, moral beauty, physical horror,
intimately knit. He must be a man very little impressionable if he recall not these
hours with an especial poignancy; he must be a man either very virtuous or very
dull, if they were not hours of self-review and vain aspirations after good.

When the Hawaiian Government embraced the plan of segregation they were
doubtless (as is the way of governments) unprepared, and the constitution of the
Lazaretto, as it now exists, was approached by blunder and reached by accident.
There was no design to pauperise; the lepers were to work, and in whole or part
be self-supporting; and when a site fell to be chosen, some extent of cultivable soil
was first required. In this, as in other conditions, Kalawao was wholly fitted for the
purpose. In the old days, when Molokai swarmed with population, the foreland
must have been a busy and perhaps a holy place; and thirty years ago it was covered with the ruins of heiaus, but still inhabited and still in active cultivation.
Terms of sale were easily agreed upon. Unhappily, the government coquetted; the
farmers were held for months under suspense; for months, in consequence, their
houses were left unrepaired, their fields untilled; and the property was already
much deteriorated before the purchase was confirmed and the clean inhabitants
ejected from the foreland. The history of misgovernment by board followed the
common course to the customary end; *too late* was coupled as usual with *too
early*; the government had procrastinated to its loss, yet even then it was unready,
and for another period of months the deserted farms lay idle. At length the first
shipment of lepers landed (1865) with a small knit of blankets, tin dishes, and the
like, but neither food nor money, to find the roofs fallen from the houses and the
taro rooting in the ground.

They were strangers to each other, collected by common calamity, disfigured,
mortally sick, banished without sin from home and friends. Few would understand the principle on which they were thus forfeited in all that makes life dear;
many must have conceived their ostracism to be grounded in malevolent caprice;
all came with sorrow at heart, many with despair and rage. In the chronicle of
man there is perhaps no more melancholy landing than this of the leper immi-

grants among the ruined houses and dead harvests of Molokai. But the spirit of our race is finely tempered and the business of life engrossing to the last. As the spider, when you have wrecked its web, begins immediately to spin fresh strands, so these exiles, widowed, orphaned, unchilded, legally dead and physically dying, struck root in their new place. By a culpable neglect in the authorities they were suffered to divide among themselves the whole territory of the settlement; fell to work with growing hope, repaired their houses, replanted the fields, and began to look about them with the pride of the proprietor. Upon this scene of reviving industry a second deportation arrived, and the first were called upon to share and subdivide their lots. They did so, not without complaint, which the authorities disregarded; a third shipment followed shortly after in the same conditions, and a further redistribution of the land was imposed upon the early settlers. Remuneration was demanded; government demurred upon the price; the lepers were affronted, withdrew their offer, and stood upon their rights, and a new regimen rose of necessity. The two first companies continued to subsist upon their farms; but the third, and all subsequent shipments, must be bed by government. Pauperism had begun, and the original design miscarried. Today all are paupers; the single occasion of healthy interest and exercise subducted, and the country at large saddled with the support of many useless mouths.

Notes

1. 'The chapters he wrote about his adventures at Kona and the City of Refuge and on the island of Molokai were omitted from most editions of his collected works.' See A Grove Day, ed. *Travels in Hawaii* (Honolulu: University of Hawaii Press, 1973), p. viii.

2. After a particularly difficult voyage, the yacht *Casco*, carrying Robert Louis Stevenson and his family (consisting of RLS, Fanny, Fanny's son Lloyd, Stevenson's mother, and the family maid Valentine Roch) reached Honolulu on 24 January 1889, where they soon received a warm welcome from the royal family: King David Kalakaua, his sister Princess (later Queen) Liliuokalani, and Princess Kaiulani at Iolani Palace. During the first several nights, the Stevensons stayed at the home of Henry F Poor (1856–1899) and his mother Caroline Bush (1836–1914) at 40 Emma Street. Later, Mrs. Bush offered Stevenson and Fanny the use of her bungalow on Waikiki Beach.

3. Stevenson did not particularly care for Honolulu, which he thought too noisy. He much preferred the remoteness and solitude of the beach. According to A Grove, 'The suburb of Waikiki, then a marshy region of rice paddies behind a fringe of shallow beach, could be reached from Honolulu in mule-drawn tram cars.' See Day, ed., *Travels in Hawaii*, p. xxii.

4. Stevenson spent a week at Ho'okena on the Kona Coast, where, according to Frank McLynn, he was 'the only white man in a Polynesian village.' See McLynn, *Robert Louis Stevenson: A Biography* (New York: Random House, 1993), p. 347.

5. Captain James Cook (1728–1779), English navigator and explorer was murdered by native Hawaiians south of Kealakekua Bay.

6. Stevenson had obtained permission from the Board of Health to visit the leper colony on Molokai. He spent twelve days on the island, seven of them in the colony. Located on Molokai's Kalaupapa Peninsula, the settlements are now located within the Kalaupapa National Historical Park. Between 1865 and 1895, the indigenous people were removed from their ancestral land. Later, from 1866 until 1969, a colony of lepers was established, first at Kalawao and then at Kalaupapa. Because of negative connotations, the term *leper* has been officially changed in the USA to Hansen's disease. See also, Frank McLynn, *Robert Louis Stevenson*, ibid.

7. Bishop's House for Girls at Kalaupapa was founded by Charles R Bishop, a Honolulu banker and run by a group of Franciscan sisters originally from Syracuse, New York, under the leadership of Mother Marianne Kopp (1836–1918). See Ernest Mehew, ed., *Selected Letters of Robert Louis Stevenson* (New Haven, Conn.: Yale University Press, 2001), p. 403 n.2. In June 1889 Stevenson described his visit to the colony to his mother: 'I went there most days to play croquet with the poor patients – think of a game of croquet with seven little lepers, and the thermometer sometimes ninety in the shade!' See Grove, *Travels in Hawaii*, p. 144.

8. Father Damien (full name: Joseph de Veuster) (1840–1889) was a controversial Belgian missionary priest who went to live and work in the Molokai leper colony in 1873.

FROM *In the South Seas*

For copyright purposes, In the South Seas *appeared in a limited edition – only 22 copies – in London in 1890 before being serialised in the* New York Sun *and the (London)* Black and White. *The American edition of the book was published in 1896 by Scribner's; the first British edition by Chatto and Windus in 1900. In the* South Seas *is Stevenson's account of his cruises on the* Casco *and* Equator *in 1888 and 1889–1890, respectively, from the Marquesas Islands to Tahiti, Honolulu, and Samoa, his final home.*

THE MARQUESAS AN ISLAND LANDFALL

FOR nearly ten years my health had been declining; and for some while before I set forth upon my voyage, I believed I was come to the afterpiece of life, and had only the nurse and undertaker to expect. It was suggested that I should try the South Seas[1]; and I was not unwilling to visit like a ghost, and be carried like a bale, among scenes that had attracted me in youth and health. I chartered accordingly Dr. Merrit's schooner yacht, the *Casco*,[2] seventy-four tons register; sailed from San Francisco towards the end of June 1888, visited the eastern islands, and was left early the next year at Honolulu. Hence, lacking courage to return to my old life of the house and sick-room, I set forth to leeward in a trading schooner, the *Equator*,[3] of a little over seventy tons, spent four months among the atolls (low coral islands) of the Gilbert group, and reached Samoa towards the close of '89. By that time gratitude and habit were beginning to attach me to the islands; I had gained a competency of strength; I had made friends; I had learned new interests; the time of my voyages had passed like days in fairyland; and I decided to remain. I began to prepare these pages at sea, on a third cruise, in the trading steamer *Janet Nicoll*.[4] If more days are granted me, they shall be passed where I have found life most pleasant and man most interesting; the axes of my black boys are already clearing the foundations of my future house; and I must learn to address readers from the uttermost parts of the sea.

That I should thus have reversed the verdict of Lord Tennyson's hero is less eccentric than appears.[5] Few men who come to the islands leave them; they grow grey where they alighted; the palm shades and the trade-wind fans them till they die, perhaps cherishing to the last the fancy of a visit home, which is rarely made, more rarely enjoyed, and yet more rarely repeated. No part of the world exerts the same attractive power upon the visitor, and the task before me is to communicate to fireside travellers some sense of its seduction, and to describe the life, at sea and ashore, of many hundred thousand persons, some of our own blood and language, all our contemporaries, and yet as remote in thought and habit as Rob

Roy or Barbarossa, the Apostles or the Caesars.

The first experience can never be repeated. The first love, the first sunrise, the first South Sea island, are memories apart and touched a virginity of sense. On the 28th of July 1888 the moon was an hour down by four in the morning. In the east a radiating centre of brightness told of the day; and beneath, on the skyline, the morning bank was already building, black as ink. We have all read of the swiftness of the day's coming and departure in low latitudes; it is a point on which the scientific and sentimental tourist are at one, and has inspired some tasteful poetry. The period certainly varies with the season; but here is one case exactly noted. Although the dawn was thus preparing by four, the sun was not up till six; and it was half-past five before we could distinguish our expected islands from the clouds on the horizon. Eight degrees south, and the day two hours a–coming. The interval was passed on deck in the silence of expectation, the customary thrill of landfall heightened by the strangeness of the shores that we were then approaching. Slowly they took shape in the attenuating darkness. Ua–huna, piling up to a truncated summit, appeared the first upon the starboard bow; almost abeam arose our destination, Nuka-hiva, whelmed in cloud; and betwixt and to the southward, the first rays of the sun displayed the needles of Ua–pu. These pricked about the line of the horizon; like the pinnacles of some ornate and monstrous church, they stood there, in the sparkling brightness of the morning, the fit signboard of a world of wonders.

Not one soul aboard the *Casco* had set foot upon the islands, or knew, except by accident, one word of any of the island tongues; and it was with something perhaps of the same anxious pleasure as thrilled the bosom of discoverers that we drew near these problematic shores. The land heaved up in peaks and rising vales; it fell in cliffs and buttresses; its colour ran through fifty modulations in a scale of pearl and rose and olive; and it was crowned above by opalescent clouds. The suffusion of vague hues deceived the eye; the shadows of clouds were confounded with the articulations of the mountains; and the isle and its unsubstantial canopy rose and shimmered before us like a single mass. There was no beacon, no smoke of towns to be expected, no plying pilot. Somewhere, in that pale phantasmagoria of cliff and cloud, our haven lay concealed; and somewhere to the east of it – the only sea-mark given – a certain headland, known indifferently as Cape Adam and Eve, or Cape Jack and Jane, and distinguished by two colossal figures, the gross statuary of nature. These we were to find; for these we craned and stared, focused glasses, and wrangled over charts; and the sun was overhead and the land close ahead before we found them. To a ship approaching, like the *Casco*, from the north, they proved indeed the least conspicuous features of a striking coast; the surf flying high above its base; strange, austere, and feathered mountains rising behind; and Jack and Jane, or Adam and Eve, impending like a pair of warts above the breakers.

Thence we bore away along shore. On our port beam we might hear the explosions of the surf; a few birds flew fishing under the prow; there was no other sound or mark of life, whether of man or beast, in all that quarter of the island. Winged by her own impetus and the dying breeze, the *Casco* skimmed under cliffs, opened out a cove, showed us a beach and some green trees, and flitted by again, bowing to the swell. The trees, from our distance, might have been hazel; the beach might have been in Europe; the mountain forms behind modelled in little from the Alps, and the forest which clustered on their ramparts a growth no more considerable than our Scottish heath. Again the cliff yawned, but now with a deeper entry; and the *Casco*, hauling her wind, began to slide into the bay of Anaho. The cocoa-palm, that giraffe of vegetables, so graceful, so ungainly, to the European eye so foreign, was to be seen crowding on the beach, and climbing and fringing the steep sides of mountains. Rude and bare hills embraced the inlet upon either hand; it was enclosed to the landward by a bulk of shattered mountains. In every crevice of that barrier the forest harboured, roosting and nestling there like birds about a ruin; and far above, it greened and roughened the razor edges of the summit.

Under the eastern shore, our schooner, now bereft of any breeze, continued to creep in: the smart creature, when once under way, appearing motive in herself. From close aboard arose the bleating of young lambs; a bird sang in the hillside; the scent of the land and of a hundred fruits or flowers flowed forth to meet us; and, presently, a house or two appeared, standing high upon the ankles of the hills, and one of these surrounded with what seemed a garden. These conspicuous habitations, that patch of culture, had we but known it, were a mark of the passage of whites; and we might have approached a hundred islands and not found their parallel. It was longer ere we spied the native village, standing (in the universal fashion) close upon a curve of beach, close under a grove of palms; the sea in front growling and whitening on a concave arc of reef. For the cocoa-tree and the island man are both lovers and neighbours of the surf. 'The coral waxes, the palm grows, but man departs,' says the sad Tahitian proverb; but they are all three, so long as they endure, co-haunters of the beach. The mark of anchorage was a blow-hole in the rocks, near the south-easterly corner of the bay. Punctually to our use, the blow-hole spouted; the schooner turned upon her heel; the anchor plunged. It was a small sound, a great event; my soul went down with these moorings whence no windlass may extract nor any diver fish it up; and I, and some part of my ship's company, were from that hour the bondslaves of the isles of Vivien.

Before yet the anchor plunged a canoe was already paddling from the hamlet. It contained two men: one white, one brown and tattooed across the face with bands of blue, both in immaculate white European clothes: the resident trader, Mr. Regler, and the native chief, Taipi–Kikino. 'Captain, is it permitted to come on board?' were the first words we heard among the islands. Canoe followed canoe till the ship swarmed with stalwart, six-foot men in every stage of undress; some in a shirt, some in a loin-cloth, one in a handkerchief imperfectly adjusted; some, and these the more considerable, tattooed from head to foot in awful patterns; some barbarous and knived; one, who sticks in my memory as something bestial, squatting on his hams in a canoe, sucking an orange and spitting it out again to alternate sides with ape-like vivacity – all talking, and we could not understand one word; all trying to trade with us who had no thought of trading, or offering us island curios at prices palpably absurd. There was no word of welcome; no show of civility; no hand extended save that of the chief and Mr. Regler. As we still continued to refuse the proffered articles, complaint ran high and rude; and one, the jester of the party, railed upon our meanness amid jeering laughter. Amongst other angry pleasantries – 'Here is a mighty fine ship,' said he, 'to have no money on board!' I own I was inspired with sensible repugnance; even with alarm. The ship was manifestly in their power; we had women on board; I knew nothing of my guests beyond the fact that they were cannibals; the Directory (my only guide)[6] was full of timid cautions; and as for the trader, whose presence might else have reassured me, were not whites in the Pacific the usual instigators and accomplices of native outrage? When he reads this confession, our kind friend, Mr. Regler, can afford to smile.

Later in the day, as I sat writing up my journal, the cabin was filled from end to end with Marquesans: three brown-skinned generations, squatted cross-legged upon the floor, and regarding me in silence with embarrassing eyes. The eyes of all Polynesians are large, luminous, and melting; they are like the eyes of animals and some Italians. A kind of despair came over me, to sit there helpless under all these staring orbs, and be thus blocked in a corner of my cabin by this speechless crowd: and a kind of rage to think they were beyond the reach of articulate communication, like furred animals, or folk born deaf, or the dwellers of some alien planet.

To cross the Channel is, for a boy of twelve, to change heavens; to cross the Atlantic, for a man of twenty-four, is hardly to modify his diet. But I was now escaped out of the shadow of the Roman empire, under whose toppling monuments we were all cradled, whose laws and letters are on every hand of us, constraining and preventing. I was now to see what men might be whose fathers had never studied Virgil, had never been conquered by Caesar, and never been ruled by the wisdom of Gaius or Papinian.[7] By the same step I had journeyed forth out of that comfortable zone of kindred languages, where the curse of Babel is so easy to be remedied; and my new fellow-creatures sat before me dumb like images. Methought, in my travels, all human relation was to be excluded; and when I returned home (for in those days I still projected my return) I should have but dipped into a picture-book without a text. Nay, and I even questioned if my travels should be much prolonged; perhaps they were destined to a speedy end; perhaps my subsequent friend, Kauanui, whom I remarked there, sitting silent with the rest, for a man of some authority, might leap from his hams with an ear-splitting signal, the ship be carried at a rush, and the ship's company butchered for the table.

There could be nothing more natural than these apprehensions, nor anything more groundless. In my experience of the islands, I had never again so menacing a reception; were I to meet with such to-day, I should be more alarmed and tenfold more surprised. The majority of Polynesians are easy folk to get in touch with, frank, fond of notice, greedy of the least affection, like amiable, fawning dogs; and even with the Marquesans, so recently and so imperfectly redeemed from a blood-boltered barbarism, all were to become our intimates, and one, at least, was to mourn sincerely our departure.

MAKING FRIENDS

THE impediment of tongues was one that I particularly over-estimated. The languages of Polynesia are easy to smatter, though hard to speak with elegance. And they are extremely similar, so that a person who has a tincture of one or two may risk, not without hope, an attempt upon the others.

And again, not only is Polynesian easy to smatter, but interpreters abound. Missionaries, traders, and broken white folk living on the bounty of the natives, are to be found in almost every isle and hamlet; and even where these are unserviceable, the natives themselves have often scraped up a little English, and in the French zone (though far less commonly) a little French-English, or an efficient pidgin, what is called to the westward 'Beach-la-Mar,' comes easy to the Polynesian; it is now taught, besides, in the schools of Hawaii; and from the multiplicity of British ships, and the nearness of the States on the one hand and the colonies on the other, it may be called, and will almost certainly become, the tongue of the Pacific. I will instance a few examples. I met in Majuro a Marshall Island boy who spoke excellent English; this he had learned in the German firm in Jaluit, yet did not speak one word of German. I heard from a gendarme who had taught school in Rapa-iti that while the children had the utmost difficulty or reluctance to learn French, they picked up English on the wayside, and as if by accident. On one of the most out-of-the-way atolls in the Carolines, my friend Mr. Benjamin Hird was amazed to find the lads playing cricket on the beach and talking English; and it was in English that the crew of the *Janet Nicoll*,[8] a set of black boys from different Melanesian islands, communicated with other natives throughout the cruise, transmitted orders, and sometimes jested together on the fore-hatch. But what struck me perhaps most of all was a word I heard on the verandah of the Tribunal at Noumea.[9] A case had just been heard – a trial for infanticide against an ape-like native woman; and the audience were smoking cig-

arettes as they awaited the verdict. An anxious, amiable French lady, not far from
tears, was eager for acquittal, and declared she would engage the prisoner to be
her children's nurse. The bystanders exclaimed at the proposal; the woman was a
savage, said they, and spoke no language. *'Mais, vous savez,'* objected the fair sen-
timentalist; *'Ils apprennent si vite l'anglais!'*

But to be able to speak to people is not all. And in the first stage of my relations
with natives I was helped by two things. To begin with, I was the show-man of the
Casco. She, her fine lines, tall spars, and snowy decks, the crimson fittings of the
saloon, and the white, the gilt, and the repeating mirrors of the tiny cabin,
brought us a hundred visitors. The men fathomed out her dimensions with their
arms, as their fathers fathomed out the ships of Cook[10]; the women declared the
cabins more lovely than a church; bouncing Junos were never weary of sitting in
the chairs and contemplating in the glass their own bland images; and I have seen
one lady strip up her dress, and, with cries of wonder and delight, rub herself
bare-breeched upon the velvet cushions. Biscuit, jam, and syrup was the entertainment; and, as in European parlours, the photograph album went the round.
This sober gallery, their everyday costumes and physiognomies, had become
transformed, in three weeks' sailing, into things wonderful and rich and foreign;
alien faces, barbaric dresses, they were now beheld and fingered, in the swerving
cabin, with innocent excitement and surprise. Her Majesty was often recognised,
and I have seen French subjects kiss her photograph; Captain Speedy – in an
Abyssinian war-dress, supposed to be the uniform of the British army – met with
much acceptance; and the effigies of Mr. Andrew Lang were admired in the
Marquesas. There is the place for him to go when he shall be weary of Middlesex
and Homer.[11]

It was perhaps yet more important that I had enjoyed in my youth some knowledge of our Scots folk of the Highlands and the Islands. Not much beyond a century has passed since these were in the same convulsive and transitionary state as
the Marquesans of to-day. In both cases an alien authority enforced, the clans dis-
armed, the chiefs deposed, new customs introduced, and chiefly that fashion of
regarding money as the means and object of existence. The commercial age, in
each, succeeding at a bound to an age of war abroad and patriarchal communism
at home. In one the cherished practice of tattooing, in the other a cherished costume, proscribed. In each a main luxury cut off: beef, driven under cloud of night
from Lowland pastures, denied to the meat-loving Highlander; long-pig, pirated
from the next village, to the man-eating Kanaka.[12] The grumbling, the secret fer-
ment, the fears and resentments, the alarms and sudden councils of Marquesan
chiefs, reminded me continually of the days of Lovat and Struan.[13] Hospitality,
tact, natural fine manners, and a touchy punctilio, are common to both races:
common to both tongues the trick of dropping medial consonants. Here is a table
of two widespread Polynesian words:–

HOUSE. LOVE.

Tahitian FARE AROHA

New Zealand WHARE

Samoan FALE TALOFA

Manihiki FALE ALOHA

Hawaiian HALE ALOHA

Marquesan HA'E KAOHA

The elision of medial consonants, so marked in these Marquesan instances, is no less common both in Gaelic and the Lowland Scots. Stranger still, that prevalent Polynesian sound, the so-called catch, written with an apostrophe, and often or always the gravestone of a perished consonant, is to be heard in Scotland to this day. When a Scot pronounces water, better, or bottle – *wa'er, be'er*, or *bo'le* – the sound is precisely that of the catch; and I think we may go beyond, and say, that if such a population could be isolated, and this mispronunciation should become the rule, it might prove the first stage of transition from T to K, which is the disease of Polynesian languages. The tendency of the Marquesans, however, is to urge against consonants, or at least on the very common letter L, a war of mere extermination. A hiatus is agreeable to any Polynesian ear; the ear even of the stranger soon grows used to these barbaric voids; but only in the Marquesan will you find such names as *haaii* and *paaaeua*, when each individual vowel must be separately uttered.

These points of similarity between a South Sea people and some of my own folk at home ran much in my head in the islands; and not only inclined me to view my fresh acquaintances with favour, but continually modified my judgment. A polite Englishman comes to-day to the Marquesans and is amazed to find the men tattooed; polite Italians came not long ago to England and found our fathers stained with woad; and when I paid the return visit as a little boy, I was highly diverted with the backwardness of Italy: so insecure, so much a matter of the day and hour, is the pre-eminence of race. It was so that I hit upon a means of communication which I recommend to travellers. When I desired any detail of savage custom, or of superstitious belief, I cast back in the story of my fathers, and fished for what I wanted with some trait of equal barbarism: Michael Scott, Lord Derwentwater's head,[14] the second-sight, the Water Kelpie, – each of these I have found to be a killing bait; the black bull's head of Stirling procured me the legend of Rahero[15];

and what I knew of the Cluny Macphersons, or the Appin Stewarts, enabled me to learn, and helped me to understand, about the *Tevas* of Tahiti.[16] The native was no longer ashamed, his sense of kinship grew warmer, and his lips were opened. It is this sense of kinship that the traveller must rouse and share; or he had better content himself with travels from the blue bed to the brown. And the presence of one Cockney titterer will cause a whole party to walk in clouds of darkness.

The hamlet of Anaho stands on a margin of flat land between the west of the beach and the spring of the impending mountains. A grove of palms, perpetually ruffling its green fans, carpets it (as for a triumph) with fallen branches, and shades it like an arbour. A road runs from end to end of the covert among beds of flowers, the milliner's shop of the community; and here and there, in the grateful twilight, in an air filled with a diversity of scents, and still within hearing of the surf upon the reef, the native houses stand in scattered neighbourhood. The same word, as we have seen, represents in many tongues of Polynesia, with scarce a shade of difference, the abode of man. But although the word be the same, the structure itself continually varies; and the Marquesan, among the most backward and barbarous of islanders, is yet the most commodiously lodged. The grass huts of Hawaii, the birdcage houses of Tahiti, or the open shed, with the crazy Venetian blinds, of the polite Samoan – none of these can be compared with the Marquesan *paepae-hae*, or dwelling platform. The paepae is an oblong terrace built without cement or black volcanic stone, from twenty to fifty feet in length, raised from four to eight feet from the earth, and accessible by a broad stair. Along the back of this, and coming to about half its width, runs the open front of the house, like a covered gallery: the interior sometimes neat and almost elegant in its bareness, the sleeping space divided off by an endlong coaming, some bright raiment perhaps hanging from a nail, and a lamp and one of White's sewing-machines the only marks of civilisation. On the outside, at one end of the terrace, burns the cooking-fire under a shed; at the other there is perhaps a pen for pigs; the remainder is the evening lounge and *al fresco* banquet-hall of the inhabitants. To some houses water is brought down the mountains in bamboo pipes, perforated for the sake of sweetness. With the Highland comparison in my mind, I was struck to remember the sluttish mounds of turf and stone in which I have sat and been entertained in the Hebrides and the North Islands. Two things, I suppose, explain the contrast. In Scotland wood is rare, and with materials so rude as turf and stone the very hope of neatness is excluded. And in Scotland it is cold. Shelter and a hearth are needs so pressing that a man looks not beyond; he is out all day after a bare bellyful, and at night when he saith, 'Aha, it is warm!' he has not appetite for more. Or if for something else, then something higher; a fine school of poetry and song arose in these rough shelters, and an air like 'Lochaber No More' is an evidence of refinement more convincing, as well as more imperishable, than a palace.

To one such dwelling platform a considerable troop of relatives and dependants resort. In the hour of the dusk, when the fire blazes, and the scent of the cooked breadfruit fills the air, and perhaps the lamp glints already between the pillars and the house, you shall behold them silently assemble to this meal, men, women, and children; and the dogs and pigs frisk together up the terrace stairway, switching rival tails. The strangers from the ship were soon equally welcome: welcome to dip their fingers in the wooden dish, to drink cocoanuts, to share the circulating pipe, and to hear and hold high debate about the misdeeds of the French, the Panama Canal, or the geographical position of San Francisco and New Yo'ko. In a Highland hamlet, quite out of reach of any tourist, I have met the same plain and dignified hospitality.

I have mentioned two facts – the distasteful behaviour of our earliest visitors, and the case of the lady who rubbed herself upon the cushions – which would give a very false opinion of Marquesan manners. The great majority of Polynesians are excellently mannered; but the Marquesan stands apart, annoying and attractive, wild, shy, and refined. If you make him a present he affects to forget it, and it must be offered him again at his going: a pretty formality I have found nowhere else. A hint will get rid of any one or any number; they are so fiercely proud and modest; while many of the more lovable but blunter islanders crowd upon a stranger, and can be no more driven off than flies. A slight or an insult the Marquesan seems never to forget. I was one day talking by the wayside with my friend Hoka, when I perceived his eyes suddenly to flash and his stature to swell. A white horseman was coming down the mountain, and as he passed, and while he paused to exchange salutations with myself, Hoka was still staring and ruffling like a gamecock. It was a Corsican who had years before called him *cochon sauvage* – *cocon chauvage*, as Hoka mispronounced it. With people so nice and so touchy, it was scarce to be supposed that our company of greenhorns should not blunder into offences. Hoka, on one of his visits, fell suddenly in a brooding silence, and presently after left the ship with cold formality. When he took me back into favour, he adroitly and pointedly explained the nature of my offence: I had asked him to sell cocoa-nuts; and in Hoka's view articles of food were things that a gentleman should give, not sell; or at least that he should not sell to any friend. On another occasion I gave my boat's crew a luncheon of chocolate and biscuits. I had sinned, I could never learn how, against some point of observance; and though I was drily thanked, my offerings were left upon the beach. But our worst mistake was a slight we put on Toma, Hoka's adoptive father, and in his own eyes the rightful chief of Anaho. In the first place, we did not call upon him, as perhaps we should, in his fine new European house, the only one in the hamlet. In the second, when we came ashore upon a visit to his rival, Taipi-Kikino, it was Toma whom we saw standing at the head of the beach, a magnificent figure of a man, magnificently tattooed; and it was of Toma that we asked our question:

'Where is the chief?' 'What chief?' cried Toma, and turned his back on the blasphemers. Nor did he forgive us. Hoka came and went with us daily; but, alone I believe of all the countryside, neither Toma nor his wife set foot on board the *Casco*. The temptation resisted it is hard for a European to compute. The flying city of Laputa moored for a fortnight in St. James's Park affords but a pale figure of the *Casco* anchored before Anaho; for the Londoner has still his change of pleasures, but the Marquesan passes to his grave through an unbroken uniformity of days.

On the afternoon before it was intended we should sail, a valedictory party came on board: nine of our particular friends equipped with gifts and dressed as for a festival. Hoka, the chief dancer and singer, the greatest dandy of Anaho, and one of the handsomest young fellows in the world – sullen, showy, dramatic, light as a feather and strong as an ox – it would have been hard, on that occasion, to recognise, as he sat there stooped and silent, his face heavy and grey. It was strange to see the lad so much affected; stranger still to recognise in his last gift one of the curios we had refused on the first day, and to know our friend, so gaily dressed, so plainly moved at our departure, for one of the half-naked crew that had besieged and insulted us on our arrival: strangest of all, perhaps, to find, in that carved handle of a fan, the last of those curiosities of the first day which had now all been given to us by their possessors – their chief merchandise, for which they had sought to ransom us as long as we were strangers, which they pressed on us for nothing as soon as we were friends. The last visit was not long protracted. One after another they shook hands and got down into their canoe; when Hoka turned his back immediately upon the ship, so that we saw his face no more. Taipi, on the other hand, remained standing and facing us with gracious valedictory gestures; and when Captain Otis[17] dipped the ensign, the whole party saluted with their hats. This was the farewell; the episode of our visit to Anaho was held concluded; and though the *Casco* remained nearly forty hours at her moorings, not one returned on board, and I am inclined to think they avoided appearing on the beach. This reserve and dignity is the finest trait of the Marquesan.

THE MAROON

OF the beauties of Anaho books might be written. I remember waking about three, to find the air temperate and scented. The long swell brimmed into the bay, and seemed to fill it full and then subside. Gently, deeply, and silently the *Casco* rolled; only at times a block piped like a bird. Oceanward, the heaven was bright with stars and the sea with their reflections. If I looked to that side, I might have sung with the Hawaiian poet:

UA MAOMAO KA LANI, UA KAHAEA LUNA,
UA PIPI KA MAKA O KA HOKU.

The heavens were fair, they stretched above,

  Many were the eyes of the stars.)

And then I turned shoreward, and high squalls were overhead; the mountains loomed up black; and I could have fancied I had slipped ten thousand miles away and was anchored in a Highland loch; that when the day came, it would show pine, and heather, and green fern, and roofs of turf sending up the smoke of peats; and the alien speech that should next greet my ears must be Gaelic, not Kanaka.

And day, when it came, brought other sights and thoughts. I have watched the morning break in many quarters of the world; it has been certainly one of the chief joys of my existence, and the dawn that I saw with most emotion shone upon the bay of Anaho. The mountains abruptly overhang the port with every variety of surface and of inclination, lawn, and cliff, and forest. Not one of these but wore its proper tint of saffron, of sulphur, of the clove, and of the rose. The lustre was like that of satin; on the lighter hues there seemed to float an efflorescence; a solemn bloom appeared on the more dark. The light itself was the ordinary light of morning, colourless and clean; and on this ground of jewels, pencilled out the least detail of drawing. Meanwhile, around the hamlet, under the palms, where the blue shadow lingered, the red coals of cocoa husk and the light trails of smoke betrayed the awakening business of the day; along the beach men and women, lads and lasses, were returning from the bath in bright raiment, red and blue and green, such as we delighted to see in the coloured little pictures of our childhood; and presently the sun had cleared the eastern hill, and the glow of the day was over all.

The glow continued and increased, the business, from the main part, ceased before it had begun. Twice in the day there was a certain stir of shepherding along the seaward hills. At times a canoe went out to fish. At times a woman or two languidly filled a basket in the cotton patch. At times a pipe would sound out of the shadow of a house, ringing the changes on its three notes, with an effect like *que le jour me dure*, repeated endlessly. Or at times, across a corner of the bay, two natives might communicate in the Marquesan manner with conventional whistlings. All else was sleep and silence. The surf broke and shone around the shores; a species of black crane fished in the broken water; the black pigs were continually galloping by on some affair; but the people might never have awaked, or they might all be dead.

My favourite haunt was opposite the hamlet, where was a landing in a cove under a lianaed cliff. The beach was lined with palms and a tree called the purao, something between the fig and mulberry in growth, and bearing a flower like a great yellow poppy with a maroon heart. In places rocks encroached upon the sand; the beach would be all submerged; and the surf would bubble warmly as high as to my knees, and play with cocoa-nut husks as our more homely ocean plays with wreck and wrack and bottles. As the reflux drew down, marvels of colour and design streamed between my feet; which I would grasp at, miss, or seize: now to find them what they promised, shells to grace a cabinet or be set in gold upon a lady's finger; now to catch only *maya* of coloured sand, pounded fragments and pebbles, that, as soon as they were dry, became as dull and homely as the flints upon a garden path. I have toiled at this childish pleasure for hours in the strong sun, conscious of my incurable ignorance; but too keenly pleased to be ashamed. Meanwhile, the blackbird (or his tropical understudy) would be fluting in the thickets overhead.

A little further, in the turn of the bay, a streamlet trickled in the bottom of a den, thence spilling down a stair of rock into the sea. The draught of air drew down under the foliage in the very bottom of the den, which was a perfect arbour for coolness. In front it stood open on the blue bay and the *Casco* lying there under her awning and her cheerful colours. Overhead was a thatch of puraos, and over these again palms brandished their bright fans, as I have seen a conjurer make himself a halo out of naked swords. For in this spot, over a neck of low land at the foot of the mountains, the trade-wind streams into Anaho Bay in a flood of almost constant volume and velocity, and of a heavenly coolness.

It chanced one day that I was ashore in the cove, with Mrs. Stevenson and the ship's cook. Except for the *Casco* lying outside, and a crane or two, and the ever-busy wind and sea, the face of the world was of a prehistoric emptiness; life appeared to stand stock-still, and the sense of isolation was profound and refreshing. On a sudden, the trade-wind, coming in a gust over the isthmus, struck and scattered the fans of the palms above the den; and, behold! in two of the tops there sat a native, motionless as an idol and watching us, you would have said, without a wink. The next moment the tree closed, and the glimpse was gone. This discovery of human presences latent over-head in a place where we had supposed ourselves alone, the immobility of our tree-top spies, and the thought that perhaps at all hours we were similarly supervised, struck us with a chill. Talk languished on the beach. As for the cook (whose conscience was not clear), he never afterwards set foot on shore, and twice, when the *Casco* appeared to be driving on the rocks, it was amusing to observe that man's alacrity; death, he was persuaded, awaiting him upon the beach. It was more than a year later, in the Gilberts, that the explanation dawned upon myself. The natives were drawing palm-tree wine, a thing forbidden by law; and when the wind thus suddenly revealed them, they were doubtless more troubled than ourselves ...

THE GILBERTS
BUTARITARI

AT Honolulu we had said farewell to the *Casco* and to Captain Otis, and our next adventure was made in changed conditions. Passage was taken for myself, my wife, Mr. Osbourne, and my China boy, Ah Fu, on a pigmy trading schooner, the

Equator, Captain Dennis Reid[18]; and on a certain bright June day in 1889, adorned in the Hawaiian fashion with the garlands of departure, we drew out of port and bore with a fair wind for Micronesia.

The whole extent of the South Seas is a desert of ships; more especially that part where we were now to sail. No post runs in these islands; communication is by accident; where you may have designed to go is one thing, where you shall be able to arrive another. It was my hope, for instance, to have reached the Carolines, and returned to the light of day by way of Manila and the China ports; and it was in Samoa that we were destined to re-appear and be once more refreshed with the sight of mountains. Since the sunset faded from the peaks of Oahu six months had intervened, and we had seen no spot of earth so high as an ordinary cottage. Our path had been still on the flat sea, our dwellings upon unerected coral, our diet from the pickle-tub or out of tins; I had learned to welcome shark's flesh for a variety; and a mountain, an onion, an Irish potato or a beef-steak, had been long lost to sense and dear to aspiration.

The two chief places of our stay, Butaritari and Apemama, lie near the line; the latter within thirty miles. Both enjoy a superb ocean climate, days of blinding sun and bracing wind, nights of a heavenly brightness. Both are somewhat wider than Fakarava, measuring perhaps (at the widest) a quarter of a mile from beach to beach. In both, a coarse kind of *taro* thrives; its culture is a chief business of the natives, and the consequent mounds and ditches make miniature scenery and amuse the eye. In all else they show the customary features of an atoll: the low horizon, the expanse of the lagoon, the sedge-like rim of palm-tops, the sameness and smallness of the land, the hugely superior size and interest of sea and sky. Life on such islands is in many points like life on shipboard. The atoll, like the ship, is soon taken for granted; and the islanders, like the ship's crew, become soon the centre of attention. The isles are populous, independent, seats of kinglets, recently civilised, little visited. In the last decade many changes have crept in; women no longer go unclothed till marriage; the widow no longer sleeps at night and goes abroad by day with the skull of her dead husband; and, fire-arms being introduced, the spear and the shark-tooth sword are sold for curiosities. Ten years ago all these things and practices were to be seen in use; yet ten years more, and the old society will have entirely vanished. We came in a happy moment to see its institutions still erect and (in Apemama) scarce decayed.

Populous and independent – warrens of men, ruled over with some rustic pomp – such was the first and still the recurring impression of these tiny lands. As we stood across the lagoon for the town of Butaritari, a stretch of the low shore was seen to be crowded with the brown roofs of houses; those of the palace and king's summer parlour (which are of corrugated iron) glittered near one end conspicuously bright; the royal colours flew hard by on a tall flagstaff; in front, on an artificial islet, the gaol played the part of a martello. Even upon this first and distant view, the place had scarce the air of what it truly was, a village; rather of that which it was also, a petty metropolis, a city rustic and yet royal.

The lagoon is shoal. The tide being out, we waded for some quarter of a mile in tepid shallows, and stepped ashore at last into a flagrant stagnancy of sun and heat. The lee side of a line island after noon is indeed a breathless place; on the ocean beach the trade will be still blowing, boisterous and cool; out in the lagoon it will be blowing also, speeding the canoes; but the screen of bush completely intercepts it from the shore, and sleep and silence and companies of mosquitoes brood upon the towns.

We may thus be said to have taken Butaritari by surprise. A few inhabitants were still abroad in the north end, at which we landed. As we advanced, we were soon done with encounter, and seemed to explore a city of the dead. Only, between the posts of open houses, we could see the townsfolk stretched in the siesta, sometimes a family together veiled in a mosquito-net, sometimes a single sleeper on a platform like a corpse on a bier.

The houses were of all dimensions, from those of toys to those of churches. Some might hold a battalion, some were so minute they could scarce receive a pair of lovers; only in the playroom, when the toys are mingled, do we meet such incongruities of scale. Many were open sheds; some took the form of roofed stages; others were walled and the walls pierced with little windows. A few were perched on piles in the lagoon; the rest stood at random on a green, through which the roadway made a ribbon of sand, or along the embankments of a sheet of water like a shallow dock. One and all were the creatures of a single tree; palm-tree wood and palm-tree leaf their materials; no nail had been driven, no hammer sounded, in their building, and they were held together by lashings of palm-tree sinnet.

In the midst of the thoroughfare, the church stands like an island, a lofty and dim house with rows of windows; a rich tracery of framing sustains the roof; and through the door at either end the street shows in a vista. The proportions of the place, in such surroundings, and built of such materials, appeared august; and we threaded the nave with a sentiment befitting visitors in a cathedral. Benches run along either side. In the midst, on a crazy dais, two chairs stand ready for the king and queen when they shall choose to worship; over their heads a hoop, apparently from a hogshead, depends by a strip of red cotton; and the hoop (which hangs askew) is dressed with streamers of the same material, red and white.

This was our first advertisement of the royal dignity, and presently we stood before its seat and centre. The palace is built of imported wood upon a European plan; the roof of corrugated iron, the yard enclosed with walls, the gate surmounted by a sort of lych-house. It cannot be called spacious; a labourer in the States is sometimes more commodiously lodged; but when we had the chance to see it within, we found it was enriched (beyond all island expectation) with coloured advertisements and cuts from the illustrated papers. Even before the gate some of the treasures of the crown stand public: a bell of a good magnitude, two pieces of cannon, and a single shell. The bell cannot be rung nor the guns fired; they are curiosities, proofs of wealth, a part of the parade of the royalty, and stand to be admired like statues in a square. A straight gut of water like a canal runs almost to the palace door; the containing quay-walls excellently built of coral; over against the mouth, by what seems an effect of landscape art, the Martello-like islet of the gaol breaks the lagoon. Vassal chiefs with tribute, neighbour monarchs come a-roving, might here sail in, view with surprise these extensive public works, and be awed by these mouths of silent cannon. It was impossible to see the place and not to fancy it designed for pageantry. But the elaborate theatre then stood empty; the royal house deserted, its doors and windows gaping; the whole quarter of the town immersed in silence. On the opposite bank of the canal, on a roofed stage, an ancient gentleman slept publicly, sole visible inhabitant; and beyond on the lagoon a canoe spread a striped lateen, the sole thing moving.

The canal is formed on the south by a pier or causeway with a parapet. At the far end the parapet stops, and the quay expands into an oblong peninsula in the lagoon, the breathing-place and summer parlour of the king. The midst is occupied by an open house or permanent marquee – called here a maniapa, or, as the word is now pronounced, a maniap' – at the lowest estimation forty feet by sixty. The iron roof, lofty but exceedingly low-browed, so that a woman must stoop to enter, is supported externally on pillars of coral, within by a frame of wood. The floor is of broken coral, divided in aisles by the uprights of the frame; the house far enough from shore to catch the breeze, which enters freely and disperses the mosquitoes; and under the low eaves the sun is seen to glitter and the waves to dance on the lagoon.

It was now some while since we had met any but slumberers; and when we had wandered down the pier and stumbled at last into this bright shed, we were surprised to find it occupied by a society of wakeful people, some twenty souls in all, the court and guardsmen of Butaritari. The court ladies were busy making mats; the guardsmen yawned and sprawled. Half a dozen rifles lay on a rock and a cutlass was leaned against a pillar: the armoury of these drowsy musketeers. At the far end, a little closed house of wood displayed some tinsel curtains, and proved, upon examination, to be a privy on the European model. In front of this, upon some mats, lolled Tebureimoa, the king; behind him, on the panels of the house, two crossed rifles represented fasces. He wore pyjamas which sorrowfully misbecame his bulk; his nose was hooked and cruel, his body overcome with sodden corpulence, his eye timorous and dull: he seemed at once oppressed with drowsiness and held awake by apprehension: a pepper rajah muddled with opium, and listening for the march of a Dutch army, looks perhaps not otherwise. We were to grow better acquainted, and first and last I had the same impression; he seemed always drowsy, yet always to hearken and start; and, whether from remorse or fear, there is no doubt he seeks a refuge in the abuse of drugs.

The rajah displayed no sign of interest in our coming. But the queen, who sat beside him in a purple sacque, was more accessible; and there was present an interpreter so willing that his volubility became at last the cause of our departure. He had greeted us upon our entrance: – 'That is the honourable King, and I am his interpreter,' he had said, with more stateliness than truth. For he held no appointment in the court, seemed extremely ill–acquainted with the island lan-guage, and was present, like ourselves, upon a visit of civility. Mr. Williams was his name: an American darkey, runaway ship's cook, and bar-keeper at The Land We Live In tavern, Butaritari. I never knew a man who had more words in his com-mand or less truth to communicate; neither the gloom of the monarch, nor my own efforts to be distant, could in the least abash him; and when the scene closed, the darkey was left talking.

The town still slumbered, or had but just begun to turn and stretch itself; it was still plunged in heat and silence. So much the more vivid was the impression that we carried away of the house upon the islet, the Micronesian Saul wakeful amid his guards, and his unmelodious David, Mr. Williams, chattering through the drowsy hours.

THE KING OF APEMAMA:
FOUNDATION OF EQUATOR TOWN

OUR first sight of Tembinok'[19] was a matter of concern, almost alarm, to my whole party. We had a favour to seek; we must approach in the proper courtly atti-tude of a suitor; and must either please him or fail in the main purpose of our voy-age. It was our wish to land and live in Apemama, and see more near at hand the odd character of the man and the odd (or rather ancient) condition of his island. In all other isles of the South Seas a white man may land with his chest, and set up house for a lifetime, if he choose, and if he have the money or the trade; no hindrance is conceivable. But Apemama is a close island, lying there in the sea with closed doors; the king himself, like a vigilant officer, ready at the wicket to scrutinise and reject intrenching visitors. Hence the attraction of our enterprise; not merely because it was a little difficult, but because this social quarantine, a curiosity in itself, has been the preservative of others.

Tembinok', like most tyrants, is a conservative; like many conservatives, he eagerly welcomes new ideas, and, except in the field of politics, leans to practical reform. When the missionaries came, professing a knowledge of the truth, he readily received them; attended their worship, acquired the accomplishment of public prayer, and made himself a student at their feet. It is thus – it is by the cul-tivation of similar passing chances – that he has learned to read, to write, to cipher, and to speak his queer, personal English, so different from ordinary 'Beach de Mar,' so much more obscure, expressive, and condensed. His education attended to, he found time to become critical of the new inmates. Like Nakaeia of Makin, he is an admirer of silence in the island; broods over it like a great ear; has spies who report daily; and had rather his subjects sang than talked. The service, and in particular the sermon, were thus sure to become offences: 'Here, in my island, I 'peak,' he once observed to me. 'My chieps no 'peak – do what I talk.' He looked at the missionary, and what did he see? 'See Kanaka 'peak in a big outch!' he cried, with a strong ring of sarcasm. Yet he endured the subversive spectacle, and might even have continued to endure it, had not a fresh point arisen. He looked again, to employ his own figure; and the Kanaka was no longer speaking, he was doing worse – he was building a copra–house. The king was touched in his chief interests; revenue and prerogative were threatened. He considered besides (and some think with him) that trade is incompatible with the missionary claims. 'Tuppoti mitonary think 'good man': very good. Tuppoti he think 'cobra': no good. I send him away ship.' Such was his abrupt history of the evangelist in Apemama.

Similar deportations are common: 'I send him away ship' is the epitaph of not a few, his majesty paying the exile's fare to the next place of call. For instance, being passionately fond of European food, he has several times added to his household a white cook, and one after another these have been deported. They, on their side, swear they were not paid their wages; he, on his, that they robbed and swindled him beyond endurance: both perhaps justly. A more important case was that of an agent, despatched (as I heard the story) by a firm of merchants to worm his way into the king's good graces, become, if possible, premier, and handle the copra in the interest of his employers. He obtained authority to land, practised his fascinations, was patiently listened to by Tembinok', supposed himself on the highway to success; and behold! when the next ship touched at Apemama, the would-be premier was flung into a boat – had on board – his fare paid, and so good-bye. But it is needless to multiply examples; the proof of the pudding is in the eating. When we came to Apemama, of so many white men who have scrambled for a place in that rich market, one remained – a silent, sober, solitary, niggardly recluse, of whom the king remarks, 'I think he good; he no 'peak.'

I was warned at the outset we might very well fail in our design: yet never dreamed of what proved to be the fact, that we should be left four-and-twenty hours in suspense and come within an ace of ultimate rejection. Captain Reid had primed himself; no sooner was the king on board, and the Hennetti question amicably settled, than he proceeded to express my request and give an abstract of my claims and virtues. The gammon about Queen Victoria's son might do for Butaritari; it was out of the question here; and I now figured as 'one of the Old Men of England,' a person of deep knowledge, come expressly to visit Tembinok's dominion, and eager to report upon it to the no less eager Queen Victoria. The king made no shadow of an answer, and presently began upon a different subject. We might have thought that he had not heard, or not understood; only that we found ourselves the subject of a constant study. As we sat at meals, he took us in series and fixed upon each, for near a minute at a time, the same hard and thoughtful stare. As he thus looked he seemed to forget himself, the subject and the company, and to become absorbed in the process of his thought; the look was wholly impersonal; I have seen the same in the eyes of portrait-painters. The counts upon which whites have been deported are mainly four: cheating Tembinok', meddling overmuch with copra, which is the source of his wealth, and one of the sinews of his power, 'Peaking, and political intrigue. I felt guiltless upon all; but how to show it? I would not have taken copra in a gift: how to express that quality by my dinner-table bearing? The rest of the party shared my innocence and my embarrassment. They shared also in my mortification when after two whole meal-times and the odd moments of an afternoon devoted to this recon-noitring, Tembinok' took his leave in silence. Next morning, the same undisguised study, the same silence, was resumed; and the second day had come to its maturity before I was informed abruptly that I had stood the ordeal. 'I look your eye. You good man. You no lie,' said the king: a doubtful compliment to a writer of romance. Later he explained he did not quite judge by the eye only, but the mouth as well. 'Tuppoti I see man,' he explained. 'I no tavvy good man, bad man. I look eye, look mouth. Then I tavvy. Look *eye*, look mouth,' he repeated. And indeed in our case the mouth had the most to do with it, and it was by our talk that we gained admission to the island; the king promising himself (and I believe really amassing) a vast amount of useful knowledge ere we left.

The terms of our admission were as follows: We were to choose a site, and the king should there build us a town. His people should work for us, but the king only was to give them orders. One of his cooks should come daily to help mine, and to learn of him. In case our stores ran out, he would supply us, and be repaid on the return of the *Equator*. On the other hand, he was to come to meals with us when so inclined; when he stayed at home, a dish was to be sent him from our table; and I solemnly engaged to give his subjects no liquor or money (both of which they are forbidden to possess) and no tobacco, which they were to receive only from the royal hand. I think I remember to have protested against the stringency of this last article; at least, it was relaxed, and when a man worked for me I was allowed to give him a pipe of tobacco on the premises, but none to take away.

The site of Equator City – we named our city for the schooner – was soon chosen. The immediate shores of the lagoon are windy and blinding; Tembinok' himself is glad to grope blue-spectacled on his terrace; and we fled the neighbourhood of the red *conjunctiva*, the suppurating eyeball, and the beggar who pursues and beseeches the passing foreigner for eye wash. Behind the town the country is diversified; here open, sandy, uneven, and dotted with dwarfish palms; here cut up with taro trenches, deep and shallow, and, according to the growth of the plants, presenting now the appearance of a sandy tannery, now of an alleyed and green garden. A path leads towards the sea, mounting abruptly to the main level of the island – twenty or even thirty feet, although Findlay gives five; and just hard by the top of the rise, where the coco–palms begin to be well grown, we found a grove of pandanus, and a piece of soil pleasantly covered with green underbush. A well was not far off under a rustic well-house; nearer still, in a sandy cup of the land, a pond where we might wash our clothes. The place was out of the wind, out of the sun, and out of sight of the village. It was shown to the king, and the town promised for the morrow.

The morrow came, Mr. Osbourne landed, found nothing done, and carried his complaint to Tembinok'. He heard it, rose, called for a Winchester, stepped without the royal palisade, and fired two shots in the air. A shot in the air is the first Apemama warning; it has the force of a proclamation in more loquacious countries; and his majesty remarked agreeably that it would make his labourers 'mo' bright.' In less than thirty minutes, accordingly, the men had mustered, the work was begun, and we were told that we might bring our baggage when we pleased.

It was two in the afternoon ere the first boat was beached, and the long procession of chests and crates and sacks began to straggle through the sandy desert towards Equator Town. The grove of pandanus was practically a thing of the past. Fire surrounded and smoke rose in the green underbush. In a wide circuit the axes were still crashing. Those very advantages for which the place was chosen, it had been the king's first idea to abolish; and in the midst of this devastation there stood already a good-sized maniap' and a small closed house. A mat was spread near by for Tembinok'; here he sat superintending, in cardinal red, a pith helmet on his head, a meerschaum pipe in his mouth, a wife stretched at his back with custody of the matches and tobacco. Twenty or thirty feet in front of him the bulk of the workers squatted on the ground; some of the bush here survived and in this the commons sat nearly to their shoulders, and presented only an arc of brown faces, black heads, and attentive eyes fixed on his majesty. Long pauses reigned, during which the subjects stared and the king smoked. Then Tembinok' would raise his voice and speak shrilly and briefly. There was never a response in words; but if the speech were jesting, there came by way of answer discreet, obsequious laughter – such laughter as we hear in schoolrooms; and if it were practical, the sudden uprising and departure of the squad. Twice they so disappeared, and returned with further elements of the city: a second house and a second maniap'. It was singular to spy, far off through the coco stems, the silent oncoming of the maniap', at first (it seemed) swimming spontaneously in the air – but on a nearer view betraying under the eaves many score of moving naked legs. In all the affair servile obedience was no less remarkable than servile deliberation. The gang had here mustered by the note of a deadly weapon; the man who looked on was the unquestioned master of their lives; and except for civility, they bestirred themselves like so many American hotel clerks. The spectator was aware of an unobtrusive yet invincible inertia, at which the skipper of a trading dandy might have torn his hair.

Yet the work was accomplished. By dusk, when his majesty withdrew, the town was founded and complete, a new and ruder Amphion having called it from nothing with three cracks of a rifle. And the next morning the same conjurer obliged us with a further miracle: a mystic rampart fencing us, so that the path which ran by our doors became suddenly impassable, the inhabitants who had business across the isle must fetch a wide circuit, and we sat in the midst in a transparent privacy, seeing, seen, but unapproachable, like bees in a glass hive. The outward and visible sign of this glamour was no more than a few ragged coco-leaf garlands round the stems of the outlying palms; but its significance reposed on the tremendous sanction of the tapu and the guns of Tembinok'.

We made our first meal that night in the improvised city, where we were to stay two months, and which – so soon as we had done with it – was to vanish in a day as it appeared, its elements returning whence they came, the tapu raised, the traffic on the path resumed, the sun and the moon peering in vain between the palm-trees for the bygone work, the wind blowing over an empty site. Yet the place, which is now only an episode in some memories, seemed to have been built, and to be destined to endure, for years. It was a busy hamlet. One of the maniap's we made our dining-room, one the kitchen. The houses we reserved for sleeping. They were on the admirable Apemama plan: out and away the best house in the South Seas; standing some three feet above the ground on posts; the sides of woven flaps, which can be raised to admit light and air, or lowered to shut out the wind and the rain: airy, healthy, clean, and watertight. We had a hen of a remarkable kind: almost unique in my experience, being a hen that occasionally laid eggs. Not far off, Mrs. Stevenson tended a garden of salad and shalots. The salad was devoured by the hen – which was her bane. The shalots were served out a leaf at a time, and welcomed and relished like peaches. Toddy and green cocoanuts were brought us daily. We once had a present of fish from the king, and once of a turtle. Sometimes we shot so-called plover along on the shore, sometimes wild chicken in the bush. The rest of our diet was from tins.

Our occupations were very various. While some of the party would be away sketching, Mr. Osbourne and I hammered away at a novel.[20] We read Gibbon and Carlyle aloud; we blew on flageolets; we strummed on guitars; we took photographs by the light of the sun, the moon, and flash-powder; sometimes we played cards. Pot-hunting engaged a part of our leisure. I have myself passed afternoons in the exciting but innocuous pursuit of winged animals with a revolver; and it was fortunate there were better shots of the party, and fortunate the king could lend us a more suitable weapon, in the form of an excellent fowling-piece, or our spare diet had been sparer still.

Night was the time to see our city, after the moon was up, after the lamps were lighted, and so long as the fire sparkled in the cook-house. We suffered from a plague of flies and mosquitoes, comparable to that of Egypt; our dinner-table (lent, like all our furniture, by the king) must be enclosed in a tent of netting, our citadel and refuge; and this became all luminous, and bulged and beaconed under the eaves, like the globe of some monstrous lamp under the margin of its shade. Our cabins, the sides being propped at a variety of inclinations, spelled out strange, angular patterns of brightness. In his roofed and open kitchen, Ah Fu was to be seen by lamp and fire-light, dabbling among pots. Over all, there fell in the season an extraordinary splen-dour of mellow moonshine. The sand sparkled as with the dust of diamonds; the stars had vanished. At intervals, a dusky night-bird, slow and low flying, passed in the colon-nade of the tree stems and uttered a hoarse croaking cry.

Notes
1. Stevenson had been fascinated with the South Seas since he was a boy.
2. Samuel Merritt (1822–1890) arrived in San Francisco during the beginning of the Gold Rush, made a fortune in real estate, and eventually served as mayor of Oakland, California, in the late 1860s.
3. The *Equator* left Honolulu with Stevenson, Fanny, Lloyd, Joe Strong and Ah Fu, their Chinese cook, on 24 June 1889.
4. The *Janet Nicholl* sailed on 11 April 1890 for a three months' cruise that took the Stevensons to the Gilbert, Ellice, and Marshall Islands.
5. Alfred, Lord Tennyson (1809–1892), English poet.
6. Alexander G Findlay, *A Directory for the Navigation of the South Pacific*. 5th ed. London, 1884.
7. Virgil (70–19 BC), Roman poet; Julius Caesar (100–44 BC), Roman general and statesman; Gaius (130–180 AD) and Papinian, Roman jurists.
8. Stevenson sailed the Pacific on the steamer *Janet Nicholl* from 26 July to 2 August 1890.
9. Noumea, capital of the French colony of New Caledonia.
10. Captain James Cook (1728–1779), English navigator and explorer.
11. Andrew Lang (1844–1912), Scottish scholar and friend of Stevenson, who translated Homer and eventually moved to London.
12. RLS is referring to a Pacific Islander.
13. Eighteenth-century Scottish chiefs.
14. Michael Scott (c.1175–c.1230), Scottish wizard; Lord Derwentwater, English Jacobite who was beheaded in 1716.
15. Tahitian legend. See Stevenson's ballad 'The Song of Rahero' in *Ballads* (1891).
16. Members of a Tahitian dynasty.
17. AH Otis was captain of the *Casco*.
18. Dennis Reid was a fellow Scot.
19. On Apemama, the Stevensons were the guests of King Tembinok, the so-called Napoleon of the Gilberts. The king had previously shunned all Westerners but he was taken with the Scotsman and his unusual family. In a letter to Sidney Colvin, Stevenson describes the king as 'a great character; a thorough tyrant, very much of a gentleman, a poet, a musician, a historian or perhaps rather more a genealogist ...' See Mehew, p. 409. After Tembinok's death in 1891, the Gilberts became a British protectorate.
20. *The Wrecker* (1892).

Miscellaneous

Walking Tours

Walking Tours *originally appeared in* Cornhill Magazine *in June 1876 and was later included in* Virginibus Puerisque, *a collection of essays published by Kegan Paul (London) in 1881.*

IT must not be imagined that a walking tour, as some would have us fancy, is merely a better or worse way of seeing the country. There are many ways of seeing landscape quite as good; and none more vivid, in spite of canting dilettantes, than from a railway train. But landscape on a walking tour is quite accessory. He who is indeed of the brotherhood does not voyage in quest of the picturesque, but of certain jolly humours – of the hope and spirit with which the march begins at morning, and the peace and spiritual repletion of the evening's rest. He cannot tell whether he puts his knapsack on, or takes it off, with more delight. The excitement of the departure puts him in key for that of the arrival. Whatever he does is not only a reward in itself, but will be further rewarded in the sequel; and so pleasure leads on to pleasure in an endless chain. It is this that so few can understand; they will either be always lounging or always at five miles an hour; they do not play off the one against the other, prepare all day for the evening, and all evening for the next day. And, above all, it is here that your overwalker fails of comprehension. His heart rises against those who drink their curacoa in liqueur glasses, when he himself can swill it in a brown john. He will not believe that the flavour is more delicate in the smaller dose. He will not believe that to walk this unconscionable distance is merely to stupefy and brutalise himself, and come to his inn, at night, with a sort of frost on his five wits, and a starless night of darkness in his spirit. Not for him the mild luminous evening of the temperate walker! He has nothing left of man but a physical need for bedtime and a double nightcap; and even his pipe, if he be a smoker, will be savourless and disenchanted. It is the fate of such an one to take twice as much trouble as is needed to obtain happiness, and miss the happiness in the end; he is the man of the proverb, in short, who goes further and fares worse.

Now, to be properly enjoyed, a walking tour should be gone upon alone. If you go in a company, or even in pairs, it is no longer a walking tour in anything but name; it is something else and more in the nature of a picnic. A walking tour should be gone upon alone, because freedom is of the essence; because you should be able to stop and go on, and follow this way or that, as the freak takes you; and because you must have your own pace, and neither trot alongside a champion walker, nor mince in time with a girl. And then you must be open to all impressions and let your thoughts take colour from what you see. You should be as a pipe for any wind to play upon. 'I cannot see the wit,' says Hazlitt[1], 'of walking and talking at the same time. When I am in the country I wish to vegetate like the country,' – which is the gist of all that can be said upon the matter. There should be no cackle of voices at your elbow, to jar on the meditative silence of the morning. And so long as a man is reasoning he cannot surrender himself to that fine intoxication that comes of much motion in the open air, that begins in a sort of dazzle and sluggishness of the brain, and ends in a peace that passes comprehension.

During the first day or so of any tour there are moments of bitterness, when the traveller feels more than coldly towards his knapsack, when he is half in a mind to throw it bodily over the hedge and, like Christian on a similar occasion, 'give three leaps and go on singing.' And yet it soon acquires a property of easiness. It becomes magnetic; the spirit of the journey enters into it. And no sooner have you passed the straps over your shoulder than the lees of sleep are cleared from you, you pull yourself together with a shake, and fall at once into your stride. And surely, of all possible moods, this, in which a man takes the road, is the best. Of course, if he *will* keep thinking of his anxieties, if he *will* open the merchant Abudah's chest and walk arm-in- arm with the hag – why, wherever he is, and whether he walk fast or slow, the chances are that he will not be happy. And so much the more shame to himself! There are perhaps thirty men setting forth at that same hour, and I would lay a large wager there is not another dull face among the thirty. It would be a fine thing to follow, in a coat of darkness, one after another of these wayfarers, some summer morning, for the first few miles upon the road. This one, who walks fast, with a keen look in his eyes, is all concentrated in his own mind; he is up at his loom, weaving and weaving, to set the landscape to words. This one peers about, as he goes, among the grasses; he waits by the canal to watch the dragon-flies; he leans on the gate of the pasture, and cannot look enough upon the complacent kine. And here comes another, talking, laughing, and gesticulating to himself. His face changes from time to time, as indignation flashes from his eyes or anger clouds his forehead. He is composing articles, delivering orations, and conducting the most impassioned interviews, by the way. A little farther on, and it is as like as not he will begin to sing. And well for him, supposing him to be no great master in that art, if he stumble across no stolid peasant at a corner; for on such an occasion, I scarcely know which is the more troubled, or whether it is worse to suffer the confusion of your troubadour, or the unfeigned alarm of your clown. A sedentary population, accustomed, besides, to the strange mechanical bearing of the common tramp, can in no wise explain to itself the gaiety of these passers-by. I knew one man who was arrested as a runaway lunatic, because, although a full-grown person with a red beard, he skipped as he went like a child. And you would be astonished if I were to tell you all the grave and learned heads who have confessed to me that, when on walking tours, they sang – and sang very ill – and had a pair of red ears when, as described above, the inauspicious peasant plumped into their arms from round a corner. And here, lest you should think I am exaggerating, is Hazlitt's own confession, from his essay 'On Going a Journey,' which is so good that there should be a tax levied on all who have not read it: –

'Give me the clear blue sky over my head,' says he, 'and the green turf beneath my feet, a winding road before me, and a three hours' march to dinner – and then to thinking! It is hard if I cannot start some game on these lone heaths. I laugh, I run, I leap, I sing for joy.'

Bravo! After that adventure of my friend with the policeman, you would not have cared, would you, to publish that in the first person? But we have no bravery nowadays, and, even in books, must all pretend to be as dull and foolish as our neighbours. It was not so with Hazlitt. And notice how learned he is (as, indeed, throughout the essay) in the theory of walking tours. He is none of your athletic men in purple stockings, who walk their fifty miles a day: three hours' march is his ideal. And then he must have a winding road, the epicure!

Yet there is one thing I object to in these words of his, one thing in the great master's practice that seems to me not wholly wise. I do not approve of that leaping and running. Both of these hurry the respiration; they both shake up the brain out of its glorious open-air confusion; and they both break the pace. Uneven walking is not so agreeable to the body, and it distracts and irritates the mind. Whereas, when once you have fallen into an equable stride, it requires no conscious thought from you to keep it up, and yet it prevents you from thinking earnestly of anything else. Like knitting, like the work of a copying clerk, it gradually neutralises and sets to sleep the serious activity of the mind. We can think of this or that, lightly and laughingly, as a child thinks, or as we think in a morning dose; we can make puns or puzzle out acrostics, and trifle in a thousand ways with words and rhymes; but when it comes to honest work, when we come to gather ourselves together for an effort, we may sound the trumpet as loud and long as we please; the great barons of the mind will not rally to the standard, but sit, each one, at home, warming his hands over his own fire and brooding on his own private thought!

In the course of a day's walk, you see, there is much variance in the mood. From the exhilaration of the start, to the happy phlegm of the arrival, the change is certainly great. As the day goes on, the traveller moves from the one extreme towards the other. He becomes more and more incorporated with the material landscape, and the open-air drunkenness grows upon him with great strides, until he posts along the road, and sees everything about him, as in a cheerful dream. The first is certainly brighter, but the second stage is the more peaceful. A man does not make so many articles towards the end, nor does he laugh aloud; but the purely animal pleasures, the sense of physical wellbeing, the delight of every inhalation, of every time the muscles tighten down the thigh, console him for the absence of the others, and bring him to his destination still content.

Nor must I forget to say a word on bivouacs. You come to a milestone on a hill, or some place where deep ways meet under trees; and off goes the knapsack, and down you sit to smoke a pipe in the shade. You sink into yourself, and the birds come round and look at you; and your smoke dissipates upon the afternoon under the blue dome of heaven; and the sun lies warm upon your feet, and the cool air visits your neck and turns aside your open shirt. If you are not happy, you must have an evil conscience. You may dally as long as you like by the roadside. It is almost as if the millennium were arrived, when we shall throw our clocks and watches over the housetop, and remember time and seasons no more. Not to keep hours for a lifetime is, I was going to say, to live for ever. You have no idea, unless you have tried it, how endlessly long is a summer's day, that you measure out only by hunger, and bring to an end only when you are drowsy. I know a village where there are hardly any clocks, where no one knows more of the days of the week than by a sort of instinct for the fete on Sundays, and where only one person can tell you the day of the month, and she is generally wrong; and if people were aware how slow Time journeyed in that village, and what armfuls of spare hours he gives, over and above the bargain, to its wise inhabitants, I believe there would be a stampede out of London, Liverpool, Paris, and a variety of large towns, where the clocks lose their heads, and shake the hours out each one faster than the other, as though they were all in a wager. And all these foolish pilgrims would each bring his own misery along with him, in a watch-pocket! It is to be noticed, there were no clocks and watches in the much-vaunted days before the flood. It follows, of course, there were no appointments, and punctuality was not yet thought upon. 'Though ye take from a covetous man all his treasure,' says Milton[2], 'he has yet one jewel left; ye cannot deprive him of his covetousness.' And so I would say of a modern man of business, you may do what you will for him, put him in Eden, give him the elixir of life – he has still a flaw at heart, he still has his business habits. Now, there is no time when business habits are more mitigated than on a walking tour. And so during these halts, as I say, you will feel almost free.

But it is at night, and after dinner, that the best hour comes. There are no such pipes to be smoked as those that follow a good day's march; the flavour of the tobacco is a thing to be remembered, it is so dry and aromatic, so full and so fine. If you wind up the evening with grog, you will own there was never such grog; at every sip a jocund tranquillity spreads about your limbs, and sits easily in your heart. If you read a book – and you will never do so save by fits and starts – you find the language strangely racy and harmonious; words take a new meaning; single sentences possess the ear for half an hour together; and the writer endears himself to you, at every page, by the nicest coincidence of sentiment. It seems as if it were a book you had written yourself in a dream. To all we have read on such occasions we look back with special favour. 'It was on the 10th of April, 1798,' says Hazlitt, with amorous precision, 'that I sat down to a volume of the new *Heloise*, at the Inn at Llangollen, over a bottle of sherry and a cold chicken.' I should wish to quote more, for though we are mighty fine fellows nowadays, we cannot write like Hazlitt. And, talking of that, a volume of Hazlitt's essays would be a capital pocket-book on such a journey; so would a volume of Heine's[3] songs; and for *Tristram Shandy*[4] I can pledge a fair experience.

If the evening be fine and warm, there is nothing better in life than to lounge before the inn door in the sunset, or lean over the parapet of the bridge, to watch the weeds and the quick fishes. It is then, if ever, that you taste Joviality to the full significance of that audacious word. Your muscles are so agreeably slack, you feel so clean and so strong and so idle, that whether you move or sit still, whatever you do is done with pride and a kingly sort of pleasure. You fall in talk with any one, wise or foolish, drunk or sober. And it seems as if a hot walk purged you, more than of anything else, of all narrowness and pride, and left curiosity to play its part freely, as in a child or a man of science. You lay aside all your own hobbies, to watch provincial humours develop themselves before you, now as a laughable farce, and now grave and beautiful like an old tale.

Or perhaps you are left to your own company for the night, and surly weather imprisons you by the fire. You may remember how Burns,[5] numbering past pleasures, dwells upon the hours when he has been 'happy thinking.' It is a phrase that may well perplex a poor modern, girt about on every side by clocks and chimes, and haunted, even at night, by flaming dial-plates. For we are all so busy, and have so many far-off projects to realise, and castles in the fire to turn into solid habitable mansions on a gravel soil, that we can find no time for pleasure trips into the Land of Thought and among the Hills of Vanity. Changed times, indeed, when we must sit all night, beside the fire, with folded hands; and a changed world for most of us, when we find we can pass the hours without discontent and be happy thinking. We are in such haste to be doing, to be writing, to be gathering gear, to make our voice audible a moment in the derisive silence of eternity, that we forget that one thing, of which these are but the parts – namely, to live. We fall in love, we drink hard, we run to and we drink hard, we run to and fro upon the earth like frightened sheep. And now you are to ask yourself if, when all is done, you would not have been better to sit by the fire at home, and be happiest thinking. To sit still and contemplate, – to remember the faces of women without desire, to be pleased by the great deeds of men without envy, to be everything and everywhere in sympathy, and yet content to remain where and what you are – is not this to know both wisdom and virtue, and to dwell with happiness? After all, it is not they who carry flags, but they who look upon it from a private chamber, who have the fun of the procession. And once you are at that, you are in the very humour of all social heresy. It is no time for shuffling, or for big, empty words. If you ask yourself what you mean by fame, riches, or learning, the answer is far to seek; and you go back into that kingdom of light imaginations, which seem so vain in the eyes of Philistines perspiring after wealth, and so momentous to those who are stricken with the disproportions of the world, and, in the face of the gigantic stars, cannot stop to split differences between two degrees of the infinitesimally small, such as a tobacco pipe or the Roman Empire, a million of money or a fiddlestick's end.

You lean from the window, your last pipe reeking whitely into the darkness, your body full of delicious pains, your mind enthroned in the seventh circle of content; when suddenly the mood changes, the weather-cock goes about, and you ask yourself one question more: whether, for the interval, you have been the wisest philosopher or the most egregious of donkeys? Human experience is not yet able to reply; but at least you have had a fine moment, and looked down upon all h of the infinite.

Notes
1. William Hazlitt (1778–1830), English essayist who had a major influence on Stevenson.
2. John Milton (1608–1674), English poet.
3. Heinrich Heine (1797–1856), German poet and critic.
4. Laurence Sterne (1713–1768), English novelist and author of *Tristram Shandy*.
5. Robert Burns (1759–1796), Scotland's national bard.

From a Railway Carriage

In this timelessly charming poem from A Child's Garden of Verses *(1885),*
Stevenson captures, in a few vivid sentences, the magic of travel as seen through
a child's eyes from a moving train.

Faster than fairies, faster than witches,
Bridges and houses, hedges and ditches;
And charging along like troops in a battle,
All through the meadows the horses and cattle:
All of the sights of the hill and the plain
Fly as thick as driving rain;
And ever again, in the wink of an eye,
Painted stations whistle by.

Here is a child who clambers and scrambles,
All by himself and gathering brambles;
Here is a tramp who stands and gazes;
And there is the green for stringing the daisies!
Here is a cart run away in the road
Lumping along with man and load;
And here is a mill and there is a river:
Each a glimpse and gone for ever!

Evensong

This touching poem was written at Vailima and appears in Songs of Travel
*(1895). The usually restless Stevenson appears to be at peace with himself and
with whatever his fate shall bring. The traveller has come home.*

The embers of the day are red
Beyond the murky hill.
The kitchen smokes: the bed
In the darkling house is spread:
The great sky darkens overhead,
And the great woods are shrill.
So far have I been led,
Lord, by Thy will:
So far I have followed, Lord, and wondered still.

The breeze from the embalmed land
Blows sudden toward the shore,
And claps my cottage door.
I hear the signal, Lord – I understand.
The night at Thy command
Comes, I will eat and sleep and will not question more.

Further Reading

Aldington, Richard. *Portrait of a Rebel: Robert Louis Stevenson*. London: Evans Brothers, 1957.

Angus, David. 'Stevenson's Bridge of Allan.' *Scots Magazine*, 1978.

Balfour, Graham. *The Life of Robert Louis Stevenson*. London: Methuen & Co., 1901.

Bathurst, Bella. *The Lighthouse Stevensons: The extraordinary story of the building of the Scottish lighthouses by the ancestors of Robert Louis Stevenson*. New York: HarperCollins Publishers, 1999.

Bell, Gavin. *In Search of Tusitala: Travels in the Pacific After Robert Louis Stevenson*. London: Picador, 1994.

Bell, Ian. *Dreams of Exile: Robert Louis Stevenson, A Biography*. New York: Henry Holt, 1992.

Bevan, Bryan. *Robert Louis Stevenson: Poet and Teller*. New York: St. Martin's Press, 1993.

Booth, Bradford A, and Ernest Mehew, eds. *The Letters of Robert Louis Stevenson*. New Haven, Conn.: Yale University Press, 1994.

Buchan, John. 'The Country of Kidnapped.' *The Academy*, May 1898.

Buell, LM 'Eilean Earraid: The Beloved Isle of Robert Louis Stevenson.' *Scribner's Magazine*, 71 (February 1922): pp. 184–95.

Calder, Angus, ed. *Robert Louis Stevenson: Selected Poems*. London: Penguin Books, 1998.

Calder, Jenni. *RLS: A Life Study*. London: Hamilton, 1980.

_____. *The Robert Louis Stevenson Companion*. Edinburgh, 1980.

Calder, Jenni, ed. *Stevenson and Victorian Scotland*. Edinburgh: Edinburgh University Press, 1981.

Callow, Philip. *Louis: A Life of Robert Louis Stevenson*. Chicago: Ivan R Dee, 2001.

Campbell, James. 'Travels with RLS', *New York Times Book Review*, 2001.

Chalmers, Stephen. *The Penny Piper of Saramac: An Episode in Stevenson's Life*. Preface by Lord Guthrie. Monterey, Calif.: Old Monterey Preservation Society, 1995.

Chesterton, GK *Robert Louis Stevenson*. London: Hodder & Stoughton, 1927; New York: Dodd, Mead & Company, 1928.

Colvin, Sidney, ed. *Letters of RLS to His Family and Friends*. London, 1911.

_____, ed. *Vailima Letters*. London, 1899.

Commins, Saxe, ed. *Selected Writings of Robert Louis Stevenson*. New York: The Modern Library, 1947.

Daiches, David. *Edinburgh*. London: Hamish Hamilton, 1978.

_____. *Robert Louis Stevenson*. Glasgow: William Maclellan, 1947; Norfolk, Conn.: New Directions, 1947.

_____. *Stevenson and the Art of Fiction*. New York, 1951.

_____. *Robert Louis Stevenson and His World*. London: Thames & Hudson, 1973.

Davies, Hunter. *The Teller of Tales: In Search of Robert Louis Stevenson*. New York: Interlink Books, 1996.

Day, A Grove, ed. *Robert Louis Stevenson: Travels in Hawaii*. Honolulu: University of Hawaii Press, 1973.

Doyle, Brian. 'A Head Full of Swirling Dreams.' *The Atlantic Monthly*, November 2001.

Dutton, Joan Parry. *They Left Their Mark: Famous Passages through the Wine Country*. Calistoga, Calif.: Sharpstreen Museum Association, 1998.

Ferguson, De Lancey, and Marshall Waingrow, eds. *RLS: Stevenson's Letters to Charles Baxter*. New Haven, Conn.: Yale University Press, 1956.

Fisher, Anne Benson. *No More a Stranger*. Stanford, Calif.: Stanford University Press, 1946.

Fitzpatrick, Elayne Wareing. *A Quixotic Companionship: Fanny and Robert Louis Stevenson*. Monterey, Calif.: Old Monterey Preservation Society, 1997.

A Friendship: Robert Louis Stevenson, Jules Simoneau. San Francisco: Taylor, Nash, & Taylor, 1911.

Furnas, J C *Voyage to Windward: The Life of Robert Louis Stevenson*. New York: Sloane, 1951; London: Faber & Faber, 1952.

Golding, Gordon, ed. *The Cévennes Journal: Notes on a Journey through the French Highlands*. Notes by Jacques Blondel, Gordon Golding, and Jacques Poujol. Edinburgh: Mainstream Publishing, 1978; New York: Taplinger Publishing, 1975. First publication of the complete manuscript notebook kept by Stevenson on his journey. Includes some material never before published, and also his additions for the published form.

Hart, James D, ed. *From Scotland to Silverado*. Cambridge, Mass.: The Belknap Press of Harvard University Press, 1966.

Hennessy, James Pope. *Robert Louis Stevenson*. New York: Simon and Schuster, 1974.

Hill, Robin. *Pure Air and Good Milk: Robert Louis Stevenson at Swanston*. Edinburgh: Privately printed, 1995.

_____. *RLS in Germany. Edinburgh*: Privately printed/RLS Club, 2001.

Holmes, Richard. *Footsteps: Adventures of a Romantic Biographer.* London: Hodder & Stoughton, 1985.

Issler, Anne Roller. *Stevenson at Silverado*. Idaho, 1939.

_____. *Happier for His Presence: San Francisco and Robert Louis Stevenson*. Stanford, Calif.: Stanford University Press, Calif., 1949.

_____. *Our Mountain Hermitage: Silverado and Robert Louis Stevenson*. Stanford, Calif.: Stanford University Press, 1950.

Johnstone, Arthur. *Recollections of Robert Louis Stevenson in the Pacific*. London: Chatto, 1905.

Jones, William B Jr., ed. *Robert Louis Stevenson Reconsidered: New Critical Perspectives*. Jefferson, NC: McFarland & Company, 2002.

Jordan, John E, ed. *Silverado Journal*. San Francisco: Book Club of California, 1954. An early version of the author's Silverado Squatters. This transcript of the manuscript is located in the Henry E Huntington Library in California. Contains Stevenson's revisions and additions.

Robert Louis Stevenson's Silverado Journal. San Francisco: Book Club of California, 1954.

Kemper, Steve. 'On foot through the Cévennes: Retracing the steps of Robert Louis Stevenson, we discover a forgotten region of France that's still hushed and secluded.' *National Geographic Traveler*, May/June 2002.

Knight, Alanna. *Robert Louis Stevenson in the South Seas*. Edinburgh: Mainstream Publishing, 1986.

Lamb, Jonathan, Vanessa Smith, and Nicholas Thomas, eds. *Exploration and Exchange: A South Seas Anthology, 1680-1900*. Chicago: University of Chicago Press, 2001.

Letley, Emma, ed. *Travels with a Donkey in the Cévennes and Selected Travel Writings*. The World's Classics. New York: Oxford University Press, 1992.

Lockett, WG *Robert Louis Stevenson at Davos*. London: Hurst & Blackett, 1934.

MacGaw, Sister Martha Mary. *Stevenson in Hawaii*. Honolulu: University of Hawaii Press, 1950.

Mackenzie, Compton. *Robert Louis Stevenson*. London, 1968.

McLaren, Moray. *Stevenson and Edinburgh*. London: Chapman & Hall, 1950.

McLynn, Frank. *Robert Louis Stevenson: A Biography*. New York: Random House, 1993.

Masson, Rosaline. *The Life of Robert Louis Stevenson*. London: Chambers, 1923.

Mehew, Ernest, ed. *Selected Letters of Robert Louis Stevenson*. New Haven, Conn.: Yale University Press, 2001.

Moors, HJ *With Stevenson in Samoa*. Boston: Small, Maynard & Company, 1911.

Morgan, Edwin. 'The Poetry of Robert Louis Stevenson' in *Essays*. Manchester, 1974.

Murphy, Jim. *Across America on an Emigrant Train*. New York: Clarion Books, 1993.

Neider, Charles, ed. *The Complete Short Stories of Robert Louis Stevenson: With a Selection of the Best Short Novels*. New York: Da Capo Press, 1998.

_____, ed. *Our Samoan Adventure*. London: Weidenfeld, 1956.

Neillands, Robin, intro. *Travels with a Donkey in the Cévennes by Robert Louis Stevenson*. Illustrated Edition. London: Chatto & Windus, 1986.

Noble, Andrew, ed. *From the Clyde to California: Robert Louis Stevenson's Emigrant Journey*. Aberdeen: Aberdeen University Press, 1985.

Osbourne, Katherine Durham. *Robert Louis Stevenson in California*. Chicago: AC McClurg & Company, 1911.

Osbourne, Samuel Lloyd. *An Intimate Portrait of RLS* New York: Charles Scribner's Sons, 1924.

Rankin, Nicholas. *Dead Man's Chest: Travels After Robert Louis Stevenson*. London: Phoenix Press, 2001.

Rennie, Neil, ed. *In the South Seas*. Penguin Classics. New York: Penguin, 1999.

Rice, Edward. *Journey to Upolu: Robert Louis Stevenson, Victorian Rebel*. New York: Dodd, Mead, & Co., 1974.

Robert Louis Stevenson Club of Monterey, *Monterey Peninsula: Showing Sites Visited by Robert Louis Stvenson in 1879*, Monterey, Calif.: RLS Club of Monterey, 1999

Royle, Trevor, ed. RL Stevenson. *Travels with a Donkey, An Inland Voyage, The Silverado Squatters*. Rutland, Vt.: Everyman's Library, 1992.

Sanchez, Nellie Van de Grift. *The Life of Mrs. Robert Louis Stevenson*. New York: Charles Scribner's Sons, 1920.

Scally, John. *Pictures of the Mind: The Illustrated Robert Louis Stevenson*. Edinburgh: Canongate, in association with the National Library of Scotland, 1994.

Scott-Moncrieff, George, ed. *Selected Essays: Robert Louis Stevenson*. Chicago: Henry Regnery Company, 1959.

Simpson, Eve Blantyre. *RLS's Edinburgh Days*. London: Hodder, 1898.

Skinner, Robert T., ed. *Cummy's Diary*. London: Chatto, 1926.

Smith, Janet Adam, ed. *Henry James and Robert Louis Stevenson: A Record of Friendship and Criticism*. London: Hart-Davis, 1948.

_____, ed. *Robert Louis Stevenson: Collected Poems*. London, 1950.

Stanton, Ken. *Mount St. Helena and Robert Louis Stevenson State Park: A History and Guide*. St. Helena, Calif.: Bonnie View Books, 1997.

Steinbeck, John. *Travels with Charley: In Search of America*. With an Introduction by Jay Parini. New York: Penguin Books, 1997.

Stevenson, Fanny. *The Cruise of the Janet Nichol*. New York: Charles Scribner's Sons, 1915.

Stevenson, Margaret Isabella. *From Saranac to the Marquesas and Beyond*. Edited by Marie Clothilde Balfour. London: Methuen, 1903.

Stott, Louis. *Robert Louis Stevenson and the Highlands and Islands of Scotland*. Milton-of-Aberfoyle: Creag Darach Publications, 1994.

Strong, Isobel. *Robert Louis Stevenson*. Saranac Lake, NY: Stevenson Society of America, 1920.

Strong, Isobel, and Lloyd Osbourne. *Memories of Vailima*. London: Constable, 1903.

Swearingen, Roger G. *The Prose Writings of Robert Louis Stevenson: A Guide*. Hamden, Conn.: Archon Books, 1980.

_____. 'Robert Louis Stevenson.' In *The Cambridge Bibliography of English Literature*. 3rd ed. Vol. 4, 1800-1900. Edited by Joanne Shattock. Cambridge: Cambridge University Press, 2000.

_____. *Robert Louis Stevenson's Edinburgh: A Concise Guide for Visitors and Residents*. Edinburgh: Writers' Museum, 2002.

Roger G Swearingen, ed. *The New Lighthouse on the Dhu Heartach Rock, Argyllshire*. St. Helena, Calif.: The Silverado Museum, 1995.

Swinnerton, Frank. *RL Stevenson: A Critical Study*. New York: Doubleday, Doran & Company, 1923.

Terry, RC, ed. *Robert Louis Stevenson: Interviews and Recollections*. Iowa City, Ia.: University of Iowa Press, 1996.

Torrey, Bradford. 'Robert Louis Stevenson: A Review.' *The Atlantic Monthly*, June 1902.

Treglown, Jeremy, ed. *The Lantern-Bearers and Other Essays*. New York: Farrar, Straus, & Giroux, 1988; reprint, New York: Cooper Square Press, 1999.

Waterston, Elizabeth. *Rapt in Plaid: Canadian Literature and Scottish Tradition*. Toronto: University of Toronto Press, 2001.

Watt, L MacLean, ed. *The Hills of Home, with the Pentland Essays by Robert Louis Stevenson*. London and Edinburgh: T N Foulis, 1913.

White, John Manchip, ed. *Travels with a Donkey in the Cévennes*. Marlboro Travel. Marlboro Press, 1996.

STEVENSON: SELECTED WORKS

Across the Plains, With Other Memories and Essays. London: Chatto & Windus, 1892; New York: Scribners, 1892.

The Amateur Emigrant: From the Clyde to Sandy Hook. Chicago: Stone & Kimball, 1895.

An Appeal to the Clergy. Edinburgh and London: Blackwood, 1873.

Ballads. London: Chatto & Windus, 1890; New York: Scribners, 1890.

The Black Arrow: A Tale of the Two Roses. London: Cassell, 1888; New York: Scribners, 1888.

The Body-Snatcher. New York: Merriam, 1895.

Catriona. London: Cassell, 1893; New York: Scribners, 1893.

A Child's Garden of Verse. London: Longmans, Green, 1885; New York: Scribners, 1885.

With Lloyd Osbourne. *The Ebb-Tide*. Chicago: Stone & Kimball, 1894; London: Heinemann, 1891.

Edinburgh: Picturesque Notes. London: Seeley, Jackson, & Halliday, 1879; New York: Macmillan, 1889.

Essays of Travel. London: Chatto & Windus, 1905.

Familiar Studies of Men and Books. London: Chatto & Windus, 1882; New York: Dodd, Mead, 1887.

Father Damien: An Open Letter to the Reverend Dr. Hyde of Honolulu. London: Chatto & Windus, 1890.

A Footnote to History: Eight Years of Trouble in Samoa. London: Cassell, 1892; New York: Scribners, 1892.

Hitherto Unpublished Prose Writings. Boston: Bibliophile Society, 1921.

The Best Thing in Edinburgh: An Address by Robert Louis Stevenson to the Speculative Society of Edinburgh in March 1873. San Francisco: John Howell, 1923.In the South Seas. New York: Scribners, 1896; London: Chatto & Windus, 1900.

An Inland Voyage. London: Kegan Paul, 1878; Boston: Roberts Brothers, 1883.

Island Nights Entertainments: Consisting of The Beach of Falesa, The Bottle Imp, The Isle of Voices. London: Cassell, 1893; New York: Scribners, 1893.

Kidnapped. London: Cassell, 1886; New York: Scribners, 1886.

Lay Morals and Other Papers. London: Chatto & Windus, 1911.

The Master of Ballantrae: A Winter's Tale. London: Cassell, 1889; New York: Scribners, 1889.

Memoir of Fleeming Jenkin. London & New York: Longmans, Green, 1887.

Memoirs of Himself. Philadelphia: Privately printed, 1912.

Memories and Portraits. London: Chatto & Windus, 1887; New York: Scribners, 1887.

The Merry Men and Other Tales and Fables. London: Chatto & Windus, 1887; New York: Scribners, 1887.

With Fanny Van de Grift Stevenson. *More New Arabian Nights: The Dynamiter*. London: Longmans, Green, 1885; New York: Holt, 1885.

Napa Wine. With an Introduction by MFK Fisher. St. Helen, Calif.: James E Beard, 1965.

Napa Wine. With Notes and Introduction by Brian McGinty. San Francisco: Westwind Books, 1974.

New Arabian Nights. 2 vols. London: Chatto & Windus, 1882; 1 vol. New York: Holt, 1882.

The Old Pacific Capital: Robert Louis Stevenson's Story of Monterey. California Classics. San Francisco: Colt Press, 1944.

Padre Dos Reales. Monterey, 1879.

The Pentland Rising. Edinburgh: Privately printed, 1866.

Prayers Written at Vailima. With an introduction by Mrs. Stevenson. New York: Scribners, 1904; London: Chatto & Windus, 1905.

Prince Otto: A Romance. London: Chatto & Windus, 1885; Boston: Roberts Brothers, 1886.

Records of a Family of Engineers. London: Chatto & Windus, 1916.

The Scottish Stories and Essays. Edited by Kenneth Gelder. Edinburgh: Edinburgh University Press, 1989.

The Silverado Squatters. London: Chatto & Windus, 1883; New York: Munro, 1884.

Songs of Travel and Other Verses. London: Chatto & Windus, 1896.

St. Ives: Being the Adventures of a French Prisoner in England. New York: Scribners, 1897; London: Heinemann, 1898.

The Strange Case of Dr. Jekyll and Mr. Hyde. London: Longmans, Green, 1886; New York: Scribners, 1886.

Treasure Island. London: Cassell, 1883; Boston: Roberts Brothers, 1884.

Travels with a Donkey in the Cévennes. London: Kegan Paul, 1879; Boston: Roberts Brothers, 1879.

Underwoods. London: Chatto & Windus, 1887; New York: Scribners, 1887.

Virginibus Puerisque and Other Papers. London: Kegan Paul, 1881; New York: Collier, 1881.

Weir of Hermiston: An Unfinished Romance. London: Chatto & Windus, 1896; New York: Scribners, 1896.

A Winter's Walk in Carrick and Galloway. Chicago: Herbert S Stone & Co., 1896.

With Lloyd Osbourne. *The Wrecker*. London: Cassell, 1892; New York: Scribners, 1892.

With Lloyd Osbourne. *The Wrong Box*. London: Longmans, Green, 1889; New York: Scribners, 1889.

COLLECTED EDITIONS

Aberdeen Edition. 10 vols. Boston: Edinburgh Society, 1908.

Beacon Edition. Edited by Charles Curtis Bigelow and Temple Scott. 10 vols. Boston and New York: Charles A Lind & Co., 1906.

Biographical Edition. 31 vols. New York: Charles Scribner's Sons, 1905–12.

Edinburgh Edition. Edited by Sidney Colvin. 28 vols. London: Constable, 1894–98.

Household Edition. Edited by Charles Curtis Bigelow and Temple Scott. 10 vols. New York: Lamb Publishing Co., 1906.

Manhattan Edition. Edited by Charles Curtis Bigelow and Temple Scott. 10 vols. New York: Bigelow, Smith & Co./Davos Press, 1906.

New Century Library Edition. 6 vols. New York: Thomas Nelson & Sons, 1912.

Pentland Edition. Edited by Edmund Gosse. 20 vols. London: Cassell in association with Chatto & Windus, W Heinemann, and Longmans, Green, 1906–7.

Skerryvore Edition. Edited by Lloyd Osbourne and Fanny van de Grift Stevenson. 30 vols. London: Heinemann, 1924.

South Seas Edition. Edited by Lloyd Osbourne and Fanny van de Grift Stevenson. 32 vols. New York: Scribners, 1925.

Swanston Edition. With an Introduction by Andrew Lang. 25 vols. London: Chatto & Windus in association with Cassell, Heinemann, & Longmans, Green, 1911–12.

Thistle Edition. 27 vols. New York: Charles Scribner's Sons, 1895-99, 1911–12.

Tusitala Edition. Edited by Lloyd Osbourne and Fanny van de Grift Stevenson. 35 vols. London: Heinemann, 1924.

Vailima Edition. Edited by Lloyd Osbourne and Fanny van de Grift Stevenson. 26 vols. London: Heinemann, 1922-23; New York: Scribners, 1922–23.

Waverley Edition. 4 vols. London: Waverley, 1924.

Appendix

HISTORIC SITES AND LANDMARKS

IN THE EDINBURGH AREA

Colinton Manse

Colinton

Edinburgh village; Stevenson's maternal grandfather Lewis Balfour was the minister of Colinton Parish Church for nearly forty years. Stevenson spent many happy days there as a child.

8 Howard Place

RLS was born in this two-story Georgian terrace on 13 November 1850. From 1926 to 1963 it housed the headquarters of the Robert Louis Stevenson Club and museum.

.Hawes Inn

Newhalls Road

South Queensferry

RLS immortalised the Hawes Inn in *Kidnapped* (1886). The abduction of David Balfour was planned here. No. 13 is the Robert Louis Stevenson Room; appropriately enough, next door is the David Balfour Room.

RLS Memorial

West Princes Street Gardens

Consists of birch trees surrounding a simple stone column designed by the Scottish artist-poet Ian Hamilton Finlay.

17 Heriot Row

RLS lived here from 1857 to 1880. It is now a bed & breakfast.

Stevenson family grave

Calton New Burial Ground

Stevenson's parents and grandparents are buried here.

Stevenson House

1 Baxter Place

Robert Stevenson, the paternal grandfather of RLS, lived and worked in this building located at the top of Leith Walk. From here, he designed and supervised many engineering works, including the famous Bell Lighthouse.

St Giles Cathedral

Parliament Square

On the west wall is a bronze memorial to RLS by sculptor Augustus St Gaudens.

Swanston Cottage

Swanston

One of Edinburgh's villages. The cottage served as the Stevenson family retreat from 1867 until 1880.

25 Regent Terrace

RLS' uncle Alan Stevenson, builder of the Skerryvore lighthouse, lived here.

IN THE USA

Portsmouth Square

Chinatown

San Francisco

A fifteen-foot memorial to Stevenson erected in 1897 by the RLS Fellowship stands in the heart of Chinatown, a spot that RLS frequently visited.

608 Bush Street

San Francisco

A plaque erected in 1972 commemorates the spot where once stood a two-story wooden lodging house run by an Irish woman named Mary Carson. Stevenson stayed here for three months from December 1879 to March 1880.

Robert Louis Stevenson State Park

3801 Highway 29, near Calistoga, California

In 1880, RLS and Fanny spent their honeymoon at Silverado, an abandoned silver mine at the top of Mount Saint Helena (4,339 feet), the setting of *The Silverado Squatters*. A five-mile trail leads to the summit. Stevenson's bunkhouse is gone of course but a monument in the shape of an open book marks the honeymoon spot. About a mile along the switchback trail is the site of Stevenson's cabin.

Simoneau House

456 Van Buren Street

Monterey, California

Jules Simoneau lived here with his wife. Stevenson was a frequent visitor. The slightly remodeled cottage is now used as offices by the Monterey Institute of International Studies.

Simoneau Plaza

Monterey, California

A triangular-shaped plaza located at the intersection of Munras, Pearl, and Tyler Streets in the heart of Old Monterey is the site of Jules Simoneau's restaurant. Features historical panels and a pastel painting by local artist NJ Taylor of Simoneau and Stevenson playing chess inside the restaurant.

Kalaupapa National Historical Park

Kalaupapa

Molokai

Hawaii

Established by President Jimmy Carter in 1980, Kalaupapa National Historical Park contains the historic settlements of Kalaupapa and Kalawao. All visitors must receive a permit from the Department of Health to enter the settlement.

MUSEUMS AND LIBRARIES

IN SCOTLAND

National Library of Scotland, George IV Bridge, Edinburgh
Letters from Stevenson and other Stevenson memorabilia, including 106 of his letters to Frances Sitwell; letters to WE Henley; materials collected by Graham Balfour, Stevenson's biographer; juvenilia and essays; Stevenson's copies (then presented to his parents) of *Virginibus Puerisque* and *Underwoods* with notes (65 in all) on where he wrote each essay and poem; photographs (from the Gorrie collection).

The Writer's Museum, Lady Stair's House, Lady Stairs Close, Lawnmarket, Edinburgh
Collection of many personal items (including Stevenson's pipe, fishing rod, ring, riding boots, and cap), and the 'Davos' printing press on which he and Lloyd Osbourne, his stepson, produced *Moral Emblems* and *The Graver and the Pen*, manuscripts (including many of Stevenson's letters to WE Henley and Alison Cunningham), paintings, and an extensive archive of photographs relating to his life and work.

IN THE USA

Carmel Mission, Rio Road, off Highway 1, Carmel, California
Stevenson visited Carmel Mission in 1879 and wrote about the annual return of the Carmel Indians to the ruined mission to celebrate the old patronal feast of San Carlos. A display features a small bust of RLS by Alan Hutchieson, a sculptor who visited Stevenson and his family in Samoa.

The Huntington Library, Art Collections and Botanical Gardens, 1151 Oxford Road,
San Marino, California
Contains many important Stevenson-related journals and notebooks (the Cévennes journal, the Silverado journal, and the Equator cruise journal; a notebook with an early draft of *John Nicholson*); 32 poems, 25 prose pieces (including manuscripts of all or part of the final version of *Kidnapped*, *In the South Seas*, 'The Beach of Falesà', the final version of *St. Ives*), 91 letters (including most of Stevenson's letters to Will H Low), 3 drawings, 1 sketchbook, and 11 music scores.

Monterey State Historical Museum, Stevenson House, Stevenson Museum, 530 Houston Street, Monterey, California
Stevenson lived here from September to December 1879, while waiting for Fanny Osbourne's divorce to become finalised. It is now a memorial museum containing articles of furniture, first editions, manuscripts, scrapbooks belonging to Stevenson's mother, Fanny's Samoa diary, and photographs and other family memorabilia.

Built circa 1830s, the two-story adobe house was originally owned by Don Rafael Gonzalez before a Swiss businessman by the name of Girardin bought it and added the Houston Street section. For a time it was known as 'The French Hotel'. In 1937 the house was purchased by the late Edith C van Antwerp and Mrs. C Tobin Clark, who in turn gave it to the State of California as a memorial. Stevenson worked on *The Amateur Emigrant*, 'Pavilion on the Links,' and his essay on Thoreau while staying here.

Sharpsteen Museum, 1311 Washington Street, Calistoga, California
A terrific local museum that chronicles the history of the town and surrounding area through dioramas and shadowboxes. The museum was founded by Benjamin Sharpsteen, a producer and production artist who worked for Walt Disney for several years. Includes a replica of the Stevenson's honeymoon cabin at Silverado as well as a bronze sculptor of RLS and Fanny at the site.

The Silverado Museum, 1490 Library Lane, St. Helena, California
Founded in 1969 by Norman H and Charlotte Strouse, the museum has a wide-ranging collection including letters (7 volumes of Fanny's letters); manuscripts (including Lloyd Osbourne's Casco diary, poems, and essays); first editions; paintings; photographs; and memorabilia, as well as some of Stevenson's childhood letters; his marriage license; manuscript notes on *The Master of Ballantrae*; chapter 1 of *Travels with a Donkey*; and over a hundred books from his library in Samoa. His lead soldiers, the desk at which he worked, and his wedding ring are also among the memorabilia.

The Stevenson Society of America, Robert Louis Stevenson Cottage (Baker Cottage), 11 Stevenson Lane, Saranac Lake, New York
Stevenson stayed here with his mother, Fanny, and stepson Lloyd Osbourne from October 1887 to April 1888. While here he wrote several essays for *Scribner's Magazine* (including 'A Chapter on Dreams' and 'The Lantern Bearers'), he began writing *The Master of Ballantrae*, and he and Lloyd worked on *The Wrong Box*.

The museum contains books and manuscript materials originally from the Stevenson Society of America (seven albums of photographs and newspaper cuttings), Davos woodcuts, and memorabilia.

University of South Carolina, Thomas Cooper Library, University of South Carolina, Columbia, South Carolina
Houses most first editions and reprints of Stevenson's work culled from the university's Department of Rare Books and Special Collections and from the G Ross Roy Collection of Scottish Literature. During summer 1994–spring 1995 the University of South Carolina marked the centenary of Stevenson's death with a special exhibition and accompanying symposium.

Yale University, Beinecke Rare Book and Manuscript Library, 121 Wall Street, New Haven, Connecticut
The world's largest collection of first and early editions of RLS (including translations); books from Stevenson's library or with annotations by him; artwork; scrapbooks; photos; memorabilia; manuscripts; juvenilia (including *The Sunbeam Magazine*); early essays; poems; the first Samoa notebook; letters to, from, and about Stevenson (including the Baxter correspondence). The Beinecke Library contains over half of the 2800 surviving letters written by Stevenson.

IN FRANCE

Association Sur le Chemin de RL Stevenson, Le Pont-de-Montvert, France
In 1994, the Stevenson Trail was created during the centenary year of the author's famous journey to the Cévennes. Several companies organise hikes along the trail.

SAMOA

Robert Louis Stevenson Museum, Apia District, Upolu, Western Samoa
Contact (in USA): Jim Winegar, PO Box 842, Provo, Utah 84604. (In Samoa): Leaupepe Latu Leaupepe, Samoa RLS. Museum at Vailima, PO Box 850, Apia, Western Samoa.
Stevenson spent the last four years of his life at his home here at Vailima. He is buried on the top of Mount Vaea. On 5 December 1994, one hundred years after his death, the Robert Louis Stevenson Museum/Preservation Foundation dedicated the completely restored building of Vailima and opened it to the public as the Robert Louis Stevenson Museum.

ORGANISATIONS, etc

SCOTLAND

The Robert Louis Stevenson Club, 37 Lauder Road, Edinburgh
Founded in 1920, the club's main objective is to foster interest in Stevenson's life and works. Organises exhibitions, lectures, and readings, as well as literary competitions and the maintenance of the first Edinburgh museum dedicated to RLS at his birthplace at 8 Howard Place. Regularly publishes the *RLS Club News*.

USA

The RLS Club of Monterey, PO Box 2562, Monterey, California
Based at the Stevenson House in Monterey, the Club promotes conservation and commemoration activities and publishes a newsletter, *RLS Club of Monterey: News and Views*. Special activities are usually celebrated around Stevenson's birthday. The Club is reportedly planning to erect a life-size sculpture of Stevenson and Jules Simoneau along with an interpretative mural at Simoneau Plaza in Monterey.

Schramsberg Vineyards, 1400 Schramsberg Road, Napa Valley, California
Stevenson stopped here during his stay at Silverado. Founded by Jacob Schram in 1862, it was in a state of ruins by 1965 when Jack and Jamie Davies restored it as a producer of sparkling wines. The original winery building stands next to the old Schram home. A small display features rare editions of *The Silverado Squatters* and a bust of Stevenson. Tasting and tours daily by appointment only.

MUSIC INSPIRED BY RLS

Wally Allan and John Shedden
Souvenirs of Modestine:
A Musical Journey in Stevenson's Footsteps
A celebration in words and music that marks the 120th anniversary of Stevenson's journey to the Cévennes. In 1998 the French Association sur le chemin de RL Stevenson organised a 12-day walking festival along the route. Contact: Wally Allan, 72 Colinton Mains Drive, Edinburgh EH13 9BJ.

Ted Jacobs
A Child's Garden of Songs: The Poetry of Robert Louis Stevenson in Song
(Music for Little People/Rhino Records)
Includes 'The Wind,' 'Pirate Story,' 'The Land of Counterpane,' 'From a Railway Carriage,' and 'Foreign Lands.'

Songs of the Silverado: Music and Narrations inspired by the writings, letters and poems of Robert Louis Stevenson (American Concert Association)
Features mezzo soprano Margery Crockett Tede, baritone Marvin Klebe, narrator Al Covala, and the Kronos String Quartet performing 'Child's Garden of Song.'

Jekyll & Hyde: The Musical
(Atlantic)
Music by Frank Wildhorn, Book & Lyrics by Leslie Bricusse
Original Broadway cast. Originally produced in 1990 at the Alley Theatre in Houston, this adaptation made its Broadway debut at the Plymouth Theatre on 28 April 1997.

Ronald Stevenson
Sing a Song of Seasons
(Musaeus)
Song cycles by the English pianist-composer of mixed Scots and Welsh descent, including RLS' *A Child's Garden of Verses*. For more information on the composer and his works, contact the Ronald Stevenson Society, 3 Chamberlain Road, Edinburgh EH10 4DL

Savourna Stevenson
Tusitala (Teller of Tales)
(Eclectic Records)
Original music from Stevenson's Travels, the BBC production on the life of RLS. Features Savourna Stevenson (daughter of classical composer Ronald Stevenson) on harp and keyboards, Aly Bain on fiddle, Fred Morrison on bagpipes, Dave Tulloch on percussion, among others.

Bryn Terfel

The Vagabond & Other Songs by Ralph Vaughan Williams, Butterworth, Finzi, & Ireland (Polygram Records)

Includes such Stevenson poems as 'The Vagabond,' 'Youth and Love,' 'In dreams, unhappy, I behold you stand,' 'The infinite shining heavens,' 'Let Beauty awake in the morn from beautiful dreams,' 'Bright is the ring of words,' 'Whither Must I Wander' ('To the Tune of Wandering Willie'), and 'I have trod the upward and the downward slope' – all from Stevenson's *Songs of Travel* (1895)